Political Leadership in

Do political leaders matter for development in Africa? Political leaders south of the Sahara have taken center stage since countries in the region gained independence in the 1960s, yet a "leadership trap" soon emerged with power-holders overstaying in office and chronic instability caused by coups resulting in decades of disappointing developmental performances. The beginnings of change are found in political reforms of the early 1990s, with many sub-Saharan countries introducing multiparty elections and an increasingly regular succession of leaders. But what impact did the new mechanisms for selecting leaders have on the political stabilization of African states, on the growth of their economies, and on the welfare of ordinary citizens? Drawing on a new dataset called the Africa Leadership Change (ALC), this innovative analysis of political leadership in Africa investigates the distinct leadership dynamics and development processes across the region from 1960 to 2018, revealing how, as Africa began to change its leaders and the way they reach power, these new leaders themselves began to change Africa.

GIOVANNI CARBONE is Professor of Political Science at the Università degli Studi di Milano and Head of the Africa Programme at ISPI (Istituto per gli Studi di Politica Internazionale). His research focuses on the comparative study of politics, geopolitics, and economic development in sub-Saharan Africa. He has been the Principal Investigator of a European Research Council (ERC) funded research project and is the author of articles in journals including *Governance, Journal of Development Studies,* and *Journal of Modern African Studies.*

ALESSANDRO PELLEGATA is Assistant Professor of Political Science at the Università degli Studi di Milano where his research is based within the field of comparative politics. He is the author of several articles in journals including *European Political Science Review* and *Journal of European Public Policy.* In 2011 he was awarded the Santoro Prize for the best paper presented by a young scholar at the SISP Annual Congress.

Political Leadership in Africa

Leaders and Development South of the Sahara

GIOVANNI CARBONE
Università degli Studi di Milano

ALESSANDRO PELLEGATA
Università degli Studi di Milano

CAMBRIDGE
UNIVERSITY PRESS

University Printing House, Cambridge CB2 8BS, United Kingdom

One Liberty Plaza, 20th Floor, New York, NY 10006, USA

477 Williamstown Road, Port Melbourne, VIC 3207, Australia

314–321, 3rd Floor, Plot 3, Splendor Forum, Jasola District Centre, New Delhi – 110025, India

79 Anson Road, #06–04/06, Singapore 079906

Cambridge University Press is part of the University of Cambridge.

It furthers the University's mission by disseminating knowledge in the pursuit of education, learning, and research at the highest international levels of excellence.

www.cambridge.org
Information on this title: www.cambridge.org/9781108423731
DOI: 10.1017/9781108529266

© Giovanni Carbone and Alessandro Pellegata 2020

This publication is in copyright. Subject to statutory exception and to the provisions of relevant collective licensing agreements, no reproduction of any part may take place without the written permission of Cambridge University Press.

First published 2020

Printed and bound in Great Britain by Clays Ltd, Elcograf S.p.A.

A catalogue record for this publication is available from the British Library.

Library of Congress Cataloging-in-Publication Data
Names: Carbone, Giovanni, author. | Pellegata, Alessandro, 1981– author.
Title: Political leadership in Africa : leaders and development south of the Sahara / Giovanni Carbone, Alessandro Pellegata.
Description: Cambridge, United Kingdom ; New York, NY : Cambridge University Press, 2020. | Includes bibliographical references and index.
Identifiers: LCCN 2019037725 (print) | LCCN 2019037726 (ebook) | ISBN 9781108423731 (hardback) | ISBN 9781108438315 (paperback) | ISBN 9781108529266 (epub)
Subjects: LCSH: Political leadership–Africa, Sub-Saharan. | Africa, Sub-Saharan–Politics and government–1960-
Classification: LCC JQ1875.A55 L444 2020 (print) | LCC JQ1875.A55 (ebook) | DDC 320.967–dc23
LC record available at https://lccn.loc.gov/2019037725
LC ebook record available at https://lccn.loc.gov/2019037726

ISBN 978-1-108-42373-1 Hardback
ISBN 978-1-108-43831-5 Paperback

Cambridge University Press has no responsibility for the persistence or accuracy of URLs for external or third-party internet websites referred to in this publication and does not guarantee that any content on such websites is, or will remain, accurate or appropriate.

Contents

List of Figures	*page* viii
List of Tables	x
Acknowledgments	xii
List of Acronyms	xiii

	Introduction	1
	The Structure of the Book	2
1	Leadership, Politics, and Development	7
	Searching for Political Leadership	7
	What Is Political Leadership?	12
	Political Leadership and African Politics	14
	The Leadership/Development Nexus in Africa	20
	The Institutionalization of Political Power and Development	26
2	Coming to Power and Using It: Leaders' Selection, Change, and Government Performance	35
	Leadership and National Development	35
	Electoral Mechanisms: Democratic and Beyond	42
	From Regime Transitions to Leadership Changes	46
	Counterarguments and Limitations	54
	Methodological Issues	57
3	The Africa Leadership Change (ALC) Dataset	60
	The Rationale for a New Dataset	60
	The Africa Leadership Change Dataset: Structure, Scope, and Coding Rules	62
	Comparing ALC to Alternative Datasets and Measures	68
	The ALC Dataset: Setting the Stage for the Empirical Analyses	77
4	The Changing Dynamics of African Leadership: Rulers before and after 1990	79
	Africa's Two Postindependence Syndromes: Overstay in Power and Violent Takeovers	79

	Successful Successions: Exceptions to Rule	92
	New Rules for Different Rulers: The Constitutional and Multiparty Transitions of the 1990s	93
	The Decline of Violent Takeovers	103
	More Rotation, Shorter Stays in Office	107
	Electoral Outcomes, Country Trajectories, and Challenges to Multiparty Rules	113
	Many Leaders, Some Clear Trends	119
5	When the Military Strikes	120
	The Rise and Fall of Modern Military Coups	120
	Coups in Africa	121
	What Is a Coup, and What Is Not	125
	Why Coups	128
	Military Investigations	133
	The African Union and Unconstitutional Changes of Government	135
	Is There Such Thing as a "Good Coup"?	139
	The Social and Economic Impact of African Coups	144
6	Lessening Africa's "Big Men": Term Limits	149
	When, How, and Why Were Term Limits Adopted	149
	To Limit or Not to Limit? The Arguments for and against	153
	Do Term Limits Matter in Africa?	157
	On Course Manipulation: Targeting Term Limits	160
	The (Relative) Resilience of Tenure Limitations	163
	Explaining Attempts to Alter or Eliminate Term Limits	168
	No-Limit Families: Dynastic Succession in Africa	171
7	Leading for Development? (I). Economic Growth	176
	Assessing Progress: Selected Dimensions of Development	176
	Leadership Dynamics and Development: Drivers and Hypotheses	177
	Explanatory Factors	181
	Research Design and Methodological Issues	184
	Economic Growth	188
8	Leading for Development? (II). Social Welfare, State Consolidation, and Corruption Control	208
	Social Welfare	208
	State Consolidation	225
	Corruption Control	238
	A Synopsis of Key Empirical Findings	252

9	Autocrats, Hegemons, Democrats, and Transients	255
	A New Typology for African Leaders	255
	Trending Leaders	260
	New Leaders, Better Outcomes?	267
	Fast Service: Transient Leaders as Fixers	270
	The Battle for Leadership	275
10	Leaders to Come	277
	Africa's Coming Leaders and Development Scenario	279

Appendix	281
References	345
Index	363

Figures

2.1 Leadership selection: the combination of elections and leadership changes across regimes	page 49
3.1 Structure and logic of the ALC dataset	67
4.1 Number of multiparty elections by year, 1960–2018	98
4.2 Modes of leadership change in 1960–1989 and 1990–2018	104
4.3 Number of coups and proportion over total number of leadership changes, by decade, 1960–2018	104
4.4 Average annual frequency of leadership changes, 1960–2018	109
4.5 Average tenure of African leaders, 1960–2018	110
4.6 Average tenure of leaders by mode of entry into power, 1960–2018	113
4.7 Election outcomes: incumbents, successors and alternators, 1960–2018	115
4.8 The jigsaw puzzle of democratization by elections in sub-Saharan Africa, 1990 to June 2015	117
5.1 Successful coups d'état in the world	122
6.1 The adoption of presidential term limits since 1989	153
6.2 Democratic improvements following electoral alternations and electoral successions favored by term limits	159
7.1 Multiparty elections, electoral changes, and economic growth in sub-Saharan Africa	195
7.2 Economic growth under non-elected, elected, and democratic leaders in sub-Saharan Africa, by decade	198
8.1 Elections, electoral changes, and social welfare in sub-Saharan Africa	214

List of Figures

8.2 Social welfare under non-elected, elected, and democratic leaders in sub-Saharan Africa, by decade	217
8.3 Elections, electoral changes, and state consolidation in sub-Saharan Africa	233
8.4 State consolidation under non-elected, elected, and democratic leaders in sub-Saharan Africa, by decade	234
8.5 Corruption, elections, and leadership changes in sub-Saharan Africa, 1960–2018	245
8.6 Political and executive corruption under non-elected, elected, and democratic leaders in sub-Saharan Africa, by decade	247
9.1 A new typology of African leaders: criteria (I)	257
9.2 Types of leaders in Africa, 1960–2018	265

Tables

3.1 Episodes of electoral succession and alternation at different levels of democracy	page 70
3.2 Breaking down Archigos cases of "regular" entry into power according to ALC coding rules and categories	75
4.1 The fate of Africa's founding fathers	81
4.2 Longest-serving rulers in Africa, 1960–2018	86
4.3 Number of leadership changes in African countries, 1960–2018	90
4.4 Non-multiparty elections in African countries, 1960–1990	95
4.5 Multiparty transitions: post-1990 founding elections	99
4.6 Post-2000 coups d'état in Africa	106
4.7 Coups d'état and time elapsed from last coup, 1960–2018	108
4.8 Average tenure of African leaders, 1960–1989 and 1990–2018	112
5.1 African coups d'état and regime effects in the new millennium, 2000–2018	143
5.2 Military coups and development performance	146
5.3 Leader's mode of entry and development performance	147
6.1 The adoption of presidential term limits since 1989	152
6.2 Parliaments, referenda, and courts: how incumbents bypassed term limits	163
6.3 Failed and successful attempts to overcome presidential term limits	164
7.1 Regression results for GDP growth	200
7.2 Regression results for GDP per capita growth	203

List of Tables

8.1	Summary of main regression results for social welfare (health spending, school enrolment, life expectancy at birth, and under-5 mortality rate)	220
8.2	Summary of main regression results for state consolidation	236
8.3	Summary of main regression results for corruption control (political corruption and executive corruption)	248
9.1	A new typology of African leaders: criteria (II)	259
9.2	Four categories of African leaders: empirical distribution	261
9.3	Regression results of performance indicators on leader's type (transients excluded)	268
9.4	Transient leaders: regular versus irregular exit from power	272
9.5	The association between transient leaders and political performance: regression results	273

Acknowledgments

We would like to thank the many friends and colleagues who contributed, in different ways, to shaping our views and work by offering time, advice, debate, empirical material, or something else. They include Chama Armitage, Paolo Bellucci, Jaimie Bleck, Alessandro Bozzini, Andrea Cassani, Nicolas Cheeseman, Tiziana Corda, Robert Elgie, Maurizio Ferrera, Anna Maria Gentili, Marco Giuliani, Arthur Goldsmith, Maddalena Procopio, Albert Trithart, Matteo Villa, and Francesco Zucchini.

We are particularly grateful, in addition, to Anita Bianchi, who helped compile the very first version of our Africa Leadership Change (ALC) dataset, and to Chiara Accinelli and Simone Minisi, who at a much later stage worked creatively to generate the data visualizations hosted on the ISPI website (Istituto per gli Studi di Politica Internazionale). The full dataset itself can be freely downloaded from the same website.

Giovanni dedicates this book to his sons Lupo, Martino, and Nico. Alessandro dedicates this book to Laura.

Acronyms

ALC	Africa Leadership Change
ANC	African National Congress
ASEAN	Association of Southeast Asian Nations
AU	African Union
BTI	Bertelsmann Transformation Index
CAR	Central African Republic
CC	Control of Corruption
CCM	Chama Cha Mapinduzi
CPI	Corruption Perceptions Index
DPP	Democratic Progressive Party
DRC	Democratic Republic of the Congo
ECM	Error Correction Model
EU	European Union
FRELIMO	Frente de Libertação de Moçambique
GDP	Gross Domestic Product
GNI	Gross National Income
HP	Hypothesis
ICRG	International Country Risk Guide
IPU	Inter-Parliamentary Union
IRT	Item Response Theory
KANU	Kenya African National Union
LC	Leadership Change
MMM	Mauritian Militant Movement
MPLA	Movimento Popular de Libertação de Angola
MSP	Mauritian Socialist Party
NELDA	National Elections across Democracy and Autocracy
OAS	Organization of American States
OAU	Organisation of African Unity
OLS	Ordinary Least Squares

PCSE	Panel-Corrected Standard Errors
PDCI	Parti Démocratique de la Côte d'Ivoire
PRI	Partido Revolucionario Institucional
RDPC	Rassemblement Démocratique du Peuple Camerounais
RENAMO	Resistência Nacional Moçambicana
RPF	Rwandan Patriotic Front
RPT	Rassemblement du Peuple Togolais
SSA	Sub-Saharan Africa
TANU	Tanganyika African National Union
TSCS	Time-Series Cross-Sectional
UCDP	Uppsala Conflict Data Program
PRIO	Peace Research Institute Oslo
UDF	United Democratic Front
UK	United Kingdom
UN	United Nations
UNIP	United National Independence Party
UNSC	United Nations Security Council
US	United States
V-Dem	Varieties of Democracy
WDI	World Development Indicators
WGI	Worldwide Governance Indicators

Introduction

Political leaders loom large in African politics and development processes. They took center stage in public life after newly independent states emerged in the region, mostly in the early 1960s, and they grew ever more prominent over the better part of subsequent decades, favored by a widespread and persistent weakness of political institutions. As the developmental failures of most sub-Saharan economies became manifest, particularly from the 1980s onward, the ruinous leadership of many among them became obvious, if often only implicitly.

A "leadership trap" appeared to characterize postcolonial African polities.[1] This was manifest in the two distinct political syndromes for which the region became widely known: the long overstay in power of many power-holders and a chronic instability due to the frequency of coups d'état. While the two phenomena seem to contradict each other, they stemmed from a common cause, that is, the virtual absence of regularized procedures for replacing political leaders, or, more broadly, for political change and adjustment. Unregulated handovers of power contributed to a political environment that was dominated by a concern to retain political office rather than use it to promote a country's development effectively.

A season of political renaissance appeared to begin in the early 1990s. As the overwhelming prevalence of military and single-party authoritarianisms on the continent gave way to the introduction of multiparty elections, it seemed that sub-Saharan states had finally found a way to ensure the orderly and regular succession of their leaders – though still often failing to fulfill democratic standards. Was this actually the case? Were the modes and the timing of leadership renewal effectively altered by the wave of multiparty reforms?

---

[1] Unless otherwise specified, in this book "Africa" and "African" refer to sub-Saharan Africa.

And what broader impact was exerted by the new mechanisms for selecting political leaders on the political stabilization of African states, on the growth of their economies, and on the welfare of ordinary citizens? These are the key issues that we address in this book, first by conceptually framing the role of political leadership in development processes, and then by empirically investigating this issue across the African continent.

When trying to assess the extent to which the reforms and regime transitions of the 1990s actually affected the dynamics of leadership selection and performance, however, one is confronted with an abundance of democratization measures but a surprising lack of systematic data on how African leaders attain and relinquish power (that is, via guerrilla takeovers, coups d'état, competitive elections, dynastic successions, or in some other way). Available data collections – such as the Archigos dataset of political leaders (Goemans et al. 2009) – are not specifically designed for Africa. They therefore overlook many aspects that are crucial for understanding leadership dynamics in the region and the incentives that power-holders face to promote or hinder good governance and development processes. We wanted to fill this gap and investigate empirically the intriguing issue of the role and rule of African leaders by means of a sound and comprehensive analysis. We therefore decided to undertake an innovative examination of political leadership in Africa by building an entirely new dataset and by empirically exploring the developmental impact of the different ways in which office-holders in the region are selected and replaced. In this book, we therefore present the Africa Leadership Change (ALC) dataset, covering all countries in the region from 1960 to 2018 (June 30), and we employ it to address the question of the role of political leadership in the progress of sub-Saharan countries. ALC is intended to become an important tool available to researchers with an interest in African political issues and their relationship with processes of economic and social development.

The Structure of the Book

Political leadership is an understudied subject in contemporary political science and development studies. Chapter 1 looks at the notion of political leadership and presents an overview of the few works that have addressed the topic in the political science literature. The study of

African politics departs from mainstream political science in that it has traditionally underscored the role that individual power-holders play in sub-Saharan polities. Single-party and military authoritarian rule has been the perfect ground for neopatrimonial regimes to flourish in Africa, and the latter, in turn, has favored the weakening of African states and the gradual deterioration of political stability, economic development, and social welfare. While political leadership has often been considered a key cause of political and economic decay in post-colonial Africa, however, the leadership/development linkage has never been examined in a systematic manner. The new electoral regimes introduced in the region since the 1990s have been intended to redress the unsuccessful development trajectories of African states by altering the way in which national leaders reach and leave power and thus their political incentives for more effective policies.

Chapter 2 presents the general framework we adopt to examine the impact of changes in how African leaders are selected and replaced. In Africa, unregulated stays in office by political leaders have coincided with the high personalization of authoritarian power, with the spread of neopatrimonial practices and with a growing disregard for public goods and government performance. There are good reasons to expect that the performance of African leaders should have improved subsequently to the adoption of political reforms in the 1990s. Democracy affects how leaders reach and leave power and what they do while they are in office. Electoral concerns induce them to be more mindful of the consequences of their government actions and policies for the population that they rule. Moving a step further, however, we hypothesize that also multiparty elections *short of democracy* may generate an impact on performance – particularly in an African context where mechanisms for selecting leaders and holding them accountable were previously in such short supply. We thus work within the stream in democratization studies that focuses on the socioeconomic consequences of political regimes. The specific perspective that we adopt, however, is one in which leadership change and alternation in power through multiparty elections constitute a key link between politico-institutional arrangements and mechanisms, even when they do not fulfill democratic standards, and performance outcomes.

Chapter 3 presents the Africa Leadership Change (ALC) dataset, an original and comprehensive dataset designed to give better and fuller account of the various modes in which sub-Saharan leaders attain and abandon power, as well as to examine the evolution of these processes. The Africa Leadership Change dataset covers all changes in a country's top political office (be this a presidential, a prime ministerial, or a king's position) in all sub-Saharan states from 1960, or subsequent year of independence, to 2018. The dataset covers the complete historical series of leaders who were in power south of the Sahara in that period. It details how they entered power and how they left it; the amount of time that they spent in office; the changing sources of their power and legitimacy during their tenure; the country's main political arrangements under their rule; a country's frequency of leadership changes, and several other related aspects.

Chapter 4 provides a detailed picture of key empirical trends in Africa's leadership changes. It compares, in particular, the pre-1990 period with the post-1990 one. It shows that the primary effect of the new multiparty political arrangements has been a drastic reduction in the incidence of coups d'état and containment of African strongmen's average duration in power. In many cases, elections helped impose an endpoint on the incumbent's terms of office – often with the help of constitutional limits – forcing ruling parties to organize an internal succession process with a view to retaining the country's presidency. In a more limited but highly significant number of cases, the outcome of the election has led to alternation in power between opposite political forces. What was only an exceptional occurrence between 1960 and 1989 has become considerably more common over the past 30 years.

Chapters 5 and 6 single out some crucial aspects in the evolution of Africa's leadership transitions for closer inspection. Chapter 5 focuses on military coups. It begins by examining the root causes and the practice of such irregular takeovers, which featured so prominently in postcolonial politics. Comprehensive data show significantly different occurrences across Africa's geographical sub-regions. West Africa, for example, displays a particularly high frequency of coups (a feature shared with Central Africa), an above-average number of leaders per country, and a correspondingly lower length of stay in office. Southern Africa, by contrast, has the highest incidence of multiparty elections and a congruently low occurrence of military interventions and other violent takeovers. For some time, the continent as a whole appeared to stand out, among comparable world regions, in terms of the permanence of coups as relatively recurrent political events. Yet military coups evolved from being a most common way of capturing office to a much less frequent phenomenon also south of the Sahara. Regional bodies – particularly the African Union (AU) – appeared to play an important deterring role in strengthening coup-free political environments. Over the past two decades they were increasingly accompanied by immediate pledges, on the part of the soldiers seizing power, that political authority would be rapidly handed back to civilian rulers via the introduction, or reintroduction, of competitive elections. Some observers went as far as to suggest that coups may be "good" for democracy. But the democratic as well as the developmental performance of most *golpistas* remains disappointing.

Chapter 6 explores the highly mediatized issue of constitutional limits to the number of mandates that African presidents can serve, whether consecutively or not. It looks at how term limits were widely adopted on the continent during the reforms of the 1990s, and how in many countries they became the object of fierce political struggles and social tensions that in a number of cases turned violent. We look at the factors that explain why some leaders respected the term limits to which they were subject, while others tried to bypass such constraints, and, among the latter group, why some succeeded while others failed. The role of constitutionally limited mandates is examined in the broader context of the changing dynamics of leadership duration in office and increased rotation in power. Finally, the comparatively few cases of dynastic or familial successions in office are discussed to complete this overview of unlimited (and postdeath) continuity in power.

Chapters 7 and 8 consider the developmental implications of leadership changes in Africa through an extensive empirical analysis. They examine the impact of leaders' duration in power and of the diverse modes of leadership transfers on the provision of public goods, notably, economic growth, social welfare, state consolidation, and control of corruption. It is postulated that electoral competition and alternation in office – even when they fall short of genuine democracy – help African citizens improve the accountability of their leaders, at least to some extent. The risk of being removed from power generates incentives to provide public goods for incumbents who want to maximize their reelection chances. At the same time, elections help opposition parties monitor the behavior of rulers and expose wrongdoings and maladministration. We advance several specific hypotheses on the effect that leaders can have on economic and social progress as well as on a better and less corrupt functioning of state apparatuses. We test these hypotheses empirically using a time-series and cross-sectional research design that includes all the 49 countries of the sub-Saharan region between 1960 and 2018. Much of the evidence confirms our underlying argument about African development: political leaders and the modes in which they rotate in office matter.

Before concluding, Chapter 9 resumes a widely known conceptualization of leadership in postcolonial Africa – the one formulated by Jackson and Rosberg in the early 1980s – and updates it to illustrate the most recurrent features and practices displayed by sub-Saharan power-holders by including the predominant leadership styles and behaviors that have emerged following the political reforms of the late twentieth century. A revised typology identifies four main leadership types on the continent, namely "transients," "autocrats," "hegemons," and "democrats." Only the latter two types – hegemons and democrats – are leaders operating within multiparty frameworks, although hegemons do not normally allow important political and electoral challengers to emerge, whereas democrats by and large do so. Finally, we also carry out a brief analysis of an understudied topic, that of the peculiar role of interim leaders (i.e., leaders who remain in office for less than one year), with a focus on the frequency with which they made their appearance – over time and across different countries – and on whether short-term rule was related to specific political developments.

Chapter 10 draws the conclusions of our empirical analyses by summing up the broader implications of the changes in the ways that leaders reach and leave power south of the Sahara for the development processes in the region and their future prospects. As vast and consequential the transformations undergone by Africa's political landscape and related leadership dynamics have been, so too are the challenges that lie ahead for the continent at a time when democratic ideals and practices have come increasingly under attack across the globe.

1 Leadership, Politics, and Development

Searching for Political Leadership

Political leaders are pivotal and inescapable figures in the political life of all countries. Understanding leadership has been a foundational element in the study of politics, with the early writings of Niccolò Machiavelli and Max Weber exerting enormous influence upon the way in which the subject was subsequently addressed. The ideas of today draw heavily on their reflections concerning the manner in which the exercise of political leadership is linked to such notions as power, legitimacy, and charisma. It was Machiavelli, for example, who famously raised the issue of whether it is safer for a leader to repress and control (and "be feared") or instead to build consensus and support (and thus "be loved"). But it is Weber's classification of the three sources of legitimate authority – traditional, legal-rational, and charismatic – that has become a constant reference and a starting point in leadership studies. This is notwithstanding the fact that, by focusing on legitimacy and essentially excluding coercion, Weber's tripartite framework fails fully to accommodate the innumerable despots and tyrants that have shaped a large part of human history.

Despite these noble antecedents and the unmatched centrality and visibility of national political leaders, contemporary political science has not always paid much direct attention to this core concept (Blondel 1987:1; Lyne de Ver 2008:9; Verzichelli 2011; Bell 2014; Rhodes and 't Hart 2014:17; Elgie 2015). Scholars have proved somewhat reluctant to scrutinize the phenomenon of leadership, which was seen "from both an etymological and a normative point of view ... to be in tension with the idea and practice of democracy" (Musella and Webb 2015:223). As Beerbohm puts it, "democratic leadership may be incoherent, even paradoxical ... leadership is a counternormative activity within a democracy" (Beerbohm 2015:639).

In the nineteenth century, the popular Great Man theories of history stressed the decisive role of particular individuals in molding human and political developments – "the history of what man has accomplished in this world, is at bottom the History of the Great Men who have worked here" wrote Thomas Carlyle (1841) – while in the early twentieth century the conceptual frameworks of elite theorists such as Gaetano Mosca, Vilfredo Pareto, and Robert Michels were grounded on more systematic analyses of empirical behaviors. Weber himself had allowed for a substantial impact of individuals, particularly charismatic leaders, albeit under certain conditions. But the tide was turning. In the place of the "great men in history" theories, large part of the twentieth century was dominated by the "leaders-do-not-matter" thesis of a Tolstoyan or Marxian kind. Social scientists – particularly economists and sociologists, but also some historians – tended to emphasize the role that powerful and impersonal "underlying forces" played in driving the course of history and the development of human societies. These perspectives not only contested the notion that leaders are "prime movers" but also maintained that they do not matter at all.

This is not to say that the subfield died away. In the 1930s and 1940s, an innovative and influential focus on the psychological attributes of leadership was inaugurated by the works of Harold Lasswell (1930, 1948). Attention to personality traits would shape many subsequent inquiries. Leadership studies then moved toward more emphasis on *styles*, and between the 1960s and the early 1980s, they adopted *contingency* approaches stressing that a leader's degree of control typically varies from situation to situation (cf. Nye 2008:22).

In Western pluralist systems, the focus was on the leader/followers interaction, while more or less explicit suspicion long lingered concerning the notion and the practice of robust leadership. As said, democratic ideals and strong leadership were uneasy bedfellows. In nondemocratic states, on the other hand, dictators naturally attracted a large amount of the overall energy devoted by scholars to leadership issues. In democratic and nondemocratic regimes alike, researchers concerned with the theme of leadership were often keen to investigate "the pathologies associated with leaders' exercise of power" (Ahlquist and Levi 2011:3; see also Bell 2014:140).

In the late 1970s and early 1980s, interest shifted to charismatic and "transformational" power-holders as the publication of some outstanding works revived interest in the topic. The in-depth investigations of leadership types that induced Burns (1978) to distinguish between transactional and transformational leadership and Paige's (1977) endeavor systematically to explain leaders' behavior on the basis of a set of interacting variables – that is, personality, role, organization, task, values, and setting – became two foundational works of contemporary leadership studies. Burns' conceptual framework, in particular, has since become a classic in the field. However, a period of decline of attention followed that essentially led to the neglect of the subject.

It was only from the 1990s onward that there was a partial return to examining the role of individual leaders as "prime movers" rather than "corks in the waves" (Bell 2014:141; see also Rhodes and 't Hart 2014:17), both with works based on historical analysis (e.g., Skowronek 1997) and more formalized studies (e.g., Bueno de Mesquita et al. 2003; see also Ahlquist and Levi 2011:19). Political reality also contributed to this revitalization. The rise of new forms of mass communication and the decline of parties and stable political alignments turned attention to the importance of leadership even in democratic institutional settings that, at least in principle, are averse to personal power. A more direct electoral link and a new emphasis on the personality and image of candidates, as well as on the psychological dimension of voting behavior, transformed democracy and led to a greater capacity of "personalized leadership" to shape policy, and ultimately to a widespread "leaderization" or "presidentialization" of politics (Poguntke and Webb 2005; Blondel and Thiebault 2010).

But different attitudes toward leadership in distinct geopolitical regions also affected how the subject was approached and understood (Blondel 2014:706ff.). In the United States, the lack of a monarchical past and a respected presidential tradition legitimized the role of popularly elected leaders and the expectation that they could make an impact. Several scholars thus delved into the personalities of American presidents – Greenstein (1969, 2004) produced influential works on their traits and styles – while occasionally interacting with the large literature on business leadership. Among Europeans, by contrast, the historical struggle against absolute sovereigns and the scars left by the Nazi-fascist dictators in the first half of the twentieth century nurtured a culture of suspicion toward power-holders. In this context, parliamentary cabinets and strong parties seemed to reflect that trust was placed in collective rather than individual endeavors. Britons, for example, were long said to find leadership "foreign" and to "mistrust charisma."[1] Marxist ideas about historical materialism further downplayed the role of personalities and emphasized that of social and economic forces. In developing areas, on the other hand, the problematic experience of *caudillismo* in Latin America since the early nineteenth century was subsequently compounded by the spread of corrupt military or one-party dictatorships in the newly independent, weakly institutionalized states of Africa. There, the urgent need to hold young multiethnic societies together and speed up economic modernization had initially legitimized strongman rule. But the failure of developmental promises led to negative perceptions, widespread criticisms, and a focus on the malfeasances of national leaders.

Besides the overall narrow attention commanded by the topic of political leadership, the methodological approach that long prevailed in the field also had evident limitations. The subfield was dominated by biographic narratives largely based on historical-political accounts of individual experiences, with a focus on leaders' personalities, particularly their psychological and even physical features, ideas and beliefs, political skills, decision-making styles, and so on. But individual life histories are far from being the best way to identify generalizations. All the more so since the vast majority of investigations looked at exceptional leaders, thus ruling out by default what was more conventional or "normal." In addition, a disproportionate amount of attention was paid to the power-holders of a small set of countries – notably the United States, but also, to a much lesser extent, France and the United Kingdom. Study after study dug deeply into the vicissitudes of national leaders such as John Kennedy and Richard Nixon, Charles De Gaulle and François Mitterrand, Winston Churchill and Margaret Thatcher. More recently, however, comparative investigations have been undertaken to complement, if not to replace, the case-by-case approach, and repeated calls have been made for leadership studies to move beyond the investigation of exceptional, charismatic, flamboyant and "transformational" leaders to examination of the more stolid, normal and "minimalist ... leadership that is common in functioning societies and is more appreciated in retrospect" (Bell 2014:156).

The little theorization that existed largely sought to explain the phenomenon of leadership – what makes for a strong leader, under

---

[1] "Follow my leader. Why leadership makes Britons queasy," *The Economist*, October 21, 2004.

what conditions leaders emerge, what forms the leader/followers relation takes, and so on – hardly ever employing it as a potential explanatory factor or an independent variable. As Bunce (1981:15) observed, "a truncated notion of succession – emphasizing the 'who' and the 'how' – has meant little concern for what is an equally, if not more important question: so what?" The political leadership-economic development link, in particular, was entirely ignored (Lyne de Ver 2008:4; see also Bell 2014). Blondel was only a partial exception. He did recognize the need to shift the focus from the mechanisms through which the power of leaders can be constrained, so that they can no longer encroach on the lives of their citizens, to how leaders affect the social and economic history of their nations. Development had to be placed squarely at center stage: "if the power of leaders can be exercised to control, dominate and subjugate, it can surely also be exercised to uplift, improve and develop ... it is essential to assess how far, and under what conditions, leadership is likely to be good ... we are interested in the impact of leaders ... to what extent they can modify the society they rule" (Blondel 1987:3–4, 28ff.). His aim was thus to combine explanations based on personality as social and psychological background with an analysis of the instruments that power-holders have at their disposal to initiate policy and implement change. Ultimately, however, Blondel did no more than conduct some general conceptual reflections about how leadership and its social effects should be investigated. His inquiry did not involve any empirical material. This was no isolated case, but reflected a more widespread tendency: "assumptions abound, yet evidence eludes us ... linking succession to public policy and generalizing from that to the role of political leadership are tasks that still await rigorous scrutiny" (Bunce 1981:3–6). The more recent and highly influential work by Bueno de Mesquita et al. (2002, 2003), on the other hand, coupled sophisticated theory with sound empirical analyses. It emphasized a political logic whereby, under certain politico-institutional arrangements, national leaders – who by default want to prolong their stay in power – have incentives to improve their policy performance by increasing the provision of public goods as opposed to private ones. Yet also the work by Bueno de Mesquita and his colleagues was only a partial exception to the general lack of interest in the socioeconomic impact of leaders, since the attention that it gave to policy performance and development outcomes was only a by-product and an "implication" of a primary focus on the political survival of leaders.

What Is Political Leadership?

There is no classic definition of political leadership of the kind to be found for other core political science notions, such as state (Weber, Tilly), democracy (Schumpeter, Dahl, Przeworski), or political parties (Burke, Weber, Sartori). Classic definitions are also often contested definitions. Nevertheless, they are useful because they provide a shared starting point – even for those scholars who criticize and discard them – from which to begin discussing, theorizing, and empirically researching a given subject.

The absence of classic definitions of political leadership does not mean there is no common ground at all on the topic. At a general level, for example, Ahlquist and Levi (2011:5) identify five necessary conditions normally recognized by most leadership studies, whether or not these conditions are explicitly mentioned by their authors. Leadership is typically seen as relational (i.e., no followers, no leader), asymmetric (one side of the relationship commands a deference and obedience that the other side does not), salient (i.e., the leader has the attention of his or her followers), domain specific (i.e., being a leader in a given domain does not prevent one from being a follower in another domain), and instrumental (i.e., a leader aims at getting his or her followers to do something). Two further features are that leaders typically, if not always, operate within durable organizations and, as a consequence, they are in a position to enforce their decisions, at least to a degree. To return to political leadership more specifically, Blondel (1987) offered an additional insight. If power is defined as the capacity of individual A to have individual B do something he or she might not otherwise do, "in the case of leadership the 'A' who gives the order, who has power, exercises this power over a large number of 'Bs', that is to say, over the whole nation" (Blondel 1987:3).

Of course this concerns political leadership, which is a political phenomenon and is analytically distinct from political leaders as individuals. What attention scholars have devoted to the subject of political leadership, however, has long emphasized a top-down, leader-centered view. This was partly rebalanced in the 1980s, when a new interest in leadership as an interactive, two-way process between leader and followers was added to the traditional focus on individuals at the top (Rhodes and 't Hart 2014:6). That the relationship was intrinsic to the notion of leading and that it needed to be studied and understood was a key if obvious recognition. One broader implication was the need to investigate how leaders derive the authority that they require to lead, which in turn placed emphasis on the institutional and contextual factors that define how the political game is played out (Rhodes and 't Hart 2014:6; Elgie 2015:5–12).

An analysis of institutional arrangements raises the question of whether there is actually a distinction to be drawn between leaders and power-holders: that is, whether those occupying a country's highest government office are proper "leaders," or just "managers" and "office-holders." In principle, "real leaders" should be analytically distinguished from office-holders, since the overlap between the two concepts is incomplete (Blondel 1987:13; see also Ahlquist and Levi 2011:2). The King of Spain, for example, is not a political leader despite the fact that he occupies what is formally the highest rank in the country. The secretary general of the Communist Party of the Soviet Union, on the other hand, was a political leader – the top decision-maker – despite not holding any state office. In practice, however, someone who reaches the uppermost position in a state's institutional hierarchy of political jobs is likely to become a leader as a result, so that office-holding partly determines political leadership.

The perspective that we adopt here is in line with what Ahlquist and Levi (2011:6) define a structural theory of leadership whereby "the leader is someone who occupies a particularly important position in some predefined institutional structure. By virtue of her position, the leader is by definition salient." A political leader is the individual that occupies the top decision-making position in a country's institutional setup. The extent to which power is actually concentrated in his or her hands and how he or she wields it are empirical questions. A full range of possibilities exist, in particular, between the two extremes of the simplistic yet deeply engrained dichotomy that classifies leaders as "real leaders" as opposed to office-holders or managers. The former group comprises great men with exceptional skills: the heroes – and often the villains – of history, with exceptional charisma, often emerging from crises, promising revolutionary change and transformative action to reshape society and make a country's history. The latter consists of mere power-holders: ordinary men that emerge in "normal" times, are prone to a transactional administration of power, often with the mediation of political parties, largely concerned to preserve existing conditions and with scant capacity to affect historical events (see also Blondel 1987:20). For our purposes here, we reject this dichotomy and question Greenstein's (1969) contention that "leader-centred explanations of public events are most likely to be powerful where leaders have a reputation for holding and wielding much power and influence" (cited in Rhodes and 't Hart 2014:7). Leaders perceived as unremarkable figures may in fact turn out to head governments whose policies are highly consequential in terms of development impact (cf. Easterly and Pennings 2018:3).

In comparative politics, political changes have been commonly framed as regime transitions rather than as leadership successions. The attention of scholars has primarily concentrated on the former rather than the latter, with the partial exception of violent government takeovers (Govea and Holm 1998:131). We take a mid-ground position that considers changes in how leaders take power – often implying broader transitions – but also leadership changes in the context of regime continuity. Political regimes are arrangements that determine who exercises power and how. They include both formal and informal rules of the political game. In principle, these rules define sets of incentives that shape the goals, strategies, and behavior of leaders. They thus represent the "chessboard" on which leaders play. In many of Africa's poor and developing countries, state building is still an ongoing and often troubled process. Accordingly, politico-institutional structures in Africa can be much more fluid, less clear, and less binding than is generally the case in advanced economies. The extent to which formal institutions actually shape political leadership – that is, the extent to which structures orient agency – is thus an open question. Also open is the question of the direction – whether predatory or developmental, for example – toward which leadership is oriented.

Political Leadership and African Politics

While political leadership struggled to gain center ground in mainstream political science, it quickly became a cornerstone in the study of African polities, which from the outset appeared to revolve to an extraordinary extent around a country's ruler. The newly forged states that gained independence in the late 1950s and early 1960s were personified by Africa's founding fathers. Kenneth Kaunda *was* Zambia, Kwame Nkrumah *was* Ghana, Jomo Kenyatta *was* Kenya. Nationalist heroes catalyzed the attention of domestic public opinions as well as of external observers. Expectations ran high that they would know how best to lead the way and deliver the full emancipation of their fellow citizens and a rapid modernization of their countries. It is for this reason that, for example, Nkrumah was revered by Ghanaians as *Osagyefo*, or "the Redeemer" in the Akan language. As Senegalese president and writer Léopold Senghor put it at the time, "the spirit of Negro-African philosophy ... is based not on the individual but on the person. The president personifies the Nation as did the Monarch of former times his people. The masses are not mistaken who speak of the 'reign' of Modibo Keïta, Sekou Touré or Houphouët-Boigny, in whom they see, above all, the elected of God through the people."[2] The first president of Equatorial Guinea, Macías Nguema, went so far as to outlaw Christianity and require that all prayers in the country must begin with the words: "In the name of Father Macías, our savior and redeemer ..." (Sylla 1982:18). The cult of personalities at the top was often linked to a generalized perception that their dignity, actions, and successes – including, at times, their wealth and well-being – were inextricably intertwined with the fate of the country and its people. In state after state, the pivotal figure in national politics acquired an extraordinary prominence, as conveyed by the title of "life president" that many leaders arrogated to themselves, contrary to the notion that individuals only temporarily occupy institutionalized political offices, and that the latter by their nature outlive the former. Indeed, strongly centralized and personalized leadership reflected the feebleness of young institutions and a related tendency toward elitist or "de-participation" politics (Kasfir 1976). It was even argued to be a necessary counterbalance to such frailty. The "tough-man system" embodied by Haile Selassie, for example, was deemed of "immense importance to Ethiopian politics" for, "in times of imperial weakness, the different elements in the state immediately start to drift apart" (Clapham 1969:111). While the study of politics in advanced economies with strongly institutionalized systems has tended to focus on

---

[2] Léopold Senghor, "La démocratie africaine," Discours à l'Université de Strasbourg, November 21, 1964.

institutions, individual personalities have retained the largest possible role in weakly institutionalized polities such as Africa's.

As early as the late 1960s, Kenyan scholar Ali Mazrui (1967) denounced a growing "monarchical tendency" in postindependence Africa that resulted from the combination of "four elements of political style." The first was a quest for an aristocratic effect, that is, social ostentation often taking the form of conspicuous consumption. This was followed by the personalization of authority through personality cults and the use of titles resembling those of monarchies. Thirdly, the sacralization of authority, particularly through the glorification and even "spiritualization" of national founding leaders, to which divine rights were accorded in recognition of their epic role in the birth of a new country. A number of African rulers, including Omar Bongo of Gabon, Francisco Macías Nguema of Equatorial Guinea, Mobutu Sese Seko of Zaire, and Gnassingbé Eyadéma of Togo, even claimed a privileged relationship with the supernatural sphere better to establish their control over society (Ngolet 2000:56; Yates 2017:344). The fourth element was the quest for a royal historical identity that, by rechristening the new nations with names from a magnificent past ("Mali," "Ghana," "Malawi," and "Zimbabwe" were all derived from past kingdoms and empires), helped fulfill a feeling of national dignity. Mazrui stressed the contribution of "tribal" traditions, colonial occupation, and national integration projects to the subsequent emergence of this monarchical tendency. But he had no initial interest in examining the developmental consequences of the latter.

Mazrui furthered his exploration of leadership styles in Africa through a four-fold distinction among intimidatory, patriarchal, reconciliation, and mobilization leaders (Mazrui 1970:538–539). His conceptual framework was subsequently expanded to include a greater number of categories (Mazrui 1977, 1995, 2007), with the caveat that "pure" types would rarely be found in political reality. Rather, individual power-holders would often mix distinct styles. The latter could be charismatic and mobilizational (for the likes of Kwame Nkrumah in Ghana and Julius Nyerere in Tanzania), patriarchal (for fathers of the nation such as Houphouët-Boigny or Kenyatta – the latter popularly known as *Mzee*, meaning the Elder, the Old Man), disciplinarian (Nigeria's military dictators Murtala Muhammad and Muhammadu Buhari in the 1970s and 1980s), reconciliatory (including Milton Obote in Uganda during his first spell in power and, certainly a less controversial example, South Africa's Nelson Mandela, who was also a patriarchal figure), housekeeping (i.e., driven by minimalist visions and purposes, as with Daniel Arap Moi in Kenya), technocratic (Jerry Rawlings in Ghana, though he was also a disciplinarian), personalistic (the long dominance of Hastings Banda in Malawi), and monarchical (as with Jean-Bédel Bokassa in Central Africa).

The way in which Africa's core political dynamics closely revolved around national presidents was further articulated through the notion of "personal rule" (Jackson and Rosberg 1982) and the somewhat more wide-ranging idea of "big man politics" (Price 1974; see also Hyden 2012:97ff.). Jackson and Rosberg's analytical framework and empirical account would prove especially influential upon scores of scholars. They conceived personal rule as an inherently authoritarian system resulting from the elimination of constitutional rights and counter-powers, including open political participation and opposition parties, and a concentration of power into the hands of the head of the state or of government. This view of African politics hinges on two essential features. The first is a practice whereby there is no distinction between the individual at the helm of a country and the political office that he or she occupies. This is in line with the broader literature on neopatrimonial politics in Africa (Bach 2011:280, 279; see also Médard 1979, 1991; Bayart 1993:224; Bratton and van de Walle 1994, 1997:61; Sandbrook and Oelbaum 1999:2; van de Walle 2001:52). In spite of their modern state trappings, public offices have all too often been treated as private resources or patrimonies. The leader's identification with the state, his ample degree of discretionary power and private use of public resources, and the essential absence of regular procedures for his removal and replacement turned many African strongmen into the highest embodiment of the neopatrimonial paradigm. This also contributed to legitimizing corrupt behaviors. Formal institutions and the rule of law remained largely ineffective; nor were citizens' needs and demands able significantly to influence political processes. However, rulers did have to take account of informal and particularistic norms such as ethnic ties, factional affiliations, and patronage networks, which resulted in the spread of corrupt and clientelistic practices. The second key feature is the intrinsic insecurity of personal rulers, which largely turned the nature of the political game into a politics of survival. Little or no sense of political direction could be detected except for the overarching goal of shielding the top power-holder and his position from the frequent threats raised by factional struggles, plots, coups, schemes for succession, and the like. Politics in Africa was consequently transformed into "a fight rather than a contest," and governance became "more a matter of seamanship and less one of navigation – that is, staying afloat rather than going somewhere" (Jackson and Rosberg 1982:18). Of course, strategies on how exactly to stay afloat could differ widely, with Senghor or Kenyatta presiding over (and even exploiting) factional competition, and Banda virtually eliminating it.

These shared features, as well as the idiosyncrasies of individual rulers, are illustrated by the political biographies of 17 presidents from 16 sub-Saharan countries as diverse and remote as Swaziland (recently renamed eSwatini) and Sudan, Gabon and Tanzania, Liberia and Ethiopia. Overall, they would eventually hold power for a total of 373 years, that is, 22 years each on average, ranging from Idi Amin Dada's "short-lived" (i.e., eight-year) grip on Uganda to Omar Bongo's record-breaking 42 years in Gabon. These 17 leaders were famously grouped into four types based on their predominant rulership style, namely princes, autocrats, prophets, and tyrants. The majority of African rulers were dubbed "princes," including the likes of Léopold Senghor in Senegal, Jomo Kenyatta in Kenya, Haile Selassie in Ethiopia, Sobhuza II in Swaziland, Gaafar Nimeiri in Sudan, and the William Tubman/William Tolbert duo in Liberia. These were pragmatic manipulators of lieutenants and clients. They tended to rule jointly with other oligarchs and preside over never-ending factional struggles. More power was concentrated into the hands of "autocrats," who were able to direct, command, and manage not just the state or the party, but the country itself, like absolute monarchs who had successfully eliminated other autonomous powers. Well-known cases include Félix Houphouët-Boigny of Côte d'Ivoire, Omar Bongo, Hastings Banda of Malawi, and Mobutu Sese Seko of Zaire. A number of national rulers were distinguished by a highly charismatic form of leadership that they directed toward the achievement of visionary transformations, through state planning, of the societies that they governed. These ideological "prophets" were certainly epitomized by the widely respected figure of Tanzania's Julius Nyerere. A lack of state capacity and misguided policies prevented him and the likes of Kwame Nkrumah in Ghana or Sékou Touré in Guinea from actually fulfilling their visions. The last type of personal rulers were "tyrants," whose shared features were recourse to unrestrained and abusive rule, with complete personal discretion, as well as an extensive and brutal use of violence. While Francisco Macías Nguema of Equatorial Guinea was less widely known, Idi Amin in Uganda and Bokassa of the Central African "Empire" – as the country was renamed during the last years of his rule – long embodied the stereotypical sub-Saharan combination of dictatorship, developmental failure, and human-inflicted sufferings.

The key aim of the large body of literature on personal rule was primarily descriptive and interpretive, rather than explanatory. *Personal rule in black Africa* maintained a close focus on the dynamics of national political games, with relatively little or no attention paid to their socioeconomic developmental impact. This reflected the initial primacy assigned to holding Africa's young states and the nations together – that is, a search for political order – in contrast to the shift of priorities that would take place in later years. As Mkandawire aptly observed, "whereas the first generation of African leaders concentrated their energies on the *politics* of nation building, there are signs of a new generation whose focus is on the *economics* of nation building. These new leaders swear by economic growth and seem to view good growth as the main source of their legitimacy" (Mkandawire 2001:296). Angola's new president, João Lourenço, echoed this view when he observed that, while Agostinho Neto accomplished the historic fight for the country's independence and José Eduardo dos Santos left peace and democratic openings as his main legacies, "my mission will be to revive the economy ... I would like to be recognised in history as the man of Angola's economic miracle."[3] The message was similar to the one conveyed in Namibia by the ruling party's 2014 election banner, which – under the motto *The legacy continues* – associated the country's first president Sam Nujoma with peace, his successor Hifikepunye Pohamba with stability, and the incoming office-holder Hage Geingob with prosperity (Melber 2015:50). In the public discourse at least, leadership and development issues were bound to come together.

---

[3] AFP, "Angola heads to polls as Dos Santos ends 38-year rule," *The Times* (South Africa), August 23, 2017. See also "Discurso de João Lourenço na cerimónia de investidura como Presidente da República," *Jornal de Angola*, September 27, 2017.

The Leadership/Development Nexus in Africa

Explanations of economic development (or the lack thereof) in Africa rarely include political leadership as a relevant factor. Besides considering the classic determinants identified by development economists – such as level of development, investment rates, human capital, and government consumption – most accounts have relied on other macro or structural drivers, including the colonial legacy of African states, their size, ethnic heterogeneity, and geographical location, demographic dynamics, natural resource endowments, a position of dependence within the international economy, the prevalence of authoritarian regimes, the absence of the rule of law/property rights and the diffusion of corruption, international aid, and the adoption of ill-conceived development strategies (see e.g., Collier and Gunning 1999 for an overview; Easterly and Levine 1997; Sachs and Warner 1997; Acemoglu et al. 2001; Barro 2003; Ndulu and O'Connell 2008). This is in line with a prevailing approach in leadership studies that, when relationships are drawn, treats leadership as a dependent variable rather than an independent one, as pointed out (Lyne de Ver 2008:27–28). Leadership is virtually absent from the vast array of drivers examined by the broader economic growth literature. Empirical analyses suggesting that leaders matter for growth are thus rather exceptional (see Jones and Olken 2005; Brady and Spence 2010a,b; Berry and Fowler 2018; Easterly and Pennings 2018).

Besides macro-level accounts, there are a number of micro explanations – grounded in both qualitative and quantitative analyses – that do stress the role that leaders play. Although personal rule and neopatrimonial accounts adopt a mostly ideographic approach and primarily focus on political order, they do not lack theoretical implications for Africa's development. They typically provide descriptions of how – if not always explicit explanations of why – African strongmen failed to adopt good policies (Blondel 2014:707,712; Mkandawire 2015). In spite of the differences among the leadership styles of prophets, tyrants, autocrats, or princes, for example, personal rule regimes are considered to share an elitist political process that "is primarily asocial insofar as it is largely indifferent to the interests, concerns, and problems of social strata beyond the political class" (Jackson and Rosberg 1984:424). Little pressure is thus brought to bear for them to adopt public interest measures. Moreover, while powerful rulers are relatively autonomous in making decisions and policies, they are rarely in the position to actually implement them because of the dysfunctionality of the state apparatuses. Even when a power-holder does pursue progress for the society that he rules, limited state capacity prevents him from achieving it. The result of this kind of reasoning is a watering down of the actual differences among distinct leaders, programs, and policies. The seven "princes" examined by Jackson and Rosberg, for example, include four civilian single-party rulers, two dynastic sovereigns, and a *golpista* military officer. Nor are there substantial dissimilarities in the development achievements of "prophets" – supposedly more oriented toward the well-being of their citizens – as opposed to "autocrats" or "princes." Thus, what was largely seen as a near-systematic pathology in the exercise of power in Africa implicitly turned into something akin to a pathology in the continent's development: that is, the absence of long-expected progress. Of course, African leaders themselves hardly shared this view, as they collectively made clear in the early 1980s by declaring that Africa remained the poorest continent, "unable to point to any significant growth rate, or satisfactory index of general well-being, in the past 20 years ... *despite all efforts made by its leaders.*"[4]

The similarities displayed by personal rulers led to a downplaying of the importance of leadership changes and government turnovers, possibly misreading the impact that leadership successions may have even in contexts of high personalism and weak states (Govea and Holm 1998:131). When one looks beyond Africa, rare exceptions were two works by Bunce (1981) and Jones and Olken (2005). Bunce found leadership succession to work as a mechanism for policy innovation across deeply diverse regimes such as those of Western industrialized countries and communist states. Whether innovation was development-oriented or not, however, was not central to her inquiry. In a seminal study on the growth effects of leadership worldwide, on the other hand, Jones and Olken find that randomly timed changes at the helm of a country (due to natural or accidental death) correlate with dramatic reversals of growth – post-Mao Tse-tung China being a case in point – although this is true for powerful autocrats but not for

---

[4] Organization of African Unity, *Lagos plan of action for the economic development of Africa, 1980-2000*, Organization of African Unity, Lagos, 1980. pp. 3–5.

more constrained democratically elected leaders. They thus "reject the deterministic view where leaders are incidental to the evolution of their national economies" (Jones and Olken 2005:840) and list a number of reasons why it may be otherwise, including the incompleteness and weakness of institutional constraints, growth theories pointing at roles for decision-makers, and the extreme volatility of medium-term growth within countries (Jones 2009). The large impact that leaders appear to exert on economic growth induced Jones and Olken to call for the careful design of institutional rules and other features that would foster the emergence of the right kind of national leaders (Jones 2009:8).

More recently, two further studies picked up the issue where Jones and Olken had left it. Easterly and Pennings (2018) uniquely look at the *individual* growth contribution of each of 750 national leaders who held office for three years or more during 1951–2014. They point that, among the 1-in-15 minority of leaders for whom they find a statistically significant growth effect, autocrats are no more likely to be significant than democrats, thus challenging Jones and Olken's (2005) original findings. In spite of their high methodological sophistication, however, Easterly and Pennings operate a dramatic and consequential oversimplification when they classify countries and their leaders: (a) *dichotomously*, with "established democracies" opposed to a group that bunches together "autocracies" and "transition countries"; (b) through a *higher threshold* for democracy than is commonly used for Polity scores (i.e., ≥7.5 instead of a more conventional 7 or, as suggested by the Polity Project itself, 6); (c) according to the *average Polity2 score* for the entire period (so that if a country transitioned to high-level democracy, say, in 1985, it is labeled as consistently non-democratic in case its previous scores were somewhat unsatisfactory – which does not exactly mean "negative"); (d) *banding together a country's leaders* as either all democrats or all autocrats. The unfortunate combination of these choices produces results that seem rather out of place. The authors end up with a highly questionable list of "autocracies/transition countries" – implying, due to their criteria, that *all* their leaders are labeled "autocrats" – which includes not only the likes of Botswana (in spite of an average score of 8 in 1987–2014) or Cape Verde (9 in 1991–2014), but also Brazil (8 in 1985–2014), Chile (9 in 1989–2014), Mexico (8 in 1997–2014), Paraguay (8 in 1992–2014), Uruguay (10 in 1985–2014), South Korea (8 in 1993–2014), Taiwan

(9 in 1992–2014), and even Romania (9 in 1996–2014), Greece (9 in 1975–2014), Portugal (10 in 1976–2014) and Spain (10 in 1978–2014)[5]. In terms of individual leaders, it is an African, namely Botswana's Seretse Khama, that tops their list of growth-contributing world leaders, but here he is a "famous" and "celebrated" "benevolent *autocrat*" (Easterly and Pennings 2018:24) – not quite the prevailing view, and in spite of the fact that the country always scored at least 6 (1966–1986) and, for the most, even higher than that (7 for 1987–1996 and 8 for 1997–2014).

The second work is by Berry and Fowler (2018) and is primarily meant to introduce a new methodology, yet it suffers from similar problems. When applied to the growth contribution of world leaders from 153 countries over a 135-year period, their method shows an overall leader's effect similar in size to that found by Jones and Olken (2005) and also, specifically, that the effect is there for autocratic and "transitional" countries, while not so much for democratic ones (Berry and Fowler 2018:24). But their 29 autocracies and 35 democracies only include countries that have consistently been so for the entire period. Those that changed status once or more at some point along the way – maybe by democratizing as far back as 30 or 40 years ago – are deemed "transitional" (89 cases), again implying that *all* their leaders for the entire period also end in this mixed and questionable category, far larger in size than the sum of the other two, raising doubts on the findings of the study.

In Africa, the underlying assumption was that correcting the political vices of personal rulers would go a long way toward establishing the premises for development progress (see Blondel 2014: 707, 712). Leaders of a different type could radically transform the political landscape and engender true socioeconomic change. Among the most committed supporters of the saliency of individual agency – leaders matter, and they matter a great deal for the material and physical wellbeing of their fellow citizens – is Robert Rotberg (2004, 2013:189ff.). South of the Sahara, he points out, "the idiosyncratic behaviors of individual leaders have mattered more than colonial legacies, arbitrary borders, inherited national deficiencies, and the like" (2013:192). However, although Rotberg's work contains some useful accounts of successful as well as detrimental leadership stories in the region, much

---

[5] See the Online Appendix to Easterly and Pennings (2018).

of it is little systematic and strongly normative, with a stress on the visionary skills that make for truly "transformational" (as opposed to "transactional") leaders, as epitomized by Nelson Mandela in South Africa and Seretse Khama in Botswana. Other studies similarly cite the importance of better leadership to spur growth and development in Africa; but their analyses remain rather generic, with calls for the formation of broad coalitions for change (Gray and McPherson 2001:729) or even the creation of training schools for aspiring leaders (Rotberg 2013). Radelet (2010) also mentions a new generation of leaders among the factors behind the success of sub-Saharan emerging economies; but his attention is on policy-makers, activists, and business leaders rather than on national power-holders.

Around the mid-1990s, a number of guerrillas-turned-presidents had seemed to embody a long hoped-for break with Africa's past sins and to show the way forward (Connell and Smyth 1998; Ottaway 1999). First, as early as 1986 the charismatic Yoweri Museveni had overthrown the government in Uganda and began rebuilding the entire structure of the state from the bottom up (Carbone 2008). Ethiopia's Meles Zenawi and Eritrea's Isaias Afwerki soon followed in his footsteps, and Paul Kagame joined in after his Rwandan Patriotic Front (RPF) ended the 1994 genocide and took over in Kigali. These four assertive political figures had all come to office through the gun. They turned their insurgent movements into governing parties and, by maintaining a firm authoritarian grip on state power for two to three decades or more, set their countries on a new and impressive developmental path (although in the Eritrean case this only lasted until the war with Ethiopia at the end of the 1990s). The advent of the "new breed" and their reconstruction of both state apparatuses and the economy was widely celebrated. But their relationship with the reformed institutions of their countries remained complex and soon displayed an evident antidemocratic streak, leading some observers to question the actual distinctiveness and novelty that they represented.

Only a handful of scholars have adopted large-N approaches to the study of African leaders and their government performances. Franck and Rainer (2012) start from the well-known thesis whereby Africa's high ethnic diversity has hindered common decisions on the provision of public goods and thus the adoption of policies supportive of economic growth (Easterly and Levine 1997; Alesina et al. 2003). But they choose an unusual perspective. They examine the role of sub-Saharan leaders in welfare by selectively focusing on ethnic favoritism, and they show how the ethnic background of a ruler is positively related to education (primary school enrolment and completion, and literacy rates) and health improvements (infant mortality rates) among his fellow co-ethnics. Their findings, based on a sample of 18 sub-Saharan countries, are consistent with the argument that ethnic heterogeneity is harmful for growth.

Profiling the biographical features of African power-holders was also the aim of a simple survey conducted by the Developmental Leadership Program (Theron 2011, 2012). Data on the age, education, professional backgrounds, and careers of 158 leaders who held office for at least four years between 1960 and 2010 were collected. The aim of the survey was primarily descriptive, and it showed, for example, that the leaders' average age when they took office – i.e., 49 years – hid wide variations. They ranged from the very young age of some military rulers, such as Valentine Strasser (25 years old when he captured the presidency in Sierra Leone, in 1992), Michel Micombero (26, ruled Burundi for ten years from 1966), or Yahya Jammeh (president of the Gambia between 1994 and 2017), to much older figures like Mandela (76) in South Africa, Ntsu Mokhehle (76) of Lesotho, or Abdoulaye Wade (74) of Senegal, all of whom were voted into office. More generally, office-holders who reached power in 2000–2010 were on average 12 years older than those who came to power during the 1960s – with military rulers as a lot averaging 40 years. Yet the aim of these profiles was not just descriptive. An explicit if simplistic association was established between these profiles, on the one hand, and the political behaviors and developmental achievements of power-holders, on the other. It turned out that the leaders of the countries recording the best economic performances in the post-2000 period were typically older and better educated than those who ran poorly performing states.

A more sophisticated effort is that by Goldsmith (2001, 2004), who theorizes on the conditions under which presidents as rational actors would or would not pursue development policies. He looks at 228 leaders between 1960 and 1999 and provides a rational-choice explanation of predatory rule. In the high-risk political environment outlined by the personal rule literature and empirically confirmed by the region's comparatively high rate of military coups and wars, African power-holders tend to adopt short-term survival strategies that prove harmful to the development of their countries. With 17 percent of leaders assassinated while in power, the job of leading an African country is about 170 times more dangerous than the three most perilous occupations in the United States, namely commercial fisherman, logger, and small plane operator (Goldsmith 2001:82). Reflecting this political uncertainty and high-risk context, utility-maximizing office-holders apply a political discount rate. This induces them to opt "rationally" for the low but immediate returns of short-term policy-making and political corruption, rather than for investments in long-term reforms and public goods.

Goldsmith, however, was also quick to realize the potential of the political reforms that sub-Saharan states underwent in the early 1990s (2004:107). It is likely that constitutional changes and multiparty elections were altering the incentives for national rulers and encouraging them to focus more on public goods. The manifest decline of military coups implied a reduction in perceived risks. Accordingly, national leaders were probably becoming less inclined to short-termism and more to longer time-horizons allowing them to invest in policies that would improve developmental performances. The institutionalization of elections produces at least three additional benefits (Goldsmith 2001:86). The first is that the penalties of losing office are softened. The prospect of being defeated is plausibly more tolerable than that of being killed, detained, or exiled, as often happens after a coup. Reduced political risks, as pointed out, enhance the performance of office-holders. Secondly, scheduled elections can drastically cut speculation about when and how the next leadership transition will take place. Policy, rather than survival strategies, can thus return to center stage. Finally, periodic elections (and the related term limits) also facilitate leadership handovers and foster a view of political offices as temporary jobs rather than entitlements. At the turn of the century, Goldsmith argued that the time was ripe for better governments and that the latter could positively contribute to the rise of a new, "emerging Africa."

The Institutionalization of Political Power and Development

In the 30 years after independence, African countries became synonymous with non-performing authoritarian states. In a context of prevailing economic stagnation, politics in the region came to be overtly dominated by personalities rather than by formal rules, organizations, and institutions. The politics of succession proved particularly problematic, as the case of little-known Togo illustrates. On January 13, 1963, the president of this small West African country was overthrown and killed by his soldiers, who left his body at the gates of the US embassy in the capital Lomé. Sylvanus Olympio had ruled Togo for less than three years when he became the first victim in a series of 85 coups d'état that took place in Africa over the following 55 years. A few years later, one of Olympio's murderers, Gnassingbé Eyadéma, took over as new head of state. Like Olympio, he too would die in office. Yet this only happened in 2005, after 38 years of uninterrupted rule. Eyadéma was one of Africa's longest serving presidents.

The cases of Olympio and Eyadéma exemplify the trouble with leadership transitions in postcolonial Africa. Two distinct and yet related political syndromes were at work. The first had to do with frequent political instability. In many countries, the military took power sooner or later after independence, on the initiative of army chiefs of staff (as in the case of David Mountsaka in Congo-Brazzaville in 1963, Joseph-Desiré Mobutu in Congo-Kinshasa in 1965, Jean-Bédel Bokassa in the Central African Republic in 1966, Yakubu Gowon in Nigeria in 1966, Idi Amin of Uganda in 1971, or Juvénal Habyarimana in Rwanda in 1973), high-ranking officers (for example, Gaafar Nimeiry in Sudan in 1969 and Mathieu Kérékou in Benin in 1972) or junior military officers (the likes of Moussa Traoré in Mali in 1968 and Jerry Rawlings in Ghana in 1981). The embryonic armies of the new African states were able to claim a governing role in the fragile context created by ethnic fragmentation and expectations of rapid economic development. External backing was easily obtained from the West or the Communist bloc in exchange for Cold War allegiance. Once military leaders had managed to take power, they were often replaced through further military overthrows. Thus, for example, Nigeria's 1966 coup by Major General Johnson Aguiyi-Ironsi, largely a reaction to Igbo marginalization in the army, was quickly followed by a second coup that restored the Hausa-Fulani's primacy over the military. In Burkina Faso, the 1966 and 1982 coups were followed by Thomas Sankara's takeover in 1983, and then by the 1987 *golpe* in which Sankara himself was assassinated. Benin, Burkina Faso, Burundi, the Comoros, Ghana, Guinea-Bissau, Mauritania, Niger, Nigeria, and Sierra Leone each had between four and seven coups d'état, which contributed to significant periods of political instability.

The second political syndrome of post-colonial Africa was the excessively long stay in power of many of its rulers. Omar Bongo, the longest serving office-holder south of the Sahara, became president of Gabon in 1967, on the death of his predecessor, Leon M'ba. He remained in power until his own passing in 2009, when he was succeeded by his son, Ali Bongo Ondimba. José Eduardo dos Santos governed Angola for almost four decades since 1979, whereas Cameroon has seen only one succession in the presidency during its 55 years as an independent nation, in 1982, when Ahmadou Ahidjo peacefully handed over power to Paul Biya. The same occurred in eSwatini – Africa's last absolute monarchy besides Morocco – where king Mswati III succeeded his father Sobhuza II after the latter's death in 1983, and in Zimbabwe, if only with Mugabe's fall in 2017. Eritrea, *de facto* independent since 1991, is yet to see the back of its first leader. In all of these countries, leadership stability reached the point where the same person remained at the helm for two, three, and at times even four decades.

The swift manifestation of these two prevailing political trends was not missed by early observers of politics south of the Sahara:

Thirty-one black African nations have gained their independence in the past decade, and they all share a curious distinction: in not a single one of them has any government ever been voted out of office. The record is not exactly a testimonial to democratic stability. Political assassinations and military coups have transformed half of the continent's emerging nations into emergency nations, and the governments of most of the rest have hung on either by openly rigging elections or outlawing their political opposition entirely.[6]

In some cases, the first syndrome evolved toward the second syndrome. Colonel Joseph-Desiré Mobutu, for example, turned the 1965 military takeover of Congo-Kinshasa into a strongly personalized rule that lasted for 32 years. Equatorial Guinea, on the other hand, is still under the control of Teodoro Obiang Nguema Mbasogo, who took office in a 1979 coup. In several African states, long tenure in office was accompanied by the consolidation of single-party rule. Two years after taking over in Cotonou, Major Kérékou set up the Parti de la

---

[6] "Sierra Leone. End of the exception," *Time*, March 31, 1967.

Révolution Populaire du Bénin to have this sole political organization allowed prop up his Marx-Leninist regime, together with the army. In Zambia, the United National Independence Party (UNIP) was instrumental to Kenneth Kaunda's power system, enabling him to control nominations for one-party parliamentary elections in the 1970s and 1980s. The same applies to the Chama Cha Mapinduzi (CCM) in Tanzania, established with the merger of the Tanganyika African National Union (TANU) and the Afro-Shirazi Party under the auspices of Julius Nyerere, or to the Kenya African National Union (KANU) of Jomo Kenyatta and Daniel Arap Moi. At the time, it must be noted, supporters of one-partism ranged much wider than would subsequently be the case, and included many Western analysts:

> the tendency towards single-party systems in West Africa ... my argument is that mass parties are created by African leaders out of the very liberating and egalitarian forces we in this country generally associate with democracy. Some of the mass parties encourage the growth of forces and institutions which may ultimately make possible the machinery of democratic systems familiar to us: as, for instance, competition for every citizen's vote by more than one organized team of candidates. At this stage of West African party history ... the number of parties is far too simple a criterion upon which to decide whether or not a system is democratic. (Schacther 1961:294)

In an early, rare quantitative study of pre-1987 African rulers, Bienen and van de Walle (1989) investigated the reasons for the puzzling combination of rapid turnovers, on the one hand, and durable rule on the other. They found that the length of time already spent in power was the best predictor of whether a leader would lose his position at any given point during his stay in office. Neither the personal characteristics of the 165 rulers examined (age on assuming power, military versus civilian background, etc.) nor the features of the 51 countries that they governed (level of development, growth rates, colonial background, ethnic conflict, etc.) proved to be substantially relevant factors. The main exception was the advantage enjoyed by founding fathers as opposed to subsequent leaders, with the former significantly less likely to fall during the early years of their tenure, probably due to the legitimacy that they derived from a newly gained independence and large patronage opportunities. Other than that, the main explanation, as mentioned, was time itself. The risk of losing power generally declined over time. Over one-third of leaders lost office in the first three years since they took over, arguably as a result of a selection process whereby the least skilful among them were unable to hold on and were ousted. Thereafter, the risk decreased sharply and the trend was not subsequently reversed, as the authors had hypothesized, by a leader growing very old or by his/her "excessively long" (say, more than two decades) stay in power. Time fostered the consolidation of a leader's power base rather than weakening his or her grip.

After three decades of one-party and military authoritarianism and neopatrimonialism, economic and state weakness intertwined, reaching their zenith between the 1980s and early 1990s. By that time, as a result of both domestic and external pressures, many African countries had embarked on political reforms that radically altered the political landscape of the region. Within a few years, most states had embraced multiparty politics, albeit with great variations as to the substance of political change (Bratton and van de Walle 1997; Cheeseman 2015). Elections contested by multiple parties became the norm in a continent that, with the notable exceptions of Botswana and Mauritius, had long stood clear of them. This represented a political watershed. Take Mozambique, for example. Following independence, the ruling Frente de Libertação de Moçambique (Frelimo) party had to fight the Rhodesia-sponsored guerrillas of the Resistência Nacional Moçambicana (Renamo). The country plunged into a civil war that lasted until a peace agreement was signed in 1992. By 1994 – and every five years thereafter – formally democratic elections were organized in which Frelimo and Renamo competed for the votes of Mozambicans. Frelimo's hegemonic hold on power, however, *de facto* remained unchallenged. In faraway Mali, a 1991 coup opened the way to a democratic transition in the following year. In Nigeria, the military handed power to an elected president in 1999 and since then has refrained from taking over again. In Equatorial Guinea, Gabon and Cameroon, incumbent presidents allowed multiparty contests that they were in fact able to control. While the outcome of political reforms differed widely from country to country, Africa had entered the age of multiparty elections.

Leadership selection processes in the region were deeply affected by institutional changes. Political developments in Malawi provide a good illustration. For large part of the country's history as an independent nation, the national government was controlled by a single individual. True to his self-assigned "president-for-life" title, Hastings Kamuzu

Banda remained uninterruptedly in office for 30 years following independence day in 1964. He was only ousted from power in 1994, at the age of 96, when opposition candidate Bakili Muluzi defeated him in the country's first multiparty election. After ten years in office, Muluzi himself stood down due to constitutional term limits that he had failed to remove. He was succeeded by Bingu wa Mutharika, also belonging to the United Democratic Front (UDF). Soon after his 2004 election, however, president Mutharika broke ranks with the UDF and went on to win a second mandate, in 2009, with the newly formed Democratic Progressive Party (DPP). His sudden death, in 2012, seriously challenged the soundness of Malawi's institutional framework. In the ensuing power struggle, Mutharika's estranged deputy Joyce Banda was installed as the country's new president and one of Africa's rare female heads of state. Banda, however, was defeated at the 2014 poll by opposition leader Peter Mutharika, the brother of the deceased president. Thus, over the last two decades, four different presidents held the country's top office. Through some testing times, Malawi succeeded in significantly strengthening its constitutional norms and multiparty setup.

African polities thus took a few timid but clear steps toward the depersonalization of politics. Post-independence Africa, as said, had been dominated by "big man" politics and personal rule to such an extent that the terms had developed into a paradigm somehow implying that the continent was a place unto itself, a place where "rules [did] not shape leaders' behaviour; leaders' behaviour trump[ed] rules" (Posner and Young 2007:127). As the 1990s reforms extended the use of multiparty elections to virtually all African countries, formal institutions began to matter more. Some constraints were gradually being brought to bear upon African power-holders. When Daniel Arap Moi, Joaquim Chissano, Benjamin Mkapa, and Olusegun Obasanjo initially tried to seek a third term that was prohibited by the constitution, for example, they were eventually convinced to desist by existing rules (and by political oppositions crying foul). One key result is that, today, there is "more to African politics than personalist rule" (Govea and Holm 1998:147; Posner and Young 2007:137).

It is quite a striking paradox, from a comparative perspective, that the politics of advanced countries have followed an opposite trajectory that also started in the 1990s. Several scholars had long emphasized the decline of political parties in the West. Evidence of a growing personalization of politics in European countries – or "a shift of power to the benefit of individual leaders" (Poguntke and Webb 2015:249) – was an added feature manifest in the increased role of individual office-holders in terms of executive powers and resources, primacy within their parties, and direct links and communications with the electorate (Poguntke and Webb 2005, 2015; Blondel and Thiebault 2010). In the words of Musella and Webb, "the rise of personal leaders has produced a Copernican revolution in party politics ... they are becoming the *dominus* of governmental activities ... the emergence of 'personal leaders' is the expression we use to describe both the political reinforcement of individual leaders and the direct relationship they share with citizens" (2015:223). And again: "personalization is not a contingent factor ... but rather, it appears to indicate a structural change to the benefit of leaders" (2015:226).

Africa, as mentioned, was moving in the opposite direction. In their analysis of the entire post-independence period, Posner and Young (2007) refer to a gradual "institutionalisation of political power" that took place between the early 1990s and 2005 as a result of a variety of mechanisms. A number of incumbent presidents, for example, decided to accept constraints on their personal power out of a political urgency to respond to donors or to popular pressures, of arranging a succession, of working out inter-elite accommodation (Jackson and Rosberg 1982:286). Regular leadership successions imply "that there is an understood set of basic limits on how long a head of state may stay in power, as well as on how his opponents may seek to replace him. It therefore marks the most important step toward restraining executive power and institutionalizing political authority more broadly" (Posner and Young 2007:130). Earlier, Govea and Holm (1998) had also looked at how constitutional and other rules, such as established political practices, governed leadership transitions in the 1963–1988 period. They posited that leadership successions are time-bound events, and that how they take place – notably the extent to which they follow established procedures or rather are sanctioned by the use of force or a claim to control it – represents "a kind of 'critical experiment'" whose study helps illuminate whether and to what extent a system is in the process of institutionalizing (Govea and Holm 1998:130). Two or more successions are needed to allow any inference as to whether handover processes have been institutionalized. As Jackson and Rosberg (1982:284–285) had observed, "time for a series of situations and actions to recur" is the key factor in telling us whether a process of institutionalization leading to a clearer distinction between office and office-holder has occurred. Violent overthrows have become significantly less common, making Africa in this respect more similar to other world regions. Reversals of the current institutionalization process are of course possible. Indeed, this is how recent coups and constitutional amendments enabling sitting presidents to prolong their stays in power should be read.

Both the works by Posner and Young (2007) and Govea and Holm (1998) share an interest in whether successions at the helm of a country are "regulated" as opposed to "unregulated." In this sense, they come close to what we set out to do in this book. In both cases, however, leadership handovers are investigated as a dependent variable explained by such factors as a country's level of development, domestic crises, public opinion attitudes, donors' pressures, and leaders' age. Govea and Holm (1998:132) do not miss the broader implications of their analysis. They hint at the causal role that political successions may play by pointing out that, in African states, they offer a unique opportunity for policy changes. Nevertheless, we depart from these and virtually all other existing analyses since our focus is on the impact of leadership selection processes on development progress.

The rationale of this book on leadership change stems from the kind of political evolution that has prevailed in Africa over the past 25 years. Political leaders – "personal rulers" in the language of the African politics literature – dominated postcolonial Africa's regimes. The multiparty reforms of the 1990s were meant to change how and when they were selected, held accountable, and replaced. Did the reforms actually affect the evolution of leadership in Africa? Do leadership trends, in their turn, influence government socioeconomic performances and a country's development? We address these issues on the assumption that individual leaders, institutional frameworks, and government policies are inextricably intertwined, as we explain in Chapter 2. Political leaders seek to maximize their tenure. Institutions determine how and the extent to which they can achieve this goal. The shape and effectiveness of government policies is crucially affected by the inducements that national leaders face within a given institutional framework. We postulate that electoral competition and alternation in office help African citizens to improve the accountability of their leaders. The risk of being removed from power generates incentives for incumbents wanting to maximize their reelection chances to provide public goods and increase the level of social welfare. At the same time, elections help opposition parties to monitor the behavior of rulers and to unmask their malfeasances. Politico-institutional reforms introducing competition for popular votes, in other words, alter a ruler's incentives to provide effective public policies. Based on new and comprehensive data on all African leaders since independence, we will be able to capture major trends in leadership change patterns – with a particular focus on the role of contested elections, coups d'état, constitutional successions, political alternations, tenure length, and so on – and systematically investigate the social, economic or political *consequences* of leadership changes in Africa. Ultimately, our analysis and empirical findings will challenge the pessimism of those observers who emphasize the capturing of electoral processes in Africa by dominant elites, and especially political leaders, able to use state power to buy support without having to provide public goods and welfare in return.

2 | Coming to Power and Using It
Leaders' Selection, Change, and Government Performance

Leadership and National Development

Leadership has long been a surprisingly neglected topic in political science. For all the daily as well as historical attention we pay to national power-holders, the study of politics has only devoted relatively limited efforts to digging into the dynamics of political leadership. When this has been done, it was rarely aimed at examining the extent to which a country's trajectory is affected by the actions of he or she who governs it. The leadership and development nexus, in particular, has been ignored in empirical studies of African politics and development, in spite of the fact that a large majority of politicians, citizens, and observers systematically acknowledge not only that such a link exists, but also that it has a very important bearing. In this work, we posit that leadership matters.

The hallmark of a leader's success is not so much his or her survival in power per se – albeit, of course, time is a relevant component – but his or her leading a country *toward* development. History records a large number of prominent figures that are at least notionally associated with national economic or socioeconomic advancement, from Otto von Bismarck to Franklin Delano Roosevelt, from Margaret Thatcher to Augusto Pinochet, from Lee Kuan Yew to Luiz Inácio Lula da Silva. These and several others stand opposite to the many that are remembered as power-holders who were deleterious to, or entirely ruined, their countries' progress, including the wildly different experiences of the United States' Herbert Hoover, Zaire's Mobutu Ssese Seko, the Philippines' Ferdinand Marcos, North Korea's Kim Jong II, or Haiti's François and Jean-Claude Duvalier. Besides national independence or international war, the most important legacy attributed to a political leader is typically success or failure in the pursuit of a country's social and economic improvement.

While acknowledging that academic research has thus far failed to demonstrate the relevance of leaders for economic development, a reexamination of the 13 high-growth stories from the second half of the twentieth century originally included in the World Bank's *Growth Report* (2008) led Brady and Spence to make the point again:

> leadership plays a role in generating sustained growth ... There is no one style of leadership ... nor is leadership the only input ... [Yet] practitioners and observers and a wide range of scholars are right in believing that, at least at times, leadership makes a difference in terms of altering the trajectory of a developing economy ... The obvious first stage is where the leadership chooses an economic model or strategy ... The second stage ... concerns how leaders adjust strategies and choices to changing circumstances. (Brady and Spence 2010b:2–5)

It is straightforward that there are bound to be limits to the extent to which any leader can impose his or her actions, choices, and policies so as to affect the course of a nation's trajectory. Political leadership has to contend with several other factors. The latter include domestic impediments, external restraints, and structural forces. Domestic constraints primarily hinge on the presence and role of additional politico-institutional actors. Top office-holders are never alone in making and implementing decisions, and what they can or cannot do depends on a country's context in terms of institutions (e.g., the constitutional framework, the level of state capacity, the baseline that existing policies represent) as well as of political hindrances or counterweights (e.g., a governing coalition, organized actors and interests, including ruling party factions, the military, the bureaucracy, the oppositions, and so on). Studies such as Bueno de Mesquita et al.'s (2003) and Svolik's (2012), for example, have emphasised the importance of the coalitional dimensions of leadership. Secondly, external limitations are also at play in terms of resources and policy space. During the Cold War, for example, the logic of international alignments and competition implied that most states in either of the two coalitions were potentially subject to substantial domestic interference on the part of an external heavyweight, whether located in Washington or Moscow. More recently, it is the interdependences that globalization has brought about – such as a significant dependence on aid, commodity prices, or financial markets – that have tended to narrow the scope for action of national governments, while potentially expanding the capacity of foreign actors such as multinationals, donor countries, international organizations, or regional bodies to affect domestic policy-making. Finally, structural factors and forces – think, for example, of the role of massive demographic expansion, infectious disease epidemics or climate change effects in regions such as Asia or Africa, or just merely the importance of a country's level of development and resource endowments – can also heavily shape national advances and retreats.

Even when we take into account these constraints, leaders do generally retain a scope for producing an impact on a country's course of development. But when and why do they use this room for maneuver and developmental initiative, as opposed to adopting conducts and measures that are unfavourable to their nation's overall progress?

In a rare and early work bordering our approach, Valerie Bunce (1981:44) asked whether "*new* leaders make a difference" in terms of "policy priorities":

leadership succession is the most visible and salient aspect of the political process ... whether through election or *coup d'état*, [it] is considered important not only because it concerns power and the powerful but also because of its implications for change. New leaders may mean new policies ... or a change in government performance ... Thus ... the central importance of leadership succession is not the process itself, but rather its expected impact. (Bunce 1980:373)

An initial empirical analysis of seven democracies confirmed that "leadership change means policy change" (Bunce 1980:384): rather than being "dispensable actors," as claimed by Greenstein (1969), elected chief executives proved to be pivotal players that did affect policy processes (Bunce 1980:391). Her conclusion that new leaders matter and that they do precisely because of their *newness* was subsequently extended to also include succession dynamics in socialist states. In spite of the vast politico-institutional differences distinguishing these from Western democracies, in both sets of countries a government's budgetary priorities appeared to be substantially altered soon after an individual at the top was replaced, resulting in "a succession cycle" whereby "new leaders make a difference in the rhythm of policy change and the types of policies that are advocated ... succession is a mechanism of policy innovation ... a regularized process of policy evaluation and change" (Bunce 1981: 223–224, 239).

While we obviously share Bunce's focus on leadership as a potentially consequential factor, there are several fundamental differences with the perspective we adopt. For a start, Bunce looked at leadership changes as such, regardless of the underlying politico-institutional features. On the contrary, we deem the latter to be crucial in setting key behavioural incentives for any incoming leader. Secondly, she adopted a cyclical notion of policy innovation centred on a leader's honeymoon period. Accordingly, she focused on the occurrence and the amount of policy change regardless of its direction, that is, of whether such change led to development progress or failure. This was in line with her choice of budgetary adjustments as the dependent variable in her quantitative analyses (although she also added case studies of agricultural and welfare policies). Bunce justified this as "a fair, but tough, test" since, "if elites can alter budgetary allocations by virtue of their rotation in office, then succession would indeed be an important political variable" (1981:50). A similar approach, however, once again deflects attention away from the development outcomes that are central to our perspective. Finally, she examined cases drawn from the so-called first and second worlds. At a minimum, her hypotheses would need retesting under the conditions prevailing in developing countries, particularly under the relative dysfunctionality of many African nations, including the frequency of irregular takeovers (as opposed to regularized or managed successions of most of the cases she investigated) and the prevalence of weak state capacity for policy implementation.

Departing from the main focus of leadership studies – namely, a leader's peculiar features, such as personality traits, ethnic, social, or political background, decision-making style, and the like – we believe that the behavior (and thus performance) of power-holders can be at least in part traced to context-induced pressures. A leader's course of action is shaped by the environment in which the political game is played out. In particular, choices and actions are largely responses to the prevailing incentives that are set by political institutions. The essence of the institutional environment office-holders are confronted with, and thus the main sets of incentives that shape their behavior, is best revealed by the way they reach and leave power – that is, by the dynamics of leadership selection and change, the central variables in our analysis.

We thus see a fundamental triangular interaction at play between individual leaders, the politico-institutional environment they operate in, and a country's development achievements. This triangulation does not occur in a vacuum, but rather in a given socioeconomic and state context that defines the terms of the core triangular relationship. State capacity and a country's existing socioeconomic conditions are essential factors influencing the extent to which policy decisions can be turned into concrete actions. At the same time, both the socioeconomic context and the capacity of a state are, in the medium and long term, inevitably affected and even profoundly transformed by a nation's development progress or regress.

We expect a ruler's behavior to contribute decisively to whether a country's politics have a prevalence of predatory activities as opposed to development-oriented policies and outcomes. Our perspective on individual agency within a given institutional framework, with the related political incentives and development achievements, is somewhat close to the influential work by Bueno de Mesquita and his colleagues, who set off from the assumption that "all actions taken by political leaders are intended by them to be compatible with their desire to retain power ... the critical question is how political institutions shape the goal of some leaders to produce peace and prosperity" (Bueno de Mesquita et al. 2003:8). They posit, in particular, that office-holders provide a combination of public goods (including such "intangible" things as the rule of law, human rights or national security) that benefit all members of society, and private goods that, on the contrary, are selectively distributed to specific individuals or constituencies. The latter type of goods may include jobs, government-granted monopolies or concessions, access to credit or hard currency, or the bribes and other inducements that only state officials can secure (Bueno de Mesquita et al. 2002:561). In this perspective, institutional arrangements – notably the "selection institutions" that the authors call the "winning coalition" (W) and the "selectorate" (S) – determine incentives, a leader's behavior, and ultimately his or her performance.

Yet our work also differs substantially from the approach of the selectorate theory. Contrary to what we do, when Bueno de Mesquita and his co-authors mention "leaders" they do not always refer to single individuals. Rather, the term is used indistinctly for individual as well as collective actors: "the smallest set of individuals is the leadership ... *one or more central individuals* with the authority to raise revenue and allocate resources ... a country's political leadership or leader ... one might, loosely speaking, think of the leadership in the United States as the president, speaker of the House and majority leader in the Senate" (2003:39). Moreover, in practice, the selectorate theory focuses on political regimes rather than leaders (if in an original way rather than through classic categorical classifications of regimes). The operationalization of what the authors call "selection institutions" – that is, S and W – is essentially based on some of the component variables of the widely used Polity index (Mesquita et al. 2003:134ff.). In choosing these components, the authors do set them apart from other features that are often deemed crucial to distinguishing between democratic and nondemocratic regimes (such as constraints on executive power or protection of civil and political rights). Yet their emphasis remains on some key "rules of the game" that typically last significantly longer than an individual's stay in office. In this way, they are unable, for example, to account for the impact of leadership successions or alternations in power that take place under unmodified rules. Through our Africa Leadership Change dataset (see Chapter 3), on the other hand, we focus on individual leaders and on how they access power as an indicator of the pressures and incentives that are likely to shape their actions. We are thus able to distinguish not only between leaders who enter office legally (via an election or otherwise) as opposed to unconstitutionally (via a coup or an armed rebellion), but, within the former group, we can tell apart those who replace a sitting leader in the context of ruling-party continuity from those who win office by electorally defeating an incumbent. These are crucial distinctions since a country's power transfers may signal dramatic adjustments *under the surface of regime continuity*, such as when a leader who originally took over illegitimately through a coup d'état is "laundered" and legitimized by transition elections, with a subsequent handover to a successor hailing from the ruling party and unconnected to the military, and maybe later to an opposition leader who succeeds in ousting the incumbent through the ballot box, and so on.

The notion that leaders matter implies that consequential political change often occurs precisely at the level of individual power-holders, rather than just political regimes. We thus look at leadership in a way that is partly separated from regime classifications. Our focus on power handovers is both narrower than democracy measures (since it allows us to single out individual leadership episodes, rather than regimes as lasting sets of rules and practices) as well as more comprehensive and fine-grained than democracy measures (for example, it accounts for nondemocratic handovers that take place in autocratic settings via coups or through non-electoral but peaceful transfers of power; see Chapter 3). We deem this to be a crucial point, since, as Govea and Holm observe, "in African polities, political successions provide one of the only opportunities for policy and structural changes ... a window during which policies and objectives come into question. To overlook successions because of the self-centred motives of the players ... is to miss key events in the evolution of African polities" (1998:132).

Because leaders may matter even more where formal political institutions are relatively weak, Africa is a context where we expect the impact of leadership to be at its starkest. But there is one caveat. Our expectation that leaders make a difference cannot but hinge on the precondition of a minimally functioning administration in a sufficiently stable environment, as Blondel (1987:25) aptly noted. Where state capacity is entirely absent or excessively low – notably, where it is wrecked by domestic conflict – any power-holder may hold little power. He or she becomes toothless, as any measures and initiatives that are taken are bound to remain largely on paper and fail to affect society or the economy. Where regulatory and administrative capacity is virtually absent, a leader's effort and the resources he or she may devote to the achievement of progress – such as welfare spending or reforms – are most likely to be derailed or to fail in some other way. The formal introduction of, say, a new agricultural or health policy will have limited consequences in such dysfunctional or spoilt places as Afghanistan, Yemen, or South Sudan currently are, where the basic political and administrative framework for turning ideas into actions is largely missing. It is only when a state's presence is sufficiently, if minimally, established that a leader can try and achieve meaningful change. We thus share the idea that "any attempt to understand the independent effects of democracy" – or, for that matter, of other politico-institutional setups – "should control for state institutional capacity" (Korolev 2016:443–444; cf. Norris 2012), which we shall empirically proxy through a measure of political order as a prerequisite for policy implementation and development achievements. Nor does this exhaust the complex leadership-stateness connection, since individual leaders themselves, as we shall discuss next, possess significant potential for contributing to building and consolidating a state, thus affecting the level of state capacity and ultimately their own room for making public action effective.

Electoral Mechanisms: Democratic and Beyond

Our core causal argument is about national leaders affecting development outcomes in sub-Saharan Africa. We expect the conditions under which a leader comes to power – that is, the modes of leadership change – to shape the extent to which he or she will pursue and promote a country's development. This is tantamount to saying that we do not assume democratic politicians to be innately different from autocratic rulers, since "politicians differ not in their goals but in the institutional contexts in which they seek to satisfy their desires ... when politicians are not tightly bound by the citizens they oversee, they use the monopoly power of the state to earn rents for themselves" (Lake and Baum 2001:617). The causal conditions we look at vary primarily in terms of leaders being elected in a multiparty context as opposed to being unelected (or elected under one-party systems), but we also investigate a number of additional possibilities and features related to the way power-holders come to office (e.g., peaceful non-electoral handovers, number of elections, genuinely democratic votes, succession via the ballot box, alternation between opposite political forces). We expect a country's development progress to be empirically connected to the abovementioned starting conditions. The baseline is that, overall, elected leaders will produce development outcomes that are comparatively better than those produced by non-elected leaders. And the more so when leaders are elected through open democratic votes, in highly competitive contests, and maybe even winning power from the opposition.

With regard to Africa, the perspective we adopt implies a relatively positive view of the often incomplete "democratic reforms" that the continent underwent since the early 1990s. Observers who take a different, pessimistic standpoint claim that several entrenched leaders on the continent have been able to use ethnic identities and communal divides, patronage distributions, and clientelist networks to capture, manipulate, or bypass electoral processes. As a result, the region is now littered with pseudo-democracies in which politics is merely "business as usual." We do not deny that the reforms of the 1990s were to a significant extent derailed and that they certainly achieved much less than what was promised. Yet, on balance, they fundamentally altered the prevailing political processes and dynamics and ushered in a largely new political scenario. With all its ups and downs, as well as its many limits and continuities, the post-1990 political landscape never went back to what was in place before 1990. The newly established multiparty elections, with the leadership changes and the alternations in office that they favored, did contribute to establishing a better political environment throughout much of sub-Saharan Africa. It is hard to question that the room for rights and freedoms has expanded. But we move beyond a mere assessment of the actual extent of regime change, which has thus far been the main task political scientists and area studies scholars embarked upon. In such a comparatively poor and needy setting as Africa generally remains, one has to ask whether political reforms actually translated into improved governmental action, better provision of public goods and, ultimately, development progress, as much democratic theory explicitly predicts or indirectly implies (cf. Lake and Baum 2001; Bueno de Mesquita et al. 2002; Brown et al. 2009). This is all the more important since development failures had been prevalent among the region's postcolonial states, regimes, and rulers.

In principle, the idea that adopting political reforms should have improved the government performance of African leaders seems plausible. Open and democratic politics affect the way leaders take and leave office, how long they stay in power, and what they do while they are in charge. Any democratic contest implies at least a minimum of uncertainty about who will win office among competing candidates. Because neither the incumbent nor the political party he or she belongs to can rule out defeat, they might both want to work hard to maximize their chances of being reelected. This pressure is bound to foster a degree of electoral accountability – if certainly a variable one – since an elected ruler who wants to retain power and offset the opposition will try to respond to bottom-up demands, needs, and concerns by adopting vote-winning public policies and by furthering the government's overall performance. A reasonably free flow of information plays a critical role in allowing a degree of transparency and responsibility. The other side of the electoral accountability link consists of citizens' empowerment, whereby voters become increasingly aware of the opportunity they have of exerting pressure through the ballot they cast. They learn to use their "voice" and "exit" options to maximize the chances that rulers behave and perform well, and to replace non-performing ones with more promising candidates. In this perspective, open and inclusive multiparty competition becomes a key precondition for accountable governments, and the main incentive for them to build the strongest possible performance record, especially when an electoral defeat looms as a real possibility. Actual alternation in office is deemed a vital step in democratization processes by leading scholars such as Huntington (1991) and Przeworski et al. (2000, 2015). In Africa, Bratton similarly found "a very strong relationship between the proximity of an electoral alternation and shifts in the amount of democracy people perceive in their country" (2004:155). The very prospect of losing office creates incentives for incumbents, who aim at being reelected, to contain corruption and respond to citizens' demands for public action. It also makes voters conscious of their ability to "throw the rascals out" of government, inducing them to raise their voices in demanding adequate responses to their social and economic concerns. Ultimately, democracy is expected to work as a self-correcting mechanism that helps gradually improve government performances.

Studies that focus on the socioeconomic consequences of political regimes – notably on what happens *after* new democratic institutions are introduced – have grown stronger in recent years (Carbone 2009), partly rebalancing the overwhelming predominance of inquiries into how democracy is first established. Under effective democratic conditions – as the thrust of the "consequences of democratization" stream in the literature goes – party pluralism, electoral competition, and government alternation strengthen the political responsiveness of those in power to the evolving environment and related popular demands, and thus favor economic and policy performances that are comparatively better than those of "closed" regimes.

Our work further expands this perspective. The specific approach we adopt assumes that also multiparty elections *short of democracy* – by which we refer to regimes that fail to meet minimalist Schumpeterian standards for procedural democracy – may produce a progressive political impact, particularly in an African context where mechanisms for selecting, holding accountable, sanctioning, and replacing leaders were previously largely absent. As other analysts also observed, "even where elections did not contribute to processes of democratization, they transformed the relationship between political leaders and their supporters and so had a profound impact on African societies" (Cheeseman 2015:182). In our view, leadership change through pluralist elections proxies the presence of performance-enhancing politico-institutional arrangements and mechanisms, even when these do not fully satisfy democratic requirements.

Borrowing from Svolik's (2012) reasoning on authoritarian rule, we see the politics pursued by an unelected, dictatorial leader as being typically aimed at the exercise of both *external* control over the governed, through a mixture of cooptation and repression, as well as *internal* control to minimize the chances of being challenged by members of his/her own dominant coalition, that is, the "inner circle" of the regime. Both endeavors are meant to guarantee as much as possible an undemocratic ruler's prolonged stay in power. Controlling the inner circle, in particular, is a delicate but crucial task, since this is where contenders who successfully ousted authoritarian rulers have historically emerged from. Autocratic power-holders are thus largely bound to focus on a stick-and-carrot approach in which carefully balanced, selectively targeted distributive measures become a key activity, whereas public goods and development issues take a back seat.

When a leader comes to power through a vote, on the other hand, the focus of his or her political survival activities is not limited to the abovementioned control needs, but partly shifts toward earning and retaining electoral support. For leaders who are elected in a multiparty but still authoritarian state, there will be a significant overlap between control and consensus. Control over the governed requires stage-managing the electoral process toward the legitimation of the status quo. Yet being able to actually show substantial popular support becomes itself a tool for the retention of power.

The broader point is that legitimacy concerns are far from alien to most authoritarian rulers. Over time, explanations of autocrats' endeavors to prop up their legitimacy have emphasized distinct factors, from the role of ideology and terror to the relevance of socioeconomic performances, to the strategic use of institutions (Gerschewski 2013). Neo-institutionalist approaches, in particular, "recently entered the research on autocracies and ... highlighted the stabilizing effect of institutions. The role of political parties, legislatures, and elections as co-optation mechanisms" (Gerschewski 2013:16). Our work partly overlaps with this literature on legitimation strategies in authoritarian settings, notably with two of its main strands and the way they intertwine, as we focus on how *(electoral) institutions* likely add to African autocrats' efforts in delivering *development performances* that help further legitimise their rule and thus prolong their stay in office. While autocratic rulers may strategically adopt democratic trappings – whether to preempt protests and the need for costly repression, to respond to external pressures from international actors, or for other reasons – they may ultimately also have to adapt to formal democratic practices and "pay a price" by devoting greater energies to pleasing voters by somehow meeting their needs or demands. Accordingly, the room for public good-oriented measures that help cement voters' backing is likely to expand somewhat.

It is in the case of leaders that are elected in a more open and democratic political environment, however, that attention to voters turns into more of a priority. The emphasis on the need to build and retain consensus will be clearer – and so will be efforts to adopt broad-based policies that supposedly nurture it – whereas the scope for exerting control over the governed through repression and other forms of coercion shrinks. In principle, top-down control is entirely reversed when democratic standards are met: it is now ideally the electorate that, from the bottom up, holds sway over leaders both by voting them into office and by ejecting them from power.

To assess the actual impact of different forms of leadership on the provision of public goods, we will look empirically at key developmental consequences of government action, notably economic growth performances, social welfare progress, corruption containment, and state consolidation. In line with an established tradition, we assume that elected rulers are incentivized to allocate resources toward larger rather than narrower segments of the population and that this favors the promotion of developmental policies (cf. Brown and Mobarak 2009:195). In this view, elected and unelected leaders are not intrinsically different, but they are bound to act differently because they pursue their goals in highly diverse institutional contexts. Since the former are, at least to a degree, mandated from and accountable to their citizens, they are more likely to pay attention to the latter's demands and consent. This in turn reflects on an increased provision of public goods, as a critical intermediate goal for elected leaders. The electoral connection approach in which this perspective is moulded looks at political agency primarily as a reduced-form model of a broader economic theory of politics as utility maximization (Lake and Baum 2001:617).

From Regime Transitions to Leadership Changes

A number of chain-like connections bring together the different modes of leadership selection to development outcomes. At a general level, we assume a causal sequence whereby the *conditions* under which a leader takes office shape the *incentive* structure he/she faces, the latter affect his/her *behavior*, which in turn influences *policy decisions*, ultimately resulting in the promotion or hindering of *development achievements*. As should be clear, we do not see a dichotomous scenario at work in which democratic leadership handovers (and the settings in which they occur) are juxtaposed to nondemocratic power transfers (whether in electoral or non-electoral settings), but rather a continuum: to the extent that a leader's concern with actually obtaining and maintaining popular consensus grows, he/she will become more responsive toward the needs of the populace, whether these are explicitly articulated and expressed or not.

Therefore, we adopt a two-level framework. At a first level, the roots of the perspective we follow lie in "democratic advantage" or "consequences of democratization" theories, an approach that looks at what democratic polities, as opposed to the authoritarian, are likely to produce in terms of social, economic, and even political by-products. This approach rests on the basic assumption that incentives generated by the combination of expanded participation and open competition drive freely elected leaders toward striving more for the achievement of development progress than unelected rulers would do. Lest the former will lose their jobs. Democracies, it has been observed, "are distinctive ... not because they always identify the best policy but because they institutionalize the right to change leaders or policies when things go poorly" (Siegle et al. 2004:66). Since "the most important lesson to be learned by democratically elected elites is that growth performance matters for their political future" (Gerring 2005:331), the argument goes that democracies also make a better use of information in the processes of preference identification, policy choice, and disaster avoidance, as well as favoring the stability of the political system (cf. Khan 2005, who is actually skeptical). Several works support the notion that elections do contribute to shaping policy and progress in Africa as a result of interparty competition, campaign programs and commitments, information flows, retrospective voting, and more (e.g., Mattes 2008; Carbone 2011; Weghorst and Lindberg 2013; Harding and Stasavage 2014; Seekings 2014), although other scholars remain unconvinced and point to the prevalence of voting behaviors all-too-often driven by manipulation, clientelism, rent-seeking, ethnic bonds, or a sheer lack of information and sophistication (e.g.,

Keefer 2007; Booth 2011; Kelsall 2013; Booth et al. 2015). We shall examine more closely some of these arguments in Chapters 7 and 8.

At a second level, we want to frame and address more directly the issue of leadership change. As much as this is rarely the focus of research, we already stressed the reasons why it can offer an essential vantage point from which to examine politics and development in Africa, as leadership transfers represent potentially crucial events leading to significant political and policy adjustments. Looking at when and how one comes to office opens up important insights into how he or she will use power, and what he or she will pursue and achieve. We thus consider each individual leader's specific mode of entry into power or selection process (coercion, legitimacy, inclusion, procedural rules and constraints, timing, duration, succession, and alternation in office) as an indicator of key aspects in the relationship with other potentially relevant political actors (the ruling elite, the oppositions, and citizens at large) – for example, in defining time horizons or in assessing risks and opportunities – that will affect his or her behavior. We expect this to orient and shape policies toward a certain kind of balance in the pursuit of personal interest and common good, of private and public goods.

It is at this second level, therefore, that we move beyond the sheer question of the presence of a specific politico-institutional setup and emphasize the role of individual decision-makers, i.e., national leaders. In doing this, the features we look at cut across regime types. In particular, we assume voting mechanisms to be potentially consequential even where democracy is not accomplished and pluralist elections disguise a hybrid, if not a more fully authoritarian regime – a familiar situation in many parts of Africa. Figure 2.1 shows the range of possible intertwining of elections and leadership changes *across* as well as *within* regimes. The possibility of political alternation remains the defining feature of democratic regimes, located toward the righthand side in the figure. But whether leadership change actually takes place or not – and how it happens, that is, whether in the form of succession or alternation – is an empirical question. On the other hand, contemporary nondemocratic governments across world regions can be divided into closed regimes that do not hold multiparty elections (monarchic, military, and single-party systems, such as Saudi Arabia, Thailand, or Vietnam) and regimes displaying a façade of electoral contests that are actually stage-managed (present-day Russia or Turkey would fit the

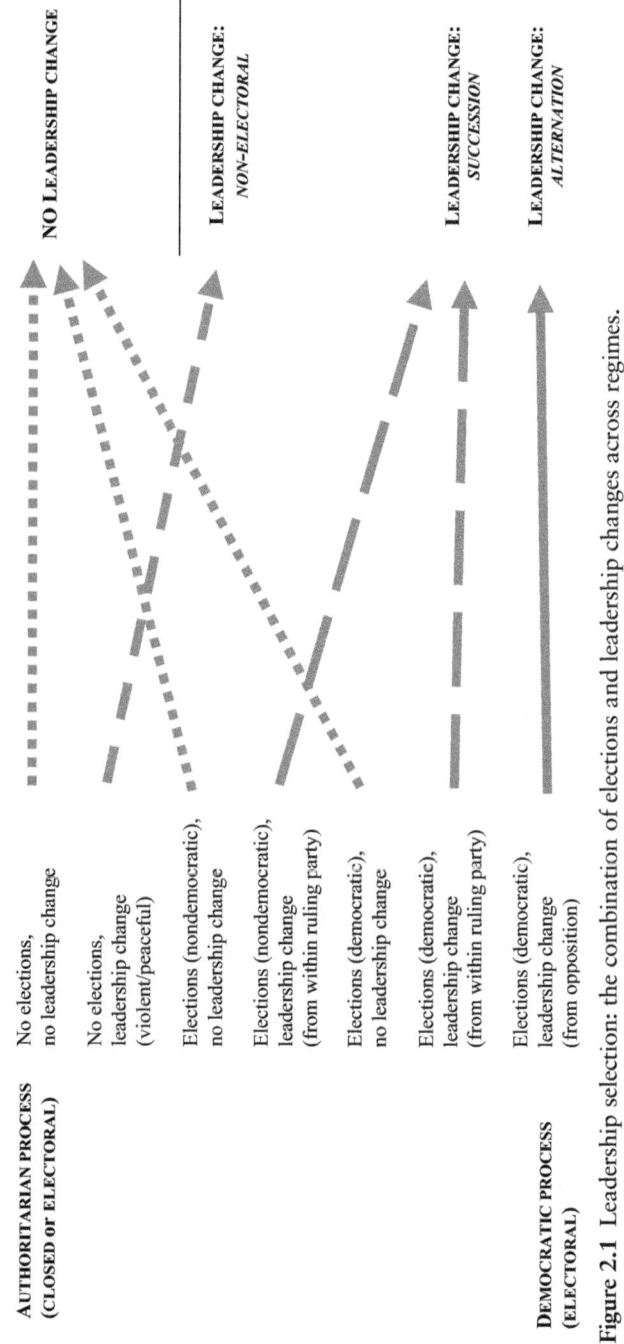

AUTHORITARIAN PROCESS (CLOSED OR ELECTORAL)	No elections, no leadership change	**NO LEADERSHIP CHANGE**
	No elections, leadership change (violent/peaceful)	
	Elections (nondemocratic), no leadership change	**LEADERSHIP CHANGE:** *NON-ELECTORAL*
	Elections (nondemocratic), leadership change (from within ruling party)	
	Elections (democratic), no leadership change	
	Elections (democratic), leadership change (from within ruling party)	**LEADERSHIP CHANGE:** *SUCCESSION*
DEMOCRATIC PROCESS (ELECTORAL)	Elections (democratic), leadership change (from opposition)	**LEADERSHIP CHANGE:** *ALTERNATION*

Figure 2.1 Leadership selection: the combination of elections and leadership changes across regimes.

bill). The latter are distinctive, since, at the time of voting, they are formally open to electoral pressures and leadership successions. But under such nondemocratic elections power handovers between opposite political forces are by definition impossible. Virtually all handovers to the opposition take place in countries deemed, for example, "electoral democracies" by Freedom House. When, on the contrary, an incumbent ruler (and his or her party) in a regime previously seen as authoritarian suddenly cedes power by allowing the first instance of alternation to surprisingly occur, in principle that is the precise moment the regime democratizes. A similar, exceptionally rare event implies a vote sufficiently free to disprove the supposed absence of minimal democracy, if *ex post*. The regime *de facto* if unexpectedly satisfies the procedural notion of democracy as an "institutional arrangement for arriving at political decisions in which individuals acquire the power to decide by means of a competitive struggle for the people's vote" (Schumpeter 1947:269). Take the case of Mexico, for example, which, in spite of formal multiparty politics, was deemed undemocratic during the 71 years of unchallenged rule by the Partido Revolucionario Institucional (PRI). But then presidential election day came, in 2000, and produced the shocking victory of opposition leader Vicente Fox. A truly pivotal election that instantly turned the Mexican political trajectory toward democracy, as imperfectly as it has thus far advanced. Gambia, an entirely different country and political setting, is possibly the African case that reached closest to a similar outcome. In late 2016, Yaya Jammeh's 23-year-old regime was unanimously categorized as a repressive dictatorship. Freedom House (2017), for example, assigned it a highly negative score of 6 both for civil freedoms as for political rights, and deemed it one of the three countries with the largest ten-year deterioration. Yet, due to a combination of domestic opposition dynamics and external support, a window of opportunity opened abruptly, which led to Jammeh's surprise defeat at the ballot box and his removal from power in early 2017.[1]

The problem these cases pose is thus different from circumstances in which alternation took place during founding elections, as happened in Zambia 1991 or Malawi 1994. The latter reflected a planned process

---

[1] While both Freedom House and Polity2 scores for Gambia in 2017 show a significant improvement, in neither case does the country technically make it to a democratic status.

of political opening that brought with it a potential for leadership change. Gambia, on the other hand, was an example of backfiring in the authoritarian use of multiparty voting, when an established routine of periodically calling voters to renew the incumbent's legitimacy suddenly and unexpectedly ushered in an entirely new scenario. We are not so much interested in explaining how competitive authoritarianism can evolve toward an election that actually leads to alternation in government, however, but rather in what happens after similar changes at the top.

We are well aware of how frequently elections are the subject of authoritarian manipulation, and that this so often reaches the point where popular voting becomes totally unfree and de facto emptied of its raison d'être (see, for instance, Cheeseman and Klaas 2018). Yet we posit that the *potential* for the virtuous effects of an electoral connection is established the moment multiparty elections are first introduced, and that this same potential culminates in full when an incumbent leader is ousted and replaced by an opponent through the ballot box. In between the starting point and the end point stand the crucial processes of reiterating the voting and expanding the actual level of competitiveness and contestability.

We thus expect an electoral connection mechanism to work in a step-by-step fashion in which each of four possible stages tends to strengthen the previous one. The four steps are: (1) *election*, (2) *reiteration*, (3) *competitiveness*, and (4) *alternation*. *Election* first establishes the new type of connection between the leader and the public through the introduction of voting, as compared to no-election settings. *Reiteration* implies that the electoral connection becomes recurrent and is gradually routinized. Continuity is necessary, among other things, for leaders' promises to gain credibility and thus for electoral accountability, with its sanctions and rewards, to potentially prevail over other types of relationships, including a clientelistic logic (cf. Keefer 2005). *Competitiveness* raises the stakes and deepens the weight of the leader-voter connection by lowering the margin of a leader's electoral success and thus eroding his "comfort zone." *Alternation* involves achieving the ultimate scenario implied by the very notion of electoral connection and accountability, that is, leadership replacement through the ballot box. While we may conceptually think of these four stages as a succession of cumulative steps, the practical order in which they appear allows for some flexibility. Competitiveness or even alternation, for example, may take place already at the time of founding elections – that is, prior to the routinization of voting. A key aspect of the perspective we adopt, however, is the fact that the presence of *a democratic environment is not a precondition* for any of these four kinds of occurrences to come about. Not only, as is widely acknowledged, do step one (election) and two (reiteration) tell us little about the actual presence of democracy – think of multiparty voting in places such as Algeria, Belarus, or Turkmenistan – but also step three (competitiveness) can be a feature displayed in what ultimately remain nondemocratic settings, as was the case with the incumbent's narrow win in the Gabonese presidential election of 2016.

It is thus not just a functioning democracy that we see as "the instrument that allows the state to do good while tempering its capacity for exploitation ... and [the mechanism that] improves the material conditions of everyday life" (Lake and Baum 2001:617). It is also the broader if formal opportunity for election-based leadership changes – but also whether and how the latter occur – that we see as the manifestation of pressures to perform and we therefore expect to shape outcomes. There is in fact some evidence that elections have affected policy decisions under authoritarian electoral regimes. This was the case in Uganda and Tanzania over 1995–2010, for example. The "landmark decisions" adopted in the taxation, education, and agricultural sectors examined by Kjær and Therkildsen (2013) share some key features: they were implemented through state interventions; they aimed at countrywide coverage; and they produced immediate and visible results that were clearly attributable to the ruling party. None of the two East African countries had ever allowed proper democratic processes. Freedom House, for example, never recognized them as electoral democracies during the period considered. Yet both cases "show that elections, although not always free and fair nor with a high degree of competition, significantly motivate political elites to pursue policies that they perceive will help them to win elections" (Kjær and Therkildsen 2013:596). Casting a ballot, for example, crucially "enable(d) smallholders in rural areas, who are the majority of voters in most African countries, to use their votes to make their preferences known" (Kjær and Therkildsen 2013:593). In this sense, the multiparty but authoritarian regimes of Uganda and Tanzania are all the more interesting since they represent "least-likely cases": if elections can affect policy in such nondemocratic settings, one would expect them to be even more likely to do so under genuine democratic pressures.

Bates and Block's (2013) investigation reaches a conclusion similar to Kjær and Therkildsen's. Building on Bates' (1981) classic work on the urban-biased policies that disenfranchised and demobilized rural voters in postindependence Africa, leading to the decline of agriculture, they contend that, since the late 1980s, "the reform of political institutions and the consequent enfranchisement of Africa's farmers influenced the performance of its rural sector, thereby shaping the continent's economic trajectory" (Bates and Block 2013:372; cf. Bates et al. 2012), and notably the economic revival experienced across the region during the early part of the twenty-first century. In practice, the authors count as "reformed" any countries that introduced multiparty elections during the 1961–2007 period – regardless of whether ballots were truly free and fair – only also looking at the vote share that parties other than the ruling organization were allowed to obtain as an additional non-decisive feature.[2] Bates and Block attribute to this kind of (limited) political change substantial increases in total factor productivity in a country's agricultural sector. Crucially, they suggest that the provision of public goods such as roads, education, and agricultural research by elected governments play a mediation role in the relationship.

Any discussion about leadership change and performance has to address the issue of time. All other things being equal, time can be expected to mediate a leader's impact on performance in two distinct ways. The first one concerns total length of stay in office and the notion that things require time to accomplish. Interim leaders who remain in power for no more than one year, for example, will hardly have the opportunity to plan, promote, implement and achieve socio-economic advancements (see Chapter 8). In general, the shorter a ruler's duration, the less likely that he or she will be in a position to substantially affect the country's progress or regress – and the less able we are to

---

[2] The authors adopt Beck et al.'s (2001) *Executive Index of Electoral Competition*. They also include as a robustness check a dummy variable that sets apart regimes deemed "competitive" (i.e., with a 9 or 10 score on the well-known Polity scale), as opposed to "non-competitive" (i.e., 8 or below). It is worth noting that Polity only assumes a value of 9 or 10 for 98 out of 3,025 country-year observations for sub-Saharan states in 1960–2013, or just about 3 percent of all observations, and even less when one stops at 2007.

establish a clear connection between leadership and performance. A second time-related implication has to do with a possible trend whereby new leaders – regardless of their length of stay in office, at least in principle – will be more likely to innovate and introduce discontinuity measures in the early phases of their mandates, while later periods will see a steep decline in their interest in bringing about change. As Bunce put it, this will lead to "a policy cycle, calibrated by succession, in which more innovative priorities will alternate with more incremental modes of decision-making. This follows from ... the ebb and flow in the incentives and capacity of chief executives to put through new public policies, an ebb and flow which reflects the distinction between politics as usual and honeymoon policy-making ... succession functions as a mechanism for policy innovation" (Bunce 1981:10). Other observers have been even more suspicious about the effects of business-as-usual politics, suggesting that "long-lived governments will have scope and incentives to implement a broader range of corrupt policies than short-lived governments" (Horowitz et al. 2009:108).

We thus hypothesize that, over time, a leader's performance will on average get worse. In addition, however, we also speculate that, particularly for elected officeholders, duration in office may have a curvilinear impact on development progress. At the outset, any newcomer to power will need time to reduce political fluidity and uncertainty by settling in, strengthening his or her position, and learning how to master the machinery of government. He or she will thus only gradually be able to better formulate and impose his or her priorities and make sure his or her preferred policies will be adopted and implemented. Subsequently, however, as time goes by incentives to perform will decline and a more conservative, less dynamic, or even sclerotic attitude merely aimed at holding on to power will set in and prevail.

Counterarguments and Limitations

There are two main sets of objections that can be leveled at the argument we outlined in the previous sections. The first concerns the possibility that unelected dictators could be just as capable of and willing to propel their country's progress forward. The second type of objection is that the virtuous mechanisms supposedly at play when leaders are selected and replaced in certain ways, favouring on their part a more vigorous push toward social and economic achievements, may simply fail to materialize. We address them hereafter.

As history teaches, it is far from impossible for unelected dictators to actually adopt a developmental attitude. A number of past and present rulers who reached power outside of the ballot box are renowned for their apparent commitment to the economic or socioeconomic progress and transformation of their countries, from Augusto Pinochet in Chile to Paul Kagame in contemporary Rwanda. Olson and McGuire argued that "the encompassing interest of the secure autocrat leads him to take account of the welfare of his subjects" (McGuire and Olson 1996:80; cf. Olson 1993). Autocrats with long-time horizons may thus provide public goods as if guided by an invisible hand. East Asian developmental dictatorships are typically brought in as examples. It is rational for a "self-interested actor with unquestioned coercive power ... to act in ways that are, to a surprising degree, consistent with the interests of society and of those subject to that power" (McGuire and Olson 1996:73). Yet, as Svolik (2012) reminds us, in practice dictators' almost constant concern is to try and shore up their uncertain political fate, leading to predatory behaviors, since, as McGuire and Olson (1996:80) also concede, "autocrats, whenever they have short time-horizons, become, in effect, roving bandits." Goldsmith offers evidence that, in Africa between 1960 and 1999, it was this kind of short-term survival strategy that prevailed and led most autocrats to opt for priorities other than the progress of their country and the welfare of their people (Goldsmith 2001, 2004; see Chapter 1). By implication, the kind of staunchness displayed by some "benevolent" or "developmental" dictators is rarely induced by the pressures and constraints of an external institutional context. Rather, it likely rests on personal motives or some other factors. Ultimately, an unelected dictator's commitment towards his country's progress will largely remain an occasional rather than a systematic occurrence.

Secondly, skeptics question the fact that the hypothesized electoral connection will actually turn real and promote policy measures that favor tangible improvements. Keefer and Khemani (2005), for example, object that a number of political market imperfections may hinder the expected functioning of electoral incentives as something that serves the interests of voters, whose majority in developing countries consists of the poor. Voters may not possess the necessary information to properly evaluate – and thus to reward or punish – the performance of those in government. Moreover, social services pledges may be inherently difficult to assess, leading politicians to prefer more targeted and clientelistic distributions. Finally, identity-based voting – such as ethnic or religious voting – may cut across the electorate and fragment its socioeconomic priorities. Khan similarly points that, at low levels of development, democratic elections are unlikely to favor progress and transformation, as the needs of the poor will most probably take a back seat in the face of patron-client networks and neopatrimonial factions that are better organized (Khan 2005:707, 721–722). For these and other reasons, elected leaders too may end up favoring public spending that privileges targeted programs, such as the distribution of jobs, licenses, and other benefits, or infrastructure investments, rather than expanding social services aimed at satisfying the needs of a broader section of the electorate. Even when officeholders do decide to raise social expenditure levels, this may not necessarily lead to better outputs (such as education enrolment or immunization rates) or outcomes (such as literacy or infant mortality rates). Education or health spending surges may in fact produce little or no social impact unless they are accompanied by institutional reforms or resource reallocations (Nelson 2007:80ff.), or they may simply fail to ameliorate the living standards of the poor because they are captured by – that is, targeted to – the middle classes (Ross 2006:861).

From a slightly different perspective, it has also been suggested that different dimensions of democracy may actually pull in opposite directions. Accordingly, "regime responsiveness to people's basic needs is ... largely driven by participation, whereas competition can cause harm by hindering responsiveness" (Korolev 2016:450). The reason why higher levels of participation have a positive impact on social outcomes is that active engagement favors both citizens' learning processes – whereby they become more aware of social needs – as well as helping them establish the collective goals of society. Participation thus promotes the convergence of "subjective wants and objective needs in a society" (Korolev 2016:451–452). But this is not the case with competition, whose negative impact is due to low variability, nonmalleability, and lower visibility. First, basic needs vary slowly, over the long run, implying that needs-oriented policies are not a rewarding investment for politicians bound to face electoral contests in the short or medium term. Secondly, politicians may have, or prefer, to focus on responding to opinions and wants through malleable symbolic measures that can more easily generate public satisfaction, and thus electoral payoffs, rather than work out complex and non-malleable policy answers to survival, health, or nourishment issues. Thirdly, basic needs may simply be "off the radar of public debate" (Korolev 2016:452) not only because, in general, it is not easy for voters to identify and give political saliency to such issues, but also because the have-nots are least capable of articulating them.

Whether and to what extent elected leaders – and particularly but not only democratically elected ones – favor the speeding up of economic growth, the advancement of social welfare, the promotion of more transparent administration, and the consolidation of the state is therefore a question for empirical investigation. We shall assess the abovementioned opposite claims by examining whether elected leaders do indeed make a greater effort to make sure tangible improvements reach citizens and voters so to maximize their chances of harvesting electoral returns.

Methodological Issues

Our work moves beyond the classic consequences of the democratization approach by adding to the existing literature an innovative understanding of the socioeconomic and political implications of leadership change, in general, and of leadership handovers of different natures in particular (e.g., coups as opposed to peaceful takeovers, non-electoral as opposed to electoral transfers, successions as opposed to alternations). In doing so, the ALC dataset that we introduce in the next pages also offers a new empirical foundation for examining broader leadership issues in Africa across space and time.

In principle, we expect elected leaders – particularly when they enjoy a democratic mandate – to try and improve the living conditions of their fellow citizens, and to do so more than their unelected peers. For an elected leader, economic growth, welfare progress, rule of law, and the like are not necessarily valuable per se – as ideological aims, altruistic ideals or "development goals" – but because these and other tangible advances for the population are thought to promote his/her chances of political survival in a somewhat competitive environment. Our causal argument is thus large in breadth or generality – that is, it aims at capturing a considerably sized *explanandum* – whereas it is parsimonious in terms of the lever or *explanans* that it employs, both worthy aspects of a social research endeavor (Gerring 2005:173–174).

The boundaries of the propositions we advance are spatially confined to the 49 states of the sub-Saharan region, which, for all its rich internal diversity, represents a relatively homogeneous area for comparative purposes. An area across which a broad *ceteris paribus* clause can be assumed to apply to distinct countries, in terms of such aspects as precolonial contexts and colonial history, levels of development, political systems, demographics, and so on. Of course there are noteworthy subregional and national differences. Yet the range of variation within the region is significantly reduced when compared to that of virtually any possible population of cases combining African and non-African countries.

At the same time, while our predictions are narrowed to one world region only, they concern the entire set of cases the latter contains; that is, they posit relationships between leadership experiences and development outcomes that are meant to hold – if probabilistically – for all sub-Saharan leaders in all of the region's states, for every year since independence. We expect the causation process that we outlined – from the way leaders rise to office to development achievements – to be most evident in Africa due to the high degree of variance of our independent variable(s) across time and space. The majority of postcolonial leaders were unelected, yet most of today's are used to the ballot box; similarly, while a number of contemporary power-holders were democratically voted into office, several have been elected in settings lacking continuity in the practice of voting, or showing no instances of electoral succession, or no government/opposition alternations in office, with deficits of competitiveness, or an altogether absence of democracy. The regional scenario thus lends itself to significant intertemporal and cross-sectional variation.

We operationalize our independent variable primarily by looking at whether a leader is elected or not (plus whether he/she is or not democratically elected, an elected successor, an elected "alternator," etc.). We then examine selected development outcomes – notably economic growth, welfare advancement, state consolidation, and rule of law – that are operationalized through a number of well-known and widely accepted indicators. Within this framework, the cause and the effect are clearly differentiated and independent from each other, and we postulate the former to happen prior to the latter, with a relatively clear temporal distance that supports an explanatory understanding of the relationship between the two. We are aware of the potential problems of endogeneity and reciprocal causality between our dependent variables and the various modes in which leaders rotate in office. One should expect for instance that a leader's ousting from his or her office may be favored by worsened political, macroeconomic, and social conditions. Therefore, we address this concern by entering in the statistical models our explanatory factors in lag and controlling for the value of each individual dependent variable at the time when a leadership change occurred. Our empirical tests are also designed to include an account of possible alternative or complementary causes of development performance as controls, including geographic and demographic factors (land size of country, landlockedness, population growth, etc.), the macroeconomic and financial (government spending, levels of external aid, natural resources rents, etc.) as well as political and sociocultural variables (conflict involvement, ethnolinguistic fractionalisation, colonial legacy, etc.).

To the extent that empirical findings confirm our expectations, they support the notion that democratization reforms and progresses are worth promoting and sustaining, and that even electoral regimes that actually fall short of truly democratic standards may deserve recognition as improvements over non-electoral settings. Of course, the latter remains a thorny issue that demands careful case-by-case consideration, and should not be misunderstood as a call for unqualified support for undemocratic regimes.

3 The Africa Leadership Change (ALC) Dataset

The Rationale for a New Dataset

For the first three decades in the postindependence history of African states, many political leaders rotated in office through irregular and violent means – namely, coups d'état and guerrilla takeovers. Even where transfers of power were peaceful, they were rarely regularized by dynastic, constitutional, or other types of procedures. Electoral handovers were relatively uncommon, typically occurring in single-party contexts where the head of the ruling organization would handpick his successor, whereas turnovers based on opposition victories at the polls were virtually unheard of. As described in the previous chapters, however, the early 1990s represented a major watershed for African politics. As a consequence of both domestic and external pressures, many African political systems embarked on reforms that introduced new constitutions – or amended existing ones – and other formal rules aimed at opening to multipartism and regulating how leaders should take turns in office. In rapid succession, the vast majority of the existing one-party or no-party regimes thus legalized opposition political forces and allowed them to contest elections that were at least formally competitive. Multiparty polls did not remain unique or isolated events, as had often been the case at the time of independence. Rather, countries in the region began holding elections at regular time intervals, as prescribed by their constitutions. It appeared that even incumbent authoritarian leaders now had to stand for election, against whoever wanted to challenge them, and to strive for popular support to legitimize their rule. Did constitutional and legal reforms actually lead to more substantial changes in African polities, societies, and economies? The next chapters answer this crucial question by investigating whether and how institutional reforms altered the modes and timing of the selection and replacement of African leaders and, most importantly, whether elected leaders and electoral turnovers produced an impact on the political and economic development of sub-Saharan countries. This chapter prepares the ground by introducing an original collection of data instrumental to the previously mentioned investigations.

The literature that considers the determinants of political and economic development usually relies on data collections that focus on political *regime* variables. In their influential study, Przeworski and his coauthors examined the democracy/development relationship by drawing a dichotomous distinction between democratic and nondemocratic regimes based on a minimalist notion of democracy (Przeworksi et al. 2000; Cheibub et al. 2010). Other datasets widely employed in the comparative study of the consequences of democracy are *Polity IV* (Marshall et al. 2013), which gauges the levels of specific democratic and authoritarian features of a given political regime and combines them into a single index, and the equally well-known *Freedom in the World Index* developed by Freedom House (Gastil 1985), which assesses the extent of the political rights and civil liberties enjoyed by the citizens of each country in the world. Our approach shares with this literature and data sources an awareness of the importance of free and fair elections and multiparty competition – that is, the cornerstones of modern representative democracy – in the political development of nations.

However, a thorough assessment of the impact that different modes of leadership change generate with respect to the development of African states requires more fine-grained data that look more comprehensively at the possible ways in which countries select and remove their rulers. For this same reason other data collections that focus precisely on elections, electoral results, and electoral competitiveness – such as Hyde and Marinov (2012) and Lindberg (2006) – do not include information that is specific enough for the aim pursued by this book. A project closer to the purpose of our study, on the other hand, is the comprehensive Archigos dataset on political leaders, which includes information on how country rulers take and leave office, as well as their post-tenure fates, for the 1875–2015 period (Goemans et al. 2009). With reference to the rotation of leaders in power, Goemans and his colleagues relied on the basic distinction between regular and irregular forms of leadership change (see the next section for a more precise discussion). This dichotomy, however, appears insufficient to shed proper light on the complex dynamics underlying leadership transitions in contemporary Africa. In particular, Archigos does not make it possible to disentangle handovers that take place through multiparty elections from other regular-but-not-electoral transfers of power. As we explain shortly, this difference acquires particular saliency when we compare Africa's postcolonial period (1960s–1980s) with the post-democratic reform years (1990s to date).

The *Africa Leadership Change (ALC)* dataset that we present in this chapter overcomes these shortcomings by focusing directly on the leadership changes that took place in African countries during the 1960–2018 period and by providing data that make it possible to disentangle all the conceivable ways in which political leaders rotate in office. The next section provides a detailed description of the core structure of the ALC dataset, of its variables, and of the coding rules that we followed to classify all changes in the top political leadership occurring in all African countries. We then compare ALC to the existing datasets and illustrate its main strengths for the purpose of studying the relationship between leadership and development in Africa.

The Africa Leadership Change Dataset: Structure, Scope, and Coding Rules

The overall purpose of ALC is to offer a comprehensive account of the ways in which leaders attain and relinquish power in Africa, to detail how these practices have evolved since independent countries emerged on the continent, and to enable investigations into their broader political, social, and economic implications. Thus, the dataset covers all leaders that held office in all 49 African states from 1960 (or subsequent year of independence) to June 30, 2018.[1]

In the absence of a standard definition of political leadership, as we mentioned, our starting point is the notion that the leader is the person who occupies the top decision-making position in a country's political and governing hierarchy, be he or she a president elected directly by the

---

[1] No new African leader took office in the second half of 2018. Yet our dataset formally stops at June 30, 2018 due to technical reasons. While the focus of this book is sub-Saharan Africa, and we will thus use data covering the 49 countries of the region, the complete ALC dataset also includes full information on the leaders of the five Mediterranean nations of Africa (Morocco, Algeria, Tunisia, Libya, and Egypt).

citizens (e.g., Mwai Kibaki in Kenya, 2002–2013) or by a legislative assembly (e.g., Nelson Mandela in South Africa, 1994–1999), a prime minister (e.g., Meles Zenawi in Ethiopia, 1995–2012), a near-absolute monarch (e.g., Mswati III in eSwatini, 1983–to date) or the chief of a military junta (e.g., Jerry Rawlings in Ghana, 1981–1992). In the overwhelming majority of cases, the identification of who is primarily in charge is noncontroversial and normally depends on the type of regime (parliamentary, presidential, or semi-presidential republic; military regime; absolute monarchy). For transitional governments, we considered the interim executive and who headed it. In a limited number of cases, a country's leader may not be the official head of state or government. Paul Kagame, for example, was formally the vice president of Rwanda between 1994 and 2000, yet nobody doubts where political authority lay in Kigali at the time. Of course, the extent to which power is actually concentrated in the hands of a leader and the way he or she wields it are empirical questions, as reality presents vast and complex variations.

Since our primary focus is on the dynamics of leadership change – i.e., the ascension to and the abandonment of power – rather than the careers of individual leaders, our dataset adopts country-years as units of analysis[2]. With a standard country-year structure, ALC can be easily merged with many other datasets, such as the World Bank's World Development Indicators, the Quality of Government dataset (Teorell et al. 2018) or the UCDP/PRIO Armed Conflict dataset (Gleditsch et al. 2002), so that other researchers will also be able to use it to fully investigate and understand the impact of leadership changes on the political and economic performances of African countries.

We began by recording the entire series of leaders that held power in each country on the continent and reporting their birth and death dates, the dates on which they took (*date entry*) and left (*date exit*) power, and the length of their tenure in terms of days and years (*duration in office*). Leaders that remained in power for less than 12 months were coded as *interim* leaders. Minor interruptions in a leader's stay in office due to a short interim leadership interlude – such as when Léon M'ba was restored by the French after a coup lasting two

---

[2] The procedures summarized in this section are detailed in full in the Codebook of the ALC dataset. An additional file accompanying the dataset briefly describes special leadership change episodes in particular countries better to explain how we accounted for and coded them.

days in Gabon, in 1964, or when João Bernardo Vieira briefly ceded power to Carmen Pereira, Africa's first female president, if only acting, while Guinea-Bissau's new constitution was introduced in 1984 – do not lead to a new duration count. We further distinguished between interim leaderships ending with a legal or nonviolent replacement (*interim regular*) and those resulting in a violent change, be it a coup, a guerrilla takeover, or a foreign imposition (*interim irregular*).

With regard to the main focus of ALC – leadership changes – we first used a simple dummy variable to code every country-year in which one or more *leadership changes* took place. We thus opted for the expression "leadership change" to refer to any instance in which power was passed on from one leader to the next, regardless of how this took place. We find this expression generally preferable to the terms "transition" or "turnover" adopted by Goldsmith (2001, 2004) and others, since the former is widely employed in the political regimes literature while the latter is used in the study of electoral alternation between different political parties or forces (Horowitz et al. 2009).

One basic distinction that we drew was between *non-electoral changes* and *electoral changes*: that is, power transfers that occur via *multiparty elections for the executive*. Within the first set of cases, we separated *peaceful* from *violent/irregular* non-electoral leadership changes. The former included handovers that follow the *natural (or incidental) death* of the incumbent leader, as in the case of Joaquim Chissano, who took over in Mozambique after Samora Machel's sudden death in a 1986 air crash, as well as those due to *voluntary retirement/resignation*, as exemplified by Abdou Diouf's coming to power in Senegal when Léopold Senghor decided to leave office in 1981. Violent transfers, on the other hand, include the vast number of *coups d'état* that have plagued the continent – regardless of whether they were bloodless, since they nevertheless involved the threat of violence – such as the military intervention that brought Siad Barre to power in Somalia in 1969; a much lesser number of *guerrilla takeovers*, i.e., armed movements that have successfully waged war against existing authorities, as did the Chadian insurgents led by Idriss Déby in 1990; and a few cases of *foreign impositions*, such as the French intervention that helped David Dacko retake the presidency in the Central African Republic in 1979. For all these violent power transfers, we also recorded the possibility of the ousted leader being *assassinated* in the process.

In our framework, holding *a multiparty election for the executive* was a necessary but not sufficient condition for an *electoral change* of leadership. These elections only comprise those in which the mandate of the leader of the national executive is formally at stake, whether as a direct (in presidential and semi-presidential systems) or an indirect outcome of the vote (in parliamentary systems). Legislative elections in presidential or semi-presidential regimes were not included (although we did record them as a separate variable in the dataset). We deemed an election for the executive to be a "multiparty election" when it was contested by at least two legally admitted parties or candidates – regardless of whether the vote was actually conducted in a free and fair manner.

When a leadership change took place via multiparty elections, we looked at whether the vote constituted a "founding" election: that is, one marking a transition to a new multiparty regime where the latter was previously absent (including cases in which polls are reintroduced after a regime interruption). We further distinguished electoral leadership changes in which the new leader belonged to the same political force as his predecessor from those in which an opposition candidate took over. These two coding rules – founding versus non-founding elections, and political continuity versus opposition breakthrough – enabled us to assign each electoral change to one of four different categories. *Electoral succession (in transition)*: when a new leader won power in the context of a transition to multipartism in which the outgoing unelected leader was not running, and either the new leader was the candidate of the outgoing unelected leader's party or else there is no candidate from the party of/sponsored by the outgoing unelected leader (we accounted for this latter possibility through the additional variable *incumbent party not standing for election*). Cases such as Nigeria 1979, Lesotho 1993, Sierra Leone 1996, or Niger 1999 fell in this category. Shehu Shagari, for example, won the Nigerian presidential elections that put an end to the country's military regime, albeit only temporarily. Neither the outgoing ruler nor a candidate representing his political block stood for the post. Also included were instances where an unelected leader formally left power less than six months prior to a multiparty contest only to be able to run for office, but remained a leader *in pectore*, if not *de facto* (e.g., Comoros 2002; Mauritania 2009). *Electoral alternation (in transition)*: these were power transfers in which a new leader emerged by winning an election, during a transition to multipartism, in which he/she defeated an outgoing unelected ruler – as in Zambia in 1991 or Malawi in 1994, where newly elected presidents were able to oust the countries' founding fathers Kenneth Kaunda and Hastings Banda, respectively – or else a candidate from the party of/sponsored by the outgoing unelected leader. The latter was the case in Niger in 1993, for example, when Mahamane Ousmane beat the candidate of the ruling party, and in Burundi in 2005, when Pierre Nkurunziza's party obtained the majority of legislative seats defeating the party of the outgoing acting president.

Electoral succession (elected-to-elected) identifies a handover in which a new leader belonging to the outgoing elected leader's party took power by winning a multiparty election other than a founding election. It was in this way, for example, that Levy Mwanawasa replaced Frederick Chiluba in Zambia in 2002, Bingu wa Mutharika was handed power by Bakili Muluzi in Malawi in 2004, and Filipe Nyusi succeeded Armando Guebuza in Mozambique in 2015. Leaders who replaced elected rulers as their lawful constitutional successors, such as when a power-holder naturally or accidentally died in office (e.g., in Gabon 2009 and in Ethiopia 2012) or else resigned and passed on his duties prior to an election (e.g., Botswana in 1998 and 2008), were themselves considered elected leaders. Finally, *electoral alternation (elected-to-elected)* occurred when a new leader that neither belonged to the party of, nor was sponsored by, an outgoing elected ruler took power by winning a multiparty vote other than a founding election. Cases in point are Abdoulaye Wade's takeover in Senegal in 2000, Marc Ravalomanana's in Madagascar in 2002, or Mwai Kibaki's in Kenya in 2002. This last category also includes those rare instances where an election held under an established multiparty system was contested neither by the outgoing elected leader nor by a candidate sponsored by him/her nor fielded by his/her party, as in the Comoros in 2006, Cape Verde in 2011, or Kenya in 2013.

The diagram in Figure 3.1 shows the core structure of the ALC dataset. Table A1 in the appendix provides an overview of summary data for each country: the overall number of leaders in power since independence (including interim leaders), their average duration in office, the total number of multiparty elections held in the country, and the number of electoral, peaceful non-electoral, violent leadership changes, and political alternations, respectively.

The Africa Leadership Change Dataset

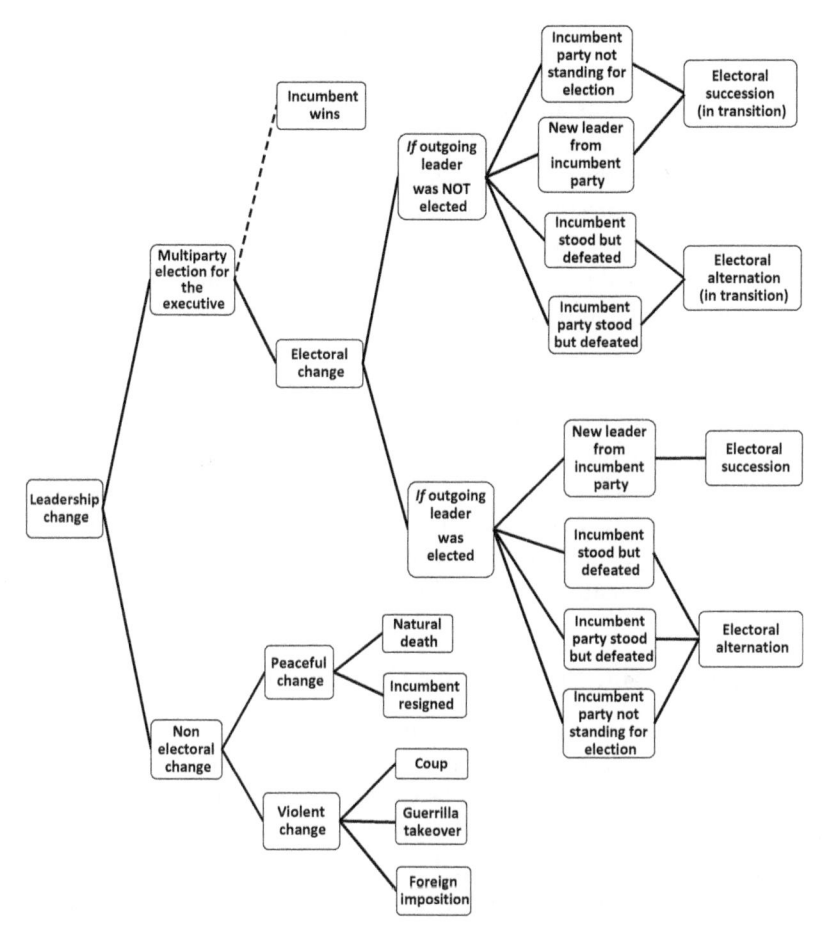

Figure 3.1 Structure and logic of the ALC dataset.
Note: leaders who replaced elected leaders as their lawful constitutional successors (e.g., following natural death in office) are themselves considered elected leaders.

In order to provide a broader picture for elected rulers, we also entered in the dataset a number of election-related variables for presidential and legislative elections, whether multiparty or not. These variables include: the election date and turnout (also those for a runoff, where appropriate); the number of contenders in presidential elections; the vote shares of the winning candidate and of his main challenger, if any, in the single or last electoral round; the vote and seat shares for governing parties and for the main opposition parties. We also detailed the name of the political party of the incumbent leader, specifying when the latter was an independent or a non-partisan leader such as a monarch or a soldier. Finally, we included political regime variables that account for the presence of multipartism, the form of government (parliamentary, presidential or semi-presidential), the presence/absence and the degree of democracy (PolityIV and Cheibub et al. 2010), a country's colonial legacy (Belgium, France, Great Britain, Italy, Portugal, and Spain) and the subregion to which it belongs (Central, West, East, and Southern Africa).

The various sources that we used to compile the ALC dataset comprise the African Elections Database, the Encyclopaedia Britannica, the World Leaders Index, the Parline Database of the Inter-Parliamentary Union (IPU), the World Bank's Database on Political Institutions (Beck et al. 2001), and Nohlen et al.'s (1999) handbook on elections in Africa.[3] A large number of more specific sources were also employed for closer examination of individual cases.

Comparing ALC to Alternative Datasets and Measures

The purpose of the ALC dataset is not to measure democracy. Its focus is on the chain of leaders at the helm of a country and on the specific ways in which they reach and leave that position. To the extent that leadership selection and removal processes involve electoral competition, there is a partial conceptual overlap with democratic procedures. But the ALC dataset does more than point to the presence or absence of democracy. When a country is deemed democratic by Polity IV or Freedom House, for example, we know that its leaders are chosen through competitive elections. But when a country is deemed undemocratic, the question remains of how its power-holders are selected and replaced – whether through (nondemocratic) voting, a coup, a peaceful non-electoral handover, etc. These, as well as how long leaders have been in power, are crucial items of information when one examines the

---

[3] The African Elections database can be found at http://africanelections.tripod.com/, the Encyclopaedia Britannica at www.britannica.com/, the World Leaders Index at www.worldleadersindex.org/homepage.html and the Parline database at www.ipu.org/parline-e/parlinesearch.asp. The Database of Political Institutions can be downloaded from the World Bank's website (www.worldbank.org/).

rulers and politics of Africa. Our dataset provides the answers to all these issues.

The ALC dataset also furnishes a more fine-grained understanding of some crucial dynamics in contemporary African politics, namely the relationship among democratic votes, electoral succession between power-holders belonging to the same political party, and electoral alternation between leaders of opposite political forces. It shows whether a proper democratic process is a prerequisite for an electoral succession to occur or for opposition parties to win office through the polls, or whether, on the contrary, successions and alternations in power can also take place in regimes that are only partially free or that are not electoral democracies. This is particularly relevant to Africa, where most countries employ multiparty politics that falls short of democratic standards (van de Walle 2002) and variously fit the categories that the literature has labeled "electoral authoritarianisms" (Schedler 2006), "competitive authoritarianisms" (Levitsky and Way 2010) or, more simply, "hybrid regimes" (Collier and Levitsky 1997; Diamond 2002; Cassani 2014).

Table 3.1 matches episodes of electoral succession and alternation detected through ALC with different regimes based on the Polity2 score and shows, for example, that electoral successions very often happen under regimes that are hybrid. Twelve out of 25 electoral successions at transition times took place in countries that did not reach the 6-point threshold on Polity IV's –10 to +10 scale (column 1).[4] This was the case of Kofi Busia in Ghana. He won the 1969 election and replaced an unelected leader to become prime minister of Ghana, but the country's score only climbed from –3 in 1969 to 3 in 1970–1971. Once elections were introduced and regularly repeated at periodic intervals (column 3), the vote helped set an end point on the tenure of elected leaders even in hegemonic-party regimes, as incumbents often (if certainly not always) had to comply with presidential term limits. Eleven out of 18 power handovers from an

---

[4] A score of 7 or more on the Polity scale is often taken as the threshold necessary to classify countries as democratic. Yet the authors of Polity IV at times lower this threshold to 6 points. Marshall and Cole, for example, explain that "countries with Polity scores from +6 to +10 are counted as democracies in tracking 'Global Trends in Governance" (see Marshall and Cole 2011:9). We believe that in the contemporary African context, which has been historically dominated by nondemocratic rule, a score of 6 signals a noteworthy democratic achievement.

Table 3.1 *Episodes of electoral succession and alternation at different levels of democracy*

		ALC		
	IN TRANSITION (*non-elected leader to elected leader*)		INSTITUTIONALIZED ELECTIONS (*elected leader to elected leader*)	
	Electoral successions (*column 1*)	Electoral alternations (*column 2*)	Electoral successions (*column 3*)	Electoral alternations (*column 4*)
Democracies (6 to 10) POLITY2	13 (52%) Burkina Faso 2015 Central African Republic 2016 Ghana 1979 Guinea-Bissau 2005; 2009; 2014 Lesotho 1993 Madagascar 2014 Mali 1992 Niger 2011 Nigeria 1979 Sudan 1965; 1986	9 (60.0%) Benin 1991 Burundi 2005 Cape Verde 1991 Liberia 2006 Madagascar 1993 Malawi 1994 Niger 1993 South Africa 1994 Zambia 1991	7 (38.8%) Comoros 2011 Malawi 2004 Namibia 2005; 2015 South Africa 1999; 2009 Zambia 2015	32 (91.4%) Benin 1996; 2006; 2016 Cape Verde 2001; 2016 Comoros 2006; 2016 Ghana 2001; 2009; 2017 Kenya 2002; 2013 Lesotho 2012; 2015; 2017 Liberia 2018 Madagascar 1997; 2002 Malawi 2014 Mali 2002 Mauritius 1982; 1995; 2000; 2005; 2014 Nigeria 2015 Senegal 2000; 2012

70

| | | | | Sierra Leone 2007; 2018
Somalia 1967
Zambia 2011 |
| --- | --- | --- | --- | --- |
| **Partial democracies (0 to 5)** | 9 (36%) | 6 (40.0%) | 8 (44.4%) | 2 (5.7%) |
| | Comoros 2002
Guinea 2010
Liberia 1997
Mali 2013
Mauritania 2007
Niger 1999
Nigeria 1999
Sierra Leone 1996
Uganda 1980 | Burundi 1993
Central African Rep. 1993
Comoros 1996
Congo, Rep. 1992
Côte d'Ivoire 2000
Guinea-Bissau 2000 | Djibouti 1999
Gabon 2009
Lesotho 1998
Mozambique 2005; 2015
Nigeria 2007
Tanzania 2015
Zambia 2002 | Côte d'Ivoire 2010
Gambia, The 2017 |
| **Non-democracies (−10 to −1)** | 3 (12%) | 0 (0.0%) | 3 (16.6%) | 1 (2.8%) |
| | Ghana 1969
Mauritania 2009
Tanzania 1995 | | Angola 2017
Tanzania 2005
Togo 2005 | Sierra Leone 1967 |
| **Total** | 25 | 15 | 18 | 35 |

Notes: For episodes occurring in 2018 we extended the Polity2 score assigned to a country for 2017.
Source: PolityIV and ALC dataset

elected incumbent to another elected leader belonging to the same political party occurred under conditions deemed less than democratic (i.e., Polity2 < 6). Tanzania was given a mere −1 on the Polity scale even after Jakaya Kikwete succeeded Benjamin Mkapa through an election in 2005. Nigeria fared only a little better, but never went beyond a 4-point rating under the rule of Olusegun Obasanjo and of his successor Umaru Yar'Adua.

When we consider alternations in office, on the other hand, it appears that African opposition leaders are essentially only able to win power either at the time of transition elections (column 2) or in sufficiently democratic regimes (Polity2 ≥ 6) (column 4). All 15 electoral alternations during transitions (i.e., an opposition leader defeating a non-elected leader at the polls) occurred between 1991 and 2006. On six occasions this took place in countries that did not satisfy democratic standards: electoral change, in other words, coincided with the introduction of hybrid regimes. For example, even after Ange-Félix Patassé defeated incumbent military ruler André Kolingba in the 1993 election, the Central African Republic only scored 5 on the Polity2 scale. The same goes for Kumba Ialá, president of Guinea-Bissau from 2000 to 2003 (maximum 5 points) and for Côte d'Ivoire after Laurent Gbagbo's election in 2000 (4 points). On the other hand, 32 of the 35 events of post-transition electoral alternation happened in 1991–2015, virtually all of them under democratic regimes. Partial exceptions were Côte d'Ivoire and the Gambia. In the 2010 poll, Alassane Ouattara defeated president Gbagbo, and yet Côte d'Ivoire retained a modest 4-point Polity2 rating for the following three years. In the Gambia, when Adama Barrow defeated long-serving autocrat Yahya Jammeh in the 2017 presidential election, the country's Polity2 score jumped from −5 in 2016 to 4, not enough to consider the small nation a democratic regime. The negative political rating of Sierra Leone in the aftermath of the 1967 vote, on the other hand, was a different case and had to do with the ousting of Siaka Stevens shortly after he won the election, leading to a sharp deterioration of the country's democratic assessment.

Besides democracy measures, as we mentioned, some other datasets exist that partly overlap with ours. *Archigos* collects data on all political leaders of all independent countries in the world for the 1875–2015 period (Goemans et al. 2009). Similarly to the ALC dataset, the focus is on "the manner by which rulers enter and leave political power," as well as the post-tenure fate of rulers and some of their personal features. In accounting for the succession of leaders, the main distinction that Goemans and his colleagues draw is between regular and irregular transfers of power (as well as recording cases of direct foreign imposition). Regular ways to reach power are based on existing institutional arrangements and conventions, including electoral mechanisms, hereditary succession, or designation by an outgoing leader. Removals from office can also be regular (e.g., voluntary resignation or electoral defeat) or irregular, with the additional possibility of natural death in office or deposition by another state. Irregular exits are further classified as the result of domestic revolts, armed rebellions, military coups, power struggles within the government or the military, or foreign intervention or threat of intervention. Finally, Archigos also records a leader's fate in the period up to one year after he/she lost power, the date of his/her birth and death, and a leader's gender.

Compared to Archigos, however, ALC is more specifically designed to investigate and understand leadership dynamics in Africa. Its purpose, in particular, is to account better for (a) the different ways in which leaders reached and left power in the postcolonial period (1960s–1980s) as opposed to the postdemocratic reform period (1990s to date) and (b) the prevailing dynamics in contemporary African regimes, which are now virtually all multiparty systems (implying elected leaders), but differ as to whether multiparty arrangements are embedded in democratic, hybrid, or authoritarian realities. For these purposes, we choose country-years rather than individual leaders (as Archigos does) as our units of analysis. Moreover, our approach allows us to account for the evolution of the source of an individual leader's power during his stay in office, for example, when a sitting military leader turns into an elected president, as with Jerry Rawlings in Ghana between the 1980s and the 1990s. This, in turn, enables us to trace processes of political institutionalization and to examine how different sets of incentives affect leadership behavior and performance.

Besides recording violent leadership changes (coups, guerrilla takeovers, and foreign impositions), the ALC dataset indicates whether a leader's regular accession to power occurs through elections or, alternatively, through a peaceful but non-electoral transfer of power. Henri Konan Bédié, for example, legitimately assumed the presidency of Côte d'Ivoire on the death of Félix Houphouët-Boigny, in 1993, with no need for a vote. Between 1960 and 2015 (the last year covered by

Archigos), there were 96 leadership changes through elections and 116 peaceful non-electoral changes in sub-Saharan Africa. Archigos does not distinguish between these diverse modes of leadership change, which it groups together in the "regular" transfer of power category. But they are crucially different phenomena, particularly when one wants to examine whether and how the spread of multiparty elections in the region has modified leadership selection processes over the past three decades. Table 3.2 shows that African cases coded "regular entry into power" by Archigos are actually a very heterogeneous set. This is somewhat misleading if one is to understand these leadership dynamics in Africa, as becomes evident when they are reclassified according to the ALC coding rules.

The ALC dataset also goes a step further. While elections are now adopted virtually everywhere on the African continent, the questions, as said, are whether voting makes a meaningful difference for leadership selection and removals, whether electoral leadership changes only occur under political party continuity, whether ballots actually allow opposition candidates to win office, whether this only happens at the time of regime transitions, and so on. Addressing these issues is beyond the scope of the Archigos dataset, but it is essential for understanding Africa's evolving political regimes. The ALC dataset thus records all multiparty elections and, for each election, whether an incumbent leader secured it, whether he was defeated, or whether he did not stand. It tracks a regime's degree of democracy – thus distinguishing democratic from nondemocratic elections – and the competitiveness of elections in terms of vote margins. It draws the decisive distinction between "electoral succession" and "electoral alternation." It separates leadership changes occurring through transition elections at the time a multiparty regime is established – implying power transfers from non-elected to elected rulers – and those handovers from elected to elected leaders that take place at subsequent voting rounds. Finally, additional political system variables are included to complete the dataset. The identity of the ruling party and its vote shares, for example, help track over time political dominance under changing political leaders.

Other datasets that partly overlap with ours are Hyde and Marinov's (2012) *National Elections across Democracy and Autocracy (NELDA)* and Lindberg's (2006) *Elections and democracy in Africa* dataset. The primary aim of NELDA is to provide detailed information

Table 3.2 *Breaking down Archigos cases of "regular" entry into power according to ALC coding rules and categories*

Archigos	ALC
Regular entry into power Angola (1979–2015); Benin (1991–2015); Botswana (1980–2015); Burkina Faso (2014–2015); Burundi (2003–2015); Cameroon (1982–2015); Cape Verde (1991–2015); Central African Republic (1993–2003; 2014–2015); Comoros (2002–2015); Congo-Kinshasa (2001–2015); Congo-Brazzaville (1992–1997); Côte d'Ivoire (2010–2015); Djibouti (1999–2015); Ethiopia (2012–2015); Gabon (1967–2015); Ghana (2001–2015); Guinea (2010–2015); Guinea-Bissau (2003–2012; 2012–2015); Kenya (1978–2015); Lesotho (1998–2015); Liberia (2003–2015); Madagascar (1975–2009; 2014–2015); Malawi (1994–2015); Mali (1992–2012; 2013–2015); Mauritania (2009–2015); Mauritius (1982–2015); Mozambique (1986–2015); Namibia (2005–2015); Niger (1999–2010; 2011–2015); Nigeria (1998–2015); Rwanda (1994–2015); Senegal (1981–2015); Seychelles (2004–2015); Sierra Leone (2007–2015); South Africa (1966–2015)*; Sudan	**Peaceful non-electoral changes (only)** Angola (1979–2015); Cameroon (1982–2015); Central Africa Republic (2014–2015); Congo-Kinshasa (2001–2015); Ethiopia (2012–2015); Gabon (1967–2015); Seychelles (2004–2015); Swaziland/ eSwatini (1983–2015). **Electoral changes** • **succession (at least one)** Botswana (1980–2015)*; Burkina Faso (2014–2015); Djibouti (1999–2015); Guinea (2010–2015); Guinea-Bissau (2003–2012; 2012–2015); Madagascar (2014–2015); Mali (2013–2015); Mauritania (2009–2015); Mozambique (1986–2015); Namibia (2005–2015); Niger (1999–2010; 2011–2015); Sudan (1986–1989); Tanzania (1985–2015); Togo (2005–2015); Uganda (1980–1985). • **alternation in transition (one)** Burundi (2003–2015); Central African Republic (1993–2003); Congo-Brazzaville (1992–1997); Liberia (2003–2015). • **alternation from elected to elected (one)** Comoros (2002–2015); Côte d'Ivoire (2010–2015); Mali (1992–2012); Nigeria (1998–2015); Sierra Leone (2007–2015); South Africa (1966–2015)*.

Table 3.2 (*cont.*)

Archigos	ALC
(1986–1989); Swaziland/eSwatini (1983–2015); Tanzania (1985–2015); Togo (2005–2015); Uganda (1980–1985); Zambia (1991–2015).	• **alternations (two or more)** Benin (1991–2015); Cape Verde (1991–2015); Ghana (2001–2015); Kenya (1978–2015); Lesotho (1998–2015); Madagascar (1975–2009); Malawi (1994–2015); Mauritius (1982–2015); Senegal (1981–2015); Zambia (1991–2015).

Notes: The table only includes the most recent period of time during which a country was uninterruptedly ruled by one or more leaders who took office via "regular means," as coded by Archigos. For the sake of comparison with the ALC dataset, we excluded each country's first post-1960 leader. Eritrea, South Sudan, and Zimbabwe are thus omitted since no leadership change has yet occurred in these countries. Chad, Equatorial Guinea, the Gambia, and Rwanda are not included because they are yet to experience a sufficiently long period of stable government following a "regular" leadership change. São Tomé and Príncipe and post-1991 Somalia are not covered by the Archigos dataset. (*) New leaders in Botswana and in pre-1994 South Africa typically took office via "peaceful non-electoral changes" shortly *before* winning an electoral mandate (based on a restricted suffrage in the case of apartheid South Africa).
Sources: Archigos and ALC datasets

on the degree of competitiveness of national elections around the world for the 1960–2012 period. ALC shares a number of important features with NELDA. Both datasets adopt a minimal definition of democracy and consider elections to be competitive irrespectively of the political regime under which they are held and of the outcome that they produce. Like ALC, NELDA too enables scholars to identify episodes of electoral succession and alternation, albeit only by reaggregating different variables included in the dataset. Besides the fact that NELDA does not provide details of election results, the crucial difference with respect to ALC is that NELDA only considers electoral leadership changes, omitting all kinds of non-electoral changes (except for post-election coups preventing the winner from taking office). Lindberg's dataset similarly considers the role of elections and government turnovers in contemporary Africa. It covers 47 countries for the 1989–2006 period, with some selected data for the 1969–1988 period, and includes a number of interesting election-related variables that we decided to omit, such as violence during election campaigns or opposition boycotts. On the other hand, the time and geographical range of Lindberg's dataset is more limited, as ALC covers the whole continent over the entire postindependence period. Similarly to NELDA, however, Lindberg's focus and scope are not just narrower than those of the ALC dataset, they are also "qualitatively" different. Our aim is to provide a more comprehensive account of the alternative modes in which African rulers reach power – not just elections – including violent takeovers and peaceful non-electoral transfers of power.

The ALC Dataset: Setting the Stage for the Empirical Analyses

The scarcity of studies addressing the relationship among leaders, their selection and removal, and political-economic development discussed in the first chapter is accompanied by a general lack of data allowing scholars to analyze this relationship empirically. Existing datasets focusing on the characteristics of different political regimes or elections permit only a partial and incomplete investigation of the topic that we study in this book. Even Archigos – a recently released dataset that collects information on all leaders in the world over an impressive 140-year period – does not allow one to disentangle the complex dynamics characterizing leadership replacement in the African continent.

As described in this chapter, to overcome the shortcomings of the extant data sources we have developed a new dataset named Africa Leadership Changes (ALC). ALC lists all national political leaders that held power in all 49 sub-Saharan countries from 1960 (or subsequent year of independence) to 2018 (June 30). Most importantly, ALC identifies all the instances of leadership changes in African countries, distinguishing between peaceful and violent/irregular changes on the one hand, and electoral changes on the other. Among the latter, our dataset further distinguishes episodes of electoral succession and electoral alternation, and specifies whether they occurred in a context of transition to multipartism or in a polity already featuring periodic elections. Several political regime and election-related variables complete the ALC data collection. The result is a dataset that permits a more fine-grained analysis of leadership changes in African countries compared to existing resources. This is a necessary starting point for investigating the relationship between leaders' replacement and political-economic developments. Before we address this task, in the next chapter we use our data to survey the emerging trends in how leaders take and leave office in Africa, with a particular emphasis on the transformations that these processes have undergone between the postcolonial period (1960–1989) and the post-democratic reform period (1990–2018).

4 | *The Changing Dynamics of African Leadership: Rulers before and after 1990*

In the political systems of postcolonial Africa, two key dynamics that played a prominent role were the ability of many rulers to cling on to power for long periods of time and, conversely, a chronic political instability mainly due to the high frequency of military-led coups d'état. Behind these two apparently contradictory phenomena lay a common cause, namely the absence of regularized procedures for selecting political leaders and of functioning mechanisms for peaceful change and political adjustment. The pervasiveness of these two syndromes, in turn, was arguably a contributing factor to Africa's developmental failures.

In the early 1990s, the overwhelming prevalence of military and one-party regimes gave way to the widespread introduction of multiparty elections that were expected to facilitate more orderly and regular leadership handovers. Political reforms were also meant to restart economic development processes that had largely become stalled. Before we turn to investigating the broader implications of the new political arrangements for Africa's development and for the welfare of ordinary citizens, we want to examine whether and to what extent the regime changes of the last decade of the twentieth century – which often failed to meet democratic standards – actually modified the modes and the timing of leadership transfers in the region. In this chapter, we thus conduct a comparative exploration of prevailing leadership trends in sub-Saharan Africa based on data from our Africa Leadership Change (ALC) dataset, which covers all countries in the region from 1960, or subsequent year of independence, to June 30, 2018.

Africa's Two Postindependence Syndromes: Overstay in Power and Violent Takeovers

Independence and postindependence politics were often overly "personal" affairs in postcolonial Africa. A key political leader typically acquired the status of "father" of the nation, similarly to what happened in other world regions. His subsequent rule would be revered to the point where few could dispute his right to lead the newly born country and to do so with a relatively high degree of discretion. This was often a premise for a lifelong reign: of the 45 founding leaders who were in power at the time of independence in sub-Saharan states, between the late 1950s and the 1970s, as many as ten – that is, little short of one quarter – ended their service only when they died of natural or accidental causes (Table 4.1). Another few long-serving independence rulers were only removed from office during the multiparty transitions of the early 1990s, when they were ultimately defeated at the ballot box. This was notably the case of Kenneth Kaunda and Hastings Banda – who had been in power since 1964 in Zambia and Malawi, respectively – but the same occurred to Cape Verde's Pedro Pires, while Djibouti's Hassan Aptidon gracefully retired just prior to a 1999 poll.

Yet the fate of other founding leaders proved that obtaining the top job before anybody else did, on the eve of independence, was no guarantee that the position was secure. Indeed, it often proved difficult not only to hold on to the job but also to get out of it safely (see Goldsmith 2001). Military coups d'état violently ousted 22 of the 45 rulers who had been at the helm since the end of colonialism, starting with the removal of Sylvanus Olympio from the Togolese presidency in early 1963. Of these 22 rulers, 5 were killed, 11 were arrested, and another 5 were exiled. In addition, the prime minister of South Africa, Hendrik Verwoerd, was also the victim of an assassination in 1966, although in his case the incident was not part of a coup attempt. Governing in Africa was undeniably a hazardous job.

While most African states had originally established "democratic" constitutions molded on Western models at independence, the vast majority of them quickly closed down most avenues for political participation and competition, as ruling leaders either banned oppositions to secure an unchallenged grip on power or were themselves removed from office by coups d'état. The resulting political landscape saw one-party systems (as in Cameroon, Angola, or Malawi) and military regimes (as in Nigeria, Ghana, or Burundi) dominating the sub-Saharan region for the better part of three decades. Africans were thus left with few or no constitutional procedures to hold their leaders to account and replace them.

Table 4.1 *The fate of Africa's founding fathers*

Country	Leader at independence	Ousted in coup (*killed, ^jailed, °exiled)	Died in office (naturally/accidentally)	Left voluntarily/peacefully	Power yet to change hands
Togo	Sylvanus Olympio	1963*			
Benin	Hubert Maga	1963^			
Congo-Brazzaville	Fulbert Youlou	1963^			
Congo-Kinshasa	Joseph Kasavubu	1965^			
Burkina Faso	Maurice Yaméogo	1966^			
Burundi	Mwambutsa IV	1966			
Central African Rep.	David Dacko	1966^			
Ghana	Kwame Nkrumah	1966°			
Nigeria	Abubakar Tafawa Balewa	1966*			
South Africa	Hendrik Verwoerd**	1966			
Mali	Modibo Keïta	1968^			
Uganda	Milton Obote	1971°			
Rwanda	Grégoire Kayibanda	1973^			
Ethiopia	Haile Selassie I	1974^			
Niger	Hamani Diori	1974^			
Chad	François Tombalbaye	1975*			
Comoros (1975)	Ahmed Abdallah	1975*			
Seychelles (1976)	James Mancham	1977°			
Mauritania	Moktar Ould Daddah	1978^			

Table 4.1 (*cont.*)

Country	Leader at independence	Ousted in coup (*killed, ^jailed, °exiled)	Died in office (naturally/accidentally)	Left voluntarily/peacefully	Power yet to change hands
Equatorial Guinea	Francisco Macías Nguema	1979*			
Guinea-Bissau	Luís Cabral	1980°			
Lesotho	Leabua Jonathan	1986^			
Gambia, The	Dawda Jawara	1994°			
Sierra Leone	Milton Margai		1964		
Gabon	Léon M'ba		1967		
Liberia	William Tubman		1971		
Kenya	Jomo Kenyatta		1978		
Angola (1975)	Agostino Neto		1979		
Botswana	Seretse Khama		1980		
eSwatini	Sobhuza II		1983		
Guinea	Ahmed Sékou Touré		1984		
Mozambique (1975)	Samora Machel		1986		
Côte d'Ivoire	Félix Houphouët-Boigny		1993		
Sudan	Ibrahim Abboud			1964	
Somalia	Aden Abdulle Osman Daar			1967	
Madagascar	Philibert Tsiranana			1972	
Senegal	Léopold Senghor			1980	
Mauritius	Seewoosagur Ramgoolam			1982	

Cameroon	Ahmadou Ahidjo	1982
Tanzania	Julius Nyerere	1985
Zambia	Kenneth Kaunda	1991
Malawi	Hastings Banda	1994
Cape Verde (1975)	Pedro Pires	1991
São Tomé and Príncipe (1975)	Manuel Pinto da Costa	1991
Djibouti (1977)	Hassan Gouled Aptidon	1999
Namibia (1990)	Sam Nujoma	2005
Zimbabwe (1980)	Robert Mugabe	2017
Eritrea (1991)	Isaias Afwerki	–
South Sudan (2011)	Salva Kiir Mayardit	–

Note: a country's year of independence is reported (in brackets) when reached after the 1960s.
Source: ALC dataset

What had happened to the founding fathers left a lasting legacy, as two broad syndromes long shaped African politics: while many national leaders managed to stay in office virtually unchallenged for extensive periods of time, an equally large number were overthrown by unlawful military interventions. Exceptions were very rare. One such exception was Aden Abdulle Osman Daar, the first African incumbent who conceded electoral defeat and peacefully handed over power after Somalia's 1967 election (two years later, however, the murder of his successor opened the way to a military takeover). That same year, in Sierra Leone, Siaka Stevens had also won an election as an opposition candidate, but he was ousted by the army almost immediately after taking office (Stevens was formally reinstated more than a year later).

Among the second- or third-generation leaders able to hold on to power for long, some were as successful as their predecessors, if not more so, in terms of duration in office. Iconic figures such as Félix Houphouët-Boigny, who ran Côte d'Ivoire from independence in 1960 until his death in 1993, were outdone by rulers who had taken over during the 1960s or 1970s, such as Omar Bongo in Gabon (1967–2009) and Gnassingbé Eyadéma in Togo (1967–2005). Others, like Juvénal Habyarimana in Rwanda (1973–1994), also stayed on for long periods. Even the "new breed" of reformers that made their appearance in some Eastern and Horn of Africa countries in the 1980s and 1990s turned out to be little different from their predecessors. On taking power through a guerrilla campaign in 1986, Yoweri Museveni had famously declared that "the problem of Africa in general and Uganda in particular is not the people but leaders who want to overstay in power." Yet in 2018 he was still in charge in Kampala, celebrating over three decades of rule. As some of his countrymen pointed out, if the Museveni of 1986 were to meet the present-day one, they would shoot each other on sight.[1] Countries whose rulers held sway for extensive periods were also the hotbeds of strongly personalized rule (Jackson and Rosberg 1982). In many such cases, taking office at a young age helped rulers hold it for a long period. At the time when they gained power, Burundi's Michel Micombero was 26, Gambia's Yahya Jammeh was 29, Museveni, Bongo, Eyadéma, and Moussa Traoré were no more than 32, while Ahmadou Ahidjo

---

[1] Will Ross, "Would Uganda's Museveni recognise his former self?," *BBC News*, May 7, 2011.

and Mobutu Sese Seko were both 35, Blaise Compaoré and Paul Kagame were 36, and José Eduardo Dos Santos and Teodoro Obiang Nguema were 37.

As Table 4.2 shows, Africa thus had a large number of long-serving rulers. As many as 90 power-holders held office for a decade or more, 36 of them for no less than 20 years, and 11 reached 30 years and beyond. A comparison with established European states is instructive. Post-war Western Europe only registered a couple of cases in which a ruler remained in office for decades. General Francisco Franco, whose sway over Spain stretched as far back as 1936, was the longest-serving one, dying in office in 1975. He was closely followed by António de Oliveira Salazar, who led Portugal's *estado novo* from 1932 to 1968. Other than these two cases, heads of the executive in major democracies since 1945 have been in power for much shorter periods. It is not surprising that, when Tony Blair and then Angela Merkel reached a decade in office, in recent years, their achievement was celebrated as rather extraordinary. If we include the current heads of government, the UK has had 15 prime ministers since 1945, averaging five years in power each, with only Margaret Thatcher and Blair achieving periods twice as long. Germany was led by Angela Merkel for 13 years at the time, by Konrad Adenauer for 14 years and by Helmut Kohl for 16 years, but the country's 8 chancellors since 1949 only averaged 8.6 years at the helm. In post-1958 France, 8 elected presidents were in office for 7.4 years each. On the other side of the Atlantic, Americans have chosen 14 presidents since 1945, with a mean stay in office of 5.6 years. By way of comparison, Houphouët-Boigny took office in Côte d'Ivoire when former World-War-II General Dwight Eisenhower was in the White House, and he was still in charge after Bill Clinton had been inaugurated, the ninth US president to become his peer.

In an apparent paradox, the longer a dictator's reign, the higher the political uncertainty that this could engender. In the absence of appropriate procedures, such might be the anxiety generated by the prospect of the fall of a long-serving ruler – the fear that the presidency would be open for the taking and that power struggles might ensue – that his clique and the public could flirt with the idea that big men never die.[2] When Omar Bongo expired, after 42 years of uninterrupted reign in Gabon, the government struggled to decide what to do: it first denied

---

[2] "Big men do not die," *BBC News*, June 18, 2009.

Table 4.2 *Longest-serving rulers in Africa, 1960–2018*

Leader	In power from/to	Consecutive years in office
1. Omar Bongo (Gabon)	1967–2009	41 and 199 days
2. Teodoro Obiang Nguema Mbasogo (Equat. Guinea)	1979–(in office)	38 and 331 days
3. Josè Eduardo dos Santos (Angola)	1979–2017	38 and 16 days
4. Gnassingbé Eyadéma (Togo)	1967–2005	37 and 307 days
5. Robert Mugabe (Zimbabwe)	1980–2017	37 and 220 days
6. Mswati III (eSwatini)	1983–(in office)	35 and 313 days
7. Paul Biya (Cameroon)	1982–(in office)	33 and 236 days
8. Félix Houphouët-Boigny (Côte d'Ivoire)	1960–1993	33 and 130 days
9. Haile Selassie I (Ethiopia)	1941–1974	33 and 8 days
10. Yoweri Museveni (Uganda)	1986–(in office)	32 and 155 days
11. Joseph-Désiré Mobutu (Congo, Dem. Rep.)	1965–1997	31 and 181 days
12. Hastings Banda (Malawi)	1964–1994	29 and 329 days
13. Dawda Jawara (Gambia)	1965–1994	29 and 161 days
14. Omar Al-Bashir (Sudan)	1989–(2019)	29 years
15. Idriss Déby (Chad)	1990–(in office)	27 and 210 days
16. William Tubman (Liberia)	1944–1971	27 and 208 days
17. Blaise Compaoré (Burkina Faso)	1987–2014	27 and 23 days
18. Kenneth Kaunda (Zambia)	1964–1991	27 and 15 days
19. France-Albert René (Seychelles)	1977–2004	26 and 320 days
20. Ahmed Sékou Touré (Guinea)	1958–1984	26 and 42 days
21. Isaias Afwerki (Eritrea)	1993–(in office)	25 and 37 days
22. Lansana Conté (Guinea)	1984–2008	24 and 167 days
23. Daniel arap Moi (Kenya)	1978–2002	24 and 136 days
24. Paul Kagame* (Rwanda)	1994–(in office)	23 and 346 days
25. Julius Nyerere (Tanzania)	1961–1985	23 and 337 days
26. Ahmadou Ahidjo (Cameroon)	1960–1982	22 and 190 days
27. Yahya Jammeh (Gambia, The)	1994–2017	22 and 181 days
28. Moussa Traoré (Mali)	1968–1991	22 and 132 days
29. Hassan Gouled Aptidon (Djibouti)	1977–1999	21 and 320 days
30. Mohamed Siad Barre (Somalia)	1969–1991	21 and 102 days
31. Meles Zenawi (Ethiopia)	1991–2012	21 and 90 days
32. Juvénal Habyarimana (Rwanda)	1973–1994	20 and 280 days

Table 4.2 (*cont.*)

Leader	In power from/to	Consecutive years in office
33. Denis Sassou-Nguesso (Congo, Rep.)	1997–(in office)	20 and 248 days
34. Maaouya Ould Sid'Ahmed Taya (Mauritania)	1984–2005	20 and 239 days
35. Leabua Jonathan (Lesotho)	1965–1986	20 and 197 days
36. Léopold Sédar Senghor (Senegal)	1960–1980	20 and 123 days

Notes: duration in office as of June 30, 2018. Leaders uninterruptedly in office for 20 years or more are included.
* De facto leader from 1994 to 2003.
Source: ALC dataset

initial reports that he had passed away; then claimed that he was in Spain for a holiday and a medical checkup after the shock of his wife's death; and finally even announced that he was about to return home. Long rule made African states unprepared for succession.

The weakness of the political institutions of African states had been exposed and debated since as early as the 1960s. Some observers specifically stressed how the region's incapacity to replace the "charismatic" leaders of independence fed into a legitimacy crisis with broader developmental implications because "agreement as to how power should be transferred is the *sine qua non* of political stability and of society's peaceful development" (Sylla 1982:11). A widespread tendency by incumbent rulers never to give up power but rather to abolish or weaken all procedures for leadership succession made coups d'état the preferred, and virtually only, mechanism for political change. In the absence of agreed-upon rules, military interventions were *de facto* accepted as a temporary solution. And they became endemic. Thus, political power and transitions on the continent often "grew out of the barrel of a gun," as Mao Zedong had put it. The region suffered a string of 85 military takeovers, and at least as many failed coups, over little more than 50 years.

Many army interventions, at times led by middle-ranking or junior officers, were bloodless and relatively welcomed by ordinary citizens (Thomson 2000:123ff.). Yet in other cases coups and civil wars, which are analytically distinct phenomena, fed into each other, with the former opening the way to the latter (e.g., Nigeria 1966, Ivory Coast 1999) as well as the other way round (e.g., Sierra Leone 1997, Mali 2012). Army takeovers were typically justified with the need to cope with economic hardship, to halt corruption, or to manage social divisions, particularly ethnic rivalries. By virtue of the alleged superior organization of the national army, and of course its control over the major means of coercion, a new leader in military fatigues would be able to portray himself and the defence forces as the country's only possible saviors and best choice.

More often than not, however, soldiers' private interests were a key motivation for seizing power. According to McGowan, in Africa's weak states at the periphery of the world economy, wealth accumulation, and upward social mobility through economic entrepreneurship was "more difficult and riskier" than capturing political office and then misuse it, which "is why ... military men and warlords have so often fought for control of the state" (McGowan 2005:10). The wealth and business interests developed by many Nigerian generals over decades of political meddling, and of illicit appropriation of the country's vast oil money, is an egregious example. But even in resource-poor Gambia, the smallest country in continental Africa by land area, Yahya Jammeh managed to amass impressive wealth in the years following his 1994 takeover, by allegedly controlling oil imports and the parallel market for foreign exchange, as well as by skimming off the financial support received from international sponsors such as Taiwan and Libya. Military dictators that gained broad popular respect for their moral rectitude, however, were far from unheard of, from populist leaders such as Jerry Rawlings of Ghana and Thomas Sankara of Burkina Faso to disciplinarian ones such as Nigeria's Muhammadu Buhari.

In all, twenty-nine countries – that is, almost two out of three sub-Saharan states – experienced at least one military overthrow after they achieved national sovereignty. In several cases, an initial takeover set off a chain of counter-coups that unfolded across the decades: 36 percent of coups (i.e., 31 out of 85) were against former *golpistas*. In Burkina Faso, more than anywhere else on the continent, this turned into a recurrent phenomenon. The Chief of Staff of the armed forces, Sangoulè Lamizana, first seized power in Ouagadougou, in 1966. Fourteen years later, it was Saye Zerbo (1980) who ousted him in a similar fashion. But Zerbo himself was soon the victim of a fellow soldier, Jean-Baptiste Ouédraogo (1982), who was in turn ejected by Thomas Sankara (1983), and the latter was eventually replaced by Blaise Compaoré (1987). More than any of his predecessors, Compaoré proved to be an extremely clever and durable power-holder, surviving almost three decades in office. Yet he ultimately shared his predecessors' fate when he was ousted by Lt. Col. Yacouba Isaac Zida in the wake of the 2014 Burkinabe popular revolt. The stormy events of 2014–2015 ultimately led to a peaceful handover of power and eventually to a more credible vote than had ever been the case under the Compaoré regime. The inauguration of a new elected president, Roch Marc Christian Kaboré, thus denoted a welcome historical dawn for the country. Burkina Faso was an extreme case, but other countries suffered similar strings of gun-based rotation in power. In Mauritania, for example, Col. Mustafa Ould Salek was forced out by Mohamed Mahmoud Ould Louly (1979), himself supplanted by Mohamed Khouna Ould Haidallah (1980), who was overthrown by Maaouya Ould Sid'Ahmed Taya (1984), himself ultimately succeeded by Ely Ould Mohamed Vall (2005).

Military interventions remained a dominant political feature longer than in any other world region, to the point that, by the mid-1980s, coups had become "almost exclusively an African phenomenon" (McGowan 2003:341), a mechanism for expressing dissent and bringing about leadership succession in closed regimes. Yet subregional differences have been profound. Since the outset, West Africa stood out as the most frequently affected area. Mauritania, Sierra Leone, Niger, Nigeria, Burkina Faso, and Ghana, for example, all suffered no fewer than four military takeovers, with Senegal, Cameroon, and Cape Verde being the only countries in the subregion that were fully spared. Southern Africa, by contrast, was only partly involved, since just 4 out of 16 capital cities south of an ideal line between Nairobi and Luanda experienced coups, and these were capitals of either very tiny (Lesotho) or island states (Madagascar, Seychelles, and Comoros).

The two patterns – overstays and overthrows – soon mixed with each other: early leadership stability was no guarantee of long-term rule, as demonstrated by Liberia, which gradually slid into a brutal domestic war following Samuel Doe's 1980 coup, or by Côte d'Ivoire, which turned unstable shortly after Houphouët-Boigny's 33-year-long dominance. Nor did an early military intervention prevent the subsequent stabilization in office of a *golpista* leader, as happened in Togo

Table 4.3 *Number of leadership changes in African countries, 1960–2018*

Number of leadership changes	Countries
18	Benin; Comoros
15	Guinea-Bissau
14	Nigeria
13	Sierra Leone
12	Ghana
11	Burundi; Somalia
10	Congo-Brazzaville; Madagascar
9	Central African Republic; Lesotho; Mauritania
8	Burkina Faso; Niger; South Africa; Sudan; Uganda
7	Chad; Ethiopia; Liberia; Mali; Mauritius; Togo
6	Guinea; Zambia
5	São Tomé and Príncipe
4	Botswana; Cape Verde; Côte d'Ivoire; Gabon; Malawi; Tanzania
3	Congo-Kinshasa; Kenya; Mozambique; Rwanda; Senegal; Seychelles
2	Angola; Gambia, The; Namibia
1	Cameroon; Djibouti; Equatorial Guinea; eSwatini; Zimbabwe
0	Eritrea; South Sudan
6.34	*Mean*
6	*Median*
4.49	*St. Dev.*

Notes: Leaders that return in office in a different period of time are counted twice. Interim leaders are included. Counts as of 30 June 2018.
Source: ALC dataset

under Eyadéma, in Congo-Kinshasa under Mobutu, and in Mali under Traoré.

An overall result of the two abovementioned dynamics is that Africa includes both countries in which changes at the top are literally or almost literally unheard of, as well as nations that have gone through a long string of handovers. Table 4.3 clusters all 49 sub-Saharan countries according to the number of leadership changes they experienced. The people of Eritrea (*de facto* independent since 1991) and South Sudan (the region's youngest nation, born as recently as 2011) are yet to see a single succession in office. Zimbabweans only witnessed it in late 2017, joining another four states that have only seen one power transfer. In Angola, the third economy in the region, José Eduardo Dos Santos had just turned 37 when he took over on the death of Agostino Neto, in 1979, and began building what would prove to be unassailable control of the state. Dawda Jawaara was in his twenty-ninth year as the president of the Gambia when he was toppled by Yahya Jammeh, who went on to consolidate his own rule. Both Dos Santos and Jammeh left office in 2017, albeit in profoundly different ways. Cameroon, Djibouti, Equatorial Guinea, and eSwatini are the other countries that had only seen one change in the period we investigate. At the opposite extreme, a number of countries each recorded a sequence of 12 or more leaders who rotated in power over the years. This special ranking is topped by some small countries, notably the Comoros, Benin, and Guinea-Bissau. Each of them has had no fewer than 4 (Guinea-Bissau) and as many as 6 coups (Comoros). This is in spite of the fact that Guinea-Bissau and the Comoros only achieved independence in the mid- and late 1970s. In each of the three countries, average tenure has been around three years per leader. Of course, this does not exclude periods of long rule. Instability in Benin, for example, was highly concentrated in the period prior to 1973, after which Mathieu Kérékou's regime stabilized domestic politics for almost two decades. But frequent turnovers are not restricted to small states. Fourth in the ranking is Nigeria, the region's giant, which counts as many as 14 rulers in its 55-year-long string of civilian and military heads of government.

Thus, the average number of leadership changes south of the Sahara – at just above 6 per country – hides wide variations. As Goldsmith (2001) pointed out, when taking power the typical postcolonial African strongman does not know what to expect, whether he will have an extremely long or an extremely short ride. Tenure was not secure. Neither was the fate of leaders after leaving office, with so many of them falling victims to murder, arrest or exile. Except for the fact that some of the countries experiencing little or no change are somewhat younger (from Djibouti and the Seychelles to Zimbabwe, Namibia, Eritrea, and South Sudan), and that many of those showing record instability are located in coup-prone West Africa (highly stable Gambia being a notable exception), there is not much that systematically distinguishes the countries at the top from those at the bottom of the table.

Successful Successions: Exceptions to Rule

Power transfers in the highly competitive but weakly institutionalized politics of Africa have almost always proved testing. Under the extremely personalized politics of many sub-Saharan states, everything appeared to hinge on the fate of the ruler. A *de facto* trade-off between leadership change and political order seemed to operate: either African citizens renounced alternating leaders in office, or they risked violence being used for that purpose. Political successions in the absence of proper procedures have thus often turned into turbulent times and full-fledged crises.

Yet this has not always been the case, as Hughes and May (1988) observed in a survey of "successful successions" across the first two decades following independence. Between one-in-four and one-in-three of all leadership changes throughout the 1965–1987 period were peaceful and "regular," as opposed to violent and "irregular." Among them were some prominent cases, such as those resulting from the graceful retirement of Léopold Senghor in Senegal, Ahmadou Ahidjo in Cameroon, Julius Nyerere in Tanzania, and Siaka Stevens in Sierra Leone. In fact, even where "the sudden or traumatic death of a powerful ruler might [have suggested] a period of anarchy or uncertainty" (Hughes and May 1988:16), reality proved otherwise, as if nature or accident removed the key obstacle to leadership turnover, namely the incumbent himself. The death in office of Sierra Leone's Milton Margai (1963) and Liberia's William Tubman (1971), as well as those of Angola's Agostinho Neto (1979) and Mozambique's Samora Machel (1986), led to quick and essentially harmonious replacements. In the latter two cases, relatively well-functioning and cohesive ruling parties such as the Movimento Popular de Libertação de Angola (MPLA) in Luanda and the Frente de Libertação de Moçambique (FRELIMO) in Maputo proved effective enough to arrange a legitimate succession process. Where internal squabbles divided a much weaker ruling organization, as with the Parti Démocratique de Guinée after Sékou Touré's death, they provided an easy justification for an army intervention. Personal background also appeared to be decisive, as all successful new leaders could count on significant political connections or administrative experience. Familial descent, on the other hand, proved to be of little significance when compared to other "Third world" regions such as Asia or Latin America. While countless African strongmen's sons and daughters acquired influential political or economic positions, and were occasionally touted as the ruler's chosen successors, no single "republican dynasty" emerged in Africa prior to the 2000s (when, in the space of a few years, within-the-family handovers occurred in Congo-Kinshasa, Togo, and Gabon). In those early decades, the only partial exception in which consanguinity played a role was Albert Margai's takeover after his brother Milton's death in Sierra Leone. This absence is rather surprising, particularly for countries that frequently lacked strong ruling parties capable of managing the transition (see Brownlee 2007). Finally, whatever the role of foreign meddling in African affairs – including controversial American and French interventions like those that led to the killing of Patrice Lumumba or to the ousting of Jean-Bédel Bokassa – leadership selection processes and related instabilities in Africa have been largely driven by domestic political forces and dynamics (see Hughes and May 1988:19).

As interesting as succession success stories are, they rarely pointed to well-institutionalized procedures for leadership change able to regulate a succession of successions, with the already mentioned exception of party-driven processes in the likes of Angola, Mozambique, and Tanzania. Ultimately, success stories revealed "ordered" *instances* of rotation in power more than ordered *systems* for turnover in office. And they remain a minority and largely unpredictable set of cases.

New Rules for Different Rulers: The Constitutional and Multiparty Transitions of the 1990s

Voting in open national polls was thus hardly a habit for the people and political systems of post-colonial Africa. For many African as well as external observers, it had long been apparent that democratic elections could offer a lasting solution to the lack of mechanisms for political change. They could allow sub-Saharan countries to move beyond coups as a short-term answer by establishing "a rational system for transferring power" (Sylla 1982:11). Prior to the 1990s, however, few leaders on the continent went down this road. One of them was Senghor, a dictator who "personally initiated a process of democratization that culminated in an orderly transfer of power" (Sylla 1982:24). He had emerged stronger than ever from Senegal's first multiparty election, in 1978, in which his Parti Socialiste (previously the Union Progressiste Sénégalaise) was challenged by the only two newly legalized political forces, namely Abdoulaye Wade's Parti Démocratique Sénégalais and the Parti Africain de l'Indépendance. President Senghor also had the constitution revised to provide for the prime minister to succeed him, should he die or retire. In 1980 he became the first long-serving leader in modern Africa to step down voluntarily. But the most notable and enduring exception was Botswana, whose citizens had regularly gone to the polls to choose their leaders since the country's independence in 1966. In late 2014, the government in Gaborone organized the tenth consecutive election since independence, an unparalleled record for the African continent in a country that had never suffered any form of political upheaval. Six years earlier, the state president, Festus Mogae, had retired following a new rule – highly unusual for parliamentary systems, but similarly adopted in neighbouring South Africa – limiting presidential mandates to a maximum ten years. The good performance of the country's institutions owes a great deal to the first president, Seretse Khama. By openly espousing democratic values, by having himself and his ministers adhere to a rigorous moral code, and by rejecting the autocratic tendencies that he saw emerging elsewhere in the region, Khama turned into one of the most outstanding examples of "accomplished leadership in the developing world," one that "created a paradigm of African leadership that was unique in his day" (Rotberg 2013:189, 201).

For two decades and a half, Botswana's remained a rather exceptional story south of the Sahara. In most countries, as we pointed out, ruling autocrats had decided to do away with pluralist elections, or else they had been removed by someone who thought and acted that way. In many places, voters were still called to the polls, but this was because most countries had shifted toward single-party elections. Table 4.4 reports the number of non-multiparty elections held under one-party regimes. One-party arrangements were justified on various grounds: a pressing need for national unity, a lack of class-based divisions and the consensus-seeking tradition of African communities, or the urgency of faster economic development (see Thomson 2000:103). The Tanganyika Africa National Union/Chama Cha Mapinduzi party, for example, for 30 years regularly held single-party elections in order to legitimize its rule in Tanzania. Admittedly, the country was somewhat unique in the extent to which the transition to a monopolistic political system had occurred peacefully through the

Table 4.4 *Non-multiparty elections in African countries, 1960–1990*

N. of elections (*non*-multiparty)	Countries (election years)
7	Tanzania (1962; 1965; 1970; 1975; 1980; 1985; 1990)
6	Cameroon (1965; 1970; 1975; 1980; 1984; 1988); Côte d'Ivoire (1960; 1965; 1970; 1975; 1980; 1985);
5	Gabon (1961; 1967; 1973; 1979; 1986); Kenya (1969; 1974; 1979; 1983; 1988); Rwanda (1965; 1969; 1978; 1983; 1988);
4	Benin (1960; 1964; 1968; 1970); Guinea (1961; 1968; 1974; 1982); Liberia (1963; 1967; 1971; 1975); Madagascar (1965; 1972; 1982; 1989); Mauritania (1961; 1966; 1971; 1976); Togo (1961; 1963; 1979; 1986); Zambia (1973; 1978; 1983; 1988)
3	Cape Verde (1975; 1980; 1985); Congo, Dem. Rep. (1970; 1977; 1984); Niger (1965; 1970; 1989); Senegal (1963; 1968; 1973); São Tomé and Príncipe (1975; 1980; 1985); Seychelles (1979; 1984; 1989); Sudan (1971; 1977; 1983)
2	Comoros (1968; 1984); Djibouti (1981; 1987); Equatorial Guinea (1968; 1989); Mali (1979; 1985); Uganda (1996; 2001)
1	Burkina Faso (1965); Burundi (1984); Central African Republic (1964); Chad (1969); Congo, Rep. (1961); Ethiopia (1987); Lesotho (1970); Sierra Leone (1985); Somalia (1986)
None	Angola; Botswana; Eritrea; eSwatini; Gambia, The; Guinea-Bissau; Malawi; Mauritius; Mozambique; Namibia; Nigeria; South Africa; South Sudan; Zimbabwe.

Notes: Presidential elections only (no-party elections for Uganda in 1996 and 2001). For Cape Verde, Ethiopia, Lesotho, and São Tomé and Príncipe parliamentary elections have been included.
Source: ALC dataset

ballot box (Nohlen et al. 1999:4). But popular consent was no prerequisite for the establishment of single-partism. The Union Nationale Camerounaise (later Rassemblement Démocratique du Peuple Camerounais, RDPC) or the Parti Démocratique de la Côte d'Ivoire (PDCI) resorted to similar "unifying" strategies over periods nearly as long as

Tanzania's. The actual governing role of these ruling organizations varied greatly. In Mozambique, Angola, and Ethiopia, the party was central to policymaking, and it retained a significant role also in countries such as Tanzania, Rwanda, Kenya, and others. In places like Uganda, Ghana, and Sierra Leone, on the other hand, it soon "deteriorated into a hollow shell" (Chazan et al. 1999:63).

So why would dictators in the region continue to call their people to polling stations if they insisted that the symbol of only one party should appear on the ballot paper? While pressures for introducing elections were generally weak – the wind of the global democratic ethos and its imperatives was yet to start blowing south of the Sahara – many leaders felt that one-party votes could perform a cathartic function as a ritual that would help them mobilize their people and reconnect with them (Sylla 1982:19). In countries that institutionalized single-party elections over relatively long periods, rulers perfected the art of presenting themselves as the nation's favorites, relying on presidential plebiscites to periodically refresh their "mandates." Julius Nyerere and later Ali Mwinyi in Tanzania typically stopped short of displays of absolute consensus, ostensibly achieving a 93-to-98 percent share of the suffrage and allowing for some 2–7 percent of "no votes." Ahmadou Ahidjo and Paul Biya in Cameroon and Félix Houphouët-Boigny in Côte d'Ivoire, on the other hand, never obtained less than a full 100 percent of valid votes (Nohlen et al. 1999). But the likes of Jomo Kenyatta, and then Daniel Arap Moi in Kenya, Grégoire Kayibanda, and Juvenal Habyarimana in Rwanda and Omar Bongo in Gabon, similarly held series of elections in which they ran unopposed. If ever, pluralism was only partly accepted where citizens were allowed to choose among alternative candidates – that is, all belonging to the ruling party – in single-member constituencies for legislative assembly seats. In countries such as Côte d'Ivoire, Kenya, Rwanda, Zambia, and many others, this kind of arrangement allowed for a degree of political renewal, but only within top-down predefined political boundaries (Bratton and van de Walle 1997:80). The elections held between the late 1960s and the 1980s in Kenya, for example, produced an average turnover of almost 60 percent of the legislators sitting in Nairobi, albeit voting choice was only permitted strictly under the umbrella of the Kenya African National Union (KANU), the sole legal party (Khapoya 1988).

It was in this scenario that, in the 1990s, political turmoil and change began to set in across the continent. In the first half of the decade, Africa underwent long-awaited constitutional and electoral reforms that profoundly altered its political landscape. The transformations initiated in the space of a few years were second in magnitude only to those experienced during the period of independence back in the 1960s. Starting with Namibia in 1989, and then Comoros and Côte d'Ivoire in the following year, multiparty politics was introduced in country after country. As shown by the bar chart in Figure 4.1, the peak came between 1992 and 1993, when presidential polls were held in 8 and 11 states, respectively. Even Liberia organized an election in 1997, in the midst of its brutal civil war – thus allowing the country's most infamous warlord, Charles Taylor, to win the presidency legally – whereas Nigeria did so twice, first with a botched poll and then with a successful one six years later, in 1999. Some latecomers also joined in during the first decade of the new millennium, notably post-genocide Rwanda in 2003, post-war Congo-DRC in 2006, and in that same year also Uganda, which hitherto had opted for no-party elections in which contenders could only participate on an individual basis (Carbone 2008). Table 4.5 shows, for each country, when the first multiparty election was held, possible interruptions to the electoral regime, and pre-1990 multiparty elections, if any.

Elections formally open to all parties quickly became the "new normal" in stark contrast to the past. By 1996 some early reformers were already running their second round of national voting, and the number of multiparty elections for the executive quickly skyrocketed, up from an average of 1.46 elections per year in 1960–1989 to 7.86 elections per year in 1990–2018. This is not to say that countries in the region made even progress toward the purported goal of the reforms, namely political renewal through the establishment of democratic politics. Far from it: many "transitions" only led to fake democratic setups that did little to hide the substantial continuity of old practices and long-standing power-holders. The strategies employed by the latter to adapt and survive in a changing political environment varied somewhat. But they typically included a mixture of buying off, containing, dividing and intimidating the opposition, while ensuring the support of specific constituencies – most often their co-ethnics, the army and the public sector – and the regulation of different stages of the transition by favourable constitutional and electoral rules (Baker 1998:121ff.). Handling and mobilizing ethnic identities was a

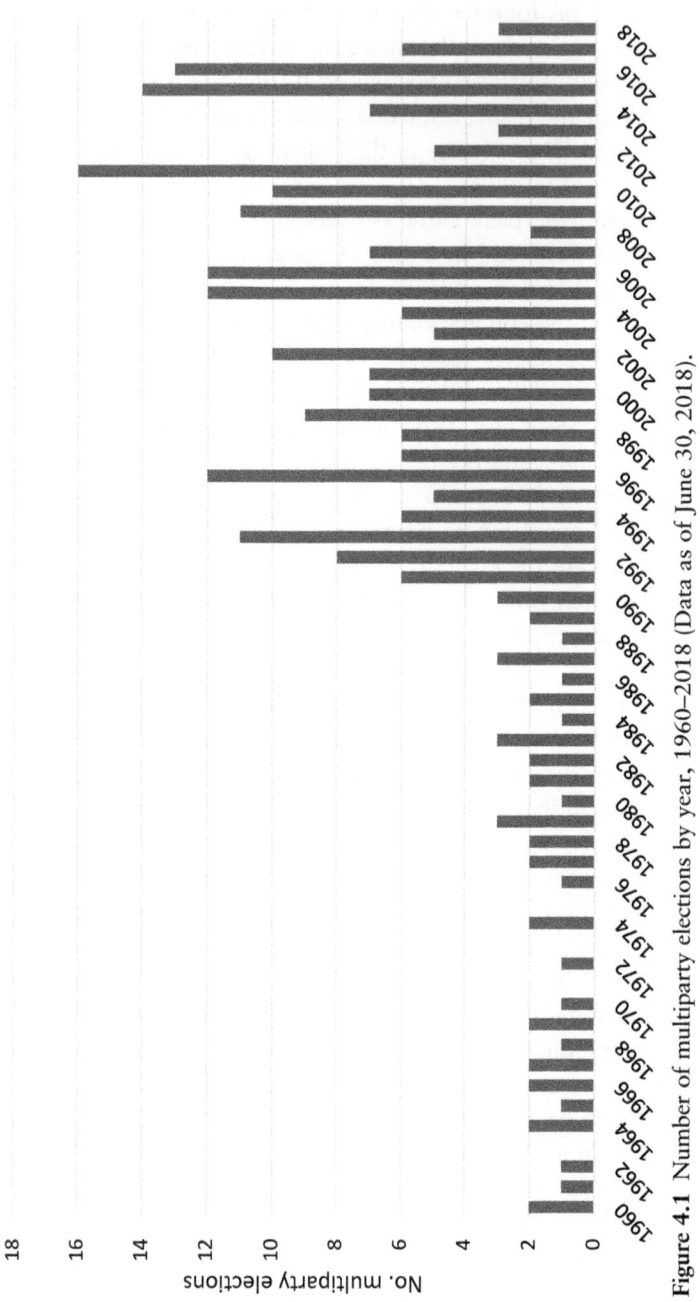

Figure 4.1 Number of multiparty elections by year, 1960–2018 (Data as of June 30, 2018).

Table 4.5 *Multiparty transitions: post-1990 founding elections*

Country	Founding election (1990 on)	Regime interruptions	Multiparty elections prior to 1990
Angola	1992	(1992–2008)§	
Benin	1991		
Botswana	-		1969; 1974; 1979; 1984; 1989
Burkina Faso	1991	2014–2015	1978
Burundi	1993	1993–2005	
Cameroon	1992		
Cape Verde	1991		
Central African Republic	1993	2003–2005; 2013–2015	1981
Chad	1996		
Comoros	1990	1995–1996; 1999–2002	
Congo, Dem. Rep.	2006		
Congo, Rep.	1992	1997–2002	
Côte d'Ivoire	1990	1999–2000	
Djibouti	1992		
Equatorial Guinea	1996		
Eritrea	-		
Ethiopia	1995		
Gabon	1993		1964
Gambia, The	1996		1966; 1972; 1977; 1982; 1987; 1992
Ghana	1992		1960; 1969; 1979
Guinea	1993	2008–2010	
Guinea-Bissau	1994	1999–2000; 2003–2005; 2009; 2012–2014	
Kenya	1992		
Lesotho	1993		
Liberia	1997	2003	1985
Madagascar	1993	2009–2014	
Malawi	1994		
Mali	1992	2012–2013	

Table 4.5 (*cont.*)

Country	Founding election (1990 on)	Regime interruptions	Multiparty elections prior to 1990
Mauritania	1992	2005–2008	
Mauritius	-		1976; 1982; 1983; 1987
Mozambique	1994		
Namibia	1989*		
Niger	1993	1996; 1999; 2010–2011	
Nigeria	1999		1964; 1979; 1983
Rwanda	2003		
São Tomé and Príncipe	1991	1995; 2003	
Senegal	1993		1978; 1983; 1988
Seychelles	1993		
Sierra Leone	1996	1996–2002	1962; 1967
Somalia	-		1967
South Africa	1994°		1961; 1966; 1970; 1974; 1977; 1981; 1987; 1989
South Sudan	-		
Sudan	1996		1965; 1986
eSwatini	-		
Tanzania	1995		
Togo	1993		
Uganda	2006		1980
Zambia	1991		1968
Zimbabwe	-		1985

Notes: §The mandates of the Angolan president and parliament elected in 1992 were extended until 2008, partly due to the civil war. *The first Namibian election is included even though it was held one year (1989) before the country gained independence (1990). °The first South African election under universal suffrage is included.

strategem frequently adopted by presidents who had found themselves with their backs against the wall:

for instance, Rawlings was able to secure 93% of the Volta region of Ghana, home of his Ewe group, in the 1992 election. Likewise, Conté mobilised his own Soussous in Guinea, Bongo his Bateke in Gabon, and Déby his fellow Muslims of north and east Chad. Other incumbents have gone so far as deliberately to manipulate ethnicity so as to promote conflict that would demonstrate the alleged ethnic divisiveness and inherent instability of multi-party democracy. Moi encouraged armed attacks by members of his own ethnic group, the Kalenjins, against the immigrant Kikuyus in the northwest. And Biya is accused of knowingly creating ethnic strife between the Foulbe and Baya in order to justify oppressive measures and to discredit the Cameroon opposition. Eyadéma, for his part, clearly exploited the fact that the Togolese army was predominantly from his own ethnic group, the Kabye, to resist the democratisation movement that was largely led by southerners. Mobutu, De Klerk and Habyarimana also engaged in ethnic provocation for political ends. When the presidential group has been the majority group, as Taya's Maures in Mauritania, it has given them an irresistible advantage. (Baker 1998:124)

Regimes such as those of Togo and Cameroon were paradigmatic cases of the tenacity of long-standing power-holders willing to use every resource at their disposal to make sure they would turn "democratization" to their own advantage. No change took place at the presidential palace in Lomé, where Gnassingbé Eyadéma and his Rassemblement du Peuple Togolais (RPT) only briefly lost their supremacy during the 1991–1994 transition. Actively backed by the army and more tacitly by France, Eyadéma survived in office and gradually regained full control of the political process. As the country's first "competitive" election was boycotted by the major opposition parties on the ground that the vote was open to manipulation by the government, the incumbent president secured 96.5 percent of the votes in 1993, survived his party's defeat in the parliamentary election held the following year, and reemerged as the uncontested master of Togolese politics until his death in 2005. Paul Biya was similarly unscathed by the reform process ignited by the "Black affair" of early 1990, when protests erupted after the arrest of Yondo Black, an attorney and Douala chief who had formed a political party outside of the realm of single-partism. During the turbulent years of the transition, the president retained a crucial if limited support base among his Beti co-ethnics, the country's public employees and the army. He weathered a nationwide "ghost towns" strike and narrowly won the 1992 first-past-the-post election by a plurality against a divided opposition. Once Biya was back in control, his tally of the vote rose exponentially, averaging around 80 percent in the subsequent three elections. As

Baker (1998:120) pointed out, awarding the nickname "the Chameleon" to Benin's Mathieu Kérékou was somewhat unfortunate. This former autocrat's attitude towards democratic openings was much closer to that of a real convert – he regained the presidency via a fair vote in 1996, and left it gracefully ten years later – when compared to many fellow authoritarian rulers turned façade democrats.

Other sub-Saharan states had much more promising beginnings, but they were subsequently diverted or abruptly interrupted. Both in Burundi and in Congo-Brazzaville, dictators who had been thrown out by voters at their country's first open polls, in the early 1990s, made their comebacks through the gun in no more than three to five years. The 1992 election of Pascal Lissouba marked an ephemeral new dawn in Brazzaville, for example, because ousted leader Denis Sassou-Nguesso managed to return to the presidential palace in the midst of the 1997–1999 war between his *Cobra* militias, backed by Angolan troops, and rival armed factions. In Madagascar, opposition candidate Albert Zafy had trumped Didier Ratsiraka, a soldier who had run the Indian Ocean's island for the better part of two decades, when the latter allowed a reasonably competitive vote in 1993. Ratsiraka's return to power via the ballot box, a few years later, initially seemed to consolidate the country's pluralist arrangements. But the latter were first shaken by a conflict-ridden election that led to the ousting of Ratsiraka himself, in late 2001, and then plunged into a deeper crisis when the mayor of the capital city Antananarivo, Andry Rajoelina, illegally took the presidency at the end of the decade.

Yet the seeds of political change had been sown in many faraway corners on the continent, and a number of former autocrats who had similarly been ousted during the transitions of the early 1990s long tried and failed to regain power. They included André Kolingba in the Central African Republic and Kaunda in Zambia. Progress was evident not only in the democratization trajectories of many countries, but occasionally also in the limited openings allowed by the new electoral authoritarianisms that mushroomed in the region (see Schedler 2006). Elections helped regularize leadership handovers in political systems that remained under the control of hegemonic parties like those in Mozambique and Tanzania. On the other hand, after Namibia became *de facto* independent in 1989, it held a string of fundamentally democratic elections that proved instrumental to orderly successions in office, if always under the ruling Swapo party. After serving as the country's first president (and prolonging his stay beyond what was initially allowed by the constitution), Sam Nujoma, the leader of the independence struggle, handed power over to Hifikepunye Pohamba in 2005, who duly passed the presidency on to Hage Geingob a decade later. In Kenya, Zambia, Malawi, Senegal, Nigeria, Ghana, Sierra Leone, Benin, and Cape Verde, progress was even more evident, as on at least one occasion opposition candidates were able to unseat incumbent presidents or ruling parties. In line with global political trends, in the space of a few years being elected under a multiparty system had become fashionable and necessary as never before among African leaders.

The Decline of Violent Takeovers

Violence had long been instrumental to reaching the top job in postcolonial Africa, as we have seen. For 30 years after the end of colonialism, almost one in two of all leadership changes in the region featured the use of armed coercion, in the form of either military coups – by far the most common – or guerrilla takeovers. Figure 4.2 shows the general shift in the shares of leadership transfer modes between the 1960–1989 and the 1990–2018 period. Figure 4.3 adds key details of this trend by plotting the absolute and relative number of coups by decade. Of the 85 military coups that occurred between 1960 and 2018, more than half took place in the early post-independence decades, namely the 1960s and 1970s. The relative frequency of armed interventions, on the other hand, peaked in the 1980s, when 17 coups accounted for as many as 51.5 percent of all leadership changes in the decade. Things then appeared to take a different course. The number of military takeovers had already begun to decline in the mid-1980s, with the 11 *golpes* recorded in 1981–1985 almost halved to 6 in 1986–1990. From 1990 onward, the balance between violent takeovers and electoral transfers of power was definitely reversed. As Figure 4.2 shows, the former diminished to less than one-fifth of all leadership transitions, whereas election-based handovers changed from being a rarity – little more than one in every 20 changes in office during the previous 20 years – to becoming the most common way in which rulers reached power, accounting for almost one in every two cases. The trend further consolidated in the new millennium, as electoral changes came to constitute a substantial majority of 60 out of 96 transfers of power, whereas army takeovers

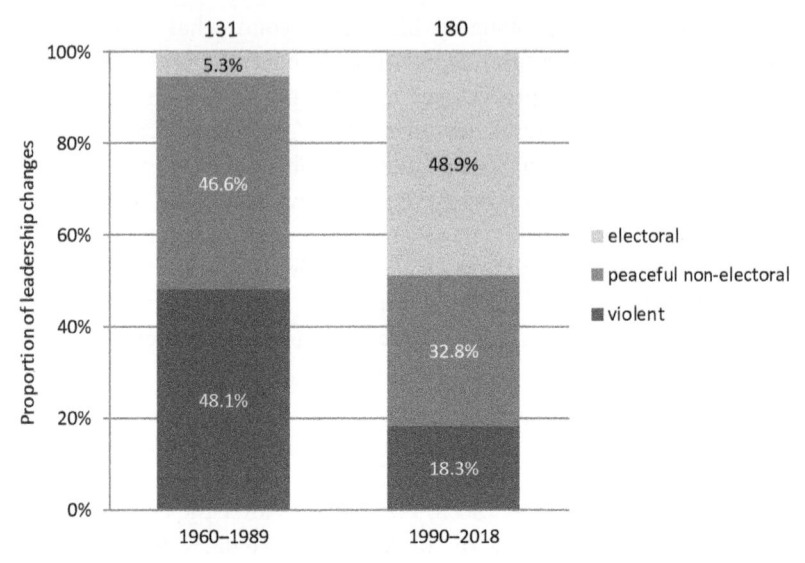

Figure 4.2 Modes of leadership change in 1960–1989 and 1990–2018 (Data as of June 30, 2018).
Source: ALC dataset

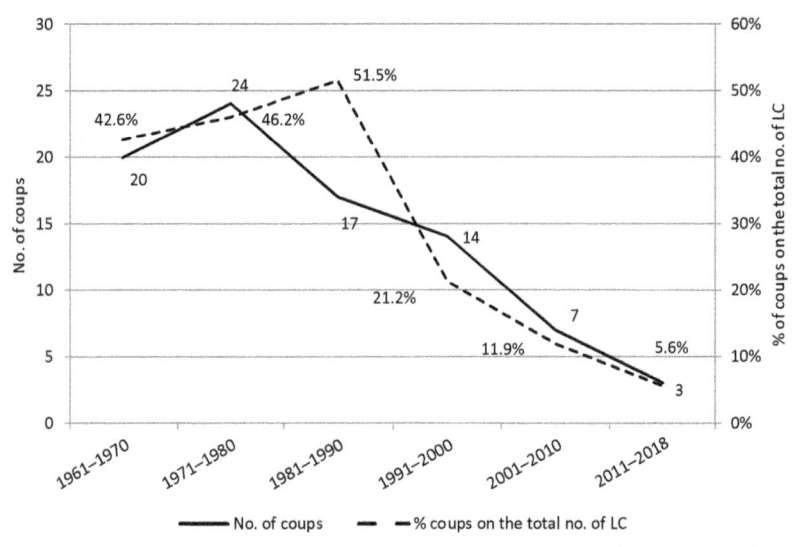

Figure 4.3 Number of coups and proportion over total number of leadership changes (LC), by decade, 1960–2018 (Data as of June 30, 2018).
Source: ALC dataset

The Decline of Violent Takeovers

dropped further to less than one per year – 10 in all in 2001–2018, or 10.4 percent of all changes – an unprecedented low level in the region.

Post-2000 coups are listed in Table 4.6 and furnish a number of insights. In all, soldiers captured power 10 times in 8 countries (they did so twice in Guinea-Bissau and Mauritania). First, there were no newcomers: all the countries that experienced a coup in the new millennium had at least one before, if not a tradition of military takeovers, as was the case of Burkina Faso, Guinea-Bissau, Mauritania, and Niger. Côte d'Ivoire was in fact the last new sub-Saharan country to join the ranks of those that have experienced military rule, back in 1999. If we extend the time frame to the past 25 years, Côte d'Ivoire was the only country, alongside the small state of Gambia, in which the army took power for the first time. Second, in all cases, elections were reintroduced within a relatively short time. With the exception of the crisis in Madagascar – a peculiar case in which power was not captured by the military but by a civilian coup-maker – all countries held a fresh election within no more than three years. In four cases, elections were organized in the year following the coup. Burkina Faso and Mauritania are possibly the most interesting instances. Both had a previous record of rotation in power only through the gun, and yet the coups of the years 2000s were for the first time rapidly followed by national votes. In Mauritania, Ely Ould Mohamed Vall turned power over to an elected civilian president (although the latter was subsequently stripped of it about one year later). Finally, only three coups took place in the most recent 2011–2018 period. These were in Guinea-Bissau and Mali in 2012, and in Burkina Faso in 2014, confirming West Africa as the most coup-prone subregion in the continent, as it had been since independence. Yet in each of the three cases power was relatively swiftly returned to a new civilian president, following the organization of fresh elections within 24 months since the military had captured power.

With all the caveats necessary when examining electoral competition in Africa, the post-1990 scenario amounted to a paradigm shift that became ever more evident in the new millennium. The gun was still there, but it had moved to the background, leaving the ballot box at center stage. The less gun/more ballot box connection was a strict one. In the words of McGowan, "the duration and quality of multiparty electoral democracy [and thus the legitimacy of the regime] is one of the factors that reduces the likelihood of military-led political instability" (McGowan 2003:358). Lindberg and Clark agree with him on the crucial importance of the time factor. They observe that the vast

Table 4.6 *Post-2000 coups d'état in Africa*

Country	Date of coup	Ousted leader	New leader	Post-coup election	Leader after the election
Central African Republic	15/03/2003	Ange-Félix Patassé	François Bozizé	2005	***François Bozizé***
Guinea-Bissau I	14/09/2003	Kumba Ialá	Veríssimo Correia Seabra	2005	João Bernardo Vieira
Mauritania I	03/08/2005	Maaouya Ould Sid'Ahmed Taya	Ely Ould Mohamed Vall	2007	Sidi Ould Cheikh Abdallahi
Mauritania II	06/08/2008	Sidi Ould Cheikh Abdallahi	Mohamed Ould Abdel Aziz	2009	***Mohamed Ould Abdel Aziz***
Guinea	22/12/2008	Aboubacar Somparé	Moussa Dadis Camara	2010	Alpha Condé
Madagascar	17/03/2009	Marc Ravalomanana	Andry Rajoelina	2014	Hery Rajaonarimampianina
Niger	19/02/2010	Mamadou Tandja	Salou Djibo	2011	Mahamadou Issoufou
Mali	22/03/2012	Amadou Toumani Touré	Amadou Sanogo	2013	Ibrahim Boubacar Keïta
Guinea-Bissau II	12/04/2012	Raimundo Pereira	Mamadu Ture Kuruma	2014	José Mário Vaz
Burkina Faso	01/11/2014	Blaise Compaoré	Yacouba Isaac Zida	2015	Roch Marc Christian Kaboré

Note: bold italics denote coup-makers who remained at the helm after an election.
Source: ALC dataset

majority of military interventions occurred shortly after a regime's "founding" election and point out that the new political legitimacy that democratic votes were meant to generate "does not necessarily materialize immediately" (Lindberg and Clark 2008:89). Rather, it is when successive rounds of elections are held that coups become less likely. But Lindberg and Clark also rightly stress that the new – if far from complete – coup-aversion of African states went somewhat beyond democracy. It was not just the spread of competitive votes under reasonably democratic conditions, but also that of electoral processes that were essentially controlled, in liberalizing or electoral authoritarian regimes, which helped curb the feasibility of coups as a path to power. As Table 4.7 shows, even when we only consider the 31 countries that have experienced military overthrows at some point in their past history, the vast majority of them are now at a significant and growing distance from the last time that they suffered one. This is true also for countries that were once considered hotbeds of militarism, such as Benin (latest coup in 1972), Ghana (latest coup in 1981), and Nigeria (latest coup in 1993). Army takeovers are still a reality in parts of Africa and a hypothetical option in others. Yet they are less and less so, and the swelling number of young Africans increasingly have no direct memories of them.

More Rotation, Shorter Stays in Office

As late as 2015, the US president, Barack Obama, used his visit to the African Union to call for all nations on the continent to establish procedures for the peaceful transfer of power, since "nobody should be president for life." The image of Africa was still associated with irremovable leaders. Yet the political landscape had in fact been shifting. Since the 1990s, national leaderships have tended to change hands more often than was previously the case. The annual frequency of leadership changes declined between the 1960s and the 1980s, testifying to a process whereby many rulers became increasingly entrenched in office. As Figure 4.4 shows, this dynamic touched its lowest point during the 1980s, when, on average, power handovers occurred in just about three countries every year. The pattern was then reversed, as the frequency recorded over the subsequent two-and-a-half decades was twice as high, with about one-in-six countries every year ushering in a new leader. When we exclude interim leaders, these differences are only slightly reduced, and the general trend remains the same.

Table 4.7 Coups d'état and time elapsed from last coup, 1960–2018

Gabon (1)	1 9 6 0			
Congo-Kinshasa (1)	1 9 6 5			
Togo (2)	1 9 6 7			
Somalia (1)	1 9 7 0			
Benin (5)				
Rwanda (1)				
Ethiopia (1)				
Seychelles (1)				
Equatorial Guinea (1)				
Liberia (1)				
Ghana (5)				
Chad (2)				
Uganda (3)				
Sudan (3)				
Nigeria (6)[a]				
Lesotho (3)				
Gambia, The (1)				
Sierra Leone (5)				
Burundi (5)				
Comoros (7)[a]				
Côte d'Ivoire (1)				
Central African Republic (3)				
Mauritania (6)				
Guinea (2)				
Madagascar (2)				
Niger (4)				
Guinea Bissau (4)				
Mali (3)				
Burkina Faso (6)				

Note: (*) indicates a coup; reported in brackets besides each country is the total number of coups that it has suffered; ([a]) Nigeria suffered two coups in 1966, the Comoros had two in 1989. Counts as of 30 June 2018.

Source: ALC dataset

108

More Rotation, Shorter Stays in Office 109

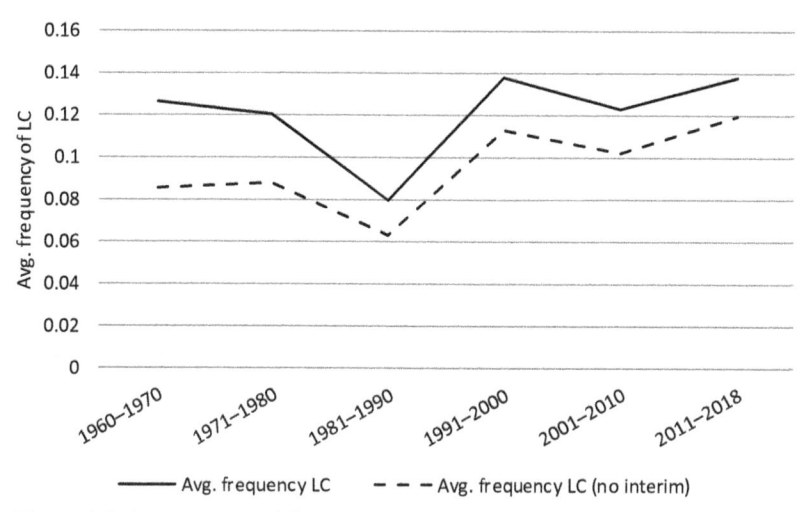

Figure 4.4 Average annual frequency of leadership changes (LC), 1960–2018 (Data as of June 30, 2018).
Note: leaders who took office in 2018 are *not* considered interim even though they had not yet reached 12 months in office at the end of the year.
Source: ALC dataset

The widespread introduction of electoral mechanisms for the selection and replacement of leaders that countries in the region had undertaken some 20 to 25 years earlier was meant to address the problem of overstays in power (alongside that of irregular takeovers). The new arrangements were first "tested against" those who held office at the time when political reforms were started: while many of them survived or even surfed the wave, as the tide rose change began to set in. In all, 41 sub-Saharan states had organized founding elections in the 1990s (that is, all but Botswana, Eritrea, Mauritius, Namibia, Somalia, eSwatini, Zimbabwe, and, of course, South Sudan, which was still to become independent). Of these, the incumbent stood for office in 34 cases (83 percent), and in a large majority of them – i.e., 25 cases, or 73.5 percent – he won the vote. Only in the remaining 9 countries (26.5 percent), or just about one in four cases, was the sitting president successfully challenged and ousted by the opposition. Yet the advent of 16 new national leaders (7 in states where incumbent autocrats did not run), all of whom were formally voted into office, marked an era of political renovation.

Political and institutional transformations were reflected in the changing length of stay in office of sub-Saharan rulers. Figure 4.5

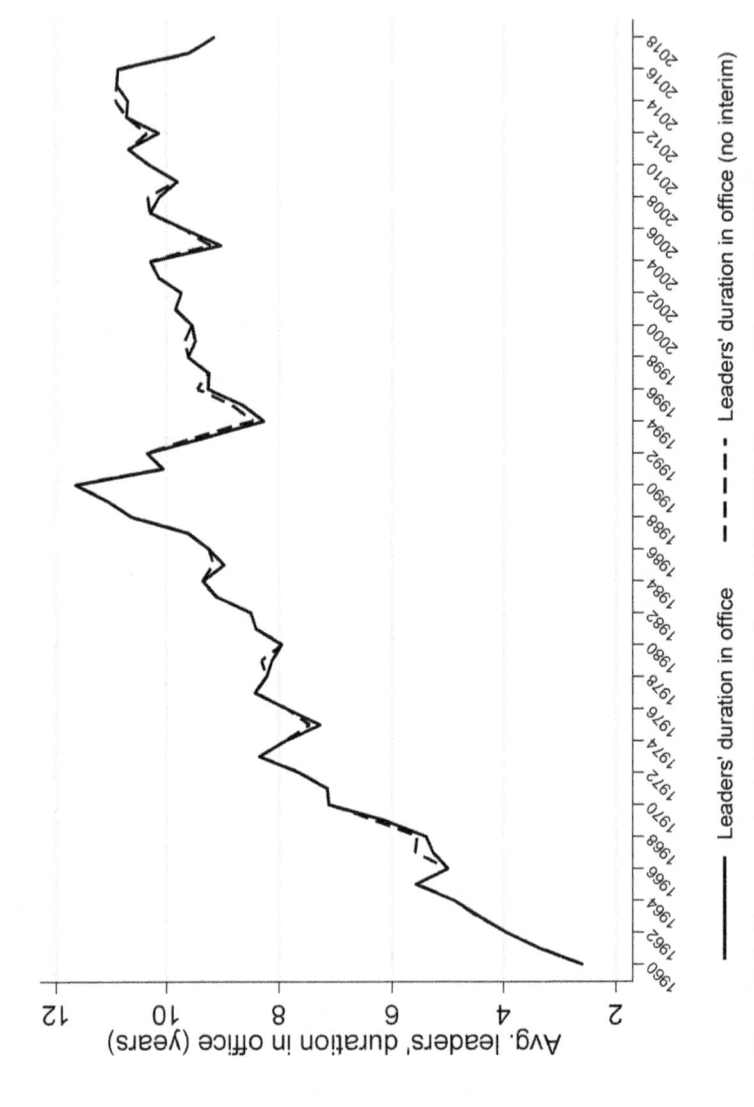

Figure 4.5 Average tenure of African leaders, 1960–2018 (Data as of June 30, 2018).

Source: ALC dataset

shows the leaders' average duration in office, by year. The solid line refers to all leaders irrespective of the length of their tenure, while the dashed line excludes interim leaders who remained in office for less than 12 months (such as Colonel Christophe Soglo's three-month tenure in 1963–1964, in Benin, or Kgalema Motlanthe's eight-month spell in 2008–2009, in South Africa). Since independence, average tenure had grown steadily, year after year, until 1990, when it peaked at 11.6 years. This trend was partly physiological (the leaders of newly independent countries had only "just started" to rule in the 1960s) and partly pathological (the result of stays in office that had gradually become excessively long in a number of cases). The subsequent multi-party transitions coincided with the demise of many long-lasting rulers – not just founding fathers like Houphouët-Boigny (who died of natural causes in 1993), Hastings Banda, or Kenneth Kaunda, but also former military putschists of the 1960s and 1970s such as Moussa Traoré in Mali, Mathieu Kérékou in Benin, and Didier Ratsiraka in Madagascar – resulting in a sharp drop in the average duration of leaders. The sitting presidents of 1994 had spent about 30 percent less time in power than their predecessors of only a few years earlier, in 1990. While a slight recovery followed, average tenure appeared to stabilize at around 10 years for the 1990–2016 period. In 2017, José Eduardo dos Santos and Robert Mugabe left power, respectively, in Angola and Zimbabwe. Since they were two of the longest-serving sitting leaders in the region, the average stay in office went down to around 9 years. Compared to the increases recorded over the previous three decades, the new trend was markedly more stable. Excluding interim leaders does not significantly modify this scenario.

But post-1990 yearly average values are pushed upward by long-standing heads of state or prime ministers from the past single-party and military era who were still hanging on to power in spite of constitutional reforms. This concerns France-Albert René of Seychelles and Obiang Nguema of Equatorial Guinea, for example, whose spells in power stretched from the late 1970s well into the new millennium. Leaders who had reached office via newly introduced elections, on the other hand, typically stayed on for a decade at most. When we separate power-holders who took office before 1990 from those who secured the top political job in or after 1990, the differences are striking. As Table 4.8 shows, office-holders reaching to power between 1960 and 1989 stayed on for periods ranging from a minimum of a few days to

Table 4.8 *Average tenure of African leaders, 1960–1989 and 1990–2018*

	N	Mean	Median	St. Dev.	Min.	Max.
Leaders who took office in 1960–1989	177	9.52	5.40	10.58	0.002	41.55
Leaders who took office in 1990–2018	183	4.87	3.09	5.36	0.005	27.59

Notes: Calculations as of 30 June 2018.
Source: ALC dataset

Omar Bongo's record-breaking 41 years (with a mean of 9.5 years and a median of 5 years). By contrast, the generations of leaders that reached power at some point in 1990–2018 remained in office between a tiny fraction of a year and 27 years (for Chad's Idriss Déby), with an average of 4.9 years and a median value of 3 years. By all parameters, the drop was quite evident. But in order fully to appreciate the difference between the two periods, one must also consider how well average values represent all individual cases within each of the two samples. For leaders who assumed office between 1960 and 1989, the standard deviation is a substantial 10.6, pointing to a considerable degree of variation largely due to the frequency of military coups in the post-colonial decades. When we turn to 1990–2018, the standard deviation is down to half (5.4) what it was, implying that under the new political arrangements leaders' lengths of stay in office were not only shorter and more stable, but also less unpredictable than in the previous period.

The evolution of time spent in office appears to be closely linked to changes in the dominant ways in which power is obtained, and particularly with ballots replacing bullets, as Figure 4.6 shows. Across the entire period, average stay in office for elected rulers, at just 6 years, is almost 40 percent shorter than the 10 years or so that unelected officeholders typically spend in power (as confirmed by a t-test with significance at $p < 0.01$). While we need to investigate the duration of *democratically* elected leaders, this seems to be in line with Bueno de Mesquita et al.'s general finding that "it is easier for autocrats (leaders with small coalitions) to survive in office than democrats (i.e., leaders with large coalitions)" (Bueno de Mesquita et al. 2002:580; cf. Bueno de Mesquita et al. 1999:152–153). Moreover, if office-holders who reached power through coups or guerrillas are singled out, it appears

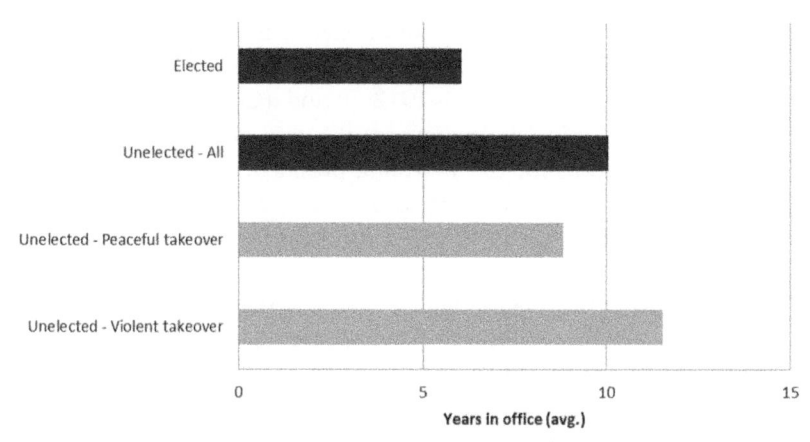

Figure 4.6 Average tenure of leaders by mode of entry into power, 1960–2018 (Data as of June 30, 2018).
Note: interim leaders (<12 months) are excluded.
Source: ALC dataset

they have an even longer average duration – over 11.5 years – when compared to unelected leaders who reached office peacefully and stop at just about 9 years.

Electoral Outcomes, Country Trajectories, and Challenges to Multiparty Rules

African elections are often won by sitting leaders. This is generally considered – and rightly so – to be a sign that the practice of multiparty politics in the region is still in its infancy and is frequently flawed, with many sub-Saharan rulers able to abuse their position, power, and resources to secure a favorable outcome of the vote under conditions of electoral authoritarianism. Incumbents, however, typically enjoy important electoral advantages in other parts of the world as well. As a matter of fact, between 1990 and 2018 African rulers won 142 out of 208 elections in which they took part, or about 68.3 percent, which is less than the share of post-1945 victories for sitting US presidents, who won 8 of the 11 contests that were not open-seat elections, or 72.7 percent. Gerald Ford, Jimmy Carter, and George H.W. Bush were the only ones who failed to obtain a second mandate. The complete 1792–2018 record only partly lowers this percentage, with 22 incumbent victories out of 32 elections, or 68.7 percent (see Mayhew 2008:212). A similarly strong advantage was also evident in Latin America over the 1953–2012 period (Corrales and Penfold 2014). From the mid-1980s onward, the rate of re-election was as high as 89.5 percent for the 19 ruling presidents who ran again for office – 17 of them were successful, the exceptions being Daniel Ortega in Nicaragua in 1992 and Hipólito Mejía in the Dominican Republic in 2004.

The bar chart displayed in Figure 4.7 plots the absolute number of multiparty elections resulting in incumbents' victories, electoral successions, and electoral alternations, respectively. Incumbent victories in Africa are down to 62.3 percent when we look at the entire set of post-1990 elections (228), including those not contested by sitting presidents. The latter cases lead to a leadership handover by definition, either to a political heir from the outgoing power-holder's circle or political force, or to a candidate from the opposition. Indeed, there is an almost 50/50 split: 39 successions – 20 of them at the time of transition elections – as against 49 alternations in office following an opposition victory. The latter turnovers include 15 cases where non-elected autocrats passed on power to elected rulers during regime transitions – the first one to admit defeat in a post-1990 vote was Mathieu Kérékou of Benin – and 34 cases where an elected president or prime minister was replaced by another elected leader. Alternations in office thus resulted from almost one in five of all post-1990 elections. This is not a lot, but neither is it a negligible share: in the past such alternations simply did not happen. Moreover, an upward trend is also apparent, with 5 turnovers in the 1990s, 11 in the 2000s – and if what happened during the first seven and a half years of the decade is anything to go by – a projected 20-plus in the 2010s. By contrast, sitting rulers had comfortably won 79.5 percent of the 44 multiparty elections held across the three decades following independence, with only 6 cases (or 13.6 percent) of succession and 3 (or 6.8 percent) alternations in office. Of the latter three cases, it was only in Mauritius that the Mauritian Militant Movement (MMM)/Mauritian Socialist Party (MSP) opposition coalition was ultimately able to replace a sitting prime minister through the ballot box, in 1982, as in the two other cases (Somalia and Sierra Leone, both in 1967) the outsider who won the vote was subsequently ousted by the military.

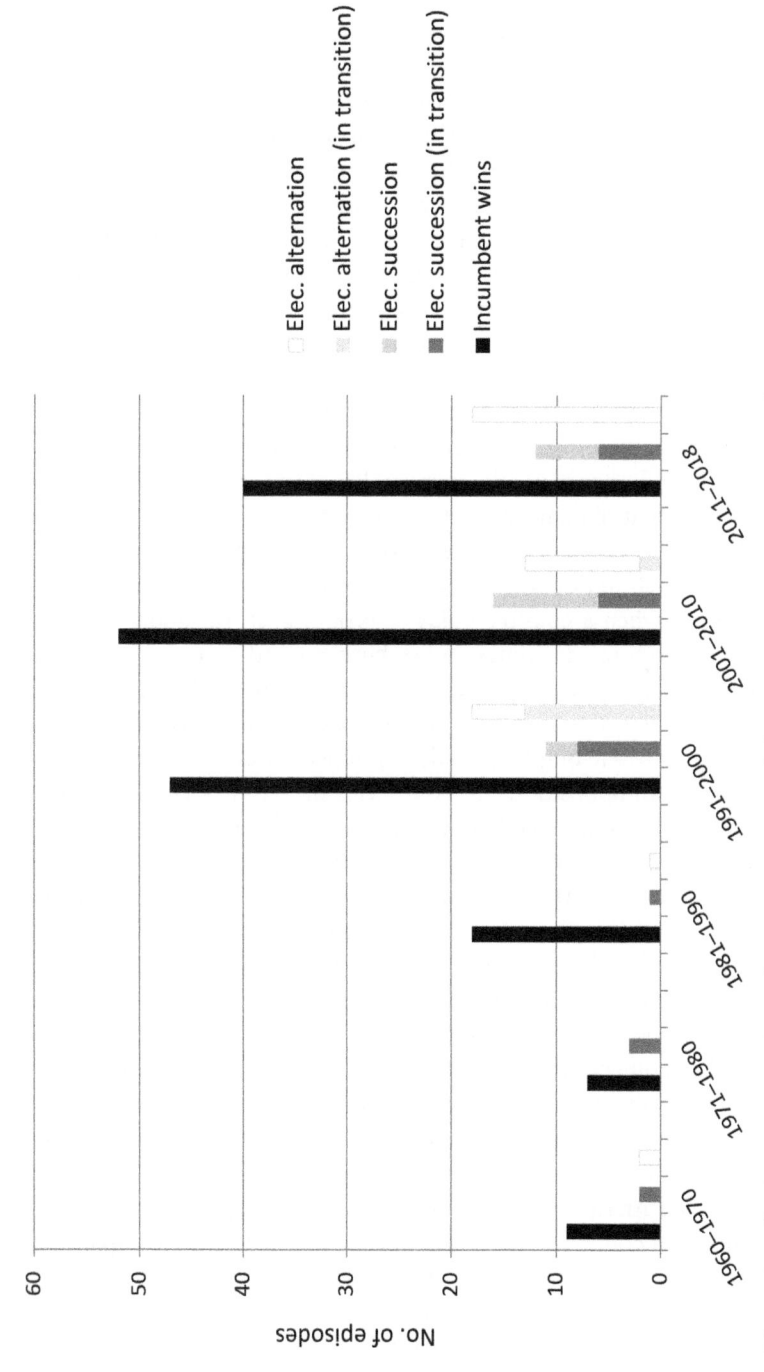

Figure 4.7 Election outcomes: incumbents, successors and alternators, 1960–2018 (Data as of June 30, 2018).

Source: ALC dataset

Closer comparative inspection of the timing and the extent to which individual African states have experienced elections and election-based leadership handovers over the past 25 years yields valuable information on the actual progress made by countries in the region with regard to the implementation and institutionalisation of basic rules for leadership change. Stimulated by Nigeria's historic vote of 2015, Carbone and Cassani (2016) recently examined the trajectories of election-related achievements of African regimes, excluding a few states with a pre-1990 multiparty tradition (Botswana, Mauritius, Senegal, and Zimbabwe). They track the ups and downs of individual countries, showing the many divergent routes they took. The latter are captured by singling out precise election-related events as crucial test-like milestones of possible progress or relapse. The underlying assumption is that elections do not equal democracy, but they can be focal points in the advancement of democratization (see Lindberg 2007). The authors hypothesize a succession of key election-related steps: a transition to a regime in which multiparty votes are introduced; the early regularization of polls when a country holds a second, post-transition election; the use of electoral deadlines to establish an end to terms of office, particularly when a leader leaves due to constitutional limits on presidential mandates; the peaceful transfer of executive power to a successor belonging to the outgoing leader's political force; the turnover that occurs when an opposition candidate wins office; the second turnover when the opposition-turned-government is itself voted out of office.

Based on the abovementioned key election-related events, Carbone and Cassani use the Africa Leadership Change dataset to trace the fits and starts of progress in sub-Saharan countries and to sum them up in a jigsaw puzzle of democratization, displayed in Figure 4.8. They identify six groups of African countries that experienced similar democratic progress, labeled *Front-runners*, *On-track*, *Stagnating*, *Back-sliders*, *Latecomers*, and *Non-starters*. These clusters are not meant to be regime categories. While no assumption is made that the countries involved will ultimately democratize, the clusters represent alternative paths of democratization through elections and help capture the way in which African countries are finding (or losing) their route. For each cluster of countries – i.e., a set of countries that made comparable democratic progress – the jigsaw-puzzle graph shows distinct configurations of election-related achievements. "Non-starters" constitute a first group and include four countries that have never used multiparty

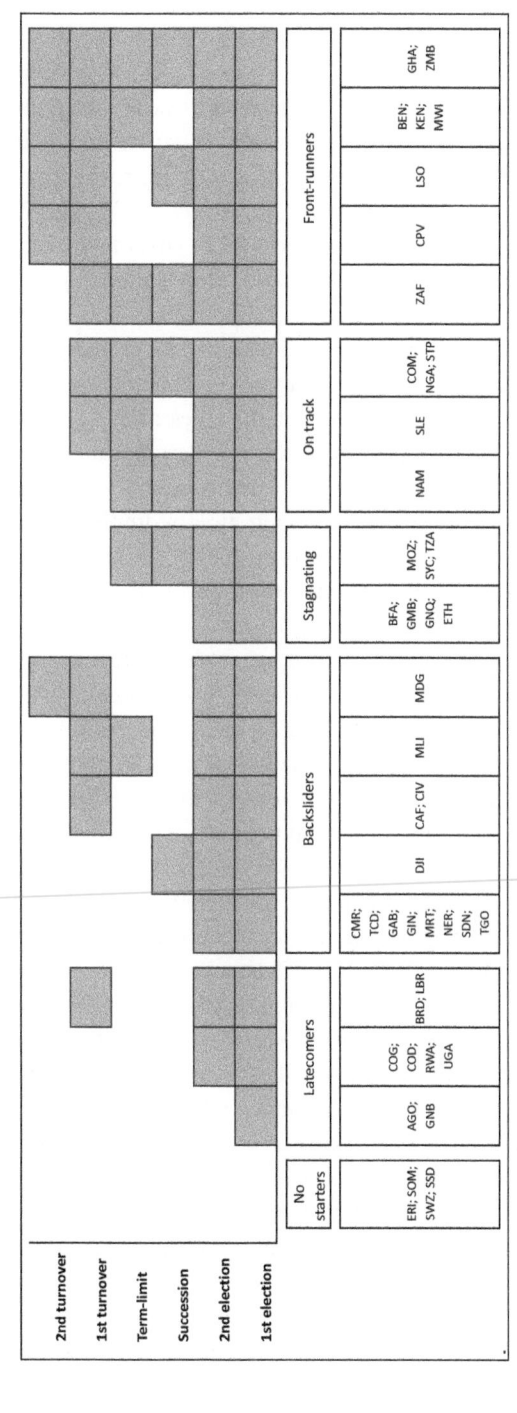

Figure 4.8 The jigsaw puzzle of democratization by elections in sub-Saharan Africa, 1990 to June 2015.
Source: Carbone and Cassani (2016)

elections since 1990. Eritrea, Somalia, South Sudan, and eSwatini show that elections are not for everybody. All of them are still to go through a process of selecting their leader through the polls. "Latecomers" consist of states that did organize one or two consecutive votes, and maybe more, but that was where their progress stopped. For different reasons, the Great Lakes states of Uganda, Rwanda, and Burundi all fall into this cluster. Two more virtuous clusters occupy the opposite extreme of the jigsaw puzzle. One is made up of regimes that appear to be "on track" where democratization is concerned. They include Namibia, Sierra Leone, Sao Tomé, and Principe and the Comoros. Elections are periodic routine in these countries; their chief executives show broad respect for the rules of the game; and at least one episode of alternation in office has already taken place. Close to them is the sizeable number of "front-runners." These are the pace-setters of African democracy, having already implemented term limits and a double-turnover test. This is in spite of the fact that some of them also experienced democratic erosion (South Africa) while others went through some very flawed voting rounds (Kenya). An inevitable "gray zone" occupies the middle of the figure. It embraces a relatively large and heterogeneous group of African "backsliders," where elections proved to be an ephemeral achievement and an outright reversion was initiated (in Cameroon, Chad, Djibouti, Gabon, and Togo this was due to incumbents removing or violating presidential term limits, whereas in Madagascar and Mali progress was halted by coups d'état) and the "stagnating" category of states such as Equatorial Guinea and Ethiopia, where the establishment and retention of political hegemony was made easier by a lack of restrictions on executive mandates (or the delayed introduction of such restrictions).

Updating Carbone and Cassani's (2016) jigsaw puzzle to account for events after 2015 would show further steps in the democratization trajectories of some countries. These would include the first ever electoral turnover in the Gambia, where, in late 2016, Adama Barrow, supported by a coalition of all major opposition parties, surprisingly succeeded in defeating long-standing incumbent Yahya Jammeh, who had seized power in a 1994 coup. The young Liberian multiparty regime, on the other hand, recorded both the fulfilment of term limits and a second electoral alternation when, in the open-seat vote of 2017, George Weah won over former vice-president Joseph Boakai. That same year Angola also made progress, as João Lourenço replaced José Eduardo dos Santos in the country's first electoral succession.

As country trajectories highlight, among the numerous leaders' initiatives that risked derailing democratic progress two warrant special attention: the time-honored tradition of military coups, and a constitutional reform trend aimed at expanding the possibility that sitting presidents may run for additional mandates. We examine these dynamics in detail in the next two chapters. Both are reminiscent of past syndromes: the tendency to capture power by extralegal means, and attempts to hold on to it indefinitely. They remind us that progress hardly ever makes its appearance without the possibility of reversing course.

Many Leaders, Some Clear Trends

Modern Africa has had 360 leaders. In the 311 episodes in which leaders handed over power, they did so in highly diverse political circumstances and in very different ways. Some of them after holding office for one day, others for some 10,000–15,000 days. Many were overthrown violently, other choose for themselves when to let go. The unpredictability of coups d'état – whereby one in every two of all African leaders was suddenly ousted during the early postindependence decades – contrasts sharply with the regular timing and organized procedures (if hardly ever flawless) of multiparty voting that led to the demise of many others. But there are clearly discernible trends in Africa's leadership change practices, with the 1990s representing a defining moment. The lack of appropriate mechanisms that had characterized three decades of African politics was supplanted with the continent-wide adoption of pluralist electoral arrangements. The new leaders that took power after 1990 typically did so via the ballot box, held it for shorter periods than their predecessors, were much more certain about their likely duration in office, and occasionally had to hand power over peacefully to a successor belonging to the opposition. While variations were very significant across the continent – including the survival of many former single-party dictators who recycled themselves as multiparty authoritarian rulers – we expect both the evolution of leadership change practices, as well as country-by-country differences, to affect the political, economic and social performance of individual leaders. This is what we shall investigate in Chapters 7 and 8.

5 | When the Military Strikes

The Rise and Fall of Modern Military Coups

Coups d'état are not a modern invention. Yet they became a much more common occurrence in the politics of Western countries and developing areas during the twentieth century. A number of coups – and occasionally also some failed coups – deeply marked the epoch. In Europe, Adolf Hitler's botched Beer Hall putsch, in 1923 in Munich, and General Francisco Franco's 1936 intervention in Spain notoriously shaped subsequent political developments. With the return and consolidation of democracy after World War II, the European continent gradually appeared to build some kind of immunity, the most notable exception being the 1967 takeover of Greece by army colonels. Latin America, on the other hand, kept recording an abundant share of soldiers' interventions. Colonel Juan Perón's seizure of power in Buenos Aires, in 1943, and, 30 years later, Augusto Pinochet's violent and infamous capture of the Palacio de La Moneda in Chile were arguably among the most consequential and certainly drew enormous international attention. In North Africa and the Middle East, military officers – among them Gamāl Nasser and Muammar Gaddafi – ended monarchic rule in Egypt, Iraq, and Libya between the 1950s and the 1960s. Several Asian nations also surrendered to the military. Thailand, in particular, experienced its first coup back in 1932 and went on to become one of the most coup-prone countries in the world, with more than ten direct interventions. Burma's 1962 power seizure ushered in a long period of army rule that only in recent years appears to be gradually overcome. In Pakistan, General Pervez Musharraf's seizure of power, in 1999, marked the last major coup of the twentieth century.

Overall, some 224 *golpes* occurred worldwide in the 70 years between 1946 and 2016, the vast majority in Asia, Africa, and Latin America (Marshall and Marshall 2017a,b). Every single year in the second half of the century recorded a successful coup – 1963 alone had the astonishing record of 12 – with the only two exceptions in 1959 and 1998. By 2017, the last globally recorded victorious coups were Abdel Fattah el-Sisi's removal of president Mohamed Morsi in Egypt in 2013, Prayut Chan-o-cha's takeover in Thailand, and Yacouba Isaac Zida's in Burkina Faso in the midst of the 2014 popular uprising. The reported number of unsuccessful coups has typically been even greater. The latter include, in recent times, a famous 2002 attempt at ousting Hugo Chávez in Venezuela and a 2016 bid at overthrowing Recep Tayyip Erdoğan, followed by notoriously brutal and widespread purges across the Turkish state and society.

Despite their pervasive presence in most developing areas of the world, a decline in the global incidence of military coups began to be apparent after the 1980s and became ever clearer in the new millennium, as Figure 5.1 shows. Economic development and the spread of the democratic ethos are arguably the two key processes that, in spite of some ups and downs, contributed most to making the military route to power a marginal strategy. For the first time since at least 1946, two consecutive years went by with no coup being recorded (in 2000–2001) followed, some 15 years later, by a longer time span of four years in a row (2015–2018).[1] In-between, occasional single years also went without an army takeover (2004, 2009, 2011).

The political autonomy and influence of the military remain features in the politics of many developing nations. In a number of them, direct interventions are at least an option that cannot be ruled out yet. From a sheer numerical perspective, however, coups have unquestionably become a much rarer phenomenon than they have ever been in recent history.

Coups in Africa

The global waning of the coup d'état in the new millennium did not prevent elected civilian governments from being ousted by the army in

---

[1] The late 2017 ousting of Robert Mugabe in Zimbabwe is an extremely thorny case. The military doubtless played a key role. Yet soldiers did not "capture" power, rather, they de facto intervened on behalf of a strong faction within the ruling party to impose an immediate civilian power transfer. Regime and ruling party continuity – in the context of a dramatic leadership change – were signaled by former vice-president Emmerson Mnangagwa taking office as president less than seven days after the military initiative.

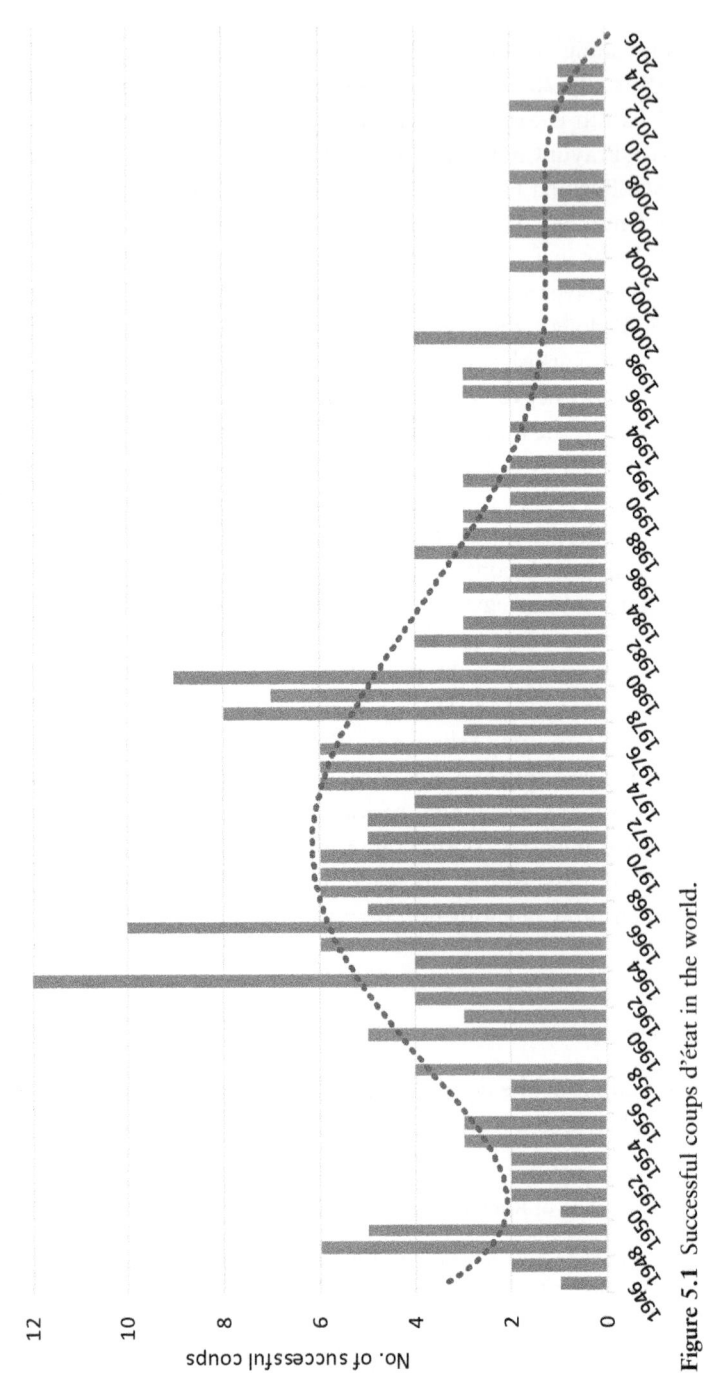

Figure 5.1 Successful coups d'état in the world.
Source: authors' elaboration based on data from Marshall and Marshall (2017)

countries as far away as Honduras in Latin America, Egypt in North Africa, or Fiji and Thailand in Asia. It was sub-Saharan Africa, however, that retained the sad record: between one half and two-thirds of all coups occurring worldwide since 2000 happened in this region.

Army interventions have historically accounted for a major share of modern power transfers south of the Sahara (see Chapter 4). Since 1960, soldiers overthrew sitting heads of states and governments on 85 distinct occasions in the region. In the immediate postindependence era, an optimistic view had prevailed that discounted the possibility of open military interventions in African polities (Wells 1974:872). But the 1963 ousting of presidents Sylvanus Olympio in Togo and Hubert Maga in Benin gave an early indication that soldiers were growing politically impatient. Africa's newly independent states typically only had small armies – some 250 soldiers in the case of Togo, 600 in the Central African Republic (Zolberg 1968:79) – but they quickly became prominent political actors and shaped the national trajectories of countries across the continent, from the small Comoros islands to giant Nigeria, from Congo-Brazzaville on the Atlantic coast to Ethiopia in the Horn of Africa, from Muslim-majority Sudan to US-established Liberia. Rather than being an unlikely setting for military rebellions, Africa promptly came to be seen as a land of endemic coups.

Africa's weak governments tended to fall all too soon when challenged, and military seizures of power thus reached such a high frequency that they became "an institutionalized pattern of African politics ... the modal form of governmental and regime change" (Zolberg 1968:77; cf. Young 1988:57). No less than 29 out of 49 sub-Saharan countries – that is, slightly less than two out of three – suffered at least one military takeover.[2] In many cases – not only Togo and Benin, but also Somalia or Congo-Kinshasa – military officers stepped in relatively soon after independence in the 1960s. Elsewhere, they did so in later decades. The latest African country to experience its "first

---

[2] Twenty-nine countries south of the Sahara suffered at least one coup between 1960 and 2018: Benin (5); Burkina Faso (6); Burundi (4); Central African Republic (3); Chad (2); Comoros (6); Congo, Democratic Republic (1); Congo Republic (2); Côte d'Ivoire (1); Equatorial Guinea (1); Ethiopia (1); The Gambia (1); Ghana (5); Guinea (2); Guinea-Bissau (4); Lesotho (3); Liberia (1); Madagascar (2); Mali (3); Mauritania (6); Niger (4); Nigeria (6); Rwanda (1); Seychelles (1); Sierra Leone (5); Somalia (1); Sudan (3); Togo (2); Uganda (3).

coup" was Côte d'Ivoire in 1999, when General Robert Guéï took the presidency following a military action he initially had no part in.

Coup-makers at times went on to rule for decades, prominent among them Teodoro Obiang Nguema (in office since 1979), Gnassingbé Eyadéma (1967–2005), Mobutu Sese Seko (1965–1997), and Blaise Compaoré (1987–2014). All too often, however, African military takeovers were not just one-off episodes, as an initial successful bid set the scene for a subsequent chain of countercoups that unfolded over the years. In more than one third of coups (i.e., 31 out of 85), the barrel of the gun was aimed at former *golpistas*. The paradigmatic cases were in West Africa. Small Benin pioneered this military-against-military syndrome with an early and impressive string of five coups in 1963, 1965, 1967, 1969, and 1972. Nearby giant Nigeria followed suit in 1966, with Yakubu Gowon's overthrow of Johnson Aguiyi-Ironsi little more than six months after the latter seized power. But no country exemplifies the coup-chain phenomenon better than Burkina Faso, as briefly described in Chapter 4.

Regardless of the actual motivation, justification and impact of soldiers' interventions in Africa, military overthrows did appear somehow to perform a systemic function for many years after independence. In a region where some three dozen rulers held office for two decades or more, military coups worked as a rare mechanism for voicing dissent and bringing about a degree of leadership rotation in office. A way of achieving political change or adjustment that, however, often bred uncertainty and instability. The frequency of African army takeovers hit the highest point in the 1980s, when 17 coups accounted for over 51.5 percent of all leadership turnovers: over one in two of all sub-Saharan leaders who grabbed the top job during this time did so through the barrel of the gun. The military was "clearly on the march across Black Africa" (Jenkins and Kposowa 1990:873), as the authors of a comparative study aptly summed up at the end of the decade.

But then the decline of the African military coup began. A period of widespread – if not always deep – reforms got under way during the 1990s. In a few years, constitutional transformations and multiparty votes were introduced in the vast majority of countries in the region, and African nations gradually appeared to find more regularized ways of rotating power to new leaders. As we have seen in previous chapters, this season of reforms led to more frequent leadership successions among elected leaders belonging to the same party (as in Mozambique or Tanzania, for example) or alternations in office among opposing political forces (as happened twice in Zambia, Ghana, and Kenya, for example). As a related development, the latter decade of the twentieth century not only recorded a lower number of coups when compared to the previous ten years (i.e., 14 as against 17), but these episodes now represented a drastically reduced share of all leadership changes, that is, slightly more than a fifth (21 percent) in the 1990s as opposed to over a half (51 percent) in the 1980s. Claiming a "lack of any effect from democratization" (Collier and Hoeffler 2005:19), and suggesting that coups had remained as common as ever, denotes missing the important transformations underway.

The new millennium saw a further, dramatic decrease in the number of coups (see Figure 4.3, in Chapter 4). While after 2000, soldiers still captured power on ten distinct occasions in eight states (Guinea-Bissau and Mauritania suffered two coups each), this averaged less than one intervention every year and a half, significantly less than in previous decades. All but one of the eight countries concerned were in West or Central Africa, and all had experienced earlier spells of military rule. For the likes of Niger, Burkina Faso, Guinea-Bissau, and Mauritania – nations with a long tradition of armed takeovers – the new episodes thus looked like business as usual in which soldiers simply came back to office. When General François Bozizé captured the top job in 2003, for example, it was the third time the Central African Republic fell under the control of the military. In Mali, a coup put an end to two decades of multiparty rule. Amadou Toumani Touré – who had been himself a coup-maker back in 1991, but had been subsequently returned to power through a free vote in 2002 – was ousted in early 2012 by elements of the army on the grounds of his inadequate response to a Tuareg rebellion in the north. These recent cases caution that the coup d'état remains a very real possibility in many African countries. Yet the declining trend is clearer than ever, and if it were to continue, future African generations may only come to learn what a military coup is by reading about it in history books.

What Is a Coup, and What Is Not

One knows a coup when one sees one, at least in the vast majority of cases. Yet definitions vary, with some well-known conceptualizations helpful in understanding the essence of the phenomenon, but not necessarily in identifying empirical instances. Edward Luttwak's famous description of coups as "the infiltration of a small but critical segment of the state apparatus, which is then used to displace the government from its control of the remainder" (Luttwak 1968:27) is a case in point. It conveys a good sense of what a coup is about, but it does not get very close to what we are likely to observe in practice. Identifying coups may not always be as straightforward as one might expect, nor as consistent across definitions and datasets. The recent cases of Egypt 2011, Burkina Faso 2014, and Ukraine 2014 – each of which involved a degree of popular participation that led to evoking "a revolution" – are deemed by some as full-fledged coups (Powell and Thyne 2011), while others categorize them as "coerced resignations" which, by definition, "do not result in a substantive change in regime leadership" (Marshall and Marshall 2017b:3).

Coups d'état are the sudden result of "relatively *covert* actions" – the plot or conspiracy, the hidden networking and preparation of an illegitimate challenge aimed at seizing power – "that ignore or bypass the regular channels or 'rules of the game' concerning the succession process" (Jackman 1978:1264). The moment coups actually unfold, they turn into "illegal and *overt* attempts by the military or other elites within the state apparatus to unseat the sitting president" (Powell and Thyne 2011:252) – or, more comprehensively, to oust the chief executive authority of a state, regardless of its formal title. To be more precise, a coup is not just "an attempt" but a successful one – otherwise analysts rightly talk of "attempted," "unsuccessful," or "failed" coup. Attempts and plots are crucially important elements, "because successful coups begin as attempted coups and attempted coups begin as plots" (Jenkins and Kposowa 1990:866). But a coup d'état definition has to include its outcome: it is a (head of) government's overthrow, it consists of "an irregular transfer of a state's chief executive" (Jenkins and Kposowa 1990:861). No transfer, no coup. This is why a seven-day minimum duration of the newly installed leadership is taken as a rather standard threshold, so to exclude short-lived and thus de facto unsuccessful coups, such as when Leon M'ba was ejected but rapidly reinstated (with a decisive hand by French paratroopers) in Gabon in 1964, or when Hugo Chávez was ousted from office in Venezuela for about two days in 2002.[3]

---

[3] Failed military interventions are an ambiguous phenomenon. They can be interpreted as evidence of a coup-prone country or, on the contrary, as an indication of a coup-proof country (Lindberg and Clark 2008:93).

By contrast, for example, a civil war is not defined by the replacement of the leadership: it has to involve systematic and widespread use of violence, resulting in a substantial number of fatalities, but it may last decades and eventually come to an end without the rebels reaching power (at times, they may not actually want to achieve office). As a matter of fact, an important difference between wars and coups concerns the key "barriers to feasibility." For rebels, these are primarily material: "a rebellion needs to acquire armaments and to finance thousands of soldiers. A coup faces no such difficulties and so overall, the barriers to a coup are likely to be lower than those to a rebellion" (Collier and Hoeffler 2005:3). While the two phenomena share some common ground, it is important to avoid conflating coups by excluding not just civil wars, but also popular protests – which also imply a more extensive involvement of the population – mutinies, assassination attempts, and so-called self-coups or *autogolpes* (as were deemed, for example, the unconstitutional shutdowns of parliament by Alberto Fujimori in Peru, in 1992, and by Boris Yeltsin in Russia in 1993).

With few exceptions, the perpetrators of a coup d'état are the armed forces or the internal security forces. Occasionally, the key actor may be another "elite who is part of the state apparatus" (Powell and Thyne 2011:250), implying that coups may originate from non-military players, as in the Malagasy power capture of 2009, where the political opposition led the way and gained crucial military backing for a civilian but unconstitutional handover. While illegality and the threat of the use of force are a prerequisite, actual violence is not. What was arguably the most consequential military intervention of the late twentieth century – namely, Pervez Musharraf's in Pakistan, in 1999 – occurred without any killing. In Africa, bloodless coups were at the origin of a number of lasting takeovers, such as with Pierre Buyoya (Burundi, 1987), Omar al-Bashir (Sudan, 1989), Sani Abacha (Nigeria, 1993), or Yahya Jammeh (Gambia, 1994). In these and many other cases, the lack of bloodshed at the outset did not prevent the new dictators from ushering in periods of internal violence and repression of various natures. In other instances, on the other hand, widespread killings occurred during the very seizure of power, particularly with the likes of Teodoro Obiang in 1979 (some 250 recorded deaths among the people of Equatorial Guinea) and Idi Amin in 1971 (75 Ugandans lost their lives).[4] In as many as nine cases, the chief executive was not only deposed but killed by those who ousted him, from the early case of François Tombalbaye, Chad's first president, who fell victim to a 1975 coup orchestrated by his former chief of staff, General Félix Malloum, to William Tolbert in Liberia, in 1980, Thomas Sankara in Burkina Faso, in 1987 – certainly the best-known case – and the most recent instance with Ibrahim Baré Maïnassara in Niger back in 1999.

The comparative literature has emphasized distinct types of coups, as in the well-known classification into "guardian" coups (primarily aimed at restoring political order and the *status quo* in the face of emerging challenges), "veto" coups (concerned with preventing political openings to the masses) and "breakthrough" coups (where radical change is on the agenda of the junior officers seizing power) (Huntington 1968). African politics scholars similarly underscored differences in the rationale behind soldiers' decisions (Zolberg 1968:79; Jenkins and Kposowa 1990:873). Relatively limited goals such as pay, pensions, or military budget increases were a common reason behind soldiers' revolts, strikes, and mutinies during an early postcolonial phase, alongside the urge to mediate in the face of escalating political standoffs between government and opposition or urban protests. Both cases allowed for a relatively easy return to the barracks, where the army belongs. But this became more complicated as takeovers were increasingly driven by the personal ambitions of military leaders, such as Mobutu Sese Seko or Idi Amin, or by the radical, populist reform agendas embodied by the likes of Jerry Rawlings or Thomas Sankara.

Why Coups

Why members of a national army or other security agencies should try and seize direct control of the political authority they are supposed to serve is not as obvious as it might at first appear. That they would do it "to gain power" is tautological. Searching for the motives and triggers behind military interventions has been the key concern for the overwhelming majority of studies of African coups. In the effort to find an explanation, or a set of explanations, for such comparatively high-

---

[4] See Marshall dataset on coups d'état available at www.systemicpeace.org/inscrdata.html (accessed August 7, 2019).

frequency and continent-wide phenomenon, coups have thus been primarily looked at as a dependent variable. The numerous accounts about why military officers decide to step into the political arena can be grouped into those that emphasize some kind of structural preconditions leading to the coup – including historical, military, political, economic, social, or ethnic drivers, or "a complex mix" of all of them (Johnson, Slater, and McGowan 1984:623; cf. Wells 1974; Jackman 1978; Jenkins and Kposowa 1990) – and those for which the reasons for taking the initiative are to be found among the personal idiosyncrasies of the actors involved (Zolberg 1968; Decalo 1973).

According to structural explanations, the emergence of developmental tensions or failures caused by one or more alternative factors – such as low growth or economic stagnation, government corruption, interethnic strife, or broader mobilizational pressures – create a situation that makes a direct military intervention appear as a solution. Economic downturns, in particular, are frequently said to be a key culprit for calling soldiers into action (Londregan and Poole 1990; Alesina et al. 1996; Arriola 2009; Kim 2016). Most readings of this kind are thus mainly based on the identification of the social and economic determinants of military coups in Africa.

A first set of analyses is rooted in the classic literature on modernization, social mobilization and political development (Deutsch 1961; Huntington 1968; Deutsch 1969). The main argument is that, in the wake of economic modernization and related processes of social mobilization and political participation, failures to forge functioning political institutions and effective government capacity fast enough to channel and respond to rising popular demands are most likely to result in the army's decision to intervene. Furthermore, once in office, soldiers will tend to promote "de-participation" strategies that close down avenues for public engagement (Kasfir 1976), particularly where preexisting social cleavages were exacerbated by postindependence mass participation and multiparty competition (Weiner and La Palombara 1966; Huntington 1968).

Given this kind of preconditions, the main barrier that would-be coup-makers face is the loyalty of the army, whether stemming from the belief that capturing the political arena is illegitimate or from the benefits derived from the existing access to power. But the very occurrence of a first coup tended to destroy the basis of this loyalty – the notion that a military challenge is unlawful – and thus to legitimize further coups. This is why, following an initial coup, countries often suffered a strong "coup trap" effect that raised the probability of new military interventions, especially in the presence of unsatisfactory economic performances, a trap effect that can only gradually wane with the passing of time (Collier and Hoeffler 2005:3,17; cf. Londregan and Poole 1990).

A second group of explanations is at times referred to as "military centrality theories" (Janowitz 1964; Nordlinger 1977; Finer 1988) due to an emphasis placed on the role of the army as the most powerful (in terms of resources) and cohesive institution (for its common training and shared corporate interests) in developing countries. Early on after independence, in particular, a prevailing positive perception depicted African militaries as "the most national, unified, disciplined, modern and efficient structure in society" (Decalo 1973:115). Janowitz (1977), for example, stressed the organizational capacity of the army. The legacy of colonial times, when soldiers were often engaged in domestic control (Jenkins and Kposowa 1990), arguably made military political involvement easier to conceive. But the very process of postcolonial "Africanization" of military corps and hierarchies contributed to the politicization of the army, turning it "into a symbol of the new national identity and creating a cohesive military leadership" (Jenkins and Kposowa 1990:867). The rise of postindependence aspirations and expectations – and the perceived risk that weak civilian governments would derail their fulfilment – ultimately favored soldiers' takeovers, as did civilian "interferences" with the military when perceived to threaten the latter's size, budget, or privileges (cf. Collier and Hoeffler 2005:15). Yet the progressive image of armies across much of Africa was quickly and dramatically eroded as internal malaise, cleavages, and dysfunctionality became exposed, together with an overall failure to deliver the much-anticipated socioeconomic or political transformations.

The politics of cultural pluralism and ethnic antagonism were a third alleged motive fostering military coups. The actual mechanisms at work were linked to the impact of modernization processes and social dislocations on ethnic revivals and groups' mobilization for power; the competition among different ethnic communities for jobs, licenses, housing, urban services, or symbolic recognition; or the fear of ethnic dominance and minority exclusion, spurring the reactions of subordinate groups (Jackman 1978). The very first coup to occur south of the

Sahara, in 1963, had "set a dangerous precedent for the rest of the continent ... as in Togo, interethnic coup attempts would emerge as the dominant type of coups in postcolonial Africa" (Roessler 2011:307, footnote 25). The small West African country illustrates how military élites may help specific ethnic groups gain advantages, and vice versa. Both Gnassingbé Eyadéma and his son and successor Faure Gnassingbé belong to a minority community from the north of the country. Despite representing little more than one fifth of the entire population, the Kabyé (or Kabre) have dominated Togolese military, politics, and institutions for over 50 years, particularly over the Ewe and Mina communities in the south (the Ewe alone comprise almost one-third of the population and gave the country its first president, Sylvanus Olympio). Between 1960 and 2005, almost two-thirds of successful and failed coup perpetrators in Africa belonged to an ethnic group other than the ruler's group. Once emerged, the "shadow of the coup d'état" prompted leaders across the continent to abandon the interethnic accommodation strategies of the early postindependence years, as ethnic exclusion appeared to be a better strategy for political survival (Roessler 2011:324).

The structural determinants of African coups have also been examined from more specific temporal and spatial perspectives. It has been argued, for example, that new sovereign countries were most vulnerable early after their independence, to the point where civilian rule appeared to be "only an interlude" – typically lasting some five years – "separating independence and military intervention" (Wells 1974:876; cf. McGowan 2003:346, 355). Geographical contagion, particularly among neighboring countries, appears to be a factor too. It mainly operates via elite linkages and the awareness of military officers, since the establishment of military rule in one country augments both the opportunities and the legitimacy of military interventions on the other side of the border, as seems to have been the case in many parts of West and Central Africa (Zolberg 1968:79; Wells 1974:875).

Finally, a number of structural analyses stressed the role of external economic dependency and political, diplomatic, or military interferences from industrialized nations. A somewhat indirect argument was made that the economic dependency of poor countries (O'Donnell 1979) contributed to producing slow and uneven development – featuring high inequality, stagnation, and unemployment – as well as the political exclusion of lower classes under authoritarian rule and military establishments (Jenkins and Kposowa 1990:867). More directly, the international legitimation of coups as a viable strategy toward stability turned out to be a potentially important supporting factor. In the late 1960s, for example, it was pointed out that "many American government officials, military leaders and academicians believe that the military in the developing areas is the best counterforce against both internal and external disruption" (Bienen 1968, quoted in Wells 1974:881). Accordingly, up until the late 1980s and the end of the Cold War, the approach that the United States adopted was broadly tolerant of army interventions. But foreign powers, from both the West and the Eastern bloc, also went well beyond tacit approvals. According to the US Central Intelligence Agency, 24 coups worldwide featured some kind of active external involvement (only succeeding in just above half of the cases), as also did the foiling of 17 conspiracies, in the 30 years between 1955 and 1985. Besides mercenaries' operations in the Comoros (1975 and 1978), the two clear-cut cases in Africa have to do with French meddling in the politics of the Central African Republic, first by supporting David Dacko's 1979 restoration (and the concomitant ousting of Jean-Bédel Bokassa) and then, only two years later, his undoing by General André Kolingba (Central Intelligence Agency 1986; cf. Médard 2005:45,50).

All the previously discussed structural or "systemic" explanations were roundly criticized by a minority of influential scholars who brushed aside the emphasis on broad quantitative or qualitative variables. The origin and incidence of "disorder," they argued, was "related to specific and circumstantial features of that country's current political and economic situation, rather than to any fundamental and lasting characteristics which differentiate that country from others on the continent ... the incidence of coups appears random" (Zolberg 1968:78). Military takeovers, in other words, can happen anywhere and at any time, depending "simply" on political dynamics and agency. Accordingly, the key to explaining coups d'état was to be found in the competition among civilian and military cliques, and particularly in "the personal and idiosyncratic element in military hierarchies, which have much greater freedom and scope of action within the context of fragmented and unstructured political systems" (Decalo 1973:113, 114). This was backed by the view that "many African armies bear little resemblance to a modern complex organizational model and are instead a coterie of armed camps owing primary clientelist allegiance to a handful of mutually competitive officers of different ranks seething with a variety of corporate, ethnic and personal grievances" (Decalo 1976:14–15). Below the surface of officially stated or apparent motivations, a closer scrutiny of individual cases was essential as it revealed how personal frictions, fears, and ambitions shaped the choices and behaviors of the likes of Soglo, Bokassa, Amin, or Ngouabi. Moreover, once a first coup took place, more and more military factionalism was likely to follow, whether along ethnic, religious, regional cleavages, or merely based on personal loyalties, rank-based networks, or the competition between the regular army and privileged units such as presidential guards or gendarmeries (McGowan 2006:238). Increased factional jockeying, in turn, was to augment the likelihood of further military involvement in politics. By the end of the century, almost half of all coups and failed coups (i.e., 89 of 188, or 47.3 percent) had targeted military rulers, signaling a high level of factional rivalries within the armed forces (McGowan 2003:347).

Military Investigations

As soon as military interventions became a frequent feature in the politics of postcolonial Africa, scholars began conducting quantitative investigations. Wells' (1974:877) early work examined 31 sub-Saharan countries of the 1960s and introduced a practice of gauging not just the frequency and the causes of successful coups, but also the unsuccessful coups and plotted coups by constructing an additive index. A similar approach was subsequently followed by Jackman (1978:1264), Johnson, Slater, and McGowan (1984), Jenkins and Kposowa (1990), and McGowan (2003), who gradually expanded the period and the number of countries covered. By the end of the century, McGowan (2003) counted some 80 coups – plus 108 failed coups and 139 plots – across 30 sub-Saharan states over almost half a century (1956–2001). The late 1960s and the late 1970s marked the highest five-year periods in terms of regimes overthrown by coups, whereas West Africa emerged as the hardest-hit region and southern Africa as the most coup-immune, with not a single episode in Angola, Malawi, Mozambique, Namibia, Botswana, South Africa, Swaziland/eSwatini, Tanzania, Zambia, or Zimbabwe (McGowan 2003:351). A more recent and comprehensive dataset helpfully compares the 94 states that, across the globe, have been affected by 227 successful and 230 failed coups over the 1950–2010 period, with Africa leading among world regions with a 36.5 percent share of all attempts, followed by Latin America with 31.9 percent and Asia with 15.8 percent, the Middle East with 13.1 percent and Europe with 2.6 percent (Powell and Thyne 2011:255).

Comparative empirical analyses, however, show limited agreement on the root causes of the phenomenon. There is broad if not unanimous evidence that Africa's economic stagnation and poverty, alongside a prior coup history, made it easier for the military to try and oust incumbent rulers (Johnson, Slater, and McGowan 1984; Londregan and Poole 1990; Alesina et al. 1996; Arriola 2009:1342; Kim 2016; Powell et al. 2016). The role of other factors is much less clear. For example, ethnic diversity per se was found not to be a factor leading to coups by Jackman (1978) nor, later, by Collier and Hoeffler (2005), whereas ethnic dominance appeared to play a role for Jackman (1978) but not for Jenkins and Kposowa (1990). On the other hand, ethnic rivalries within the military turned out to be a major driver for Jenkins and Kposowa (1990:872), not so for Collier and Hoeffler (2005:18). For some, multipartism acted as a stabilising force (Johnson, Slater, and McGowan 1984:634), contrary to prior findings (Jackman 1978). Social mobilization was related to coup events (Jackman 1978) as was economic dependency (Johnson, Slater, and McGowan 1984; Jenkins and Kposowa 1990). But these, like relevant characteristics of national armies, were mostly investigated in ways that are not comparable.

More recently, a new wave of inquiries shifted the main focus to a distinct but related issue, namely, why coups in Africa had begun to decline. In a relatively early paper, Decalo (1998) had already addressed the issue of why and when coups did *not* happen in Africa from a broad perspective. He singled out three major obstacles. The first was the presence of an external guarantor, notably Paris in the case of Francophone *pré carré* countries such as Cameroon, Gabon, Côte d'Ivoire, or Senegal. Secondly, a situation in which rulers were able to buy off military officers, as was the case in Zambia or Kenya. Finally, the origin and extent of the legitimacy of civilian rulers could help keep the military at bay. In pre-1990 Africa, this was not only the case with the occasional elected government, as in Botswana, but also of various undemocratic leaders who could claim solid legitimacy, as with the absolutist kingdom of eSwatini, Hastings Banda's tradition-derived social standing in Malawi, or the respect commanded by the *ujamaa* ideology claims in Tanzania (Clark 2007:142,144).

As one-party systems lost legitimacy in much of the post-Cold War world, political openings delegitimized military interventions and made African states less vulnerable to them. McGowan drew attention to this by pointing out that, in the continent's reformed political environment, "the duration and quality of multiparty electoral democracy [and thus the legitimacy of the regime] is one of the factors that reduces the likelihood of military-led political instability" (McGowan 2003:358). He did spot a reduction in the success rate of coup bids in the latest phases of the 1956–2001 period he investigated. But the virtual stability of overall attempts led him to stress continuity in "coup behaviour" rather than change, underscoring that "the military coup is today almost exclusively an African phenomenon" (McGowan 2003:341). Lindberg and Clark (2008), on the other hand, articulated a more direct and forceful case for the impact of political reforms. They argued that, in post-1990 reformed African states, political liberalisation ("liberalizing regimes") and particularly democratization ("electoral democracies," including liberal democracies) reduced the chances of military coups, both successful as well as failed. The key causal mechanism was the increased political legitimacy that reformed regimes were able to gain. Accordingly, time was a crucial factor since "legitimacy does not necessarily materialize immediately" (Lindberg and Clark 2008:89): coups thus appeared to become less likely as a country gradually piled up successive rounds of elections, whether in democratic, liberalizing, or electoral authoritarian regimes. More than four out of five of all post-transition military interventions took place only shortly after a first and "founding" election was held (Lindberg and Clark 2008:96). An interlude of uncertainty reminiscent of the fragility that some had observed in the immediate post-independence era.

The African Union and Unconstitutional Changes of Government

The late twentieth-century triumph of a global democratic *zeitgeist* brought with it a principled commitment to defend new democracies from domestic military threats. The normative imperative to fight coups became clear and widespread as never before. Coups had no place in a free and democratic world, and had to be rooted out altogether.

In practice, however, the anti-coup norm has enjoyed mixed fortunes at the global level. The 2015 coup in Burkina Faso did spark a robust international response (including an open condemnation by the United Nations Security Council [UNSC] and Ouagadougou's temporary suspension from the African Union). The Burkinabe *golpistas* rapidly had to cave in. But this was not the case with the Egyptian officers who ousted Morsi in 2013. While the AU suspended Egypt, the decision was not backed by UNSC condemnation, and General Abdel Fattah el-Sisi was allowed to go on and legalize his power capture *ex post* by obtaining an electoral mandate. Similarly, the 2014 coup in Thailand was not even criticized by the Association of Southeast Asian Nations (ASEAN), let alone by the UNSC (Tansey 2017).

The normative shift that followed the end of the Cold War in 1989 could not be self-enforcing. It required response mechanisms to be in place. The distant and veto-prone UN Security Council soon proved to be only partly apt at filling this role. It often failed to condemn unconstitutional seizures of power – the notable exceptions being three small African states (Burundi in 1996, Serra Leone in 1997, and Guinea-Bissau in 2012). This was partly the result of alternative, nondemocratic normative frameworks being promoted by the likes of China, Saudi Arabia, and Russia. But the United States was also selective in denouncing coup-makers; it did not do so, for example, in the case of Egypt in 2013 and in other cases where strategic interests were prioritized over normative commitments (Tansey 2017:152).

Regional organizations, on the other hand, could be in a strong position to enforce the new norms due to their vested interest in monitoring and addressing coups. They did not rise to the task in Asia nor in the Middle East, again because of powerful players espousing different world visions. But Latin America set a different standard. As early as 1991, Resolution 1080 adopted by the Organization of American States (OAS) "required each member to be a representative democracy and to be proactive in preserving democracy among its members" (Powell et al. 2016:485). This proved a rallying point for the strong reaction against the ousting of Haitian president Jean-Bertrand Aristide that same year (with economic sanctions, an arms embargo, and US pressures). The case of Haiti established a clear example. Since then, across the entire region it was only Honduras in 2009 that suffered a clear-cut coup.

Alongside Latin America, Africa too surprisingly found itself at the forefront. The very formation of the new African Union (AU), in 2002, which revamped the outdated Organisation of African Unity (OAU), proved a key step and a reinforcing factor in accelerating the (quasi) demise of the military coup on the continent (Powell et al. 2016; Souaré 2014). In establishing and enforcing a global anti-coup norm, the regional body "led the way ... with its robust and mostly consistent enforcement" (Tansey 2017:148), including the suspension of coup-born governments in Mauritania (2005 and 2008), Guinea (2008), Madagascar (2009), Egypt (2013, if readmitted after just one year), and Burkina Faso (2015).

For almost 40 years, international sanctions for coup conspirators had been low to nonexistent under the OAU due to an explicit non-intervention policy that guaranteed regional inaction and also hindered non-African interventions. As a result, the impunity of early coup leaders such as Eyadéma or Mobutu actually set a precedent that somehow invited new coups. But the African Union acted decidedly as a "norm entrepreneur" against military coups (Souaré 2014). The new body both redefined the regional standards of right and legitimate behavior, as opposed to wrong and proscribed actions, and established effective mechanisms to back this up. Its anti-coup framework began to take shape as a reaction to the army interventions that, in the 1990s, ousted democratically elected leaders or transitional governments. At the Harare Summit of 1997, the OAU had already adopted a tough stance – including open condemnation by the host Robert Mugabe – in the wake of the overthrow of Sierra Leone's Ahmed Kabbah. This was followed two years later by the OAU Algiers Declaration whereby "member states whose governments came to power through unconstitutional means after the Harare Summit, should restore constitutional legality before the next Summit."[5] The emerging approach could count on some prominent supporters in the region, most notably Nigeria's president Olusegun Obasanjo. A former army general who had twice played a crucial role in transitioning his country from military dictatorship to constitutional rule – first as a resigning military ruler in 1979 and then as an elected president in 1999 – Obasanjo

---

[5] Decision 142.1, *Algiers Declaration,* 35th Assembly of heads of State and Government, Organization for African Unity, Algiers, July 12–14, 1999.

brought his firm anti-putsch stance to bear on the rest of the continent (Sklar et al. 2006:100).

Crucially, it was three subsequent policy instruments that fully shaped the new anti-coup framework (Souaré 2014:76ff.). First, in 2000, the Lomé Declaration articulated an OAU response to "unconstitutional changes of government," that is, not just coups, but also armed insurgencies, mercenary takeovers, incumbents' rejecting electoral defeats. It explicitly acknowledged that "the resurgence of coup d'état in Africa ... constitute[s] a very disturbing trend and serious setback to the ongoing process of democratization in the continent."[6] Accordingly, coup-born regimes were banned from the policy and top organs of the Union. The problem remained, however, that the noninterventionist nature of the OAU prevented any meaningful and effective collective action. This itself contributed to justifying the replacement of the OAU with a new union. The Constitutive Act of the African Union (2000) reiterated the suspension of any member states that went through an unconstitutional transfer of power. By 2007, the African Charter on Democracy, Elections and Governance (the "Addis Charter") went a step further by proscribing the auto-legitimation of coup-makers via elections and requiring that, to avoid sanctions, constitutional order had to be restored within six months (Souaré 2014:76ff.; Powell et al. 2016:490).

In practice, the pressure increased for coup-makers to reestablish constitutional rule by handing power to the overthrown leader, a successor or a caretaker. Coup-installed leaders appeared to hasten to do it, the major exception being Madagascar. Their average duration in office went down from 25 months for the 15 coup-born regimes of the 1990s to 11.4 months for the 10 post-2000 cases, with half of them actually lasting less than one month (Souaré 2014:84,87). This is all the more remarkable since it was in the 1990s that Africa's democratic reform movement was at its strongest, before the Lomé Declaration, implying an autonomous effect of the AU anti-coup framework over the political developments of the subsequent decade. In fact, disentangling the impact of the end of the Cold War (post-1990) from that of African Union's anti-coup framework (post-2002) appears to show that, empirically, only the latter had a statistically

---

[6] Decision 5, *Lomé Declaration,* 36th Assembly of heads of State and Government, Organization for African Unity, Lomé, July 10–12, 2000.

meaningful effect, strongly suggesting that "anti-coup norms are reliant on regional institutions adopting formal commitments to effectively reduce coups" (Powell et al. 2016:484). Neither does this impact seem to depend on the extent to which aid and development levels, trade relations, or democratic neighborhood increase the leverage that can be exerted on any specific country (Powell et al. 2016:498). What the AU still relied (and occasionally over-relied) upon, however, were international partners. Both in Mauritania in 2008 and in Guinea in 2009, for example, a European Union (EU) aid suspension gave crucial additional weight to external pressures. The AU, on its part, offered Western countries "a legitimating cover" that helped them eschew the all-too-easy accusations of neo-colonial interference (Souaré 2014:90).

Is There Such Thing as a "Good Coup"?

The post-1990 political scenario did not entirely prevent national armies from occasionally taking over, even where a relatively democratic context would suggest otherwise, as in Gambia 1994. When the military did strike (or tried to), however, it increasingly seemed to happen where the legitimacy of elected leaders was being weakened by early processes of democratic erosion during the last decade of the century in places such as Guinea-Bissau, the Central African Republic, Congo-Brazzaville, and Zambia (Clark 2007:150). Similar instances, in which military takeovers or attempted takeovers appeared to be "likely to reflect popular will ... in states experiencing 'democratic backsliding'" (Powell et al. 2016:500), also occurred more recently in Niger (2010), Burkina Faso (2014), Burundi (2015), and Zimbabwe (2017), where soldiers targeted leaders trying to overstay in office (or, in the case of Zimbabwe, to position the aging president's wife as his chosen successor), often by blatantly violating the constitution.

The actions of soldiers were thus hailed by some as "good coups," based on the fact that, "while the military was instrumental in the demise of [a] regime" deemed undemocratic or at least dangerous, "it did not install a government of its own choosing" (Powell and Thyne 2011:252). Mali had pioneered this dynamic as early as 1991, when, following widespread popular demonstrations, the then chief of the presidential guard Amadou Toumani Touré moved to end Moussa Traoré's 23 years of repressive rule by arresting the head of state. Touré's interim tenure opened the way to the multiparty elections of the subsequent year. Comparable developments later unfolded both east and west of Bamako. In Niger, Major Daouda Wanké ousted the incumbent in 1999 and, in the space of a few months, swiftly passed on power to a newly elected president (albeit the latter's attempt to overstay in office led to the same "procedure" being followed ten years on, in 2009). Mauritania traced a similar path between 2005 and 2009.

Coups are illegal and "by definition profoundly authoritarian events" (Tansey 2017:146), and they have often turned out to be "unguided missiles" (Collier 2008) in terms of where they head. Yet, in an apparent oxymoron, the "democratic coup" hypothesis holds that coups can be "democratic" – and thus good and desirable – when they are ignited by popular opposition to autocratic rulers and their purpose is the introduction of democracy after a limited interim period (Varol 2012; Powell 2014). Collier went as far as to bluntly suggest that, under certain circumstances, the need for a coup must be accepted as the only way out: "there is only one credible counter to dictatorial power: the country's own army ... realistically, [murderous autocrats like Robert Mugabe of Zimbabwe or Senior Gen Than Shwe of Burma] can be toppled only by a military coup" (Collier 2008). And again, "rather than trying to freeze coups out of the international system, we should try to provide them with a guiding system" (Collier 2008).

A number of military interventions do seem to question the assumption that "the plotters ultimately seek power, when they may merely be attempting to change the political system or leadership" (Powell and Thyne 2011:252). But whether coups can play a role in fostering the democratization process has remained quite controversial. Marinov and Goemans (2013) roundly suggest that not only had "democratic" reforms favored a decline of coups at a global level, but, contrary to pre-1990 instances that typically led to durable authoritarian rule or coup traps, a surprisingly high number of post-Cold war coups were followed by democratization advances. The elections coup leaders organize are not always façade elections, rather they are often competitive, free, and fair votes in which the coup perpetrators have a good chance of being ousted from power. But why would leaders who placed power in the hands of the military organize elections? The authors solve this apparent puzzle by stressing the role of external partners. Foreign pressures matter – particularly in the form of the "democratic conditionality" of development aid – albeit they typically

Is There Such Thing as a "Good Coup"? 141

hinge on other geopolitical considerations. Both the EU (from 1991) and the United States (from 1997) are formally committed to suspending aid when an aid recipient country experiences a coup d'état. In the period prior to 2003, for example, the EU suspended aid after the coups in Burundi 1993, Comoros 1995, Gambia 1997, Haiti 1991, Niger 1996, Pakistan 1999, and Sierra Leone 1997. On average, Western aid dropped by 20 percent following a coup in the 1990s, while no similar drops could be detected between 1960–1990 (Marinov and Goemans 2013:818). Given these incentives and the expectation for quick elections, in addition, many would-be coup-plotters around the world probably dropped their destabilising plans in the first place. The authors' upbeat conclusion is that "democratic failures need not last long ... [and] democratic institutions may be more durable and less frail due to countries' changing post-coup trajectories" (Marinov and Goemans 2013:801).

Powell (2014:9) essentially agrees, if cautioning that the actual influence of coups on a country's regime trajectory depends on the starting situation. In general, the evidence he produces shows that coups targeting staunchly authoritarian states are most likely to generate some democratic advances in the post-coup period (three years). During the Cold War, this positive impact was not significant in the case of less authoritarian or "mixed" regimes, whereas coups negatively undermined the democratic trajectories of already democratic states. After the Cold War, and particularly in the African Union years, however, "a larger range of countries are now democratising following successful coups. Democratic coups are no longer reserved for toppling dictators, but could actually promote democratic gains in fledging mixed regimes that are merely leaning towards authoritarianism" (Powell 2014:10). When democracies are overthrown, on the other hand, the probability of a "democratic failure" in the post-coup period is just as likely as that of the *golpe* being followed by democratic improvements.

Credited with coining the expression "democratic coup," Varol (2012:295) warns that it represents the exception, not the norm. The Turkish *golpe* of 1960 and the 1974 *Revolução dos Cravos* in Portugal – the latter ushering in the so-called third wave of democratization – are two of his three case studies. Yet presenting the Egyptian coup that removed Hosni Mubarak from power in 2011 as one "break[ing] the traditional mold of military coup ... [and demonstrating that] some military coups are distinctly more democracy-promoting than others" (Varol 2012:293), seems, only a few years on, a premature and extremely naïve assessment to say the least. In the Egyptian case, the interim was not the coup-born government, but the elected civilian regime. This strikes a chord with critics of the "good coup" hypothesis who point out that the medium- to long-term outcomes of such coups have largely failed expectations. Global evidence does show that democracies that are overthrown by coups have been increasingly more likely to redemocratize – also because today's irregular takeovers are more likely to occur in democratic settings – and to do so relatively quickly. Yet this hardly makes such democratic interruptions "good" and desirable. For a start, it is claimed that "an example of democratic deepening after a coup-maker's [election] victory is yet to be found ... the promised improvement of democracy has remained elusive even when coup opponents have won post-coup elections" (Bermeo 2016:10), the 1994 coup in Lesotho being the exception. Moreover, when one excludes actions against democratic regimes and only considers those coups that supposedly "help" topple dictatorships, it appears they are not systematically related to democratization, neither for the entire 1950–2015 period nor for the post-Cold war period only. While a democratizing outcome does at times take place, in the majority of cases coups simply tend to replace older autocracies with new ones, and even to increase the level of repression of human rights (Derpanopoulos et al. 2016).

Africa is claimed to confirm this broader trend. When coups led to the restoration of democratic rule, Miller points out, it was never durable, as shown by Sierra Leone in 1968, Ghana in 1978, Sudan in 1985, and Niger in 1999. Moreover, the vast majority of military takeovers on the continent "led to no change or a minor adverse change in polities suggesting that most coups simply amounted to power grabs" (Miller 2011:50; cf. Souaré 2014:82).

If one looks at today's Africa and limits the observation to a regime's political trajectory, this picture is further substantiated. As Table 5.1 shows, after every single one of all ten post-2000 interventions the new rulers quickly moved to hold fresh elections within a relatively short time. In Mali, for example, a transitional government was formed as Captain Amadou Sanogo was negotiated out of power, and the country went on to organise an election in little more than a year. In the Central African Republic, François Bozizé won a vote just about two

Is There Such Thing as a "Good Coup"? 143

Table 5.1 *African coups d'état and regime effects in the new millennium, 2000–2018*

Country	Date of coup	Post-coup election	Polity2 score in pre-coup year	Polity2 score 3 years after coup	Δ Polity2 score
Central Afr. Rep.	15/03/2003	2005	5	−1	−6
Guinea-Bissau I	14/09/2003	2005	5	6	+1
Mauritania I	03/08/2005	2007	−6	−5	0
Mauritania II	06/08/2008	2009	4	−2	−6
Guinea	22/12/2008	2010	−1	1	+2
Madagascar	17/03/2009	2014	7	3	−4
Niger	19/02/2010	2011	−3	6	+9
Mali	22/03/2012	2013	7	5	−2
Guinea-Bissau II	12/04/2012	2014	6	6	0
Burkina Faso	01/11/2014	2015	0	6	+6

Source: authors' elaboration based on ALC data

years after taking power. These African instances thus appeared consistent with the new "promissory coups" (Bermeo 2016): elections were hardly ever delayed beyond a couple of years, either to legitimize the new rulers or else to return power to some other civilian leader. With the main exception of Madagascar, where an extremely atypical crisis unfolded following Andry Rajoelina's "civilian coup," all other episodes were normally followed by a multiparty vote within one to two years. A wait that was about one-fourth shorter than had been the case in the 1990s. In a few places, the poll was clearly controlled from the top to ensure the perpetuation in power of the incumbent military leader. This is what Ely Ould Mohamed Vall in Mauritania and Bozizé in the Central African Republic managed to do. Elsewhere, the election was a potential turning point as it eventually ushered in a new, elected civilian ruler, as happened in Burkina Faso where, similarly to Mauritania, rotation in office had previously occurred only when backed by the threat of violence. If we look at measures of overall post-coup democratic advancements, however, there is not much to celebrate. In four out of the ten sub-Saharan countries that suffered post-2000 coups – all ten starting off with a Polity2 score somewhere within the −6 to + 7 range – the regime's "democratic" credentials three years after the coup were indeed higher than the year before soldiers stepped in. But in an equal number of states – four – the regime harshened, and in the two remaining cases the situation was comparable to the pre-coup year. In all, the ten coups led to no improvement at all in the countries' average Polity2 rating. Africa's promissory coups and the elections they typically lead to have been, quite literally, pointless.

The Social and Economic Impact of African Coups

The objection that there is no such thing as a "good coup," however, goes beyond the lack of democratization advances, especially when one cross-examines Africa's military regimes against their own justifications for taking office (cf. Souaré 2014:82). Soldiers who seize power hardly ever fail to claim that they are doing so to redress a country's development trajectory: overturn economic stagnation, fight corruption, improve citizens' welfare, or restore stability in the face of mounting social tensions. These justifications thus typically refer to the record of the governments that are being overthrown, allegedly responsible for development failures. But do military *golpes*, in practice, usher in socio-economic advances? Do leaders who achieve power unconstitutionally bring about performances that are comparatively better than those of power-holders who reach office in a peaceful manner (if not via an election) and of elected ones? Before we move to a more comprehensive empirical analysis of the impact that the different ways in which leaders rotate in office have on development in Chapters 7 and 8, we examine some preliminary indications to answer these questions. Existing evidence is limited and for the most part not encouraging. Over 40 years back, Nordlinger and Decalo had already warned that, "if economic development results under military regimes, it is often *in spite of*, not because of, the military elite in power" (Decalo 1973:120). An inspection of the government performance of African armies shows a prevailing disrespect of the rule of law at both the highest and lowest echelons of the administrative apparatus, repression of the citizenry, a spread of corruption and mismanagement of economic resources (Agbese 2004). In the way McGowan summed this up, "the historical record shows that military rulers 'govern' no better than elected civilians in Africa, and often much worse" (2003:340), with soldiers' interventions – whether successful or failed – typically followed by a one-third reduction in GDP growth over the 1960–1986 period.

The Social and Economic Impact of African Coups 145

Based on our overall framework (see Chapter 2), we thus expect that:

HP 1 (coups). *The occurrence of a coup is not associated with improvements in a country's development performance*

HP 1.1 (irregular takeover). *Leaders who take power in an irregular manner are associated with development performances that are inferior to those of elected leaders*

A range of empirical measures show that coups are not generally followed by progress, they do not lead to improvements in a country's socioeconomic or administrative performance. This emerges clearly from Table 5.2, reporting the results of ten statistical models in which development indicators are regressed on a dummy variable measuring the occurrence of a coup at time *t* and at time *t-1*, respectively. The dependent variables measure economic growth (annual GDP and GDP per capita growth), social welfare (health spending as a share of GDP, primary and secondary school enrolment, life expectancy at birth and child mortality rate), state consolidation, and political/executive corruption. Chapter 7 and 8 offer a detailed illustration of the indicators chosen to operationalize these dependent variables, and Table A3 in the appendix provides descriptive statistics. All models include the lagged level of the dependent variable as well as country and year dummies. Models are estimated via ordinary least squares (OLS) with panel-corrected standard errors (PCSE).[7] As expected, regression coefficients of coups are never significantly associated with an improvement in the socio-economic conditions of sub-Saharan countries. On the contrary, the occurrence of a coup is linked to an immediate negative effect on economic growth, health spending and state consolidation. When one looks at corruption and secondary school enrolment, coups show a detrimental effect that becomes evident in a longer period.

In line with what is expected from HP1.1, when specifically compared to elected leaders, during their stay in office the average performance of power-holders who reached power through the gun is disappointing. The rhetoric of their supposedly superior capabilities and aptness does not stand up to the facts. Table 5.3 reports the results

---

[7] A detailed explanation of the model specifications for the different dependent variables and the reasons that induced us to opt for them can be found in Chapter 7.

Table 5.2 *Military coups and development performance*

	Economic growth				Social welfare				Stateness	Corruption	
	GDP growth	GDP per capita growth	Δ Primary school enrolment	Δ Secondary school enrolment	Δ Health spending	Δ Life expectancy at birth	Δ Under-5 mortality rate		Δ State consolidation	Δ Political corruption	Δ Executive corruption
Dep. var. $_{t-1}$	0.255***	0.232***	−0.029**	−0.045**	−0.190***	−0.028***	−0.020***		−0.106***	−0.057***	−0.077***
	(0.050)	(0.050)	(0.014)	(0.018)	(0.041)	(0.010)	(0.007)		(0.021)	(0.012)	(0.013)
Coup	−2.125***	−1.948***	−0.903	0.220	−0.220**	0.027	0.242		−0.046**	0.003	0.012*
	(0.732)	(0.704)	(0.606)	(0.248)	(0.100)	(0.042)	(0.439)		(0.019)	(0.004)	(0.006)
Coup $_{t-1}$	0.691	0.789	−1.234	0.639*	−0.455***	0.053	0.469		−0.052*	0.014**	0.025***
	(0.719)	(0.692)	(0.831)	(0.329)	(0.148)	(0.057)	(0.613)		(0.028)	(0.006)	(0.009)
Country dummies	Yes	Yes	Yes	Yes	Yes	Yes	Yes		Yes	Yes	Yes
Year dummies	Yes	Yes	Yes	Yes	Yes	Yes	Yes		Yes	Yes	Yes
Constant	3.532	1.322	14.650***	3.696***	0.312	1.798***	0.181		0.027	0.051***	0.072***
	(2.707)	(2.592)	(2.835)	(1.362)	(0.210)	(0.427)	(3.045)		(0.074)	(0.009)	(0.012)
N	2,166	2,166	1,616	1,143	887	2,288	2,224		1,970	2,459	2,460
Countries	49	49	48	48	48	49	49		45	49	49
R^2	0.177	0.165	0.156	0.174	0.124	0.213	0.146		0.139	0.085	0.089

Note: since all the dependent variables but GDP growth and GDP per capita growth are nonstationary, they are entered in the regression models in first difference (Δ). Regression coefficients of controls are omitted. Panel-corrected standard errors (PCSE) in parentheses. * $p < 0.1$; ** $p < 0.05$; *** $p < 0.01$.

Table 5.3 Leader's mode of entry and development performance

	Economic growth		Social welfare				Stateness	Corruption	
	GDP growth	GDP per capita growth	Δ Primary school enrolment	Δ Secondary school enrolment	Δ Health spending	Δ Life expectancy at birth	Δ Under-5 mortality rate	Δ State consolidation	Δ Political corruption	Δ Executive corruption
Dep. var. $_{t-1}$	0.162***	0.154***	−0.022***	−0.012	−0.254***	−0.011**	−0.017***	−0.110***	−0.018***	−0.018***
	(0.041)	(0.041)	(0.006)	(0.008)	(0.046)	(0.006)	(0.003)	(0.018)	(0.007)	(0.006)
Reference cat: Electoral										
Violent $_{t-1}$	−1.695***	−1.638***	−1.028**	−0.695***	−0.170***	−0.164***	1.147***	−0.030*	0.007***	0.001
	(0.494)	(0.482)	(0.415)	(0.135)	(0.064)	(0.046)	(0.302)	(0.016)	(0.003)	(0.003)
Peaceful $_{t-1}$	−1.483***	−1.433***	−0.270	−0.482**	0.051	−0.123**	0.830**	−0.014	0.007***	0.001
	(0.441)	(0.428)	(0.436)	(0.198)	(0.108)	(0.052)	(0.359)	(0.016)	(0.002)	(0.003)
Constant	−0.209	−0.642	6.382**	−0.321	3.131**	0.382	−2.413	−0.313***	−0.001	−0.001
	(2.768)	(2.687)	(2.638)	(1.584)	(1.465)	(0.363)	(1.935)	(0.086)	(0.010)	(0.010)
N	1,447	1,447	1,337	953	770	1,636	1,612	1,378	1,522	1,522
Countries	42	42	42	42	46	42	42	41	42	42
R^2	0.109	0.093	0.068	0.093	0.216	0.102	0.321	0.102	0.041	0.028

Note: since all the dependent variables but GDP growth and GDP per capita growth are nonstationary, they are entered in the regression models in first difference (Δ). Regression coefficients of controls are omitted.
Panel-corrected standard errors (PCSE) in parentheses. * $p < 0.1$; ** $p < 0.05$; *** $p < 0.01$.

of statistical models in which the abovementioned development indicators are regressed on two dummy variables, one coded "1" if a power-holder seized power through a coup or other violent/irregular mode (e.g., guerrilla takeover, foreign imposition) and the other one coded "1" if he comes to office via peaceful but non-electoral means. The reference category includes leaders who reached power via multiparty elections. Given the inert nature of most development indicators and considering that in Table 5.2 we already tested the short-run effects of the occurrence of a coup, the two independent variables are included in one-year lagged level. Models in Table 5.3 have the same specifications of models that will be presented and discussed in Chapters 7 and 8, where we provide a detailed description of the methodology and the controls we employ. Our findings confirm that office-holders who grabbed power via violent/irregular means tend to perform worse than elected leaders. *Golpistas* are associated to lower macroeconomic performances, school enrolment rates, healthcare expenditures and life expectancy at birth, while, on the other hand, they are associated to higher child mortality rates and political corruption levels.

Africa has come a long way since the times of postcolonial military takeovers. The window of opportunity that soldiers saw opening in the early 1960s led some pioneer coups d'état to spread and evolve into a veritable, continent-wide wave of army interventions. The image of African rulers in military fatigues became highly recurrent, if not prevailing. But the promise of brighter and faster progress under military rule failed to materialize. More often than not, generals and colonels further stifled the socioeconomic advancement of their countries, nor did they hinder the diffusion of corruption. Poor average performances in government contributed to delegitimizing military rule. Eventually, the window of opportunity begun to close and the military wave gradually dwindled – albeit it certainly has not disappeared entirely – as electoral processes were established across the region and most armies were sent back to the barracks.

6 | *Lessening Africa's "Big Men"*
Term Limits

When, How, and Why Were Term Limits Adopted

Drawing from ancient republican experiences in classical Athens and Rome, the modern practice of limiting executive tenure emerged with the birth of presidential government. Breaking with British-style dynastic succession, the US constitution of 1787 meant to avoid establishing an "elective king" of sorts while, at the same time, promoting citizens' sovereignty and a degree of rotation in power. America's first leader, George Washington, turned this idea into practice by refusing to stay on and stepping down after eight years in office. The powerful precedent he set proved overwhelming for over 140 years. It was only with Franklin D. Roosevelt's second, unprecedented reelection, in 1940, that a long-lasting legacy was temporarily broken. Roosevelt later went on to seek and win even a fourth mandate. His break with tradition, however, spurred the reaction of Congress – as soon as Republicans regained control of it in 1947, after 14 years – and the passing of the Twenty-Second Amendment, which, once the ratification process was completed in 1951, constitutionalized the maximum of two terms any US president can serve.

Formal reelection bans and term limits, meanwhile, had been pioneered in Latin America during the nineteenth century – Argentina started its own in 1853 – as democratic reformers shaped new participatory systems based on the US model but also sought ways to win their national battles "to prevent *caudillismo, continuismo,* and the concentration of power in the executive branch" (Corrales and Penfold 2014:157; cf. Maltz 2007:131). It was toward the latter part of the twentieth century, however, as the so-called third wave reforms of the 1970s and 1980s introduced or reintroduced democracy by means of new constitutional provisions, most often in the presidential mold, that the adoption of one- or two-term limits quickly spread across much of the globe, including the post-communist world and Africa (cf. McKie

2017:437). At this time, many Latin American countries, for example, adopted comparatively harsh restrictions by either banning reelection altogether (Mexico, which had done so from earlier in the century with the *sexenio*, was joined by the likes of Paraguay and Honduras) or only allowing it after a gap term (such as in Chile or Peru). Others opted for a maximum of two consecutive mandates, typically with further reelections possible after spending a full term out of office, as in Argentina and Brazil.

In Africa, few constitutions envisaged term limits prior to the 1990s. This was originally due to the fact that, at independence, European-derived parliamentary or semi-presidential models prevailed, which normally did not envisage formal tenure limitations. France itself, where the semi-presidential form of government had first been conceived in 1958, only set a maximum number of mandates 50 years later. As the introduction of direct presidential elections gradually spread south of the Sahara under one-party systems in the 1970s and 1980s, it was the parallel rise of legal and *de facto* life presidencies – the exact antithesis to limited stays in office – that contributed to ruling out similar arrangements (cf. McKie 2017:438).

Self-proclaimed "presidents for life" included Kwame Nkrumah (1964), Hastings Banda (1970), Jean-Bédel Bokassa (1972), Francisco Macías Nguema (1972), and Idi Amin Dada (1976). They did not lack illustrious non-African predecessors of the past, such as Julius Caesar's late *dictator perpetuo* designation in ancient Rome (which did not prevent him from being stabbed to death and thus removed) or Jozip Broz Tito in the Socialist Federal Republic of Yugoslavia (who successfully retained office till he passed away). None of sub-Saharan official "presidents for life," however, actually went on to serve as president until his death, all being forcefully deposed by a domestic or international intervention (except for Banda, defeated at Malawi's first multiparty poll in 1994). They ultimately proved that, for non-royal rulers, staying in power forever depends more on strongmanship than on formal titles. As Napoleon Bonaparte once explained to Count von Metternich, then the Austrian Empire's foreign minister, "my reign will not outlast the day I have ceased to be strong and therefore to be feared."[1] As a matter of fact, Africa's political stage

---

[1] Krastev, Ivan, "Welcome to the era of presidents for life," *New York Times*, March 18, 2018.

saw a number of *unofficial* presidents for life – the likes of William Tubman (Liberia), Jomo Kenyatta (Kenya), Ahmed Sékou Touré and Lansana Conté (Guinea), Félix Houphouët-Boigny (Côte d'Ivoire), Gnassingbé Eyadéma (Togo), or Omar Bongo (Gabon) – who were more successful in actually remaining at the helm until their death.

A sea change occurred beginning in the 1990s, when 28 of 37 presidential countries – that is, just over 75 percent – introduced explicit tenure restrictions, leaving only 9 African states where presidents could be reelected indefinitely (see Table 6.1 and Figure 6.1 for an overview of the adoption of constitutional term limits south of the Sahara). The establishment of term limits was part of a broader process of gradual institutionalization of political power (cf. Posner and Young 2007; Cheeseman 2015:176ff.) aimed at curbing Africa's extensive personal rule tradition as well as the practice of unconstitutional changes of government. Tenure restrictions were meant to be a pivotal and transformative ingredient: "if institutions are rules that restrain political actors, then the most important institutions that constrain the most important political actors are the rules that tell presidents how and when they must relinquish power" (Posner and Young 2018:1).

With about a quarter of its presidential and semi-presidential states retaining the possibility of unlimited executive tenure, however, the political landscape in Africa was not as uniform as in Latin America or in post-communist areas, where *all* third-wave democratizers electing their heads of state opted for limiting stays in office (McKie 2017:437). But the absence of limits to mandates in some countries cannot be explained away as the result of constitutional transitions that were controlled by incumbents. Somewhat surprisingly, in as many as one third of all cases where limitations were adopted, they came at the behest of a long-serving ruler who unilaterally introduced them. This is what happened under Hastings Banda, Daniel Arap Moi, or Omar Bongo, for example, whereas the same did not occur under peers of theirs such as Félix Houphouët-Boigny or Teodoro Obiang Nguema Mbasogo. In her detailed analysis, McKie (2017) explains a country's choice (adoption versus non-adoption) on the basis of two key factors. The first was the actors' *ability* to impose their preferred institutional outcome, that is, whether the constitution was unilaterally revised by the incumbent party or the result of a more open-ended and negotiated process. The second was the actors' *preference* for power-concentrating as opposed to power-sharing institutions, which, in turn,

Table 6.1 *The adoption of presidential term limits since 1989*

Presidential term limits adopted (year of adoption)		Presidential term limits NOT adopted (year of the first multiparty election after 1989)
Angola (1992)	Malawi (1994)	Cameroon (1992)
Benin (1990)	Mali (1992)	Cape Verde (1991)
Burkina Faso (1991)	Mozambique (1990)	Central African Rep. (1993)
Burundi (1992)	Namibia (1990)	Côte d'Ivoire (1990)
Chad (1996)	Niger (1993)	The Gambia (1996)[c]
Congo-Brazzaville (1992)	Nigeria (1999)	Mauritania (1992)[d]
Congo-Kinshasa (2005)	Rwanda (1991)	South Sudan (2011)
Djibouti (1992)	São Tomé and Príncipe (1990)	
Equatorial Guinea (2011)	Senegal (1991)	
Gabon (1990)	Seychelles (1993)	
Ghana (1992)	Sudan (1998)[a]	
Guinea (1990)	Togo (1992)	
Guinea-Bissau (1993)	Uganda (1995)	
Kenya (1992)	Zambia (1991)	
Madagascar (1992)	Zimbabwe (2013)[b]	

Notes: Three criteria were used to select the 37 cases in the table, i.e., a country: (1) holds direct presidential elections, (2) did not already have presidential term limits before 1989, and (3) held at least one multiparty election since 1989. Excluded are therefore parliamentary systems (Ethiopia, Botswana, South Africa, Lesotho, and Mauritius), kingdoms (eSwatini), states with no popular elections (Somalia, Eritrea), and those that already had tenure restrictions prior to 1989 (Liberia, Sierra Leone, Comoros, and Tanzania). Some additional notes on specific cases: (a) Sudan, not part of McKie's cases, adopted a two-term limit with the 1998 constitution that governed the 2000 election, but the new 2005 constitution reset the count, allowing Al-Bashir to stand for two more elections (2010 and 2015); (b) In Zimbabwe, constitutional changes in 1987 introduced a presidential system and removed the two 6-year term limit that the 1980 constitution envisaged for the previously ceremonial head of state under a parliamentary system; term limits were subsequently adopted with the new constitution of 2013; (c) In the Gambia, the 1996 constitution reintroduced multiparty politics, following a 1994 coup; (d) Mauritania amended its constitution to introduce a two-term limit in 2006.
Source: adapted from McKie (2017:440ff.)

hinged on whether incumbents perceived they would face electoral uncertainty, as in Kenya, or, on the contrary, they felt they were highly likely to win future elections, as in Côte d'Ivoire. Even those three states that, after initially rejecting term limits, went on to introduce

To Limit or Not to Limit? The Arguments for and against 153

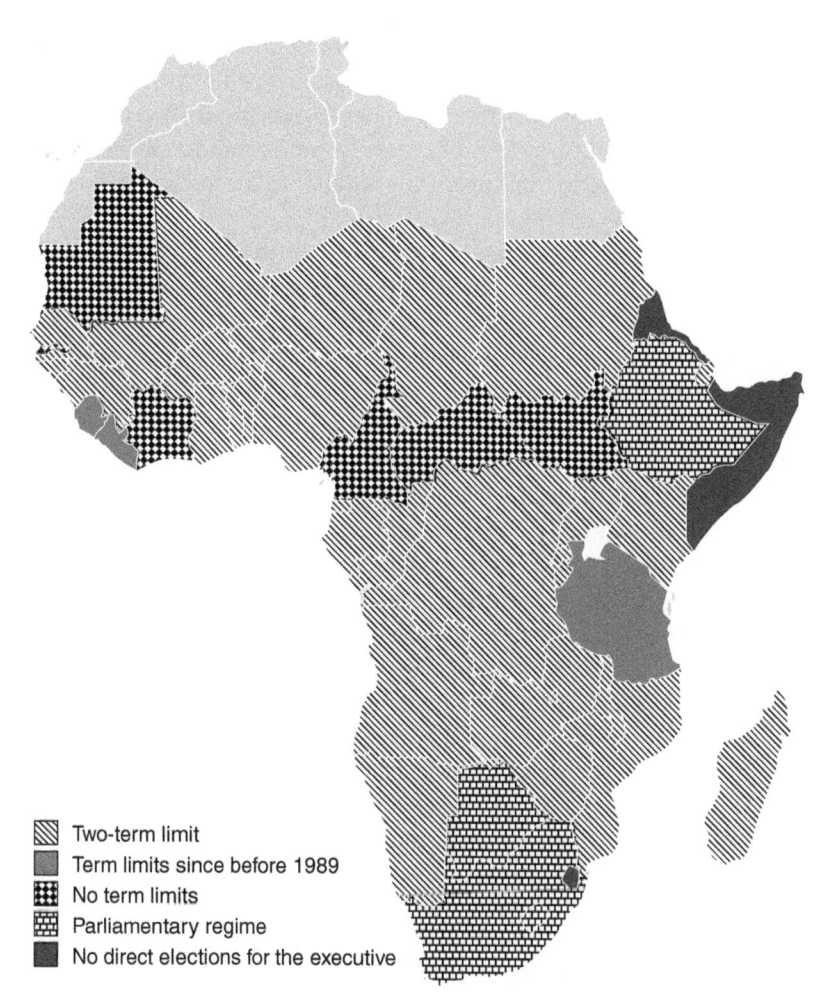

- Two-term limit
- Term limits since before 1989
- No term limits
- Parliamentary regime
- No direct elections for the executive

Figure 6.1 The adoption of presidential term limits since 1989.
Source: updated from McKie (2017:440ff.)

them before their second presidential election (namely, Cameroon, CAR, and Cape Verde), did so after the first contest proved more competitive and uncertain than anticipated.

To Limit or Not to Limit? The Arguments for and against

Constitutions around the world generally adopt one of four main ways of regulating presidential reelection. Between the two extremes of indefinite reelection, on the one side, and a total ban on reelection on the other, the typical constraints include allowing nonconsecutive reelection only or else permitting limited consecutive reelection (Corrales and Penfold 2014:159). The most common solution is by far that of admitting reelection but only for a total of two consecutive four- or five-year terms.

Establishing norms on the amount of time that a single individual can retain a country's top office is generally popular with voters (Saad 2013; Dulani 2015), at least as a principle, and may appear as a rather obvious and appealing embodiment of notions such as open participation and competition, pluralism of voices and actors, diffused political power, rule-based authority, legitimate processes of adjustment and policy change, and similar underpinnings of prevailing ideas about how a democratic regime is supposed to work. Personal political entrenchment is inimical to democratic rule. Some well-known definitions of democracy explicitly emphasise alternation in office as a *sine qua non* requisite (Przeworski et al. 2000:18ff.), or at least a key component of democratic consolidation (Huntington 1991:266–267). Any such characterizations demand, in other words, that no given political actor uninterruptedly remains in office.

The concentration of power and the risk of tyranny that may go with continuous tenure run against the principle that power must lie in the hands of the broader *demos*. Indeed, tenure breeds power, as the latter tends to grow and concentrate in the hands of long-term office-bearers, and power breeds tenure, as evidence shows that incumbents running for reelection typically have much higher chances of being successful – the so-called advantage of incumbency – than a successor candidate. Time limits thus favor alternation in office for individuals and political forces alike, as demonstrated, time and again, by departures from the job such as those, in 2000, of Jerry Rawlings in Ghana and Franjo Tuđman in Croatia. Alternation is a reflection and a reminder of the principle that the rule of law has to prevail over the rule of man, that the exercise of political power is better held in check when it is formalized and depersonalized – and thus institutionalized – by separating the rule from the ruler (cf. Huntington 1968; Tull and Simons 2017:90).

Restraining stays in office is also widely perceived to help periodically sever the links with special interests, break down established personal fiefdoms, and thus limit corruption. Countries allowing indefinite reelection for presidents, for example, are associated with worse governance quality (i.e., in terms of Worldwide Governance Indicators (WGI), including the rule of law, corruption, political stability, and governmental effectiveness) when compared to countries that adopt some kind of limits, particularly those that only allow nonconsecutive reelection (Corrales and Penfold 2014:161).

By opening up the chances for the incumbent's rivals to gain office at some point in the future, in addition, term limits help win support for the rules of the game and thus the loyalty of political oppositions to the system. This, in turn, contributes to containing the risk of rebellions on the part of actors who may otherwise feel they have few stakes in the existing political order. Moreover, the increased possibility of government turnovers – which imply an incumbent's reversal of fortunes – may incentivize the strengthening of judicial independence and the prevalence of restraint rather than abuse in the use of political power as guarantees of a safer future for current office-holders.

Yet, as recurrent or near universal as they are in presidential systems, tenure limits are hardly a defining feature of democracy as it is oftentimes claimed. This is all the more evident when one turns to parliamentary systems, where official limits to one's length of stay in office are generally deemed unnecessary (on the ground that, in principle, legislators are in a position to sack and replace their prime minister at any time) and thus virtually inexistent (South Africa and Botswana are rare exceptions). In practice, the heads of parliamentary governments frequently serve multiple terms, as with Angela Merkel's four or Tony Blair's three election wins.

The very argument whereby term limits are somewhat "undemocratic" is far from unwarranted. Even advocates of tenure restrictions acknowledge that, "limiting re-election ... limits not just a president's right but also the voters' choice" (Corrales and Penfold 2014:158). In principle, the sovereign citizens of a democratic polity should be in a position to retain an exceptional or a merely preferred politician in office indefinitely, should they wish so. This same justification was frequently voiced by sitting African presidents trying to have similar regulations removed: "'What is democracy?' Mr. Abdou Diouf said. 'It's the choice of the people. The National Assembly in a majority judged that it was not natural, if the country has a good president and wants to keep him, that it should be prevented from keeping him. It is democracy if the people have the possibility to express an opinion.'"[2]

A measure that is essentially meant to prevent abuses, overstays, and an overconcentration of power thus arguably ends up curtailing the freedom of voters and their possibility of rewarding and retaining upstanding and outstanding political leaders – a negative rather than positive outcome for democracy, the quality of government, and society as a whole (cf. Besley and Case 1995:793). In this perspective, tenure restrictions can only be justified – as an established institutional check on a majority-elected government – by the need to strike a balance between democracy and a liberal authority.

On a more practical ground, term limits inevitably create a potentially significant distinction, or even a distortion, between an elected president's non-final terms and his/her last mandate. The former are typically affected by the prospect of seeking reelection, whether this strengthens or weakens a leader's freedom of action and position in the face of other political actors. A final, nonrenewable mandate – even where this is the one and only mandate allowed – by contrast, is shaped by the awareness that there is no election to win on the horizon, and thus little need to please voters, as well as by the flimsy inducements a "lame-duck" head of government can employ to retain political backing. Indeed, it has been argued and demonstrated that the foreseeable lack of electoral sanctions and accountability may result in the removal of a key deterrent for opportunism, the shortening of one's career horizon and the risk of capture by special interests, favoring the emergence of corrupt behaviors (cf. Rose-Ackerman 2001; Alt and Lassen 2014; Ferraz and Finan 2011). Reflecting on the extreme case of Mexico – where one mandate only was allowed for presidents and legislators alike (following a 2014 reform, lawmakers will be reelectable from 2021 on) – this is how an observer described some perverse effects of term limits:

at the first moment of the first day of his first term in office, the new President of Mexico, Ernesto Zedillo Ponce de Leon, became a lame duck, and he was not alone. He accepted the red, white and green presidential sash Thursday in front of the 628-member federal legislature, 31 state governors and a number of Mexico's 2,392 mayors, *all of them freshmen who cannot run for*

---

[2] Norimitsu Onishi, "With Africa watching, Senegal casts votes that Count," *New York Times*, February 27, 2000.

re-election when their current terms end ... 'The system produced enormous mobility in the political elite,' said ... an adviser to former President Carlos Salinas de Gortari, 'but it has had a fundamental cost, which is that the Mexican electorate doesn't have any concept of accountability.'[3]

Ultimately, arguments *against* the adoption of term restrictions do not at all appear as unreasonable as they may at first seem. A more thorough assessment of their potential, however, requires considering some contextual aspects of the African political scenario, as a candidate standing for office against a long-serving president retorted to the no-limits argument:

'In a country with a fully functioning democracy, where there is a culture of democracy and credible institutions, there is no problem with having no term limits,' Mr. Djibo Ka said. 'But in a poor country like this one, where the same party has been in power for 40 years and where power has corrupted its members, it's not a bad idea to have term limits.'[4]

Do Term Limits Matter in Africa?

A sceptical view holds that post-1989 forms of rule in Africa are not much different from those that prevailed in the previous, postcolonial era. While a number of African countries did make democratic progress and brought some institutional restrains to bear on elected governments, it is claimed, the region's authoritarian leaders remain largely unconstrained, and ultimately their "power trumps institutions" (Tull and Simons 2017:97–98). Yet this conclusion is twice faulty. First because it is too simplistic to acknowledge that elections in Africa "offer only slim chances to oust incumbents, making term limits all the more relevant" (Tull and Simons 2017:80) and that "term limit compliance ... certainly marks important progress" (Tull and Simons 2017:89), only to then go on and object that, nevertheless, informal institutions have not been fully displaced. Of course they have not, it was merely naïve to expect so. All political systems are at least in part moulded by durable informal practices, and the more institutionalized they are, the more time is required before formal rules can

---

[3] Anthony DePalma, "Do term limits work? Ask Mexico," *New York Times*, December 4, 1994.
[4] Norimitsu Onishi, "With Africa watching, Senegal casts votes that Count," *New York Times*, February 27, 2000.

impose themselves, shape, and transform specific behaviors. The battle for setting and implementing time limits on presidential tenure was never going to be an easy, quick and one-off fight. Secondly, Tull and Simons' reading overlooks the fact that the likes of Daniel Arap Moi (Kenya), Ali Hassan Mwinyi (Tanzania), Joaquim Chissano and Armando Guebuza (both in Mozambique), Fredrick Chiluba (Zambia) or, ultimately, even Blaise Compaoré (Burkina Faso) did have to step aside – in countries that were at the time deemed *authoritarian* by both Freedom House and Polity2 – precisely and only because they were facing constitutional bans on their hypothetical second reelection. There are chances that Mauritania may be next, as president Mohamed Ould Abdelaziz claimed he will not ditch the legally allowed maximum of two mandates to extend his tenure and will duly retire in 2019.[5]

Term limits are no panacea for Africa's political deficits, and, in many cases, their implementation has certainly been highly problematic, as we discuss next. Yet they are part of the genuine if turbulent progress the region has made over the past 30 years. This is because they have often been for real – forcing out of office many dominant and entrenched power-holders – and, overall, they "constrain African leaders in ways that were almost unimaginable in earlier eras" (Posner and Young 2018:1).

Setting a maximum number of mandates for presidents serving in Africa, and having it respected, also contributed to further democratic advances. Figure 6.2 shows the 17 cases where voters on the continent were faced with an open seat election as a result of term limits, that is, where incumbents could no longer bid for reelection. The outcomes of these elections are rather evenly split between nine instances that resulted in an electoral succession (i.e., an incoming president representing political continuity) and eight in which electoral alternation took place (i.e., where the new president hailed from an opposition party). Thus, for a start, they appeared to greatly widen opportunities for alternation in office, as government turnovers are much less common than a one-in-two average when we look at elections in which the opposition needs to uproot an incumbent in order to win office.

---

[5] Justine Spiegel, "Mauritanie – Mohamed Ould Abdelaziz: 'Je soutiendrai un candidat en 2019,'" *Jeune Afrique*, March 5, 2018.

Do Term Limits Matter in Africa? 159

[Bar chart showing Δ Polity2 values for Electoral Alternations and Electoral Successions]

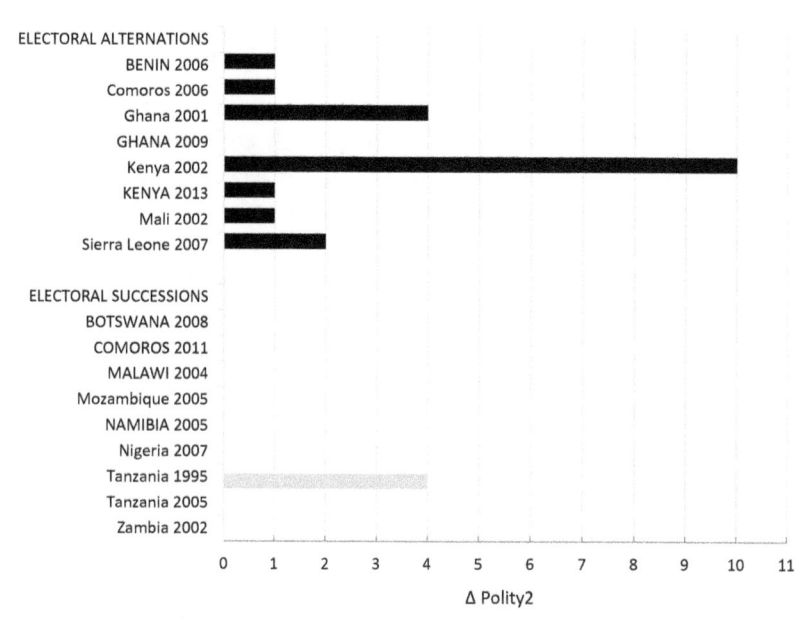

ELECTORAL ALTERNATIONS
- BENIN 2006: ~1
- Comoros 2006: ~1
- Ghana 2001: ~4
- GHANA 2009: 0
- Kenya 2002: ~10
- KENYA 2013: ~1
- Mali 2002: ~1
- Sierra Leone 2007: ~2

ELECTORAL SUCCESSIONS
- BOTSWANA 2008: 0
- COMOROS 2011: 0
- MALAWI 2004: 0
- Mozambique 2005: 0
- NAMIBIA 2005: 0
- Nigeria 2007: 0
- Tanzania 1995: ~4
- Tanzania 2005: 0
- Zambia 2002: 0

Figure 6.2 Democratic improvements following electoral alternations and electoral successions favoured by term limits.
Notes: countries in capital letters were deemed democratic (i.e., Polity2 ≥ 6) at the time of the election; no Polity2 data available for São Tomé and Príncipe (2001 succession and 2011 alternation). We include the case of Botswana in 2008, widely seen as a case of electoral succession, despite Ian Khama formally took over prior to the election.
Source: authors elaboration based on ALC dataset

The bar chart in Figure 6.2 reports the difference between a country's Polity2 score in the year a power handover favored by a term limit takes place and the score in the following year. Unsurprisingly, no country suffered a setback in terms of its degree of democracy. Whereas in only one country – Tanzania – a leadership succession through elections led to a score improvement, this happened in virtually all of the eight instances of electoral alternation (the exception being Ghana in 2009, due to the very high democratic score the country already displayed, i.e., 8 on a –10 to +10 scale). Thus, term limits in practice expanded political opportunities for alternation in power, and the latter, in turn, contributed to a country's overall democratic progress.

On Course Manipulation: Targeting Term Limits

Pressures for and attempts at eliminating – or at least relaxing – presidential term limits have grown increasingly common across world regions. As far back as the early 1990s, for example, several Latin American countries undertook to revise their rather restrictive constitutional provisions to allow elected leaders to run for a second consecutive mandate (e.g., in Peru from 1993, in Argentina from 1994, in Brazil from 1997) or, at times, for an indefinite number of mandates, as in Hugo Chávez's Venezuela following a 2009 referendum, in Daniel Ortega's Nicaragua subsequent to a 2014 reform, and in Evo Morales' Bolivia as a result of a 2017 ruling by the Constitutional Court. In a number of countries – including Argentina and Colombia – initiatives to legalize the possibility of a third term were rejected by political or judicial oppositions. Overall, however, reelection possibilities in the region are today broader than they used to be prior to the last decade of the past century. Neither was Latin America alone. Elsewhere, Alexander Lukashenko had limits on mandates in Belarus lifted in 2004. Three years later, Nursultan Nazarbayev of Kazakhstan also had them removed, but for himself alone, retaining them for future successors. When even China – where multiparty elections, real or façade, have never been allowed – did away with term limits for its head of state, in 2018, some analysts pointed out that this was a global watershed: "constraining a ruler's power was one of the key ways that non-democracies adjusted to the age of democracy," but Beijing's move now appeared to mark the end of democracy hegemony and the advent of an "emperor's moment."[6]

Once again, however, the fact is that term limits are *not* a non-renounceable component of modern democracies. As pointed out, there is no lack of democratic arguments against their adoption. In the past, US presidents Ronald Reagan and partly also Harry Truman openly spoke out against term limits. Over the years, several bills have been unsuccessfully introduced in the US Congress to try and erase them from the country's fundamental law. The underlying assumption is that "the relaxation of term limits is not, in and of itself, deleterious to democracy ... especially if negotiated across the political spectrum,

---

[6] Krastev, Ivan, "Welcome to the era of presidents for life," *New York Times*, March 18, 2018.

can enhance accountability and strengthen checks and balances ... the trouble comes when a president tries to change the constitution without much negotiation ... [as this] often provoke(s) a backlash" (Corrales and Penfold 2014:162). Starting off from comparatively stricter constraints, for example, Latin American reforms aimed at allowing more room for presidents to be reelected were in many cases less controversial, and more likely to be negotiated and accepted by the oppositions, than was elsewhere the case. Particularly in Africa, where the existing baseline was typically a constitutional two-term limit and opposition forces were more likely to resist the incumbents' unilateral attempts at further expanding their chances for remaining in office. In the process, a number of popular movements emerged, coalesced, and mobilized exactly around a common will to resist similar initiatives, as with the *Y'en a marre* ("We've had enough") protests in Senegal, the *Le Balai Citoyen* ("The citizen broom") in Burkina Faso, the *Halte au troisième mandate* ("Stop the third mandate") in Burundi, and the *Anti-kisanja* ("Anti-third term") demonstrations in Uganda. South of the Sahara, the tense controversy over the "third-term issue" was grounded in the region's political past, with memories and fears of never-ending and self-serving life presidencies, and frequently turned into violent confrontations.

Questioning term limits often started with an incumbent leader pretending he was personally uninterested in prolonging his stay in office – that is, unless "the 'people' asked or begged him to run,"[7] as claimed by the likes of Mamadou Tandja in Niger, Paul Kagame in Rwanda, or Pierre Nkurunziza in Burundi. Contrary to how events would have likely unfolded in previous decades, however, this time around Africa saw hardly any attempt to simply disregard the constitution. Virtually every would-be term evader – particularly authoritarian rulers, who proved highly likely to succeed in their bids to get rid of constitutional obstacles on their way toward a third mandate – embarked on painstaking and long political and legal maneuverings to achieve their desired goal. Following proper procedures in modifying the fundamental chart would help them claim at least a degree of legitimacy in the face of fierce international, regional, or popular criticism. In fact, despite widespread condemnation, incumbents rarely

---

[7] Lakemfa, Owei "There will be Rwanda after Kagame," *The Vanguard*, November 6, 2015.

suffered regionally or internationally imposed sanctions on the part of external partners and organizations, Niger's suspension from ECOWAS in 2009 being an exception.

Ultimately, three were the alternative strategies that African power-holders undertook to bypass term limits, namely scrapping, exempting, or restarting. First, several serving presidents intervened prior to the application of reelection rules by trying to rescind those constitutional provisions that would have forced them out of office. Secondly, a minority of them took a different route, adopting new, self-tailored measures that would ensure that limits did not apply to their particular case. Sam Nujoma in Namibia obtained being exempted from the two-term limit, and exceptionally allowed a third mandate, by virtue of being the country's first and founding president. Yet personalized solutions arguably reached their peak with Rwanda's complex way out of legal strictures. Kagame's original two seven-year mandates were supposed to last from 2003 until 2017 at most. But the constitution was duly revised in 2015, first with a parliamentary vote by both houses of parliament and then with a final approval through popular referendum. The two-term limit was still there. Indeed, the length of a single term was even reduced, down from seven to five years. But a "transitional presidential term" of seven years (2017–2024) was envisaged before the new provisions would come into force. Any person, including Kagame, would be eligible to stand for office. The "new" two-term limit would only apply after completing this transition. Thus, at least in principle, the way was opened for Kagame to stay on until 2034. Thirdly, a number of rulers – including those of Burkina Faso, Equatorial Guinea, Senegal, or Sudan – opted for a timely introduction of new constitutions whose term limits would not apply retroactively, thus setting back the clock for themselves.

Precisely how national leaders who were successful in bypassing term limits went about doing so is summed up in Table 6.2, and once again boils down to three main routes. First, classic constitutional amendments were passed by the required parliamentary majorities in places from Namibia to Djibouti. In other countries, a popular referendum was held to legally and politically back the notion that the people's will was supportive of leadership continuity. Burkina Faso's Blaise Compaoré, a pioneer and a recidivist in term manipulation, went this way as early as 1997. Rwanda's Paul Kagame used a popular vote as a complement to the parliamentary route. Finally,

Table 6.2 *Parliaments, referenda, and courts: how incumbents bypassed term limits*

Mechanisms	Cases
Change of constitution through **parliament**	Cameroon, Djibouti, Gabon, Namibia, Rwanda, Togo, Uganda
Change of constitution / introduction of new constitution through **popular referendum**	Burkina Faso, Chad, Congo-Brazzaville, Guinea, Rwanda, Sudan
Court ruling legalizing third-term bid	Burundi, Senegal

Source: Tull and Simons (2017:87)

constitutional court rulings granted Pierre Nkurunziza in Burundi and Abdoulaye Wade in Senegal the possibility to run again, albeit Wade failed to win or orchestrate the support of voters and eventually had to leave office. In Burundi, pressure had been high for the court to legitimize Nkurunziza's bid after parliament stopped one vote short of the four-fifths majority that constitutional amendments required (Reyntjens 2016:63). It is thus remarkable – and a sign of the times – that the vast majority of African power-holders went to great lengths to formally remain within the constitutional order while trying to circumvent the latter's substantive content. Simply ignoring the existing legal framework could backfire. When, in the two cases of Niger (2009–2010) and Burkina Faso (2014), the incumbents' bold initiatives stirred political or judicial opposition, even the army, somewhat surprisingly, felt it had to react in defence of the constitution and ultimately ousted the would-be term evaders.

The (Relative) Resilience of Tenure Limitations

Table 6.3 illustrates all attempts – whether failed or successful – that sub-Saharan presidents made to overcome term limits.[8] By 2018, as many as 18 countries had seen attempts at bypassing term limits by tampering with the constitution or its interpretation, starting from

---

[8] Table A2 in the appendix offers a complete overview of presidential term limits in sub-Saharan countries, the instances in which tenure limitations were met, and all the failed and successful attempts to bypass such constitutional limits by incumbent leaders.

Table 6.3 Failed and successful attempts to overcome presidential term limits[a]

		Constitution contains a two-term limit on the presidency			
Presidency does not exist, is non-executive, not directly-elected, or not term-limited	No two-term limited executive presidency	Two-term limit not reached/violated by 2018 (year limit was / will be reached)	Limit accepted, no attempt made to amend constitution	Two-term limit was reached/violated by 2018 (year limit was reached or violation attempted; Outgoing leader)	
				Attempt made to amend, by-pass or ignore constitution	
				Attempt was not successful	Attempt was successful
Cape Verde	Comoros	Angola (2028)	Benin (2006 Kérékou; 2016 Yayi Boni)	Burkina Faso II (2014 Compaoré)	Burkina Faso I (1997 and 2005 Compaoré)
Eritrea	Gambia	Central African Republic (2026)	Botswana (2008 Mogae; 2018 Khama)	Malawi (2004 Muluzi)	Burundi (2015 Nkurunziza)
eSwatini	South Sudan	Côte d'Ivoire (2020)	Congo DRC (2016/2018 Kabila)	Niger (2009 Tandja)	Cameroon (2011 Biya)
Ethiopia		Equatorial Guinea (2030)	Ghana (2000 Rawlings; 2008 Kufuor)	Nigeria (2007 Obasanjo)	Chad (2006 Déby)
Lesotho		Guinea-Bissau (2020)	Kenya (2002 Moi; 2012 Kibaki)	Zambia (2001 Chiluba)	Congo Rep. (2016 Sassou-Nguesso)
Mauritius		Madagascar (2024)	Liberia (2017 Johnson Sirleaf)		Djibouti (2011 Guelleh)
Somalia		Mauritania (2019)	Mali (2002 Konaré; 2012 Touré**)		Gabon (2005 O. Bongo)
		Seychelles (2025)	Mozambique (2004 Chissano; 2014 Guebuza)		Guinea (2003 Conté)
		South Africa (2029)	Namibia II (2004 Nujoma; 2014 Pohamba)		Namibia I (1999 Nujoma)
		Zimbabwe (2027)			Rwanda (2017 Kagame)

164

São Tomé and Príncipe (2001 Trovoada; 2011 de Menezes)	Senegal (1998 Diouf, 2012 Wade)
Sierra Leone (2007 Kabbah; 2018 Koroma)	Sudan (2005 Bashir)
Tanzania (1995 Mwinyi; 2005 Mkapa; 2015 Kikwete)	Togo (2003 Eyadéma)
	Uganda (2006 Museveni)

[a]*Burkina Faso* and *Namibia* appear twice in the table (marked by "I" & "II"), see hereafter for some details. In *Angola*, following a 2010 constitutional amendment and the 2012 parliamentary election, a two-term limit applies to a president that is indirectly elected based on the result of legislative elections and is not subject to parliamentary confidence; *Botswana, Cape Verde, Ethiopia, Lesotho, Mauritius*, and *South Africa* have parliamentary systems, with Botswana and South Africa combining it with two-term limited indirectly elected executive presidencies (in the case of Botswana this is formally "an aggregate period not exceeding 10 years," art. 34.1, Constitution as amended in 1997) and Cape Verde with a two-term directly elected presidency (first experiencing cohabitation in 2011–2016; ALC considers the prime minister to be the country's leader); in *Burkina Faso*, term limits were introduced in 1991, rescinded in 1997, reintroduced in 2000 (with duration in office reduced from 7 to 5 years), bypassed when Compaoré claimed the new provision was not retroactive and run for two additional terms in 2005 and 2010, and ultimately preserved as Compaoré himself was ousted by mass protests following a new attempt at lifting them in 2014; in *Burundi* whether or not Nkurunziza's first term was to be counted was a matter of controversy; the *Comoros*, between 2001 and 2018, adopted by constitution a four-year rotation of the directly elected presidency between the federation's three islands; in *Congo-Brazzaville*, a new constitution was approved by referendum in 2015, allowing Denis Sassou Nguesso to stand again for office in 2016; in *Congo-DRC*, Joseph Kabila's second mandate expired in 2016, but he prolonged his stay in office for two more years before abiding by the constitution; in *Equatorial Guinea*, the 2011 referendum approved constitutional changes allowing Teodoro Obiang to run in 2016 for the first of another two terms; *Eritrea* does not hold national elections; *eSwatini* is ruled by its monarch; *Gabon* removed the limit of two seven-year presidential terms in 2003, which was not reinstated, as originally pledged, by the 2018 constitutional revision; *Liberia* allows two six-year terms, a limit that was implemented in 2017; in *Mali*, Amani Toumani Touré was ousted in a coup in 2012 shortly before he was meant to step down; in *Namibia*, a 1998 constitutional amendment gave the option of a third term only to the newly independent country's first president, namely Sam Nujoma; in *Rwanda*, Paul Kagame was reelected in 2017, after a 2015 constitutional amendment allowed him to stand again for office until 2034; in *Senegal*, the maximum of two terms allowed by the 1991 constitution was removed in 1998 under Abdou Diouf, who however lost the 2000 election to Abdoulaye Wade; the latter first had term limits reinstated by a new 2001 constitution, if extended from five to seven years, but then tabled constitutional reforms that would have removed them in 2011; the plans were dropped the year prior to the 2012 election by court ruling (since he had been elected before the 2001 introduction of term limits), he lost; eventually, a 2016 constitutional reform reduced presidential terms from seven to five years; in the *Seychelles*, Danny Faure's takeover after James Michel's 2016 resignations will count as a full term toward the newly introduced two-term limit (down from the three terms previously allowed); in *Sudan*, the 2005–2010 transitional government allowed al-Bashir to prolong his stay and then claim a reset of his terms in office when he was reelected in 2010.

Source: adapted from Posner and Young (2018), Reyntjens (2016), Cassani (2014), Africa Center for Strategic Studies (2018), and various other sources.

Burkina Faso in 1997 and, so far, culminating with Burundi at the end of the period. Two of the countries involved – namely, Congo-Brazzaville and Rwanda – only completed the process with reelection of the sitting president in 2016 and 2017, respectively. Senegal was a unique case in that a term evader running for a new mandate eventually proved unable to get the support needed from voters. In certain regimes, the relaxation of presidential limits also included the removal of age requirements, as in Equatorial Guinea, Congo-Brazzaville, and Uganda, whose constitutions originally barred candidates of 70 or 75 years or more from vying for the top job.

Removing constitutional constraints obviously helped a number of long-standing African rulers further prolong their stays in office. From Cameroon to Eritrea, through Equatorial Guinea, Chad, and Sudan, "Africa's crescent of dictators"[9] appeared to perpetuate one of the continent's solid political traditions. In spite of the 2017 departure of José Eduardo Dos Santos and Robert Mugabe – Africa's longest and third-longest serving leaders at the time, respectively – the likes of Teodoro Obiang Nguema, Paul Biya, Yoweri Museveni, Omar Al-Bashir, Idriss Déby, and Isaias Afwerki still qualified among the world's longest-reigning heads of government. As they grew old in office on a continent with the world's most youthful population, some of them – Paul Biya was born in 1933 – also entered the elite group of exceptionally old leaders. While this prospect might have persuaded Dos Santos to gracefully leave power on time, Mugabe waited just too long and was forcefully ousted a very frail man at 93.

Yet, in examining Africa's presidential duration and constitutional manipulations, there is an additional side of the story one should look at. The 41 instances in which an African president's mandate was to end due to a two-term limit, during 1990–2015, were evenly split: in 21 cases, the head of state abided by the constitution and duly stepped down, whereas in the remaining 20 he looked for a way to stay on, either by having the fundamental law itself re-interpreted in his favor or by having it amended or replaced. But, while the incumbents' bids to remain in office were mostly successful – i.e., 15 out of 20 times, including twice in Burkina Faso – one in four such attempts failed (5 cases out of 20), as they were stopped by the courts, the parliament, or

---

[9] Wachira Maina, "One in four African leaders has served more than 20 years," *The East African*, March 14, 2018.

the army (cf. Posner and Young 2018). Zambia and Malawi had pioneered the success of this politics of resistance. Yet the most prominent case of failure was arguably Nigeria. At the time, its ruling president Olusegun Obasanjo was a high-profile and widely respected figure not only in national politics but also on a continental scale. His supporters' attempts to have parliament change the constitution and allow him a possible four more years had catalyzed a nationwide public debate and dangerously stirred political divisions, partly also along ethnic, religious, and regional lines. But the bid was ultimately dashed, in early 2006, by a senate vote rejecting the proposed amendment. Several observers celebrated the outcome, and the president's acceptance of it, as a historic development for the country's politics, "a victory for democratic institutions and a powerful blow against godfather politics" (Sklar et al. 2006:108). As much as Nigeria's road toward democracy remains a long one, there is no denying that a helpful precedent was set in a country with a troubled past and a difficult present. Zoom out again and, comprehensively, tenure limits in Africa were eventually respected, or made to be respected, in little short of two-thirds (63 percent) of all cases.

It should also be noted that, while many countries were dismantling or relaxing term limits, some others introduced them. The latter include Mauritania in 2006, Angola in 2010 (previously unable to organize periodic elections), Equatorial Guinea in 2011, and Zimbabwe in 2013. Here, the devil was often in the details. In the latter three countries, in particular, the new measures were meant to apply retrospectively to serving rulers, each of whom had been in office for over three decades (albeit Angola's Dos Santos subsequently left office before the end of his "first" term, if after a hefty 38 years in power). Other countries made new restrictions on the retention of power real. A 2016 constitutional reform, for example, had the two presidential mandates allowed in Senegal (a country where norms on terms have been highly unstable) shortened from seven to five years. In the Seychelles, on the other hand, James Michel won office for a third time in 2015 and swiftly had his campaign promise of limiting presidential terms to a constitutional maximum of two adopted by parliament, only a few months prior to his surprise resignation in late 2016.[10] In a rare

---

[10] George Thande, "Seychelles votes to limit presidential term limits," *Reuters*, April 5, 2016.

development, Patrice Talon, the cotton businessman and opposition leader elected to the Beninese presidency in 2016, promised to stand down after only one term. The only precedent on the continent was Nelson Mandela.

Explaining Attempts to Alter or Eliminate Term Limits

What explains whether African leaders approaching the end of their allowed stay in office decided that they would respect the word of the constitution and quit or else embarked on attempts to ignore, bypass, or remove such legal hurdles? As a baseline, the presence and reasonable functioning of democratic institutions allowing people a free vote and opposition parties and candidates some chance to gain office made it more likely that, on reaching the conclusion of presidential mandates, exit rules would be enforced and respected (Reyntjens 2016:66). A strong predictor of countries where attempts were made to set the stage for a leader's third mandate, by contrast, was the poor state or absence of democracy, suggesting that "democracy renders term limits effective … [whereas] autocrats are highly unlikely to respect term limits" (Tull and Simons 2017:94; Cheeseman 2016). Very different levels of democracy may explain the overrepresentation of French-speaking countries. If we adopt a 6-point threshold on the –10/+10 Polity scale, Africa's 20 Francophone countries count only 6 "democracies" (averaging a mere 2.2 score) as against 13 out of 20 among Anglophone states (with a 4.6 average score). French-speaking countries represent as many as 68.4 percent (13 out of 19) of all cases where a third term bid emerged, an even stronger 78.6 percent majority among successful cases (11 out of 14), but only a minority of countries where such an attempt was defeated (2 out of 5) and a smaller minority (2 out of 10) among those where no open attempt was launched. Yet, causality seems to be bidirectional. Open endeavors at manipulating term limits never happened in a regime where they had previously been complied with at least once. As with George Washington in the United States, the power of precedent thus proved highly consequential, lending support to the notion that respect for constitutional limits favors a country's democratic progress (cf. Maltz 2007:129), as we already showed to be the case south of the Sahara. When adhered to, Africa's limits on mandates have shown the potential to help remove entrenched authoritarian parties and open up the political space (as happened in Kenya), to reinforce trust between winners and losers (as was the case in Ghana), and to strengthen popular support and thus legitimacy for existing democratic arrangements (as in Benin) (Cheeseman 2010:150ff.).

Besides the level of democracy, a number of other factors played a role in determining the emergence of the so-called third term issue (Posner and Young 2007:135). First, public opinion or voters' attitudes toward the incumbent leader could be a springboard. The larger a president's electoral majority, the more likely he would attempt to prolong his tenure, as exemplified by Daniel Arap Moi's decision to retire as against Sam Nujoma's resolve to stay on. The point is a broader one and concerns the worldwide trend toward the revision of term limits, from Belarus and Kazakhstan in Central Asia to Honduras and Venezuela in Latin America. Many such revisions were spurred by a decline of electoral uncertainty – when compared to that perceived at the time of a country's regime transition – and the consequent feeling, on the part of those in power, that they "no longer require[d] the electoral insurance mechanism that term limits provide" (McKie 2017:454). A second factor appeared to be the age of the incumbent leader. In this case, the younger the ruling president, the more likely he or she would try and remain in office. Older leaders may be more amenable to leave due to their deteriorating health and energy, or because they have groomed sons or other family members in the hope that their moment will soon come. Finally, external pressures by donors have been part of the picture. Such pressures could be particularly effective in countries with larger shares of foreign aid on GDP, which potentially raised the cost of the fight and thus made it less likely that a serving president would resist stepping aside. This situation is mirrored by a higher likeliness of tampering with the two-term provisions in oil-reliant regimes. Ultimately, it was typically younger, more popular and less development aid-dependent heads of state who were more likely to strive to remain in power beyond their second mandate (Posner and Young 2018).

A closer look at East African cases also reveals that a history of frequent political upheavals and the personal background of serving leaders impacted on the shaping of different country trajectories. In the region's three landlocked states – Uganda, Burundi, and Rwanda – former-rebels-turned-presidents refused to leave office, and made sure the constitution allowed them to do so. In Kenya and Tanzania, on the other hand, the set maximum number of mandates has already been complied with by at least two leaders. The legacy of conflict appears to be bad for the deepening of democratic institutions (Cheeseman et al. 2018).

The leaders of Uganda, Burundi, and Rwanda were backed not only by key political actors but also by the security forces. Support from the army can be very important and may have additional dimensions. An army dominated by co-ethnics loyal to the serving president may contribute both to the likeliness of constitutional limits being challenged as well as to the challenge being successful (Harkness 2017). Even where civil mobilization emerged to resist and block such attempts, the outcome typically hinged on the presence of co-ethnic armies (as in Cameroon, Congo-Brazzaville, or Djibouti) as opposed to a multiethnic military (in places such as Zambia in 2001 or Burkina Faso in 2015). African armies thus continue to retain political influence even where direct takeovers have become less common.

Democratic progress, in Africa as well as elsewhere, requires a growing acceptance that constitutional charters and popular votes are meant to be the key determinants of who should govern a country, and for how long. This goes beyond election rules or military attempts at taking over. As political jockeying for position in Malawi got under way following the sudden death of president Bingu wa Mutharika, in 2012, for example, the former and first elected head of state Bakili Muluzi rose to the occasion and urged the country and its national politicians to respect "constitutional order" – "we have to avoid a situation where there is disorder ... we have no choice but to follow the constitution"[11] – and allow a vice president enjoying limited political support to take power under the existing rules of the game. But term limits, because of their high visibility and symbolic as well as political importance, will continue to be at the center of the political turf for quite some time to come. Like coups that abruptly interrupt the functioning of constitutional arrangements, third terms snatched by leaders who interfere or fail to comply with existing legal provisions represent reversals in the process of institutionalization of power (Posner and Young 2007:137), if only generally less dramatically than military interventions.

---

[11] Godfrey Mapondera, David Smith, "Malawi faces power struggle after president reported dead," *Guardian*, April 6, 2012.

No-Limit Families: Dynastic Succession in Africa

One way a degree of power continuity has been granted beyond the terms of office of some African presidents – and typically also beyond their lives – is through succession by a family member. With the only exceptions of eSwatini (an absolute monarchy) and Lesotho (a parliamentary monarchy), all of today's sub-Saharan states are republics. By definition, the latter are meant to embody nonpersonal (i.e., a *res publica* is a public thing) and thus also nonhereditary forms of rule. Yet, in practice, a formal republican set up may on occasions disguise a dynastic essence, where a dynasty is "a system where power is held by a family, a succession of rulers who belong to the same family" (Yates 2017:340).

Non-royal dynastic or quasi-dynastic politics does retain some influence across the contemporary world. The Kennedys, the Bushes, and the Clintons in the United States or the Trudeaus in Canada show that the political role of power families is not a phenomenon limited to poor authoritarian countries. Among developing areas, on the other hand, it is Asian countries that have most frequently seen the emergence of presidents or prime ministers who were the sons and daughters of former leaders, albeit not always their immediate successors. This has occurred in states of a wildly different political nature, from Syria and Azerbaijan to Pakistan, Bangladesh, and India, from South Korea to Indonesia and the Philippines.

Rulers across the world – particularly in nondemocratic regimes – look at their own succession and at how they deal with it as a key and challenging issue that will affect their political and at times even physical survival. Who follows in one's footsteps, for example, may crucially determine the outgoing leader's future individual freedom as well as material welfare. The inner circle of power, as a whole, is likely similarly concerned. Uncertainty is often heightened by the lack of succession procedures. Some recent evidence, however, seems to show that the death of dictators is not as consequential as is typically either hoped (by those who see it as an opportunity for a democratic opening) or feared (by the regime insiders who are against political change). Ultimately, political elites tend to coalesce around a successor as their best option for political continuity, rather than fragment through infighting (Kendall-Taylor and Frantz 2016).

Common wisdom sees hereditary successions as a manifestation of personalistic, neopatrimonial, and corrupt regimes. Yet this need not be necessarily the case, as it was not in Taiwan and Singapore. Given a ruler's vulnerable position and security dilemma – whereby by clearly raising a successor he positions a political contender who may then try to replace him (the so-called crown-prince problem) – Tullock's hypothesis posits that hereditary succession provides "a method for regime stability during and beyond a ruler's lifetime" (Brownlee 2007:605). The combination of a genealogical principle (i.e., a clear line of inheritance) and a generational gap (i.e., due to his younger age, a son can afford to wait, a brother may not) provides mutual security. By offering guarantees of political stability and continuity, particularly where there are no established party mechanisms for organizing a succession, the son-heir can offer "a focal point for reducing uncertainty, achieving [elite] consensus, and forestalling a power vacuum" (Brownlee 2007:597).

Successions in non-monarchic authoritarian states have not been closely scrutinized, the main exceptions being historically disciplined political successions in places such as Mexico, the Soviet Union, and China. The vast majority of dictators were in no position to choose their own successor. They were either constrained by term limits determining the end of their rule, or they were removed by their parties, by a coup, by an election defeat, or by foreign imposition. Out of 258 autocrats who were in office for at least three years over the 1946–2006 period, only 52 were able to pick their own successors, and only 9 of them were successful in preparing a hereditary handover to their offspring (Brownlee 2007). This is what Hafez al-Assad did when handing over power to his son Bashar al-Assad in Syria, in 2000. The other cases were Nicaragua (1956), Dominican Republic (1960), Haiti (1961), Taiwan (1975), North Korea (1994), Azerbaijan (2003), Singapore (2004), and Togo (2005). Post-2006 cases include at least Gabon (2009) and North Korea (2011).

Once the eSwatini monarchy is excluded, sub-Saharan Africa counts seven countries that were led by the son (in one case the brother) of a previous president[12]. Three of these were the offspring of a founding leader – namely, Ian Khama in Botswana, Uhuru Kenyatta in Kenya, and Navin Rangolaam in Mauritius – who took office through peaceful and reasonably open elections after a 13-to-34-year interlude after

---

[12] Vera Songwe, "From father to son: Africa's leadership transitions and lessons," *Brookings*, May 6, 2015.

their father left it. Africa's only democratic back-to-back, father-to-son succession occurred in Mauritius, in 2017, when Anerood Jugnauth, who had been in and out of power for almost four decades, handed it over to Pravind Kumar Jugnauth. Malawi, on the other hand, is the only country where two brothers were voted to the presidency, with only a couple of years separating Bingu wa Mutharika's death in office from the election of his sibling Peter Mutharika. The remaining three countries experienced continuous familial rule as the passing of a serving authoritarian ruler opened the way for his son's direct rise to power. While the Kabilas' hold on the Congo-DRC is a relatively more recent affair that "only" began in 1997, Togo and Gabon were ruled uninterruptedly for over 50 years by the Gnassingbé Eyadéma/Faure Gnassingbé and Omar Bongo/Ali Bongo Ondimba father-and-son duos (if, in both cases, with the brief interim of façade office-holders). In all three cases, hereditary succession was accompanied by a controlled process of electoral legitimation – generating the semblance of a "dynastic democracy" – as a way to try and appease both external actors as well as domestic ones.

A larger than proportional share of world leaders who recently died in office did so while at the helm of an African country. Since 2008, as many as 10 out of 19 serving leaders who passed away were sub-Saharan, namely Guinea's Lansana Conté and Zambia's Levy Mwanawasa (2008), Gabon's Omar Bongo and Guinea-Bissau's João Bernardo Vieira (2009) – the latter as a result of an assassination – Nigeria's Umaru Yar'Adua (2010), four colleagues who followed in 2012 alone (Malam Bacai Sanhá of Guinea-Bissau, John Atta Mills of Ghana, Bingu wa Mutharika of Malawi, and Meles Zenawi of Ethiopia), and Zambia's Michael Sata, the last name on the list, in 2014. Ethiopia, Ghana, Malawi, and Zambia are the four "latest cases of smooth succession following the death of a leader [and] provide evidence that Africa is gradually getting its transitions right."[13] In all, however, it must be noted that across Africa it was only in 3 out of 43 cases where the leader passed away in office – whether due to natural causes (23) or assassination (20) – that they were succeeded by their own sons, namely, as already mentioned, in Congo-DRC, Togo, and Gabon. This may be all the more surprising given the

---

[13] Kingsley Ighobore, "Politics of succession: coping when leaders die," *Africa Renewal*, January 2013.

authoritarian or semi-authoritarian nature of a number of regimes on the continent and the virtually omnipresent speculation that an ageing or ailing leader is lining up a member of his family as a successor. Ensuring a dynastic succession is thus the hardest goal – and a potentially destabilising one, as demonstrated by north African countries such as Egypt, Tunisia, and Libya[14] – even for the longest-serving and most entrenched among so-called personal rulers.

The list of rumored and failed attempts at dynastic successions is long. Among recent cases, two peculiar failures were Zimbabwe and South Africa. In Harare, the controversial rise of Robert Mugabe's wife, Grace, ultimately unleashed a backlash from within the old president's own circle that led to his ousting. In Pretoria, Jacob Zuma failed to have his former wife win the leadership of the ruling African National Congress (ANC), a preliminary step for her to succeed him at State House and to halt Cyril Ramaphosa's rise to the presidency. In both cases, the presence of a strong party appeared to be a decisive factor in hindering the incumbent's plans. As it possibly was in Angola, where José Eduardo dos Santos had been rumored to be working for his daughter or son to inherit power, and "yet, to the surprise of many," the president ultimately "handpicked" the former Minister of Defence, João Lourenço.[15] In Senegal, popular reactions forced Abdoulaye Wade to drop planned constitutional changes that, by appointing him vice president as well as by requiring less than a majority of popular votes to win the presidency, would have made it easier for his son Karim to succeed him. Facing widespread criticism, Wade went on to lose his own contentious bid for a new electoral mandate in 2012. But the temptation remains and a number of familial heirs-in-waiting are still to meet their fate in countries such as Uganda (for the better part of the past two decades, Maj. Gen. Muhoozi Kainerugaba is said to have been groomed and promoted through the ranks of the army in view of succeeding his father Yoweri Museveni) and Equatorial Guinea (Teodoro Obiang Nguema, who has been in office since ousting his uncle Francisco Macias Nguema and having him executed, appointed his controversial son "Teodorín" Nguema Obiang Mangue as vice president in 2012). The latter case reminds us of how difficult it is to pass on political power to be

---

[14] James Moody, "Familial succession and violence across Africa," ACLED.
[15] Tom Collins, "African ruling dynasties," *New African*, January 2, 2018.

No-Limit Families: Dynastic Succession in Africa

retained within the family network – something that in a sense already occurred once through a first handover (which in Equatorial Guinea, as said, occurred violently) and evokes Ibn Khaldoun's six-century-old warning that "as a rule, no dynasty lasts beyond the life span of three generations" (197:136, quoted in Yates 2017:357).

7 Leading for Development? (I)
Economic Growth

Assessing Progress: Selected Dimensions of Development

To where are leaders supposed to "lead" their nations? Except maybe for times of international or domestic war, the hallmark of successful leadership is not survival in office, as we pointed out, but rather a leader's will and capacity to favor his or her country's progress. Our approach posits that the diverse modes of leadership transfer – and, notably, the introduction of electoral competition and the possibility of alternation in office – impact on development by generating distinctive incentives for leaders to pursue common interests and progress. It is now time to assess in a systematic manner whether empirical evidence supports our expectations about a leadership-development nexus in African countries since independence.

As lasting debates and countless definitions aimed at capturing its essence have revealed, a nation's development has wide range of facets. In order to produce a reasonably diversified and yet parsimonious account of the expected implications of leadership – our key explanatory factor – distinct dimensions of economic, social, and political advancement need to be selected. We thus identified economic growth (which we examine in this chapter), social welfare, state consolidation, and corruption control (all explored in the next chapter), respectively, as our main dependent variables.

As much as it is a mistake to conflate economic growth with development – gross domestic product variations only capture a limited part of a country's progress and transformations – economic expansion remains a necessary component of any development process at least in the poorer regions of the contemporary world. Most if not all political leaders arguably share a concern with growth, but they do not necessarily prioritize it in the same way. With rare exceptions, however, the literature on growth and development fails to examine the actual role of leadership in fostering or hindering a country's economic progress. As we mentioned in Chapter 1, leadership is essentially absent from among the drivers of growth scrutinized by the existing literature. We want to fill this gap.

The socioeconomic transformations of a nation, as pointed out, go well beyond the expansion – or contraction – of its gross domestic product. Actual changes in the welfare and living conditions of ordinary people are only partly related to their country's overall economic improvement. To a significant degree, they also depend on the freedom individuals have to pursue their own well-being as much as on the resources and means they can use to realize it, including public interventions that are introduced as a response to social needs. Social policies are in turn affected, among others, by factors such as a country's policy tradition, party or ideological perspectives, or leadership orientations toward, and responsiveness to, distributive and social justice issues. How a leader comes to office – and what is required for him or her to remain there – arguably influences the extent to which he or she will strive to improve the social welfare of the largest part of the population.

The notion that political leadership also impacts the consolidation of the state may be less straightforward than the idea that leaders affect their countries' economic growth and social welfare. In young and often poor and fragile states, stabilizing political order and strengthening the public administrative apparatus is a core challenge and an essential component of the process of development, if not a precondition for it. Power-holders – who by definition sit at the top of the state's coercive system and administrative structure – have a role to play. As much as an orientation toward the predation of public resources and a neo-patrimonial distribution of rents and private goods likely weakens a state's functioning, institutionalization, and performance, the latter can be improved when leaders choose – or are induced – to focus more on common interests and public goods. Thus, besides state and administrative capacity, a leader's capacity to control corruption as such deserves special attention in the context of our examination of the impact of leadership effects.

Leadership Dynamics and Development: Drivers and Hypotheses

Our hypotheses build on the arguments we developed in Chapter 2 and stem from the overarching assumption that, in the presence of periodic multiparty votes as regularized procedures for leadership successions, African leaders tend to respond to electoral incentives. In doing so, they likely contribute to better development performances, including the achievement of higher growth rates, improved welfare results, gradual state strengthening, and lower corruption levels. Pressures are more likely felt when elections are reiterated, competitive, favoring succession in office, or open to alternation in power. In principle, they supposedly touch their strongest point when the electoral and non-electoral components of a country's political setup – such as respect for individual freedoms and the independent media – reach closer to those of a genuinely democratic system. Yet we posit that electoral practices are likely to produce some effects even when the system is democratically deficient. By contrast, non-elected leaders (i.e., leaders who come to office through non-electoral means, whether violent or not, including single-party or no-party voting) generally have weaker reasons to promote and improve the provision of public goods and good governance. Unregulated power grabs and stays in office, in particular, will more often go hand in hand with a type of rule that is more authoritarian, personalized, corrupt, ineffective and, ultimately, less responsive to bottom-up demands for social improvements and progress.

We list hereafter all the conjectures that we set out to investigate empirically. At this stage, they are deliberately formulated in broad reference to "development performances," as they are here meant to comprehensively accommodate the distinct aspects of development that we singled out for investigation and that we shall return to, individually, in the different sections where we present the empirical analyses.

We start by positing a general link between a leader's length of stay in office and a country's development progress. As previously pointed out, this may take a more direct and linear form, whereby new leaders concentrate their fresh efforts in the early stages of their tenure, while subsequent periods will show a decline in their interest and capacity to promote change against growing frictions, conflicts, and obstacles. Alternatively, we may expect a slightly more complex scenario where a leader will first need time to settle in and learn the ropes, move beyond the initial fluidity and uncertainty, build support, capacity and better control of the state machinery, and only then will he/she actually be in a position to plan and implement initiatives favoring a country's improvement and thus to make a more substantial impact.

Once again, however, this push will erode as time goes by, leading to a gradual slowdown of performances and thus to an overall curvilinear trend. We therefore set out with the following hypotheses:

HP 2 (duration, linear). *The longer leaders remain in office, the worse their country's development performance*

HP 2.1 (duration, curvilinear). *The association between a leader's tenure and his or her country's development performance is non-linear: it takes time to materialize, peaks and then gradually weakens*

The next hypotheses reflect our core perspective. They build on the notion that electoral incentives play a crucial role in directing a leader's efforts toward the betterment of his/her country rather than having him/her focus on shorter time horizons, narrower interests, and more private goods. We expect a more open and democratic context to raise the stakes and pressures for leaders to pursue development achievements. Yet, rather than ruling out any impact of multiparty electoral processes that take place in nondemocratic setups, we still leave room for the latter to affect the concerns and thus the behavior of powerholders in a direction more favorable to their countries' progress than is commonly the case with non-elected leaders.

HP 3 (elected). *Elected leaders are associated with better development performances than non-elected leaders*

HP 3.1 (elected, democratic). *Leaders elected in a democratic context are associated with better development performances than non-elected leaders and leaders elected in non-democratic contexts*

Time may be a relevant factor not only when reasoning about an individual leader's accomplishments, but also to account for the actual functioning of the abovementioned pressures and mechanisms. Both a nation's leaders and voters need time to understand the full implications of electoral practices as mechanisms favoring the matching of demands and responses. Learning by doing implies that an important key is the repeated practice of multiparty elections (Lindberg 2006, 2009). The more elections, the more likely that leaders and voters will make them work, at least to a degree, the way they should work. To count the number of elections a country cumulates, we opted for including all past polls regardless of temporal disconnections, since previous voting experiences may constitute something akin to a valuable electoral "capital" citizens can refer back to. This means, for example, that we consider and count Uganda's 1980 multiparty vote as a starting ground upon which the country could build when it restored multipartism in 2006. Finally, similarly to what we did with HP 3.1, we posit that recurrent votes are more likely to improve development performances when they are combined with other democratic requisites, such as the autonomy of the courts and a political environment that is open to independent media and civic activism. Therefore:

HP 4 (cumulative elections). *The longer the series of cumulative elections in a country, the better its development performance*

HP 4.1 (cumulative democratic elections). *The longer the series of cumulative democratic elections in a country, the better its development performance*

While, in principle, electoral practices are meant to offer real chances for political competition, this does not always turn out to be the case. Yet competition may remain a key stimulus for chosen leaders to accomplish more. In other words, when a president's share of votes (or, in a parliamentary form of government, his/her party's or coalition's share of legislative seats) is non-overwhelming, he or she is forced to "sweat" to get elected or reelected. Elections that are more competitive – as Strøm (1989:7) put it "elections are more contestable if voters tend to shift away from incumbents than if the opposite is the case" – raise the stakes and the incentives to engage and bear fruitful results. Thus:

HP 5 (competitive election). *The more competitive an election, the more likely an elected leader is to have a positive impact on a country's development performance*

Succession and alternation in office are critical notions in our view of leadership changes. Particularly in African contexts that have seen so many cases of long-lasting and stagnant leadership spells, power handovers can represent important renewal opportunities even when they do not amount to the advent of entirely new political forces. Succession can be a way of renovating a country's political leadership within the context of stable or relatively stable control by the same ruling party. As much as a succession at times implies little or no change, it can represent a midway stop – and an opportunity for broader political and policy change – on the way toward full-fledged turnovers. João Lourenço's recent rise to power in Angola, where he replaced long-time ruler José Eduardo Dos Santos in late 2017, is a case in point.

HP 6 (succession). *Leaders reaching power through electoral successions are associated with better development performances than non-elected leaders and incumbents confirmed in office*

Electoral turnovers, on the other hand, mark a clearer discontinuity through which power shifts to new actors and political forces, implying "a high level of electoral competitiveness" (Strøm 1989:7) that, on occasions, only becomes apparent *ex post*. Government/opposition alternation is the definitive and most concrete indication that office-holders can indeed lose power, and thus that the incumbent must take an interest in what concerns voters if he or she wants to be reelected. Alternation implies that voters were unhappy with the outgoing government and opted for someone different to adjust policy without regime interruptions. Uncertainty remains limited. Whereas irregular changes can prove to be "a disruptive source of uncertainty and instability," ordered alternation promotes "accountability and error correction through political competition ... and might yield benefits to citizens just as market competition yields benefits to consumers" (Feng 1997:397; Horowitz et al. 2009:107–108). Finally, alternations are most effective when they are repeated and cumulated, since this further engrains the notion that power is only retained when those in office achieve tangible results that are rewarded by voters.

For both of our alternation hypotheses, we consider a government turnover to take place at the time of so-called founding elections (i.e., when an electoral regime is first introduced) only if the outgoing, pre-transition leader (or a candidate from his/her party or openly sponsored by him or her) runs for election and loses the race (see also Chapter 3 on this point).

HP 7 (alternation). *Leaders reaching power through electoral alternations are associated with better development performances than non-elected leaders and incumbents confirmed in office*

HP 7.1 (cumulative alternations). *Multiparty regimes in which more electoral alternations took place over time have better development performances than multiparty regimes in which such instances were less frequent or never took place at all.*

Explanatory Factors

Before turning to a detailed description of the different dependent variables and then to a discussion of our empirical findings, we introduce hereafter the main explanatory factors that we use to test the research hypotheses advanced previously and that are shared by all our empirical analyses. Table A3 in the Appendix reports a basic description of our leadership-change related explanatory variables and descriptive statistics (including those for HP 1 and HP 1.1, which we examined in Chapter 5). To test HP2 and HP2.1, we measured the duration in office (*duration*, expressed in number of years) at time *t* for each non-interim leader, that is power-holders that remained in office for at least one year. In the statistical models aimed at testing HP2.1, which postulates a nonlinear relation between a leader's length of stay in office and a country's development performance, duration is also included as a squared term (*duration^2*).

To test HP3 and HP3.1, we developed a categorical index coded "1" when a leader takes power by non-electoral means or through non-contested elections (*non-elected leader*), "2" when a leader takes power through multiparty elections (*elected leader*), and "3" when a leader is elected in an institutional context regarded as democratic (*democratically elected leader*). We deem a political regime democratic if its Polity2 score is equal to or higher than 6. *Elected leader* and *democratically elected leader* are simultaneously included in the same model, while non-elected leader serves as a reference category.

For HP4, we recorded the total *number of multiparty elections* for the executive held prior to or at any time *t*. We count presidential elections in systems that envisage a direct vote for the chief executive, and legislative elections for parliamentary systems. HP4.1 is tested by measuring the *number of democratic multiparty elections*, namely presidential or legislative elections that take place in years for which a country is deemed democratic according to Polity2. To account for the stock of elections cumulated by any given country since independence, the count for (democratic) multiparty elections is down to zero for any year in a no-elections period (e.g., a phase of single-party or military rule), but, if and when elections are reintroduced, it resumes starting from the highest value previously reached.

To test HP5, *executive control* measures the vote share obtained by the president in elections for the chief executive (or the share of seats obtained by the governing party or coalition in the lower or single house of a parliamentary system). The higher the level of *executive control*, the less the competitiveness of an election. For elected leaders, the share of votes or seats obtained at the time of the election is

Explanatory Factors 183

reentered for each successive year until a fresh election is held or a new leader takes office. A leader replacing an incumbent who was elected via multiparty elections but subsequently resigned inherits the vote or seat share of his predecessor until a new election takes place. Leaders that were either not elected or elected via single-party or non-party elections are assigned a score of 100 (i.e., 100 percent of votes or seats) as they are assumed to exert the strongest control over the executive. Considering the latter as missing would have dramatically reduced the number of observations making an empirical test of HP5 virtually impossible.

We then construct a categorical index to test HP6 and HP7. These postulate, respectively, that a leader acceding to office by electoral succession or alternation will favor the achievement of better political, economic, and social development results than both non-elected leaders and leaders reelected via multiparty elections. The term "succession" denotes a situation in which a multiparty vote leads to the rise of a new leader belonging to the same party of the outgoing leader, whereas the term "alternation" refers to a multiparty vote leading to the replacement of an incumbent by an opposition leader. We build a categorical variable coded "0" for each country-year for which a *non-elected leader* (including leaders elected via single-party or non-party elections) is in power, "1" when an *incumbent reelected* via a multiparty vote is in office, "2" in case a new leader emerges after an *electoral succession*, and "3" when a new leader comes to office following an *electoral alternation*. A leader that comes to power via succession or alternation remains in that same category during all his/her regular terms in office, but he/she is then coded as an *incumbent reelected* for any additional terms obtained by altering or bypassing constitutional term limits. *Incumbent reelected, electoral succession,* and *electoral alternation* are entered simultaneously in the same statistical models, while *non-elected leader* serves as a reference category.

Finally, to test HP7.1 on the cumulative effect of electoral alternations we created another categorical variable. The latter is coded "1" for *regimes without multiparty systems*, "2" for countries where multipartism never led to government turnovers (*multiparty regimes with no alternation*), "3" for multiparty regimes that, at any given time *t*, had only experienced one turnover (*multiparty regimes with one alternation*), and "4" for regimes that experienced at least two (*multiparty regimes with more than one alternation*). Regimes without multiparty *system* serves as the reference category. The validity of HP7.1 was also examined through a different explanatory factor that measures the total number of multiparty alternations a country has cumulated at any time t. While this variable is more straightforward, we preferred the categorical indicator since it permits a better estimation of the impact of Huntington's (1993) "two turnover test" on a country's political, economic, and social development.

Research Design and Methodological Issues

In Chapter 3 we described the scope and structure of the Africa Leadership Change dataset, which provides a key part of the data employed in the analyses presented in this and in the next chapter. To test the research hypotheses advanced previously, we merged the ALC data on leadership dynamics with data on the political, macro-economic, and social performances of African countries that are made available by other cross-country sources and that we introduce in the following sections. The resulting dataset covers all 49 countries of sub-Saharan Africa (N = 49) from 1960, or subsequent year of independence, to June 30, 2018 (from T = 8 for South Sudan, which became independent only in 2011, to T = 59 for countries that reached or had already reached independence in 1960), that is, an unbalanced dataset with a total of 2,575 observations.

The country-year is our basic unit of analysis and we thus employed appropriate time-series cross-sectional (TSCS) techniques. Panel data offer important advantages. First, since variables vary along two dimensions, namely years and countries, the number of degrees of freedom increases, thus strengthening the efficiency of the estimates with respect to a cross-sectional dataset with the same number of observations. Second, they allow the researcher to measure the effect of a country's behavior, observable with cross-sectional data, in its temporal evolution, usually emphasized by time series data. Finally, panel data provide internal instruments: endogenous regressors can easily be replaced by transformations or lags in the independent variables, which are highly correlated with the endogenous regressors, but not with the error term.

Some temporal and spatial properties of this kind of data, however, make their use problematic. In particular, panel data violate some assumptions that lie at the basis of OLS techniques. They are likely to exhibit contemporaneous correlation of the residuals (i.e., residuals from different cross-sections in the same time-period can be correlated) in addition to the more usual time-series' property of serial-correlation and the typical cross-sections' property of heteroskedasticity. The joint effect of contemporaneous correlation, serial-correlation, and heteroskedasticity may lead to inefficient estimates and inconsistent standard errors. Therefore, following Beck and Katz's (1995) advice, we employed panel-corrected standard errors (PCSE), the commonly used technique for the analysis of panel data. More precisely, to deal with the temporal and spatial properties of our data we first regressed our dependent variable on its lagged level and the lagged levels of independent and control variables. Accordingly, the first estimated equation has the following general form:

$$Y_{it} = \alpha + \beta_1 Y_{it-1} + \beta_2 X_{it-1} + \sum \beta_j \text{Controls}_{it-1} + \varepsilon_{it}$$

Where Y_{it} is the value of the dependent variable measured in country i in year t; α is the constant, Y_{it-1} is the lagged level of each dependent variable multiplied by its estimated coefficient, β_1. X_{it-1} is the lagged level of the main independent variable – accounting for the different aspects of leaders' rotation in office – multiplied by its estimated coefficient, β_2. Finally, Controls$_{it-1}$ is a (k × 1) vector of lagged control variables, taken in levels; β_j is a (k × 1) vector of coefficients with the subscript j referring to the particular explanatory variable, ε_{it} is the error term. Given the strongly inert nature of most of development indicators, the effect of a leadership change may take time to become evident. Thus, we checked the validity of our main results by including explanatory factors and controls at one-, three-, and five-years lagged intervals, which might broadly be thought of as corresponding to different moments within or at the end of a leader's time span in office.

However, with the exclusion of variables measuring economic growth, tests for panel unit root on the indicators of social welfare, corruption, and state consolidation used as dependent variables with various lagged differences, and with and without trends, failed to reject the null hypothesis according to which all the series are stationary. The same tests, when applied to our regressors, revealed that several control variables also have unit root. To deal with the non-stationarity nature of the measures of social welfare, corruption control, and state consolidation, we applied a more sophisticated technique called the

Error Correction Model (ECM). This method appropriately manages the non-stationarity of the dependent variable. It also allows for a more sensible treatment of dynamics – notably the distinction between short- and long-term effects of our explanatory factors – thus improving our ability to link theory and quantitative analysis (de Boef and Keele 2008). This method regresses the change in the dependent variable on its lagged level, the lagged level of each potential co-integrating factor, and whatever other levels or differences theory or empirics may suggest. Provided that the coefficient of the lagged dependent variable in levels is negative, this approach provides valid estimates. Accordingly, the general form of the estimation equation is the following:

$$\Delta Y_{it} = \alpha + \lambda Y_{it-1} + \sum \beta_j \Delta X_{it-1}$$
$$+ \sum \beta_j X_{it-1} + \sum \beta_j \Delta Controls_{it-1} + \sum \beta_j Controls_{it-1} + \varepsilon_{it}$$

where ΔY_{it} is the change in the dependent variable in country i in year t from one year to the next. X_{it-1} is a vector of (k × 1) explanatory variables, with the subscript j referring to the particular explanatory variable. α is the intercept and ε is the disturbance term. Short-term effects are measured by the estimated coefficient β_j of any differenced independent variable. These refer to momentum-like relations between changes in independent and dependent variables. The long-term effects are captured by dividing the coefficient β_j of any independent variable in levels by λ, called the error correction rate. Long-term effects should be interpreted as equilibrium-like relations between independent and dependent variables in levels. $Controls_{it-1}$ is a (k × 1) vector of control variables that, according to specific theoretical justifications, are included in the model in its differenced and/or lagged level. Time-invariant control variables are included only in their lagged levels. As suggested by Beck and Katz (1995), we adopt an ordinary least square estimator with panel-corrected standard errors (PCSE) to correct for panel heteroskedasticity in the data structure.

In models employing ECM our explanatory factors are entered in both level *t−1* and first-difference. When our explanatory factor is a categorical variable, its value in first-difference should be interpreted as the discrete change between the values it assumes at time *t* and at time *t−1*. Therefore, in the case of the dummy variable coded "1" for each country-year an elected leader was in office, its value in first-difference equal to "1" indicates that in that specific country-year a leader who took office via multiparty elections replaced a non-elected leader. However, we have distinct expectations with regard to when the predicted impact on different dependent variables should come true. Given the strongly inert nature of indicators operationalizing the outputs and outcomes of social welfare – such as primary and secondary school enrolment rate, life expectancy at birth, and under-five mortality rates – we plausibly expect the effects of leadership changes to become significant only in the long period. The same goes for economic growth, though we did not employ ECM in models testing the validity of our hypotheses on this dependent variable. On the other hand, when testing our research hypotheses for health spending, state consolidation, and corruption control, in the next chapter, we expect the impact of the independent factors to also be significant in the short period.

Since the independent variables we employ to test our hypotheses refer to different aspects of leadership dynamics, they are strongly interrelated. Therefore, to appropriately disentangle the net effects displayed by every proposed explanatory factor on different dependent variables we run separate regression models, each one including only one independent variable and the controls.

As we shall discuss in the next sections, the literature on sub-Saharan Africa identifies several important drivers of development that are time-invariant. Since the latter may make the relationship between leadership changes and development spurious, we decided to include them in our analyses. Because these variables do not vary over time, their inclusion in the regression models forced us to exclude country dummies, which are collinear to them. However, as a robustness check we run regression models substituting time-invariant variables with country dummies. Furthermore, the statistical models also include a dummy coded "1" for all the observations after 1989. This variable allows us to account for the generally more positive economic and social trends experienced by much of the continent from the 1990s. Again, the robustness of our results to time trends was also examined by substituting the dummy for post-1990 observations with a series of dummies for each decade (with the 1960s as reference decade), for each year and for each year passed since the country's independence, respectively.

Finally, the robustness of our findings was assessed by regressing our dependent variables (i.e., its value at time t or in first difference) on independent and control variables in TSCS models including country-fixed effects. The inclusion of country-fixed effects has the advantage of containing the risk of missing important country-level characteristics that may confound the analysis and for which data are not available. On the other hand, this technique implies a dramatic reduction of the degrees of freedom and limits the explanatory potential of the estimated model by only allowing within-country variations. For this reason, we checked the validity of the main results obtained by PCSE models by also running TSCS fixed-effects regressions both with and without the inclusion of control variables.

Economic Growth

Theoretical Approaches and Key Determinants

The literature on the determinants of economic growth has focused extensively on sub-Saharan Africa as the locus of the "economic tragedy of the 20th century" (Artadi and Sala-i-Martin 2004; Easterly and Levine 1997). Particularly after the 1973 international oil shock, the region's young sovereign states failed not only to gain an 'independence dividend' in terms of overall economic progress, but also to increase their per capita income levels toward convergence with emerging and advanced nations. This became ever more disturbing when compared to what was being achieved in other developing regions, especially in parts of Asia.

Accounts of *why* exactly this "tragedy" took place vary. On the one hand – and rather unhelpfully as an answer – it has been argued that Africa failed to grow because it is Africa. According to Barro (1991), when an Africa dummy is added to regressions including most nations in the world, this variable explains between 1 percent and 2 percent of the annual growth shortfall experienced by the region since independence. But the mystery remained as to what laid behind the dummy itself (Englebert 2000). Thus, the economic literature also nurtured an empirical strand expressly focused on Africa that tried to unpack the actual factors constraining economic expansion in the continent.

Early accounts using cross-country data suggested that investment rates matter for growth. Countries with higher levels of physical investments grow more rapidly than countries with lower levels of investments (Barro 1991, 2003; Levine and Renelt 1992). Investments in

Africa have been comparatively lower than in other world regions. While gross capital formation as a share of GDP in East Asia increased from 29.3 percent in 1960 to 41.6 percent in 2010, in sub-Saharan Africa it only rose from 17.9 percent to 20.5 percent. This was largely due to well-documented problems of investment climate, capital flight (Collier, Hoeffler, and Pattillo 2004) and a corruption-driven diversion of resources (Shleifer and Vishny 1993).

The importance of capital accumulation can be extended to also include human capital, typically measured through education or health indicators. Glewwe and colleagues (2014), for example, find that African countries with higher levels of schooling per worker tend to grow more than relatively under-schooled nations. These findings are confirmed by Akyüz and Gore (2001) who compare the development trajectories of East Asia and Africa and link much of Africa's missed growth opportunities to its comparatively lower levels of schooling. The impact of life expectancy on economic growth, on the other hand, has recently been the subject of debate and contradictory findings (Acemoglu and Johnson 2007, Bloom et al. 2010, Desbordes 2011).

Other frequently cited factors of economic progress – or lack of it – are state intervention, demographic growth, and development aid. There is virtual consensus, among economists, that excessive levels of state intervention in the economy – typically measured as the share of government consumption on GDP – have a negative effect on growth performances. Population growth can, on the contrary, be a powerful driver of economic development (Mankiw et al. 1990). When studying growth in Africa, however, demography appears to play an unexpected role: if a "large population has been positively correlated with growth among non-African developing countries ... this effect is largely absent in SSA ... where the population-weighted data suggest, if anything, lagging performance by the larger countries" (Ndulu and O'Connell 2008:15). Finally, development assistance is also claimed to contribute to growth, particularly for Africa's recent economic trend (OECD 2010). However, the empirical literature is more cautious in drawing a positive link between aid and growth south of the Sahara (Arndt et al. 2010, Bourguignon and Sundberg 2007).

A different set of theoretical and empirical accounts of Africa's economic failures calls upon factors that are somewhat more region-specific. Broadly speaking, this literature can be divided into two main strands: the first explains the region's shortcomings by looking at its endowments, the second by focusing on its policies, institutions and governance practices. Investigations that focus on endowments, in turn, offer three main kinds of motives. First, Africa is underdeveloped because the continent is located at the tropics. Tropical climate exacts a higher price than other climates in terms of human and animal diseases, technical change, agricultural productivity, and wearing down of infrastructures (Bloom et al. 1998, Gallup et al. 1998, Sachs 2001). Second, African states lag behind in terms of development because they are geographically isolated: being landlocked (16 nations out of 49) or being distant from the most important markets implies higher transportation costs for exports (Sachs and Warner 1997) and reduces opportunities for accessing developed markets (Redding and Venables 2004). This hinders Africa's ability to trade and thus grow. The third explanation drawing on Africa's endowments has to do with natural resources. Dismal growth performances are due to the fact that many countries in the region suffer from the resource curse (Auty 2001). Resource abundance retards development because it encourages rent-seeking behaviors and conflicts (Collier and Hoeffler 1998, Herbst 2000), while at the same time it makes economic management more difficult due to resource price volatility and Dutch disease (Poelhekke and Van der Ploeg 2007).

Endowment-based explanations are discarded by studies suggesting that the reasons for Africa's poor growth record are related to its politics, policies, and institutions (cf. Acemoglu and Robinson 2012:45ff.). The dispute between the natural endowments and the governance hypotheses has profound policy implications, since the former assumes the presence of "essentially permanent sources of slow growth in Africa" (Ndulu and O'Connell 2008:43) that the second does not.

The idea that governance matters for economic development dates back to Adam Smith and was later expanded by new institutional economists led by Douglass North. Acemoglu et al. (2001a, 2001b, 2012), for example, suggest that natural conditions originally influenced the type of colonial institutions (i.e., more or less extractive) and through them a country's long-term path of development. Nunn (2008), on the other hand, dates the underdevelopment of Africa back to the slave trade period. Easterly and Levine (1997) suggested that a particularly high level of ethnic fractionalization of the continent negatively affects the quality of its political institutions and policies. Englebert (2000) articulates a not-to-distant argument when he claims that Africa's newly independent states lacked domestic legitimacy due to institutions that were superimposed over pre-colonial arrangements. This frequently led ruling élites to prefer short-term, growth-averse distributive and neo-patrimonial policies that would help them build alliances and consolidate their power, rather than opt for long-term developmental strategies. Collier et al. (2003) claim that Africa suffers from slow growth due to violent conflicts that exact a high price in terms of development. A plethora of other studies link the continent's economic failure to poor institutional qualities (cf. Aron 2000), widespread neo-patrimonial practices (cf. Bach 2011), or inadequate policies (Sachs and Warner 1997, Azam et al. 2002, Ndulu et al. 2008), at times proxied by such indicators as real exchange rate overvaluation or inflation rates (Easterly and Levine 1997).

The key point of many explanations is summed up by McGowan when he points that:

politics matters greatly for economic growth. Economic growth results from investment, and the expected profitability of investment is determined, in part, by two political factors: the extent to which the economy favours production instead of diversion and the stability of the economic environment. Poor political leadership encourages resource diversion by means of corruption, theft, and rent seeking by special interests. These act like taxes on businesses, reducing their profitability and investment attractiveness. Coups and violent conflict are extreme forms of political instability and destabilize the economic environment as well. (McGowan 2005:17)

A frequent underlying argument is that institutional arrangements could help shape the behavior of national political leaderships, inducing them to focus more on what they could deliver and how, and ultimately making them more likely to pursue growth-enhancing policies. Political variables were also part of a new wave of analyses in which attention shifted from constraining to enabling factors of growth in Africa, as the continent started expanding surprisingly fast since the turn of the millennium. It was this perspective that led to early optimistic forecasts by some observers who hinted at the "widening scope for positive interactions between politics and economic performance in Africa ... where political freedoms remain, the constraints they impose on government predation will enhance the environment for capital accumulation and growth" (Ndulu and O'Connell 1999:63–64; cf. Cohen 2015:15, 60, 181). In trying to account for Africa's economic upturn, analysts placed great emphasis on the economic value of ousting a government (or, more generally, of being able to oust it). An influential magazine, for example, adamantly pointed out that economic expansion was "happening partly because Africa is at last getting a taste of peace and decent government. For three decades ... not a single one (bar ... Mauritius) peacefully ousted a government or president at the ballot box. But since Benin set the mainland trend in 1991, it has happened more than 30 times."[1] Development analysts similarly stressed that "the movement toward democracy ... has been at the core of the renaissance ... in Africa the relationship [between democratic governance and economic success] is crystal clear" (Radelet 2010:16,18). Echoing Liberian president Ellen Johnson Sirleaf ("the most important thing is the change in political systems," quoted in Radelet 2010:5), some went so far as to suggest that democracy had become no less than "a prerequisite for growth and development in Africa" (Wantchekon 2012:197). This was in line with approaches stressing "the rational-choice assumption that leaders care about their power and want to maximize their time in office" (Englebert 2000:1825): multiparty reforms arguably altered power-holders' incentives.

Recent studies have systematically investigated the question of whether different political regimes – more or less authoritarian or democratic – produced diverse economic performances across the region, and largely found evidence of a positive impact of political reforms (Bates et al. 2012, Bates and Block 2013, Masaki and van de Walle 2014, Carbone et al. 2016), although not necessarily pro-poor growth (Cheeseman 2015:202).

Others are more cautious, if not openly sceptical, either because they soften the role of institutions and other "fundamentals" and emphasise the need for structural changes (Rodrik 2016), or because they disagree on what the most effective pro-growth institutions are. In examining successful developmental regimes in Southeast Asia and sub-Saharan Africa, for example, David Booth and Tim Kelsall ultimately downplay the merits of liberal democratic arrangements. They suggest that:

democracy is a desirable long-term goal but not a reliable route to better public policies in the short and medium term ... in most developing countries ... clientelism is cheaper and more reliable for power-hungry politicians ... [and] voters ... have little evidence of politicians' ability to

---

[1] "The hopeful continent. Africa rising," *The Economist*, December 3, 2011.

provide public goods ... it is a mistake to believe that more and cleaner elections are a reliable way to get better public policies. (Booth 2011:2)

To the extent that politics and institutions matter, they claim, this is not about "Anglo-American institutional forms" nor "inclusive institutions," as electoral deadlines and horizons actually play against good policy in Africa (Booth et al. 2015:iv, 7; Kelsall 2013:2). The authors are particularly concerned with the sustainability of extended periods of fast economic expansion (i.e., a decade or more at 7 percent annually or higher) initiated under an "exceptional political leader." The latter's death in office, or merely his declining capabilities, were met with a failure to replace him with equally apt successors in the likes of Côte d'Ivoire, Kenya, or Malawi. A leader's departure or weakening, the argument goes, undermines the confidence that past commitments will remain credible and will continue to be honored in the future – particularly with regard to *de facto* property rights – thus eroding the conditions for growth (Kelsall 2013:3, Booth et al. 2015:4). A "succession trap" and economic decline were only averted in the presence of strong institutions, particularly a well-institutionalized dominant political party with a tradition of consensual decision-making (Booth et al. 2015:7), an emphasis reminiscent of some early modernization theories (cf. Huntington 1968:420ff., 461).

Yet the analysis presents a number of weak points. First, the authors draw sweeping generalizations from a very limited set of cases, with only one of the successful-transition-cum-sustainable-growth examples, in particular, being African (i.e., Mozambique 1997–2010). Moreover, they attribute the extended growth records in this handful of cases to the role of "exceptional leaders," and the end of the golden period to their departures or declining capacity. But they fail to account for a vast array of much-less-brilliant or outright poorly performing postcolonial African power-holders propped up by the kind of strong parties they recommend – think of Angola's, Tanzania's, Zambia's, or Senegal's, for example – as well as to examine what makes it more likely that a developmentally successful leader will emerge in the very first place. Finally, from an empirical point of view, recent developments make their conclusions seem at least premature. Mozambique's strong party, Frelimo, also helped insulate a political leadership that piled up a massive hidden debt, contributing, once the scandal was brought to light, to halving (rather than sustaining) growth levels, currently forecast at around a 3.6 percent annual average for 2017–2023. Côte d'Ivoire and Kenya, on the other hand, were classified as failures in post-succession growth-sustainability due to the absence of strong parties. Yet both countries are currently outperforming Mozambique (recorded and expected growth rates point at some 7.8 percent annually for Côte d'Ivoire in 2012–2023 and 6 percent for Kenya in 2010–2023), arguably the result, at least in part, of recent improvements in political openings and renewal.

Dependent Variables

The economic growth literature often opts for GDP growth per capita as a dependent variable, rather than GDP growth per se. Looking at the expansion of per capita income is meant to more directly account for improvements or contractions in the material resources available, at least on average, to a country's ordinary people. This is a reasonable choice. However, since we also want to know whether our key factors (namely, leadership dynamics) also produce an impact on economic activities as such, even when economic advances may not accrue to the average well-being of individuals because they are offset by population growth, we ran our analysis using both GDP annual growth and GDP per capita annual growth as dependent variables. While the values recorded by the former are typically higher than those of the latter – essentially due to Africa's fast population expansion – the two variables are very strongly correlated (Pearson's r = 0.98***). Data for both indicators are from the World Bank's World Development Indicators (WDI), the same source of most of the macroeconomic and financial data used in our analyses. WDI is one of the most commonly used databanks in comparative politics and macroeconomic studies. Compared to alternative sources, WDI provides sufficiently long and complete series for most of the variables we employ. With regard to economic expansion, WDI provides data on annual GDP growth and annual GDP per capita growth for most of sub-Saharan countries from the early 1960s to 2016. For both indicators, only 10 percent of total observations are missing.

As already pointed out, the sub-Saharan region experienced reasonably high postindependence rates of growth until a period of declining performances set in in the early 1970s that lasted for about two decades. As shown by the longitudinal trend of growth for the entire 1960–2018 period, plotted in Figure 7.1, the region's growth patterns

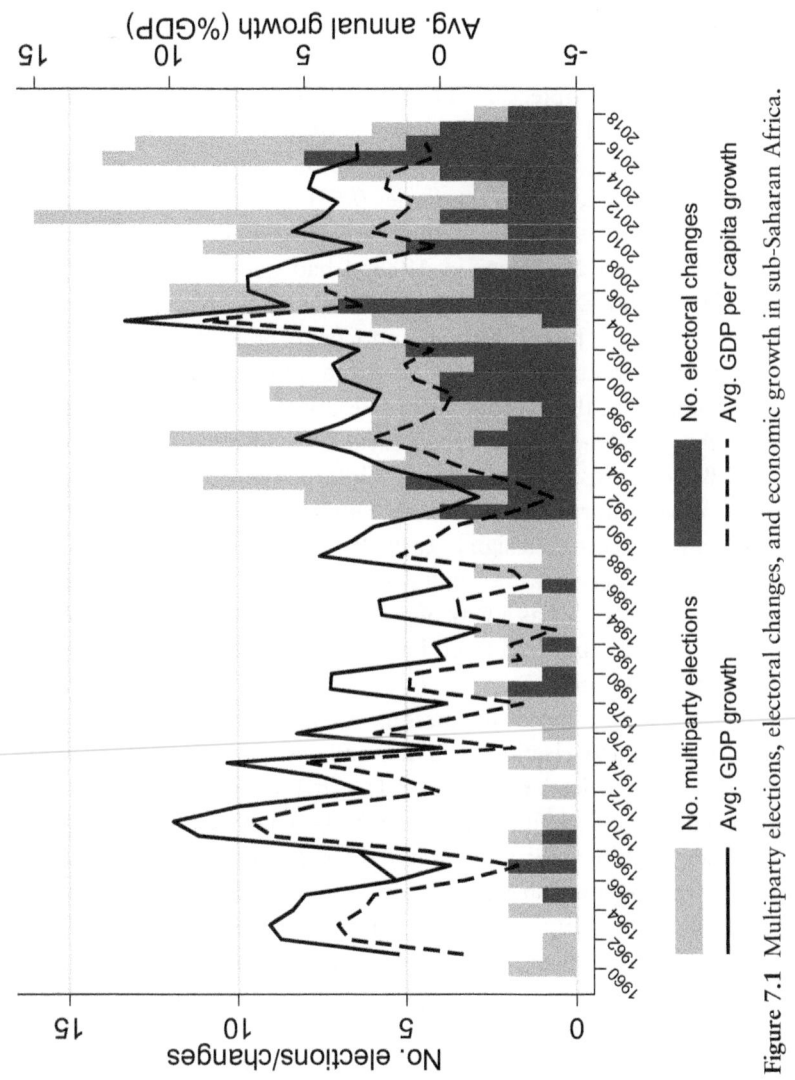

Figure 7.1 Multiparty elections, electoral changes, and economic growth in sub-Saharan Africa.

became comparatively more stable and reached significantly higher average levels from the early 1990s and for some 15 to 20 years. But how did such trends relate to the political evolution of leadership dynamics in the region?

At a glance, Africa's phase of economic renewal and expansion since the mid-1990s coincided with a generalized move away from military overthrows (see Chapter 5). The remarkable total of 75 coups d'état between 1960 and 1999, or an average of almost two (1.87) power seizures per year, dropped to only 10 instances over the entire 2000–2018 period, or less than one (0.53) coup per year. Similarly, six out of seven cases of takeovers by rebel leaders – namely, by Uganda's Yoweri Museveni in 1986, Chad's Idriss Déby in 1990, Ethiopia's Meles Zenawi in 1991, Rwanda's Paul Kagame in 1994, Congo-Kinshasa's Joseph Kabila, and Congo-Brazzaville's Denis Sassou Nguesso, both in 1997 – occurred prior to the end of the millennium. With the exception of Meles, who died of natural causes, all of the abovementioned rebels-turned-presidents still hold office today. By contrast, the only post-2000 instance of a guerrilla capturing power proved short-lived, as Michel Djotodia of the Central African Republic was forced to resign in early 2014, less than one year after he seized the presidency in the capital Bangui. Overall, violence became increasingly less viable as a way of grabbing power in Africa, and more political stability appeared to go hand in hand with relative economic stabilization and progress.

The same – if symmetrical – message is conveyed by the encouraging resort to multiparty elections as a new and widely predominant way of selecting national leaders (Figure 7.1). After independence, limits to political participation and competition had arguably contributed to the slowdown of African economies. By the beginning of the 1990s, the sub-Saharan region entered a complex period dense with political transitions and fluidity – somehow mirrored in economic instability – but the gradual regularization of electoral regimes was soon accompanied by unprecedented growth performances. Election-based leadership changes – inclusive of both successions and alternations – reflect this same trend, with 1990 acting as a visually striking watershed in the figure. An overall upturn in power handovers also meant that the average tenure of incumbent office-holders declined, after three decades of steady increases, first between 1990 and 1994 (down from a peak of 11.6 years to 8.3 years), and then again, after a period of moderate rise, between 2015 and 2018 (down from 10.9 years to 9.1 years, following the historic departure of two of Africa's longest-serving presidents such as Robert Mugabe and José Eduardo Dos Santos).

During the 1960s and 1970s, there was a linear relationship between the different ways in which leaders took office and their country's economic performance, with the few democratically elected leaders achieving better results than their peers elected through less-than-democratic votes and, especially, than unelected leaders (Figure 7.2). In the 1980s, the relationship was no longer monotonic, as unelected power-holders outdid those voted into office in the absence of democracy. But the performance of unelected leaders worsened from the 1990s on, when compared to the other two groups, and was altogether negative after 2011. It was not democratically elected leaders, however, that achieved the best overall results, but those legitimized through defective democratic practices.

Empirical Analysis

Based on the economic-growth literature examined previously, we selected a series of alternative explanatory factors that might be a source of spuriousness in the relation between different modes of leadership change and economic growth. We control for the level of income per capita to account for the notion that a country's level of development affects its growth rates. We use gross capital formation to control for the growth-enhancing role of investments and also expect natural resources rents and international development assistance, both measured as a share of the national income, to potentially inflate growth performances. On the other hand, we suppose government consumption (as a percentage of GDP) to negatively affect the latter. As a proxy for human capital, we opt for life expectancy at birth alone, rather than also including an education indicator, both to preserve the parsimony of our causal model as well as to maximise observations and thus the degrees of freedom. Higher levels of human capital (i.e., of life expectancy at birth) are predicted to positively affect growth rates. We also include population growth among our regressors, though with unpredetermined expectations. An additional control variable accounts for a country's involvement in an ongoing war (internal or interstate) through a 0–10 scale measuring the magnitude of the

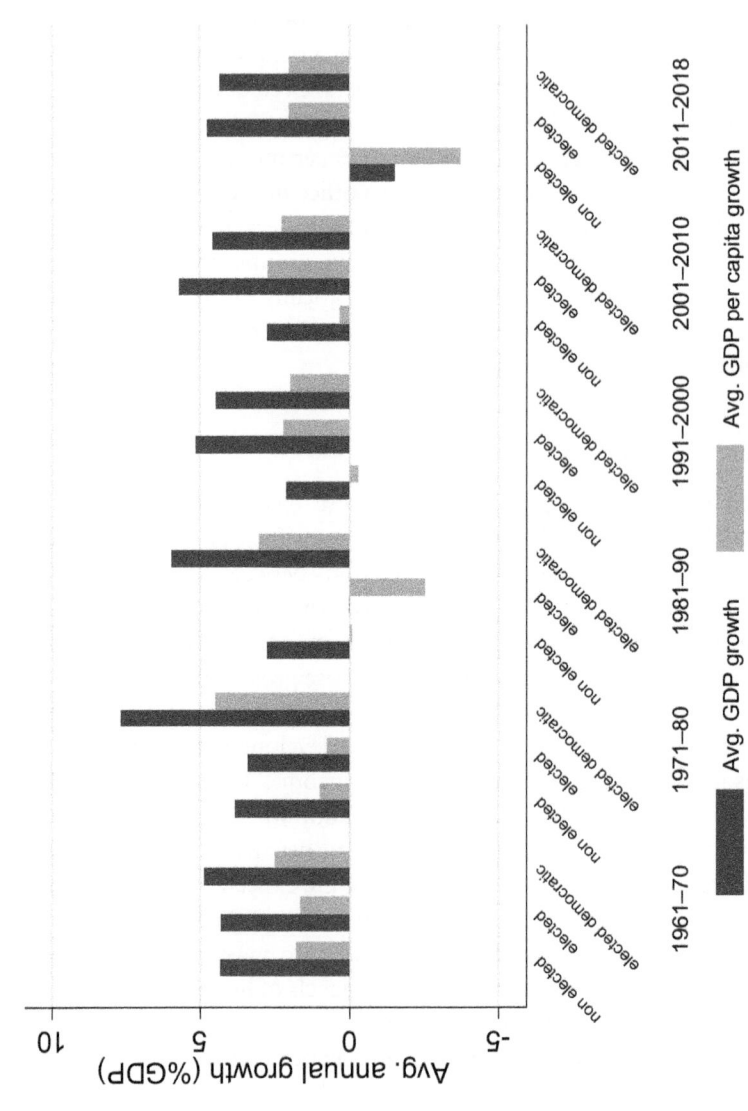

Figure 7.2 Economic growth under non-elected, elected, and democratic leaders in sub-Saharan Africa, by decade.

conflict (data are from the Center for Systemic Peace). Ethnic fractionalization and landlockedness are two other factors possibly harming economic performances. We exclude these two time-invariant control variables when we check the robustness of results by including country dummies in the regression models. We also account for time-related trends through a dummy for post-1990 observations, and we cross-check the results by substituting the latter with decade and year fixed effects, respectively. Table A4 in the appendix reports brief definitions, sources, and descriptive statistics of dependent and control variables.

Tables 7.1 and 7.2 present the results of eight model specifications in which GDP growth and GDP per capita growth, respectively, are regressed on their lagged level and the lagged level of the independent and control variables.[2]

The results of our empirical analyses are largely supportive of our hypotheses and, unsurprisingly, do not present important differences when looking at either GDP growth or GDP per capita growth. In Chapter 5, we already examined the performance of leaders who came to power via a military coup (HP1). It was shown that power seizures by the military are not generally followed by development progress and that, more specifically, the economic performances that post-coup leaders achieve during their stay in office are comparatively inferior to those of other (i.e., non-coup) leaders.

HP2 looks at the impact of duration in office and its validity is tested in the first model reported in Tables 7.1 and 7.2, respectively. Our main expectation is confirmed, as we do find that a leader's length of stay in power negatively affects a country's economic progress. The relationship is linear rather than curvilinear, disproving our alternative proposition (HP2.1), namely that a leader's effect becomes more positive as time allows him or her to make an impact, but it then gradually declines.

Our HP3, according to which power-holders who gain office via multiparty elections are more effective growth promoters than unelected leaders, is also supported by the evidence. This is a key point in our framework. The corollary hypothesis (HP3.1) – namely that it is leaders voted into office under better democratic conditions, as opposed to those elected in the absence of basic democracy or

---

[2] We estimated models also via TSCS regressions with fixed effects. Results are not shown here.

Table 7.1 Regression results for GDP growth

Dependent variable: GDP growth	Model 1	Model 2	Model 3	Model 4	Model 5	Model 6	Model 7	Model 8
GDP growth $_{(t-1)}$	0.218*** (0.040)	0.218*** (0.040)	0.163*** (0.041)	0.170*** (0.041)	0.172*** (0.041)	0.166*** (0.041)	0.162*** (0.041)	0.165*** (0.041)
Leader duration $_{(t-1)}$	−0.066*** (0.019)	−0.107* (0.059)						
Leader duration $_{(t-1)}$*Leader duration $_{(t-1)}$		0.001 (0.002)						
Elected leader $_{(t-1)}$			1.346*** (0.427)					
Democratically elected leader $_{(t-1)}$			1.748*** (0.512)					
Cumulative no. of elections $_{(t-1)}$				0.173** (0.079)				
Cumulative no. of democratic elections $_{(t-1)}$					0.184* (0.100)			
Executive control $_{(t-1)}$						−0.020*** (0.006)		
Incumbent reelected $_{(t-1)}$							1.388*** (0.423)	
Electoral succession $_{(t-1)}$							1.741*** (0.488)	

200

Electoral alternation (t−1)						1.159** (0.588)	
Multiparty regime – no alternation (t−1)							1.551*** (0.401)
Multiparty regime – one alternation (t−1)							1.030* (0.551)
Multiparty regime – more alternation (t−1)							1.544** (0.693)
Population growth (t−1)	0.946*** (0.198)	0.951*** (0.198)	0.646*** (0.217)	0.703*** (0.218)	0.686*** (0.218)	0.704*** (0.222)	0.629*** (0.217)	0.616*** (0.218)
(log)GDP per capita (t−1)	0.019 (0.271)	0.003 (0.274)	0.017 (0.277)	−0.019 (0.284)	−0.028 (0.284)	−0.099 (0.292)	0.032 (0.272)	0.063 (0.273)
Government expenditure (t−1)	−0.031 (0.025)	−0.030 (0.025)	−0.051** (0.025)	−0.046* (0.025)	−0.047* (0.025)	−0.046* (0.026)	−0.052** (0.025)	−0.048* (0.025)
Gross capital formation (t−1)	0.080*** (0.025)	0.084*** (0.025)	0.090*** (0.025)	0.089*** (0.025)	0.090*** (0.025)	0.090*** (0.026)	0.089*** (0.025)	0.089*** (0.025)
Natural resources rents (t−1)	0.002 (0.017)	0.001 (0.017)	0.002 (0.018)	0.001 (0.018)	0.003 (0.018)	0.002 (0.018)	−0.001 (0.018)	−0.001 (0.018)
Net ODA (t−1)	0.011 (0.021)	0.011 (0.021)	0.040* (0.021)	0.042** (0.021)	0.039* (0.021)	0.039* (0.021)	0.044** (0.021)	0.043** (0.021)
Life expectancy at birth (t−1)	0.065** (0.033)	0.063* (0.032)	0.033 (0.035)	0.049 (0.034)	0.052 (0.036)	0.035 (0.037)	0.041 (0.034)	0.040 (0.035)
Conflict involvement (t−1)	−0.014 (0.120)	−0.008 (0.121)	0.192 (0.120)	0.159 (0.120)	0.143 (0.120)	0.152 (0.126)	0.185 (0.120)	0.178 (0.120)

Table 7.1 (*cont.*)

Dependent variable: GDP growth	Model 1	Model 2	Model 3	Model 4	Model 5	Model 6	Model 7	Model 8
Post-1990 $_{(t-1)}$	0.243	0.221	−0.710	−0.296	−0.046	−0.243	−0.691	−0.688
	(0.506)	(0.507)	(0.526)	(0.556)	(0.532)	(0.519)	(0.534)	(0.537)
Landlocked $_{(t-1)}$	0.688	0.660	0.613	0.653	0.653	0.549	0.623	0.742*
	(0.448)	(0.449)	(0.441)	(0.439)	(0.439)	(0.461)	(0.437)	(0.441)
Ethnolinguistic fractionalization $_{(t-1)}$	−1.112	−1.176	−1.611	−1.624	−1.359	−1.344	−1.626	−1.313
	(1.098)	(1.093)	(1.114)	(1.122)	(1.101)	(1.127)	(1.127)	(1.153)
Constant	−3.389	−2.986	−1.443	−2.046	−2.271	0.956	−1.863	−2.276
	(2.548)	(2.575)	(2.773)	(2.728)	(2.744)	(3.140)	(2.657)	(2.669)
N	1,428	1,428	1,447	1,447	1,447	1,427	1,447	1,447
Countries	42	42	42	42	42	41	42	42
R^2	0.130	0.131	0.107	0.102	0.101	0.103	0.107	0.107

Notes: Panel-corrected standard errors (PCSE) in parentheses. * $p < 0.1$; ** $p < 0.05$; *** $p < 0.01$.

Table 7.2 Regression results for GDP per capita growth

Dependent variable: GDP per capita growth	Model 1	Model 2	Model 3	Model 4	Model 5	Model 6	Model 7	Model 8
GDP per capita growth $_{(t-1)}$	0.213*** (0.040)	0.214*** (0.040)	0.156*** (0.041)	0.163*** (0.041)	0.165*** (0.041)	0.160*** (0.042)	0.156*** (0.041)	0.158*** (0.041)
Leader duration $_{(t-1)}$	−0.060*** (0.018)	−0.092 (0.058)						
Leader duration $_{(t-1)}$*Leader duration $_{(t-1)}$		0.001 (0.002)						
Elected leader $_{(t-1)}$			1.336*** (0.416)					
Democratically elected leader $_{(t-1)}$			1.681*** (0.499)					
Cumulative no. of elections $_{(t-1)}$				0.170** (0.078)				
Cumulative no. of democratic elections $_{(t-1)}$					0.176* (0.098)			
Executive control $_{(t-1)}$						−0.020*** (0.006)		
Incumbent reelected $_{(t-1)}$							1.377*** (0.413)	
Electoral succession $_{(t-1)}$							1.681*** (0.475)	

Table 7.2 (*cont.*)

Dependent variable: GDP per capita growth	Model 1	Model 2	Model 3	Model 4	Model 5	Model 6	Model 7	Model 8
Electoral alternation $_{(t-1)}$							1.119* (0.574)	
Multiparty regime – no alternation $_{(t-1)}$								1.497*** (0.391)
Multiparty regime – one alternation $_{(t-1)}$								0.966* (0.536)
Multiparty regime – more alternation $_{(t-1)}$								1.452** (0.675)
Population growth $_{(t-1)}$	0.211 (0.195)	0.215 (0.195)	−0.126 (0.211)	−0.061 (0.212)	−0.077 (0.212)	−0.064 (0.215)	−0.142 (0.211)	−0.153 (0.212)
(log)GDP per capita $_{(t-1)}$	0.041 (0.265)	0.028 (0.267)	0.046 (0.270)	0.008 (0.278)	0.001 (0.277)	−0.069 (0.285)	0.058 (0.266)	0.087 (0.267)
Government expenditure $_{(t-1)}$	−0.035 (0.025)	−0.034 (0.025)	−0.054** (0.025)	−0.049** (0.025)	−0.050** (0.024)	−0.049* (0.026)	−0.055** (0.025)	−0.051** (0.025)
Gross capital formation $_{(t-1)}$	0.078*** (0.024)	0.081*** (0.025)	0.088*** (0.024)	0.087*** (0.024)	0.088*** (0.024)	0.087*** (0.025)	0.087*** (0.024)	0.086*** (0.024)
Natural resources rents $_{(t-1)}$	−0.000 (0.017)	−0.002 (0.017)	−0.001 (0.018)	−0.002 (0.018)	0.000 (0.018)	−0.000 (0.018)	−0.003 (0.017)	−0.004 (0.017)
Net ODA $_{(t-1)}$	0.010 (0.021)	0.010 (0.021)	0.037* (0.020)	0.039* (0.020)	0.036* (0.020)	0.036* (0.020)	0.041** (0.020)	0.040** (0.020)

Life expectancy at birth $_{(t-1)}$	0.071**	0.069**	0.040	0.055*	0.059*	0.041	0.047	0.047
	(0.032)	(0.031)	(0.034)	(0.033)	(0.035)	(0.036)	(0.033)	(0.034)
Conflict involvement $_{(t-1)}$	0.022	0.027	0.219*	0.187	0.171	0.180	0.212*	0.204*
	(0.118)	(0.118)	(0.117)	(0.117)	(0.117)	(0.122)	(0.116)	(0.116)
Post-1990 $_{(t-1)}$	0.257	0.240	−0.670	−0.264	−0.015	−0.208	−0.646	−0.628
	(0.492)	(0.493)	(0.512)	(0.537)	(0.516)	(0.505)	(0.519)	(0.523)
Landlocked $_{(t-1)}$	0.636	0.615	0.569	0.605	0.605	0.506	0.577	0.693
	(0.439)	(0.439)	(0.433)	(0.430)	(0.430)	(0.452)	(0.429)	(0.432)
Ethnolinguistic fractionalization $_{(t-1)}$	−1.223	−1.272	−1.711	−1.729	−1.469	−1.451	−1.719	−1.415
	(1.101)	(1.097)	(1.113)	(1.122)	(1.103)	(1.127)	(1.127)	(1.152)
Constant	−3.828	−3.523	−1.990	−2.525	−2.771	0.367	−2.365	−2.790
	(2.466)	(2.494)	(2.688)	(2.643)	(2.658)	(3.056)	(2.573)	(2.586)
N	1,428	1,428	1,447	1,447	1,447	1,427	1,447	1,447
Countries	42	42	42	42	42	41	42	42
R^2	0.106	0.107	0.092	0.087	0.086	0.088	0.092	0.092

Notes: Panel-corrected standard errors (PCSE) in parentheses. * $p < 0.1$; ** $p < 0.05$; *** $p < 0.01$.

unelected power-holders – is partially confirmed. While the regression coefficient for democratically elected leaders is positive and significant, a *t* test shows that it is not significantly higher than the regression coefficient for elected leaders. Therefore, while leaders elected in an essentially democratic institutional context are associated with levels of economic growth higher than those of unelected leaders, their performance in terms of growth is not significantly higher when compared to power holders elected under nondemocratic conditions.

Also in line with the previous findings is corroboration of the idea that the multiparty elections dividend increases with the rise of their total cumulative number (HP4 and HP4.1). This holds true for both democratic and nondemocratic voting rounds, as shown by the fourth and fifth model specifications.

HP5 stated that the degree of competition in elections – meaning smaller gaps in the votes separating winners and losers – is supportive of better efforts on the parts of the elected leaders who gain or retain office, and is similarly validated by our evidence. The higher the share of votes obtained by the winning presidential candidates (or the share of parliamentary seats obtained by the winning coalition), the lower the level of GDP growth and GDP per capita growth, respectively.

Our final set of hypotheses had to do with the economic impact of leaders' electoral replacements. They include the idea that both a leadership succession (HP6) as well as turnovers allowing opposition candidates to take power (HP7) are associated with economic improvements. Both are only partly supported by empirical evidence, as is the anticipation that more alternations in office would further strengthen a country's performance when compared to no-change multiparty governments (HP7.1). In the seventh regression model, both the coefficients for electoral succession and that for alternation are positive and significant. However, the non-significance of the *t* test adopted to examine the difference between the two coefficients, respectively, and the coefficient for incumbent reelected proves that leaders who took power through an electoral succession or a government alternation are associated with significantly higher growth rates than non-elected leaders, but not higher than those associated with incumbents that have been reelected.

With regard to a country's cumulative experience with electoral alternation, our last model specification shows that multiparty regimes experiencing no cases of alternation, regimes counting only one episode of alternation, and countries that experienced more than one alternation are all associated with significantly higher levels of economic growth when compared to non-multiparty regimes. However, regression coefficients for regimes with one episode of alternation and regimes with more cases of alternation are not significantly different from the coefficient for regimes with no experience with alternation. Furthermore, countries having gone through at least two episodes of alternation since independence are not associated with significantly higher levels of GDP growth and GDP per capita growth than those counting only one episode.

The previous results are generally robust to several statistical checks, such as the inclusion of different controls (state control over territory instead of conflict involvement, and secondary enrolment rate instead of life expectancy at birth), the inclusion of country dummies instead of time-invariant variables, and the inclusion of year or decade dummies instead of the post-1990 dummy. Finally, our findings do not change when running models with TSCS regressions with fixed effects. Overall, the results we presented prove that when and where African countries changed the ways in which they select their leaders – particularly with the introduction of elections and related dynamics – this contributed positively, across the continent, to altering the pace of economic growth.

8 Leading for Development? (II)
Social Welfare, State Consolidation, and Corruption Control

In this chapter, we complete the presentation of the results of our empirical analyses, all based on the methodological framework outlined in Chapter 7. We test the hypothesized impact of leadership dynamics with regard to issues of social welfare, state consolidation, and corruption control.

Social Welfare

Theoretical Approaches and Key Determinants

Some leaders may be better than others in fostering overall economic expansion, but for whose benefit? A country's economic growth alone is not necessarily going to improve the well-being of the wider population. The actual impact of leadership dynamics on the latter requires a more specific investigation into welfare issues.

The reasons for the emergence of welfare systems in advanced and emerging countries have been examined in depth, resulting in the identification of a number of key drivers (cf. Carnes and Mares 2007; van Kersbergen and Manow 2008). First, the rise of the welfare state has long been explained as part of modernization and economic development processes in the West (Wilensky 1975). A related account, if with a clearer political focus, linked it to the mobilisation and struggle of workers demanding broader public interventions to meet their changing social needs (Korpi 1983, Esping-Andersen 1990). Thirdly, the technocratic role of state bureaucrats in advancing new social policies has been the core of a distinct approach (Skocpol et al. 1985, Grindle and Thomas 1991:49-51), particularly where social actors proved too weak to take the initiative (cf. Carnes and Mares 2007:879). An emphasis on a "policy feedback" effect, according to which new measures typically draw on previous policy developments and on the specificity of existing contexts, is a fourth theme (Pierson

1994). Finally, external constraints and pressures, notably those coming from international actors or global economic dynamics, help us understand the direction policies take in the fights against poverty, inequality, illiteracy, diseases and the like (Garrett 1998, Weyland 2005).

The idea that opening politics to democratic competition and mass participation would force a reallocation of resources – through the introduction of new public actions – more favorable to a wider section of society has been a long-standing theoretical proposition (cf. Meltzer and Richard 1981). The social struggles for achieving universal suffrage in the West, between the late nineteenth century and the early twentieth century, were largely encouraged by the anticipation that political equality would bring about some kind of redistribution and social improvement. Voters demand that elected leaders respond to their needs: political support thus rewards the provision of public goods (Lake and Baum 2001:617).

Contemporary processes of political change appear to remain an influential factor in shaping welfare systems. The regime transitions of the 1980s and 1990s in Latin America, East Asia, and Eastern Europe, in particular, "saw renewed attention to the social question and pressures both to protect existing entitlements and to expand social insurance and services to new groups" (Haggard and Kaufman 2008:15), with important specificities in each of the three regions. This was also the case where hybrid regimes emerged, as electoral dynamics still often prompted the expansion of welfare efforts. If social and political coalitions, together with economic conditions, are key to understanding a country's welfare developments, regime type remains "an important component of any explanation of social policy" (Haggard and Kaufman 2008:3,16). Social spending and social performances, for example, are better protected in democratic polities, followed by hybrid regimes and then autocracies (Rudra and Haggard 2005:1017).

Empirically, democratic mechanisms are known to be instrumental to preventing or addressing the most severe food crises (Sen 1994; de Waal 2018). Social expenditure is often higher under democratic rule (Brown 1999, Brown and Hunter 2004), albeit poverty has been less affected by regime type (Varshney 2000), whereas inequality is only partly reduced and after some initial worsening (Bollen and Jackman 1985, Harms and Zink 2003, Chong 2004). Human development has at times been used as a proxy for the welfare dividend of different regimes. Gerring et al. (2016) find that it is the *electoral* component of democracy (rather than the extent of civil liberties or of citizens' empowerment) that impacts positively on human development, whereas Miller (2015) extends this electoral effect to the use of multiparty voting under authoritarian rule. Sharing a concern with a population's well-being, Lake and Baum (2001) focus on the provision of public services such as access to safe water or immunization rates and confirm the existence of a democratic advantage. The same goes for Brown and Mobarak (2009), who find that the provision of electricity tends to reach larger segments of the citizenry where the latter are empowered with the vote.

The welfare regimes of developing countries inevitably lag far behind those of industrialized and newly industrialized economies. This is particularly the case for sub-Saharan Africa, with the remarkable exception of South Africa. The region does not fit well into the existing welfare-state building frameworks (Hickey et al. 2018:2). To account for the prevalence of only sporadic and flimsy social policies, some region-specific characterisations have been employed – beyond that of "*welfare state* regimes" – including allusions to "informal security regimes" or even "insecurity regimes" (Bevan 2004, Wood and Gough 2006). The out-of-the-ordinary influence of external actors in policy design and implementation has also been noted, from international organizations to national donor agencies (Hickey et al. 2018:9).

Yet given the widespread, basic needs of large parts of the African populations, the new channels opened by the political reforms of the 1990s appeared highly likely to be used for voicing social discomfort and demands for measures aimed at an extensive public. The kind of distributive politics-as-usual that had prevailed for much of the post-independence politics, targeting relatively narrow segments or communities and making the provision of public goods harder, still plays an important role in African countries, if often in new forms (Lindberg 2003, 2010; van de Walle 2012; Kramon 2017). But these practices, which had already come under pressure as a result of the structural adjustment programmes of the 1980s (Herbst 1990), now also had to contend with multiparty electoral politics that made elites potentially more receptive to larger sections of society, such as, for example, rural voters. In countries at very dissimilar levels of democracy such as

Ghana, Mozambique, Tanzania, and Uganda, for instance, "political elites have clearly been responsive ... major decisions have typically aimed to benefit citizens countrywide; they are designed to have immediate and visible impact and can clearly be identified with the party in power" (Kjær and Therkildsen 2011:4).

A range of studies has produced evidence that the new electoral politics did favor the emergence of social policy issues in a number of sub-Saharan states – including the likes of Malawi, Zambia, or Uganda, but also in long-time multiparty Zimbabwe and Botswana (Seekings 2014:20) – by incentivizing governments to adopt welfare reforms. Public initiatives spanned from social protection programmes (Hickey et al. 2018) to primary education (Stasavage 2005a,b; Kjær and Therkildsen 2013; Harding and Stasavage 2014) or health insurance schemes (Carbone 2011, 2012). A recent extension of social protection measures, for example, was apparent. Despite wide differences across sub-Saharan nations, Hickey and colleagues emphasize the role of domestic political imperatives over external pressures. While some prominent cases are to be found in authoritarian electoral regimes such as Rwanda or Ethiopia, the authors conclude that the process through which they were "promoted, contested, and rolled out" included bargaining "between rulers and ruled, whereby concerns with electoral success, legitimacy, and popular pressures are increasingly influential over budgetary allocations and welfare provision" (Hickey et al. 2018:1,16). Similarly, since the late 1990s, many countries eliminated the user fees for health services that had been introduced some 10–15 years earlier. The elimination was "decided at the highest levels of government ... often, abolition was decided suddenly and in a highly politicized context (pre- or post-election)" (Ridde and Morestin 2011:4).

The few quantitative investigations that looked into these issues emphasized that political pressures for new or expanded welfare measures emerged both in countries by and large deemed democratic (Benin, Ghana, or Mali, for example) as well as in others where electoral politics stopped short of democracy (such as Uganda or Tanzania) (Harding and Stasavage 2014, Cassani and Carbone 2016). But not all observers agreed on whether competitive autocracies or "hybrid regimes" were also subject to the kind of electoral pressures that were more evident in open and democratic systems and responded by expanding welfare programmes (Kudamatsu 2012).

The notion of a democratic advantage in terms of welfare expansion – in Africa and beyond – has been challenged, as we mentioned in Chapter 2. From an empirical point of view, the example of Asian developmental states, a number of which combined autocratic rule with new welfare initiatives, shows that multiparty elections are certainly not the only factor driving leaders to adopt measures for social improvements. On the other hand, electoral accountability mechanisms may not work as predicted due to market imperfections, for example where voters lack the necessary information or where identity voting dampens socio-economic demands (Keefer and Khemani 2005). Nor is increased spending for education or health necessarily enough to translate into actual social improvements, as the amelioration of social services may require institutional reforms or resource reallocations more than just new resources (Nelson 2007:80; cf. Harding and Stasavage 2014), or because social spending is de facto tailored to the needs of the middle classes rather than to those of the poor (Ross 2006:861).

Dependent Variables

Education and health are the two key welfare areas we decided to focus on. We chose these two sectors for theoretical and empirical reasons. At a theoretical level, education and health have always represented key political issues in a region struggling with very low public service provisions. With the spread of multiparty competition across the African continent, education and health often became important campaign themes. From an empirical point of view, the choice of the indicators employed in the empirical analysis was strongly affected by data availability. Specifically, we selected one investment indicator (the level of public health expenditure as a percentage of GDP), two output indicators (the gross primary and secondary school enrollment rates), and two outcome indicators (life expectancy at birth and children under-5 mortality rate). All the variables are drawn from the World Bank's World Development Indicators. A number of alternative measures proved unviable due to their grossly incomplete series, particularly for the years prior to 1990. This is also the reason why we could not include public spending in the education sector. Figures for health expenditure, on the other hand, are only available for our sample of sub-Saharan countries from 1995 on. While the number of observations in our sample was significantly reduced by incomplete data distribution, we were able to consistently test our hypotheses across time and countries. Primary and secondary school enrollment rates cover the 1970–2016 period, while life expectancy at birth and the child mortality rate present long series that cover almost the entire period of analysis (1960–2017) for the vast majority of sub-Saharan countries.

As shown by the lines in the four graphs plotted in Figure 8.1, overall, sub-Saharan citizens' well-being clearly improved over time. This is particularly true for outcomes in the health sector. More precisely, the region experienced a substantial increase in life expectancy at birth. In 1960, sub-Saharan Africans could expect to live around 40 years on average, whereas by 2016 this was up to 60 years. Following the same general trend, the rate of children who did not reach 5 years of age was some 250 per 1,000 live births in the early 1960s, but it then declined to around 60 children in 2016. These two indicators exhibit a rather constant trend over time, with a sharper change starting from the mid-1990s. The share of people enrolled in primary or secondary school, on the other hand, shows much less impressive improvements. Yet the primary school enrollment rate (solid line) also becomes steeper from the mid-1990s and, from the mid-2000s, the average total primary school enrollment of sub-Saharan citizens, regardless of age, reaches around 100 percent. Secondary school enrollment (dashed line) is relatively constant over time, with a marked increase in recent years, after 2010. Finally, public health expenditure as a percentage of GDP displays a less clear longitudinal trend. In the 20 years (1995–2014) for which data are available, public health spending exhibits several fluctuations. It decreased in the second half of the 1990s and then recovered until 2010, only to decrease again in recent years.

This positive trend in sub-Saharan citizens' well-being can be mostly explained by scientific and technological improvements, especially in the healthcare sector. Unsurprisingly, life expectancy and under-5 mortality display the strongest improvements over the period we examine. Yet the timing of important increases in primary and secondary school enrollment and life expectancy at birth – as well as the parallel decline in child mortality – seems to follow the multiparty openings of the 1990s, the spread of elections and the increase in leadership changes through the ballot box (Figure 8.1). These preliminary illustrations are in line with the expectation that competing politicians are

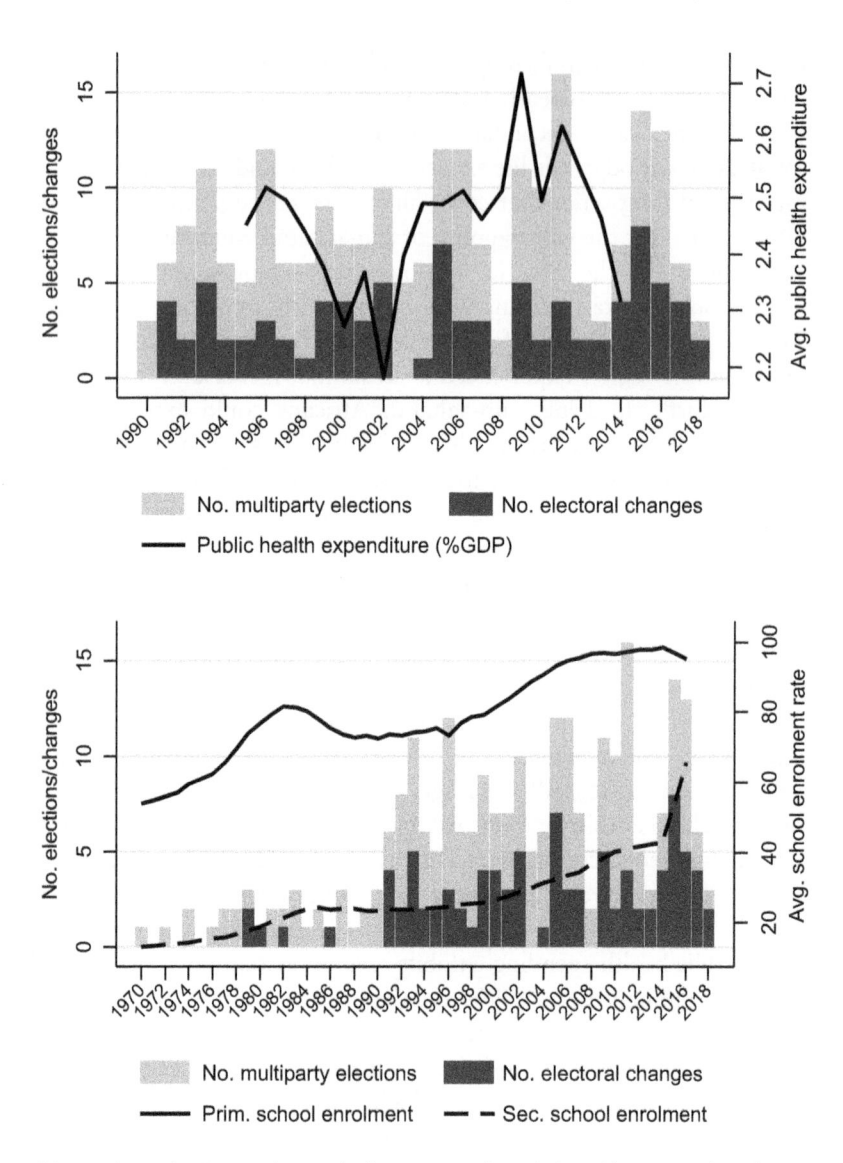

Figure 8.1 Elections, electoral changes, and social welfare in sub-Saharan Africa.

Social Welfare 215

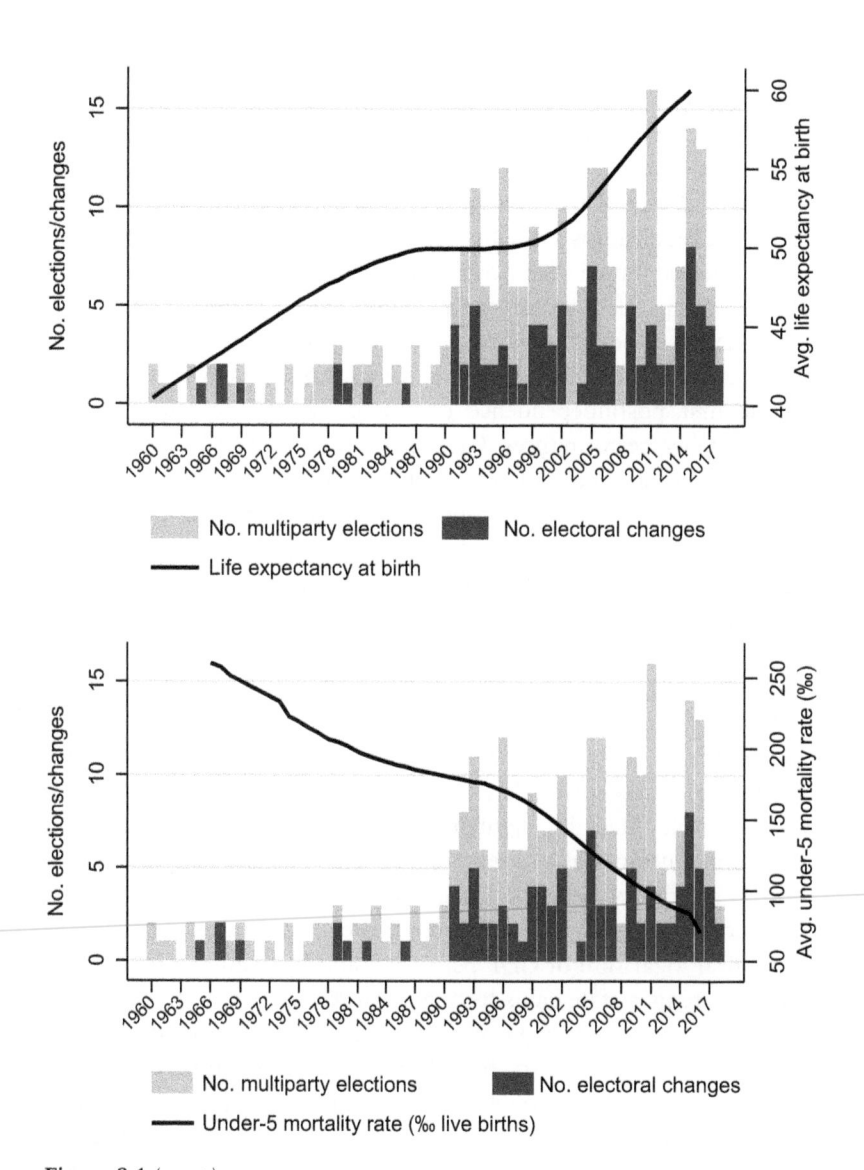

Figure 8.1 (*cont.*)

more responsive to the electorate and help improve social indicators. Data on public health expenditure, on the other hand, only cover the post-1990 period and do not allow us to detect any straightforward association.

Figure 8.2 shows the average social welfare performance of non-elected leaders, leaders elected in democratically deficient contexts, and leaders elected under democratic conditions. For all the indicators selected as dependent variables we do not detect significant differences in the levels of social welfare provided by non-elected leaders and leaders elected in institutional frameworks short of democracy, except for the first postindependence decade in which the latter present slightly higher performances. On the contrary, elected leaders in relatively democratic contexts tend to outperform all other leaders in terms of better social welfare provisions. This pattern is particularly evident during the 1970s and 1980s, whereas in more recent years the difference between democratically elected leaders and nondemocratic elected leaders thins down.

Empirical Analysis

The validity of our research hypotheses was controlled with the inclusion in the regression models of various alternative drivers of social welfare development highlighted by the literature. In the process, an important concern was to keep the model as parsimonious as possible and focused on socioeconomic factors.

We control for the level of economic development as measured by the natural logarithm of GDP per capita and for annual GDP growth rates. The rents a state gains from natural resources and official development aid as a percentage of gross national income (GNI) are also entered. Moreover, we also control for the size of the total population (natural logarithm). In models with health spending as the dependent variable, we opted for including the share of the population under 14 years of age, rather than total population size, to account for the part of the population that is supposedly less in need of health care.[1] Furthermore, we exclude the share of net development aid because it is endogenous, insofar as the indicator of public health spending already

---

[1] Main findings do not change also using the natural logarithm of total population or the percentage of population ages 65 or above.

Social Welfare 217

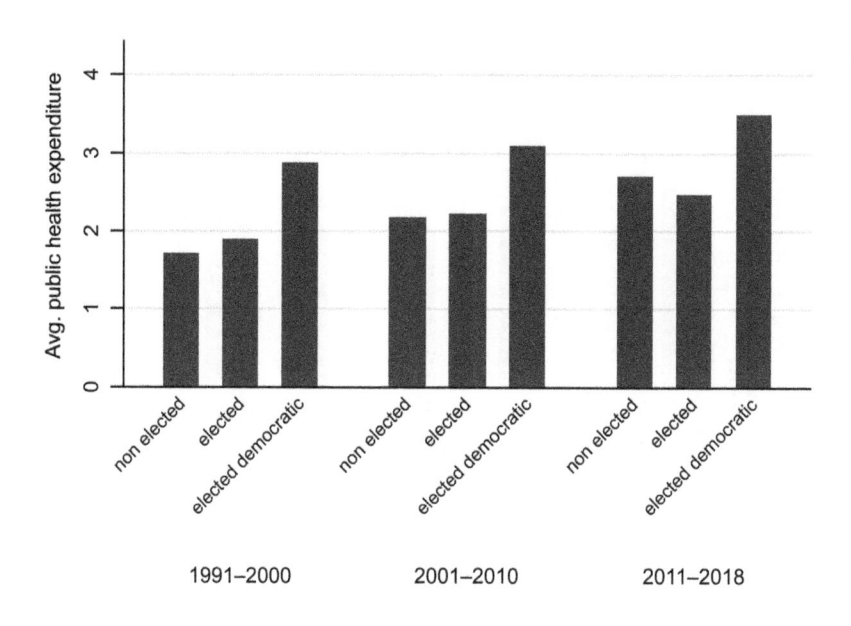

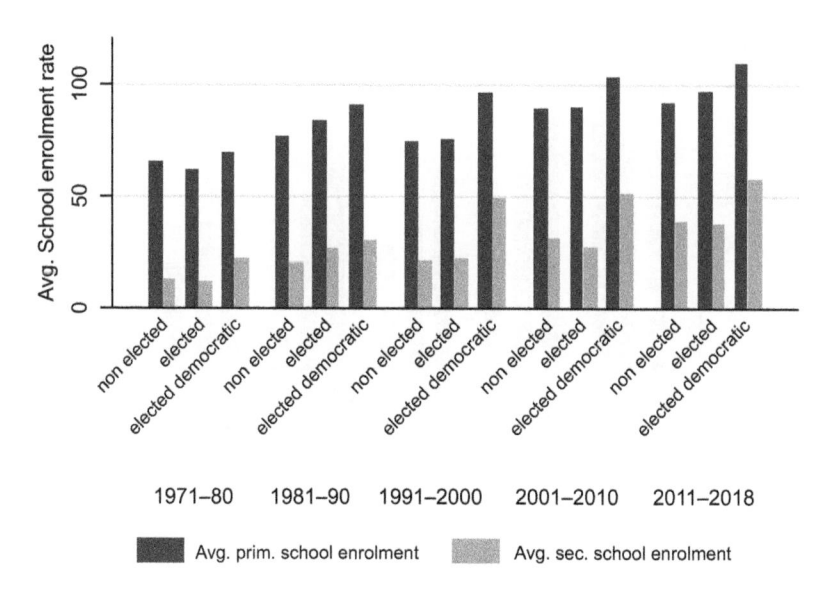

Figure 8.2 Social welfare under non-elected, elected, and democratic leaders in sub-Saharan Africa, by decade.

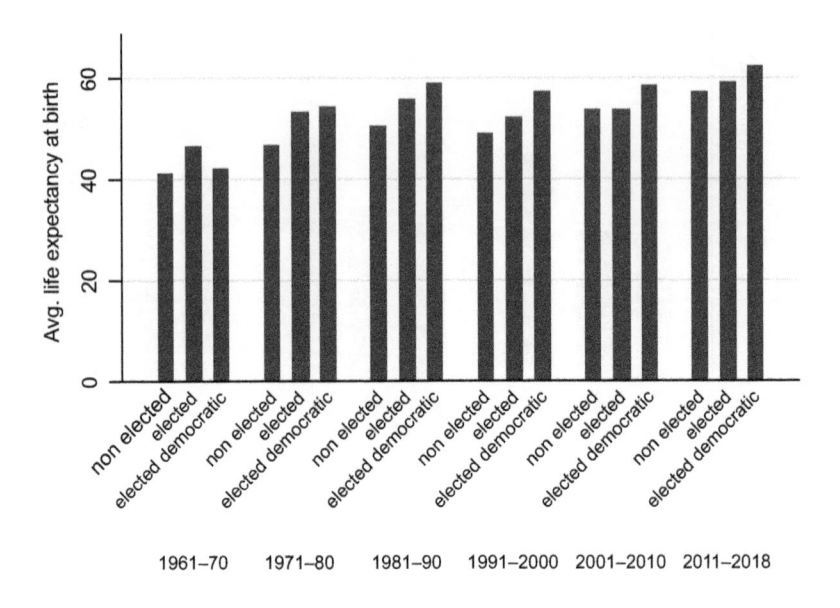

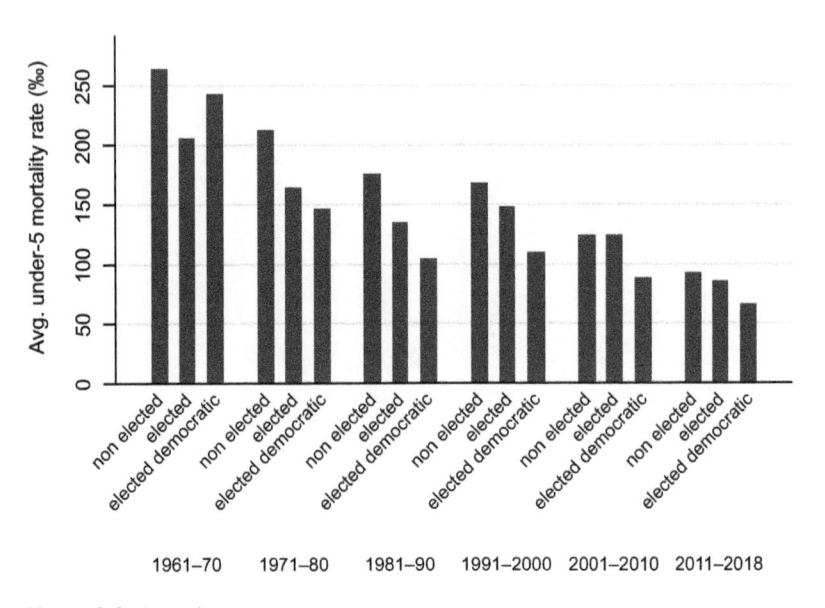

Figure 8.2 (*cont.*)

includes donations from international agencies and nongovernmental organizations, and we include a measure of general government consumption expenditure as a share of GDP. All data are from the World Bank's World Development Indicators. A country's conflict involvement (internal or interstate) is also accounted for through a 0–10 scale of conflict magnitude from the Center for Systemic Peace. Two time-invariant variables in our models are a dummy variable for countries sharing a British colonial legacy and an index of ethnolinguistic fractionalization from the Quality of Government dataset (Teorell et al. 2018). Additional time-invariant measures such as latitude and country size were also tested but, in seeking parsimoniousness, we eventually opted for leaving them out of our main models since their empirical relevance is almost nil. Finally, we add a post-1990 dummy to control for the fact that, in the latter period, several sub-Saharan countries experienced rather generalized if incomplete improvements of their economic and socioeconomic performances.[2] We also run our models by replacing the post-1990 variable with a series of dummies for each decade as well as with year fixed effects. These changes do not affect our main findings. Descriptive statistics for all of the previous variables are reported in Table A4 in the appendix.

Table 8.1 displays the regression coefficients associated with our main explanatory factors. For ease of presentation, coefficients of control variables are omitted in this table, but full regression results are reported in Table A5 to Table A9 in the appendix. To appropriately deal with the non-stationarity of the dependent variables measuring social welfare, we employed the ECM technique. The eight models that were tested regress the change of one of the dependent variables from one year to the next on its lagged level and the lagged level of every explanatory factors and their first-difference (see our general model in Chapter 7). We did the same for all controls except for time-invariant variables and the post-1990 dummy that were included only in levels.

The coefficients of the lagged dependent variables in levels are negative and statistically significant, meaning that inferences from these estimates should be free of unit-root concerns (see Tables A5 to A9 in the appendix). Results suggest that social welfare indicators

---

[2] This control could not be included in models that have health expenditure as dependent variable because data are available only since 1995.

Table 8.1 Summary of main regression results for social welfare (health expenditure, primary and secondary school enrollment, life expectancy at birth, and under-5 mortality rate)

Model		Δ Public health expenditure	Δ Primary school enrollment	Δ Secondary school enrollment	Δ Life expectancy at birth	Δ Under-5 mortality rate
Model 1	Leader duration $_{(t-1)}$	0.004 (0.003)	−0.013 (0.016)	−0.012 (0.008)	−0.001 (0.002)	0.016 (0.012)
Model 2	Leader duration $_{(t-1)}$	0.016** (0.007)	−0.117** (0.049)	−0.097*** (0.026)	−0.011** (0.005)	0.048 (0.035)
	Leader duration $_{(t-1)}$ * Leader duration $_{(t-1)}$	−0.000** (0.000)	0.004** (0.002)	0.003*** (0.001)	0.000* (0.000)	−0.001 (0.001)
Model 3	Δ elected leader	0.066 (0.071)	0.522 (0.624)	0.059 (0.331)	−0.038 (0.059)	0.565 (0.469)
	Elected leader $_{(t-1)}$	0.143** (0.070)	0.540 (0.418)	0.332* (0.191)	0.070 (0.049)	−0.558* (0.326)
	Δ democratically elected leader	0.175 (0.117)	0.810 (0.845)	−0.148 (0.315)	0.127** (0.060)	−0.632 (0.629)
	Democratically elected leader $_{(t-1)}$	0.210** (0.096)	1.014** (0.416)	0.811*** (0.213)	0.277*** (0.054)	−1.352*** (0.329)
Model 4	Δ cumulative no. of elections	0.022 (0.021)	−0.101 (0.196)	−0.010 (0.082)	0.038** (0.019)	0.037 (0.137)
	Cumulative no. of elections $_{(t-1)}$	0.037** (0.018)	−0.060 (0.060)	0.069 (0.045)	0.077*** (0.015)	−0.261*** (0.060)

Model 5	Δ cumulative no. of democratic elections	−0.025 (0.039)	0.090 (0.317)	0.002 (0.113)	−0.189 (0.191)
	Cumulative no. of democratic elections $_{(t-1)}$	0.012 (0.030)	−0.018 (0.062)	0.121** (0.051)	−0.279*** (0.071)
Model 6	Δ executive control	0.001 (0.001)	−0.009 (0.011)	−0.002 (0.006)	−0.001 (0.008)
	Executive control $_{(t-1)}$	−0.002 (0.001)	−0.009* (0.005)	−0.008*** (0.003)	0.009** (0.004)
Model 7	Δ incumbent reelected	0.075 (0.084)	0.609 (0.657)	0.190 (0.326)	0.375 (0.544)
	Incumbent reelected $_{(t-1)}$	0.148* (0.076)	0.617 (0.423)	0.447** (0.180)	−0.634** (0.319)
	Δ electoral succession	0.119 (0.089)	0.698 (0.734)	−0.015 (0.333)	0.038 (0.483)
	Electoral succession $_{(t-1)}$	0.194** (0.088)	0.539 (0.427)	0.521** (0.206)	−1.342*** (0.334)
	Δ electoral alternation	0.063 (0.098)	0.742 (0.983)	−0.374 (0.521)	−0.356 (0.610)
	Electoral alternation $_{(t-1)}$	0.168** (0.083)	1.516*** (0.510)	1.306*** (0.261)	−1.258*** (0.401)

Table 8.1 (cont.)

Model		Δ Public health expenditure	Δ Primary school enrollment	Δ Secondary school enrollment	Δ Life expectancy at birth	Δ Under-5 mortality rate
Model 8	Δ multiparty regime – no alternation	0.165*	0.559	0.129	0.017	−0.155
		(0.095)	(0.686)	(0.303)	(0.068)	(0.524)
	Multiparty regime – no alternation $_{(t-1)}$	0.156**	0.612	0.497***	0.113**	−0.729**
		(0.077)	(0.381)	(0.170)	(0.045)	(0.314)
	Δ multiparty regime – one alternation	−0.039	1.358	−0.698	0.067	−0.479
		(0.106)	(1.213)	(0.672)	(0.083)	(0.671)
	Multiparty regime – one alternation $_{(t-1)}$	0.201**	0.807	0.550**	0.304***	−2.076***
		(0.087)	(0.535)	(0.247)	(0.060)	(0.396)
	Δ multiparty regime – more alternation	−0.077	0.141	0.206	0.221*	0.289
		(0.138)	(1.678)	(0.673)	(0.124)	(0.992)
	Multiparty regime – more alternation $_{(t-1)}$	0.104	1.890***	1.452***	0.335***	−1.414***
		(0.097)	(0.571)	(0.350)	(0.077)	(0.460)

Notes: Controls are omitted. Complete regression results in the appendix. Panel-corrected standard errors (PCSE) in parentheses. * $p < 0.1$; ** $p < 0.05$; *** $p < 0.01$.

adjust very slowly. This is particularly the case for both output indicators (primary and secondary school enrollment) and outcome indicators (life expectancy at birth and child mortality rate). On average, for all these variables over 97 percent of a shock in one given year persists into the next, then more than 97 percent of that into the following year, and so forth.[3] This means that the long-run impact on social welfare indicators of any permanent shock is stronger than its immediate impact. Unsurprisingly, the associations between our independent variables and the dependent variables measuring social welfare are significant only in the long period.

As shown by the first model in Table 8.1, HP2 postulating a negative association between leaders' tenure and social welfare provisions does not find support in the data. Leaders who remained in power for longer periods are not significantly related to lower health spending, school enrollment rates, and life expectancy at birth, nor to higher child mortality rates. Even HP2.1, which posits a curvilinear relationship between duration in office and development performance – whereby a leader's positive impact takes time to materialize, peaks and then gradually weakens – only finds limited empirical support. The expectation is only partially confirmed in relation to primary school enrollment and life expectancy at birth. Shorter durations are significantly associated with lower school enrollment rates and life expectancy at birth. When leaders spend more time in government, the size of these negative associations actually decreases but turns out to be insignificant when their length of stay in office reaches 10 (primary school enrollment rate) or 15 years in office (life expectancy at birth). With regard to health spending, we found the opposite relation. Shorter durations are associated with higher levels of public health expenditure. As duration in office increases, the magnitude of this positive effect decreases and becomes negative but insignificant after 15 years of tenure. Finally, we detected no significant relationships (neither linear nor quadratic) between leaders' tenure and child mortality rates.

The association, predicted by HP3 and HP3.1, between (democratically) elected leaders and development shows interesting differences depending on whether we look at social welfare investments, outputs

---

[3] This percentage is obtained from the following formula: $1-\lambda$, where λ is the regression coefficient of the lagged value of the dependent variable included among regressors, which represents the "error correction rate."

or outcomes. Leaders with a nondemocratic electoral mandate are significantly associated with higher investments in health and higher rates of (secondary) school enrollment, but they are not related to any significant effect on outcomes. Only democratically elected leaders are significantly linked to beneficial effects in increasing life expectancy at birth and decreasing child mortality rates. They are also positively and significantly associated with higher investments in health, but a Wald test on the difference between the regression coefficients of elected and democratically elected leaders proves that the said effect is not distinguishable from that of leaders elected undemocratically.

The results of the models that tested HP4 and HP4.1 confirm that a higher cumulative number of (democratic) multiparty elections tend to positively affect a leader's performance in enhancing their citizens' well-being. A country's more extensive experience with elections is significantly related to more public investments in health, higher life expectancy at birth and lower child mortality rates. With the exclusion of health spending and primary school enrollment rates, this positive effect is confirmed for political regimes with a higher number of elections deemed democratic.

HP5 suggests a positive association between electoral competitiveness and development and finds empirical support for only three of our five social welfare indicators. More precisely, elected presidents (or prime ministers) who won relatively limited majorities of votes (or seats) are significantly associated with higher primary and secondary school enrollment rates and lower child mortality rates, but not with our remaining two indicators (life expectancy and health spending).

The analyses testing the role of electoral successions and alternations (i.e., HP6 and HP7) show the most robust and straightforward results. Across all social welfare indicators, electoral "successors" – namely, leaders replacing an outgoing leader from the same party – are associated with the best performances. Compared to non-elected leaders, successors tend to invest more in health and to promote school enrollment increases. In terms of life expectancy and child mortality, they also exhibit better performances when compared to incumbents that were confirmed in office by new elections.

Similarly, "alternators" – that is, elected leaders who win office for a party different from that of the outgoing leader – tend to perform better, in terms of raising social welfare standards, than both non-elected leaders and incumbents confirmed in office by new elections.

This is also evident when we turn to a country's total number of electoral alternations since independence (HP7.1). Countries with at least one episode of alternation present higher health expenditure, school enrollment rates, and life expectancy at birth, as well as lower levels of child mortality, than both non-multiparty regimes and multiparty regimes with no practice of electoral turnovers. More importantly, with the exception of health spending, multiparty regimes that experienced two or more episodes of electoral alternation tend to provide even higher social welfare outputs and outcomes than countries with less numerous electoral alternations or no experience with them at all.[4]

State Consolidation

Theoretical Approaches and Key Determinants

State-building and state capacity have long been associated with socio-economic development and modernisation processes, and essentially interpreted as the latter's political dimension. A classic body of literature linked the early emergence of the modern state model to the deep economic transformations European societies went through over long periods of time, as well as to the unintended by-products of wars and conflicts for political survival among would-be rulers (cf. Tilly 1990; Flora et al. 1999). Ethnic and national identity issues were also taken on board by this literature, as both key hurdles and consequences in the creation and strengthening of state entities. Others focused on the subsequent extension of state capacity, responsibilities and functions, explained either as a result of bottom-up demands from the mobilization of lower social strata, or as an outcome produced by "self-referring" state agencies in the struggle for budget increases (cf. Poggi 1992:163ff.).

A number of autonomous insights came from scholars who explored state formation and consolidation processes – or lack thereof – in developing areas. Some stressed the connection between persistently low levels of development, poor public revenues, and natural resources

---

[4] T tests were employed to estimate whether the differences between regression coefficients of variables included in Model 7 and Model 8 respectively are significant or not.

rents, on the one hand, and civil wars and political disorder on the other (Bates 2008b:4–5). The persistence, in some non-Western regions, of many weak or "quasi-states" – that is, states recognized by other states and by international organizations that nevertheless lacked "substantial and credible statehood" (Jackson 1990:22) in terms of effective control over territory and population – was also explained as a result of their colonial origins and of a subsequent international system based on principles and interests that protected their survival and prevented their disappearance (cf. Jackson and Rosberg 1982b; Clapham 1998; Herbst 2000).

More recently, democracy and democratization have likewise been looked at as factors affecting state-building processes. This is an approach that comes very close to our interest in the impact of leadership change dynamics on state consolidation, so we take this strand of the literature, which we examine hereafter, as a starting point for structuring our analysis.

Based on the Western experience of state formation largely occurring prior to state democratization, scholars have predominantly looked at the two processes as sequence-like, with few doubts on what comes first. Historical evidence seemed to be in line with the logical argument whereby a state has to be in place before it can be democratized. Democracy is nothing but the form that (the government of) an existing state can take. The early literature on political development was quick in pointing out that the distance between an ungoverned territory and a functioning state is larger and more salient that that between democratic and undemocratic rule. It was famously observed that "men may, of course, have order without liberty, but they cannot have liberty without order. Authority has to exist before it is limited" (Huntington 1968:7–8). Contemporary Somalia, whose central government collapsed in the early 1990s, has long been a textbook illustration of how a degree of order is required, based on the creation of some kind of minimally functioning institutional arrangement, before one may think of organising orderly participatory and competitive contests for power. Linz and Stepan (1996:14) brought the point home with their well-known catchphrase "no state, no democracy," echoed by Kaplan's (1997) "states have never been formed by elections." The state is first and foremost a precondition for democracy; it must simply come prior to the latter.

The argument, however, leads to the question of what constitutes a state. Political thinkers and scientists alike tend to define the state based on one or more of three dimensions, namely political order, administrative capacity, and citizens' consent. Domestic political order exists to the extent that control over the means of coercion is reasonably centralised and monopolized by a single authority. Administrative capacity refers to the existence of some sort of organized offices – a "usable bureaucracy" (Linz and Stepan 1996:11) – for translating directives that come from the top into actual actions on the ground. Finally, within the territory of any given state authority, the people should perceive the exercise of power to be rightful (Gilley 2006:500). All three dimensions are always bound to be imperfectly realized, implying that state-building processes are ultimately long and virtually never-ending affairs.

The deep political changes embarked upon by innumerable developing and emerging countries over the past 30 years or so led some observers to rethink the state-democracy relationship and to contemplate the possibility that, rather than a one-directional link, the second term of the pair may also affect the first one. Thus, an alternative view has emerged stressing the role democratic politics can play in strengthening the state. Open elections in democratized regimes, it is argued, may help the consolidation of internal political order, the building of functioning bureaucracies, and the legitimation of public authority. The underlying idea is that of a necessary distinction, in any state-building process, between the initial stage and subsequent steps. The early creation of basic political order, administrative structures, and embryonic legitimacy must be held separate from the gradual making of a *well-functioning state*, that is, "one with capable, impartial institutions and a solid capacity to develop, legislate, and implement effective policies" (Carothers 2007). The latter stages of state-building thus imply the establishment of institutions that are impartial, efficient, effective, autonomous, and legitimate. Many autocratic rulers may have little reason to walk a road that runs right up against the personal arbitrariness at the heart of their power (Carothers 2007:18–19). The original sequence is thus somewhat turned on its head, as "democratization may itself be a prerequisite for well-governed and consolidated states" (Bratton 2008:7). The dispute sets scholars supporting a more traditional perspective, according to which a state must and should consolidate before it can be democratized, against those who suggest that the very adoption of democratic processes can help strengthen existing but weak states. This has crucial consequential implications, notably prescriptions for anticipating democratic openings ("it helps!") as opposed to postponing democracy ("it hurts!").

One key mechanism through which democratic advances can promote state strengthening is a chain-like connection between democratic inclusion, legitimacy, and effectiveness. The legitimation of state authority – that is, the "popular approval of government and governors or, at least, acceptance of their right to rule" (Levi and Sacks 2009:313) – is a key objective of the democratic process. Inclusive politics help weaken resistances to the social and territorial penetration of state organizations, favoring the enforcement of domestic political order throughout a national territory. Democratic progress reportedly reduced feelings of political exclusion in the case of both the Turkish minority in Bulgaria and ethnic Albanians in Macedonia, for example, fostering the legitimation of state authority in these communities (Engström 2009). More broadly, there is no lack of developing countries whose elites introduced democratic mechanisms, in recent decades, to address severe legitimacy crises that threatened the very survival of their states (Ayoob 2001:137). To the extent that legitimacy favours citizens' cooperation and compliance with public authority, democratic states are also more likely to be effective states.

Another important mechanism has to do with an even more direct institution-building function of electoral processes. Organizing nationwide voting requires the establishment of complex election administration bodies for the registration of voters, the balloting, the counting and reporting of votes, and so on. Slater (2008) demonstrated how holding elections crucially enhanced state infrastructural power over national territories in the South East Asian cases of Malaysia, Indonesia, and the Philippines

While acknowledging the general wisdom of the "no state, no democracy" proposition as a baseline, Mazzuca and Munck (2014) thus observe that this idea often led to excessively pessimistic recommendations, overlooking the different ways in which democracy can actually offer solutions to state-related problems. In particular, they rebuke warnings that electoral competition may ignite anarchy, instability and violence, as suggested by the likes of Kaplan (1997), Snyder (2000), Bates (2008a) and Cederman, Wimmer and Min (2010:113), and retort that democratic inclusiveness more often acts as a pacification tool "and hence effectively deliver(s) political order" (Mazzuca and Munck 2014:1224).

Few empirical works directly and systematically addressed the relationship between democratic openings and state development, and they essentially produced only mixed evidence. Charron and Lapuente (2010) submit that the real effect of democracy in poor countries tends to be negative, rather than positive. Bates agrees, with regard to African regimes, when he points out that "electoral competition and state failure go together" (2008a:12). Bäck and Hadenius (2008), on the contrary, find empirical support for their thesis of a J-shaped relationship, whereby democracy needs time to grow roots and positively affect state consolidation. More recently, Wang and Xu (2018:1–2) examined a large sample of countries over a 50-year period to conclude that democratic politics does foster state capacity. The uncertainly bred by political competition, in particular, tends to favor institutional reforms – such as those separating politics from administration, including through independent accounting offices or ombudsmen, for example – that reduce the room for rent-seeking and other forms of malfeasance, and ultimately prove positive for administrative effectiveness, transparency, and state-building.

Several other studies have indirectly examined the links between democratic politics and state capacity by focusing on dependent variables that are (or can be seen as) proxies for the latter's individual dimensions, including violent conflicts (e.g., Ellingsen 2000; Hegre et al. 2001; Elbadawi and Sambanis 2002; Fearon and Laitin 2003; Marshall and Gurr 2003; Collier, Hoeffler, and Soderbom 2008), taxation (e.g., Cheibub 1998; Thies 2004; Mulligan et al. 2004; Schmitter 2005; Timmons 2010), or legitimacy (e.g., Sil and Chen 2004; Gilley 2006; Levi and Sacks 2009; Rothstein 2009; Carter 2011).

While once again empirical results are largely mixed, the abovementioned, substantial body of literature has conceptual as well as methodological lessons that we can draw upon in structuring our analysis of the relationship between leadership dynamics and state capacity. It is, in particular, a stimulus on how to conceptualize and operationalize the notion of state capacity. When studying a similar relationship, one should start from the key dimensions at the heart of most notions of stateness, identify a limited number of indicators for each of them and then combine them into a single measure. Our approach will focus on only two of the abovementioned three conceptual dimensions of the state, namely, political order and administrative capacity. This is because we posit that, as much as legitimate authority – the third dimension of the state – can be crucial, it is not a defining characteristic but rather an element that favors the sound establishment and good functioning of a state apparatus over the territory and the citizenry that a national government aims to rule (cf. Levi 2002:40; Gilley 2006). Accordingly, we expect elected leaders to be more motivated state-consolidators (because they are more likely to be concerned with meeting voters' demands or needs) as well as more effective at the job (because they are more likely to be perceived as legitimate) than their unelected peers. The pressures for them to perform and ensure the improvement of a country's political order and a functioning administration will be all the stronger when national electoral processes are characterized by respect for democratic standards, recurrent votes, competitiveness of contests, and successions and alternations in office. On the other hand, we anticipate excessively long stays in power to make rulers more self-referential and ultimately deleterious to state consolidation.

Dependent Variable

In selecting an appropriate operationalization of the notion of consolidation of state capacity among the different empirical measures adopted in the literature, we faced two main challenges. First, disagreement about the dimensions underlying the notion of state capacity led some scholars to opt for measures that are actually focused on adjacent, if related, aspects. This is the case, for instance, for quality of governance indicators such as the World Bank's Worldwide Governance Indicators (WGI) and those of the International Country Risk Guide (ICRG) compiled by the Political Risk Services Group. Some of these indicators – e.g., government effectiveness (WGI) or bureaucracy quality (ICRG) – do point to institutional aspects that have to do with state capacity, but they contribute to measuring a distinct underlying concept that refers to the impartiality of institutions that exercise government authority and the extent of citizens' control over the elites (Rothstein and Teorell 2008). The fact that ICRG data are not freely available further hinders their use. To overcome this problem, the Quality of Government dataset includes an index that is obtained by averaging three different ICRG indicators – namely, law and order, bureaucracy quality, and control of corruption. But they cannot be unpacked, and the third component of the index is an aspect that we shall examine separately, in a following section, and is not strictly related to state capacity.

A second issue stems from the fact that most existing indicators do not offer sufficient temporal and geographical coverage, particularly for sub-Saharan Africa, a region for which valid and reliable data are often incomplete. The WGI data were released every two years from 1996 to 2002 and yearly since 2003. The ICRG data cover a longer, if still limited, time span (1984–2017), but, as mentioned, they are not freely available. A third alternative, the Bertelsmann Transformation Index (BTI), suffers from similar weaknesses. While the index includes two components measuring basic administrative capacity and the monopoly of the use of force – two aspects that are strongly related to the concept of state capacity – empirical coverage is only available for seven recent years (2006, 2008, 2010, 2012, 2014, 2016, and 2018). Such a limited temporal coverage does not allow us to compare what happened during the first three postindependence decades, when most African countries were under one-party or military leaderships, with the comparatively more open politics of the subsequent period.

All these shortcomings considered, we ruled out most of the indicators of state capacity commonly used by the extant literature and opted for an operational measure that more clearly matches our notion of state consolidation while at the same time overcoming the abovementioned problems. The State Capacity Index developed by Hanson and Sigman (2013) presents a number of advantages. First, in building their index, the authors adopt a minimalist definition of state capacity, broadly conceived as the ability of state institutions to effectively implement official goals. Next, they operationalize it by focusing exclusively on core functions of the state: its extractive capacity, its administrative capacity, and its coercive capacity. The three functions refer precisely to the two underlying dimensions of state consolidation that we opted to focus on, as mentioned in the previous section, namely political order and administrative capacity. This minimalist approach enables us to avoid conflating state capacity with institutional aspects related to the way policy priorities are pursued, rather than the capability to implement these policies. Second, by aggregating 24 different measures, the index captures several important aspects related to the two dimensions we are interested in. They include, for example, bureaucratic quality and administrative efficiency, size of military personnel and spending, and tax revenues. Finally, the authors employ the latent variable estimation technique developed by Arel-Bundock and Mebane (2011), which has many advantages over traditional factor analysis, including robustness to missing data.

The State Capacity Index covers all the 163 countries mapped by the Polity project in the 1960–2009 period. It thus provides data for all sub-Saharan countries except Cape Verde, São Tomé and Príncipe, Seychelles, and South Sudan. It is a continuous measure that is normalized so to have 0 as mean and 1 as standard deviation. In sub-Saharan Africa, values of the index range from −3.5 to 1.3, with a mean of −0.08 and a standard deviation of 0.63. Unsurprisingly, sub-Saharan countries exhibit levels of state consolidation that lie below the world average. They include some of the worst global performers in terms of state consolidation, particularly Somalia, Chad, the Central African Republic, and Congo-Kinshasa. Among the region's best performers, on the other hand, we find southern African countries such as South Africa, Namibia, and Botswana.

As plotted in Figure 8.3, from a longitudinal perspective the region's average level of state capacity increased constantly during the first two decades after independence (1960–1980), as sub-Saharan countries gradually developed the fragile state apparatuses inherited from colonialism. From the early 1980s, state capacity began to decrease, falling quite markedly in the early 1990s. In the mid-1990s there was a weak recovery, but capacity decreased again in subsequent years. From an aggregate view, state consolidation does not seem to be associated with multiparty rule. The sharpest drop coincided with the beginning of the new era, nor did the continuous spread of elections and the more frequent ousting of leaders through the ballot box seemed to ignite any truly different trend. In the next section, we will conduct time-series and cross-sectional analyses that allow us to assess the actual validity of this seeming association without incurring the problem of ecological fallacy.

Before we move on, however, examining the average level of state consolidation under different types of leaders, as we do in Figure 8.4, reveals that leaders who assume office via multiparty elections tend to perform better in reinforcing state capabilities. But the association is not monotonic and changes across different decades. During the first three postindependence decades, elected leaders performed better not only when compared to unelected leaders, but also to those few leaders

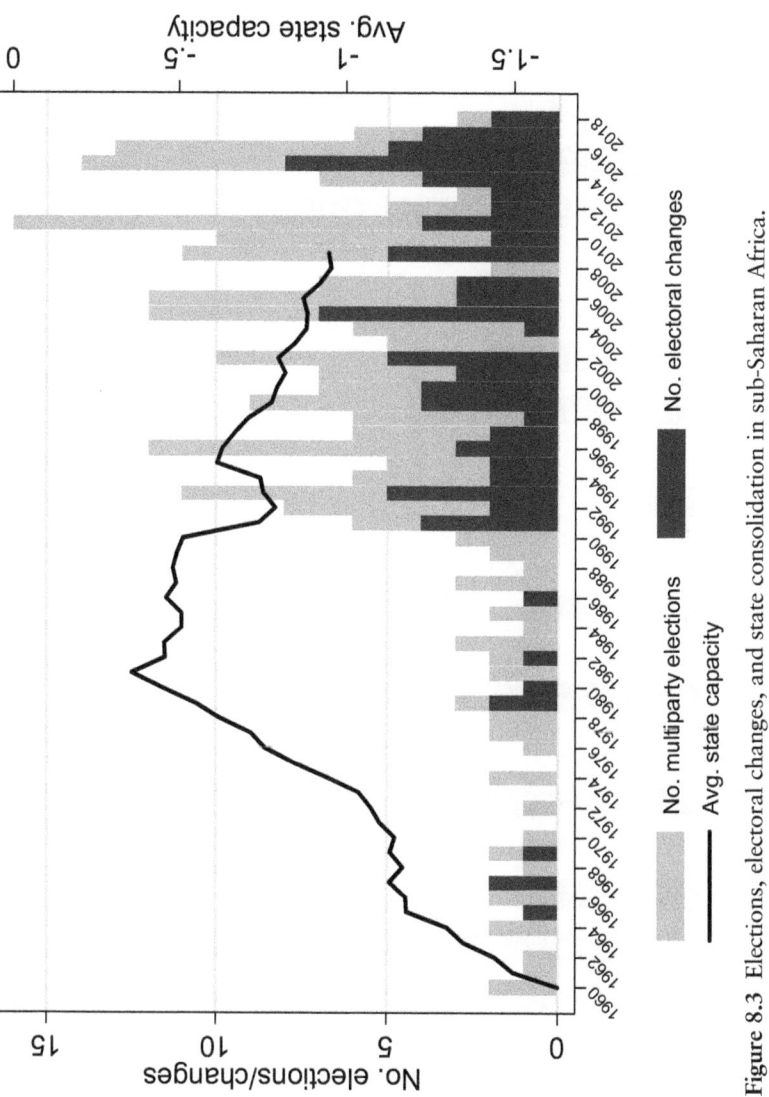

Figure 8.3 Elections, electoral changes, and state consolidation in sub-Saharan Africa.

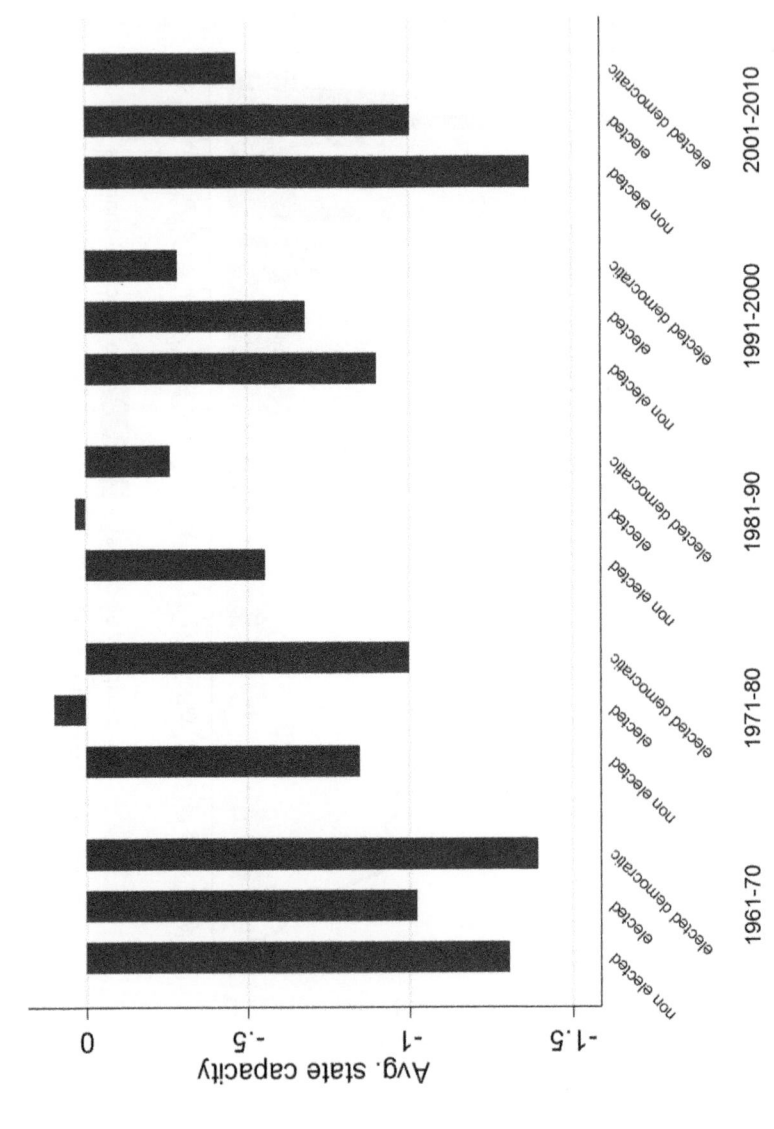

Figure 8.4 State consolidation under non-elected, elected, and democratic leaders in sub-Saharan Africa, by decade.

elected under democratic conditions. The situation changes following the political openings of the 1990s, as democratic leaders are now associated with higher levels of state consolidation than both unelected leaders and leaders elected nondemocratically.

Empirical Analysis

In the following empirical analyses, we include several control variables that may interfere with the relationship we want to shed light on. The association between democracy and state capacity may prove to be spurious, for example, because development lies at the origin of democratization as well as of state consolidation processes. Based on the literature, we thus control for the level of economic development (measured through the natural logarithm of per capita GDP) and for trade openness (the sum of imports and exports as the share of GDP). To account for the oil resource curse argument, we include the rents countries obtain from natural resources, also measured as a percentage of GDP. Three time-invariant variables are also entered in the analysis, namely, the size of a country's land area (in its natural logarithm), a measure of ethnolinguistic fractionalization, and a dummy variable coded "1" for countries that were British colonies. Finally, we account for temporal dynamics through a dummy coded "1" for the years after 1989. Brief descriptions and descriptive statistics of the control variables are reported in Table A4 in the appendix.

Overall, our regression analyses conducted on state capacity provided strong empirical support for our expectation of a positive role played by multiparty electoral competition and leadership turnovers. The main findings are summarized in Table 8.2, which reports regression coefficients of our key explanatory factors (without those of control variables). A complete overview of regression results on state consolidation can be found in Table A10 in the appendix.

First, we find a significant association between officeholders' tenure and state consolidation. As postulated by HP2, the longer sub-Saharan leaders' stay in office, the lower the level of state consolidation of their countries. This result, however, must be taken carefully when we turn to findings from the second model in Table 8.2, testing our hypothesis of a non-linear relationship between leaders' duration and state consolidation (HP2.1). As expected, the regression coefficient for the squared value of duration in office is negative and significant. For a

Table 8.2 *Summary of main regression results for state consolidation*

Model		Δ State capacity index
Model 1	Leader duration $_{(t-1)}$	−0.001*
		(0.001)
Model 2	Leader duration $_{(t-1)}$	0.002
		(0.002)
	Leader duration $_{(t-1)}$ * Leader duration $_{(t-1)}$	−0.000*
		(0.000)
Model 3	Δ elected leader	0.056**
		(0.023)
	Elected leader $_{(t-1)}$	0.023
		(0.015)
	Δ democratically elected leader	0.099***
		(0.032)
	Democratically elected leader $_{(t-1)}$	0.055***
		(0.019)
Model 4	Δ cumulative no. of elections	0.007
		(0.009)
	Cumulative no. of elections $_{(t-1)}$	0.008**
		(0.004)
Model 5	Δ cumulative no. of democratic elections	0.013
		(0.014)
	Cumulative no. of democratic elections $_{(t-1)}$	0.007
		(0.004)
Model 6	Δ executive control	−0.001***
		(0.000)
	Executive control $_{(t-1)}$	−0.001***
		(0.000)
Model 7	Δ incumbent reelected	0.034
		(0.028)
	Incumbent reelected $_{(t-1)}$	0.020
		(0.017)
	Δ electoral succession	0.085***
		(0.033)
	Electoral succession $_{(t-1)}$	0.051***
		(0.016)

Table 8.2 (*cont.*)

Model		Δ State capacity index
	Δ electoral alternation	0.133***
		(0.034)
	Electoral alternation $_{(t-1)}$	0.056**
		(0.022)
Model 8	Δ multiparty regime – no alternation	0.032
		(0.027)
	Multiparty regime – no alternation $_{(t-1)}$	0.024*
		(0.015)
	Δ multiparty regime – one alternation	0.102***
		(0.039)
	Multiparty regime – one alternation $_{(t-1)}$	0.041**
		(0.020)
	Δ multiparty regime – more alternation	0.177***
		(0.065)
	Multiparty regime – more alternation $_{(t-1)}$	0.062**
		(0.030)

Notes: Controls are omitted. Complete regression results in the Appendix. Panel-corrected standard errors (PCSE) in parentheses. * $p < 0.1$; ** $p < 0.05$; *** $p < 0.01$.

correct interpretation of these results, we computed the marginal effect of duration in office on state consolidation at changing values of the duration itself. This further confirmed that long-serving leaders are detrimental to the consolidation of the state apparatus only when they last in office for more than 15 years. For shorter durations, we did not detect a significant association with the dependent variable.

HP3 and HP3.1 postulate a positive role of elected and democratic leaders compared to leaders who came to power without contesting multiparty elections. Both also found support from our data. When a leader wins office through a vote contested by two or more candidates/parties and replaces a non-elected power-holder, we see an immediate positive effect on state consolidation. This beneficial effect, however, fades away in the long run as shown by the non-significance of the coefficient for *elected leader*$_{(t-1)}$. On the other hand, when the elected leader obtains the presidency (premiership) under democratic conditions, this is significantly associated with improvements in state capacity both in the short and in the long period. Our data also proved that democratically elected leaders tend to perform better than both unelected leaders and leaders winning nondemocratic elections.

In line with the previous findings, countries with a longer history of multiparty elections are positively and significantly associated with bureaucratic apparatuses stronger than those of countries with shorter or no experience with multipartism, thus confirming our HP4. The association, however, is not necessarily reinforced when such multiparty votes are also deemed democratic, as we would have expected (HP4.1).

More competitive electoral contests are linked to improvements in state consolidation, validating our hypothesis (HP5). Presidents (or prime ministers) who won office with lower margins of victory are better performers, in terms of strengthening state bureaucracies, than their peers who secured larger shares of votes (or seats).

As posited by HP6 and HP7, leaders who assume office after electoral changes – be they "successors" belonging to the party already in power or "alternators" emerging from the opposition – are related to higher levels of state capacity compared to unelected leaders and reelected incumbents. The rise of a successor or an alternator produces immediate positive effects that persist in subsequent years. We only found partial confirmation, on the other hand, for HP7.1, which suggested a positive influence of the cumulative number of electoral alternations on state consolidation. Multiparty regimes that experienced two or more episodes of alternation are associated with higher levels of state capacity than both one-party/no-party regimes and multiparty regimes that never experienced turnovers. However, a Wald test shows that the regression coefficient of multiparty regimes with two or more alternations is not significantly different from the coefficient of multiparty regimes with only one alternation.

Corruption Control

Theoretical Approaches and Key Determinants

In 1996, the then president of the World Bank, Jim Wolfensohn, delivered his famous "cancer of corruption" speech, in which he forcefully stressed how "corruption diverts resources from the poor to the rich, increases the cost of running businesses, distorts public expenditures and deters foreign investors," and that, for these very reasons, "it is a major barrier to sound and equitable development" (Wolfensohn 1996). His strong statement coincided with a period in which academics had started to pay increasing attention to the detrimental consequences of corruption for economic growth, regime stability, and citizens' confidence in national institutions and political authority (Mauro 1995; Seligson 2002; Anderson and Tverdova 2003).

A plethora of studies has exposed the endemic corruption in large sections of the public sectors of African countries. Venality pervades the everyday activity of many public-desk officials and elected representatives, up to the highest political authorities, undermining the political, economic, and social development of a poor region (Kempe 1999; Blundo and Olivier de Sardan 2006; Mbaku 2010; Aborisade and Aliyyu 2018).

Several theoretical arguments have been made to explain the widespread reach of the phenomenon south of the Sahara. A cultural approach linked corruption to social norms and widely accepted behaviors that, in most African societies, emphasize gift-giving and loyalty to family or clan, rather than Western-style rule of law. Olivier de Sardan (1999) refers to this as the "moral economy of corruption" and points out that the incidence of corruption is not so much a deviation of public actors' behavior from formal rules, but is rather the divergence of the latter rules from accepted conducts. This argument is strictly related to the notion of neo-patrimonialism, first applied to Africa by Médard (1979) for the case of Cameroon and referring to "the incorporation of patrimonial logic into bureaucratic institutions ... [as] the *core* feature of politics in Africa" (Bratton and van de Walle 1997:62).

A partially related explanation – at times referred to as "revisionist" – was articulated between the late 1960s and early 1970s by scholars who claimed that the universality of corruption was to be attributed to the specific stage of development of African countries (Leff 1964; Huntington 1968; Scott 1972). These scholars argued that, in modernizing societies and underdeveloped economies, a certain level of corruption is efficiency-enhancing. It provides incentives to mobilize an otherwise rigid bureaucratic apparatus, alleviate problems of capital formation, and act as a lubricant in easing the path toward modernity.

A more recent perspective originates from the public choice school and looks at corruption as the consequence of a lack of competition in both the economic and the political arenas (Rose-Ackerman 1999). By restricting markets through their legislative and regulatory powers, in particular, government officials can distribute highly lucrative public contracts. This discretionary power allows them to extract illicit profits, for instance through bribes, from private economic actors. The argument fits well with the postcolonial experience of several sub-Saharan countries, where many leaders established one-party regimes and nationalized industries in key economic sectors. This gave high-level public officials and their cronies a direct control over public companies and the opportunity to extract rents through the issue of public contracts and trade licences.

In the political arena, the lack of electoral competition made it difficult for African citizens to sanction and replace those responsible for corrupt activities. For about three decades, most postindependence regimes in Africa lacked procedures for their leaders' transparent and accountable rotation in office.

Political competition has the potential to reduce officials' incentives to engage in corruption through three interrelated mechanisms. The first mechanism is institutional accountability, that is, politicians must periodically compete in elections. Office-seeking politicians, in order to maximize their (re)election chances, have to maintain reasonably honest behavior (Rose-Ackerman 1999). The principal-agent theory sees corruption as a source of agency loss, i.e., the damage suffered by the principal (the citizen) because an agent (the public official) lacks the skills or incentives to complete the task delegated to her/him (Lupia 2003). The second mechanism is political alternation, which discourages corruptors from bribing elected officials, especially those who hold executive powers. As those in office could be replaced, they cannot credibly promise that the particular laws and regulations they adopt will remain in effect in the future. A new government might change such rules simply to benefit different interest groups. This raises the costs of corruption and encourages individuals and businesses to respect the rule of law (Horowitz et al. 2009; Montinola and Jackman 2002). Finally, a third mechanism derives not so much from the procedures of democracy as from its broader functioning. Freedom of information and association helps to monitor public officials, thus limiting opportunities for corrupt behaviors. The media and opposition parties are in a position to act as watchdogs of the government and its administration.

A number of cross-national studies empirically scrutinized the public choice arguments about an association between democracy and corruption control. These studies typically rely on a country's level and duration of democracy as proxies for the presence and effectiveness of electoral competition and political accountability. Evidence failed to provide support for a positive role of the level of democracy. Rather, it is democracies with longer histories that, due to the more solid accountability relationship that is established between politicians and voters through repeated elections, perform better in constraining corruption (Sandholtz and Koetzle 2000; Treisman 2000; Blake and Martin 2006).

To account for the non-significance of the level of democracy, some scholars hypothesized a non-linear relationship (Montinola and Jackman 2002; Pellegata 2013; Sung 2004). In flawed democracies and hybrid regimes, contested elections coexist with authoritarian practices such as an uninterrupted political dominance of the ruling party. This combination weakens political accountability and encourages corrupt practices by powerful officials who abuse their position to benefit particular interest groups in exchange for private gains. Empirical evidence confirmed that hybrid regimes tend to present higher levels of corruption than both closed authoritarianisms and consolidated democracies.

Only a few studies explored the relationship between competition and corruption by focusing on political actors and how they rotate in power, rather than on political regimes. Horowitz et al. (2009) demonstrated that, among the post-communist regimes of Central and Eastern Europe, those that more frequently experienced government turnovers also exhibited a better respect for the rule of law. Similarly, Pellegata (2011) examined a sample of 32 consolidated democracies in the 1945–2000 period to show that higher levels of alternation (measured in terms of ideological or policy distance between different governments) are associated with lower levels of corruption. We are not aware of any study that directly and empirically investigates the effect of different modes of leadership change on corruption in sub-Saharan Africa.

Dependent Variables

Given its conceptual ambiguity and clandestine nature, defining and measuring corruption are challenging tasks. Political corruption is a complex phenomenon that can only be defined in general terms as it encompasses a wide range of activities that vary according to the sector in which they occur, the actors involved, their impact, and the degree to which they are formalized. A narrow but widely used definition considers corruption "the misuse of public office for private financial gain" (Andersson and Heywood 2009). Each corrupt activity thus involves elected officials and/or appointed bureaucrats who exploit the power and authority with which they have been entrusted to obtain private advantages. Such activities take place at the expense of the broader community, thereby violating the norms that regulate public office.

Few attempts in the literature tried to develop objective measures based on actual cases of corruption, such as criminal records for corruption charges included in official police reports or reported by the media. The latter, however, are only spurious indicators of corruption and hardly the basis for valid and reliable measures that can be used in cross-national analyses. For this reason, the vast majority of existing studies relies on perception-based indicators of corruption based on experts' evaluations of the extent of corruption in the public sectors of different countries. The most commonly used are Transparency International's *Corruption Perceptions Index* (CPI) and the World Bank's *Control of Corruption* (CC), which is part of the Worldwide Governance Indicators (Kaufmann et al. 2006; Lambsdorff 2006). Both CPI and CC are built by aggregating a large number of partially similar individual data sources, including polls of experts, surveys of businessmen, senior managers, and individuals, and the assessments of commercial risk agencies, nongovernmental organizations, and multilateral aid agencies. CC combines elite and mass perceptions, but gives much greater weight to the former.

Both CPI and CC, however, present some shortcomings that hinder their use for the purpose of our study. CPI data are released annually, but only since 1995. Moreover, while the dataset currently covers almost all independent countries in the world, up until the early 2000s it only included a few sub-Saharan countries. CC data are available starting from 1996 and covered all African countries from the outset. From 1996 to 2002, however, CC was only published every two years, implying a significant reduction in the number of comparable points in time. More generally, the limited coverage offered by these two measures makes a comparison of Africa's post-1990 multiparty period with the previous three decades, which were dominated by no-party or one-party regimes, quite problematic.

To overcome this problem, we opted for using the corruption data recently released by the Varieties of Democracy project (V-Dem)[5]. These data are also based on expert surveys but they cover all countries of the world from 1900 to the present day. Multiple coders, at least three fifths of whom are native to the country under examination, were used to code each country-year observation, and the coder recruitment procedures and coding procedures were consistent over time and across countries. An item response theory (IRT) measurement model was used to aggregate the experts' responses. The resulting V-Dem Political Corruption Index is a factor index that aggregates six indicators for distinct types of corruption. They cover both different areas and levels of the polity, distinguishing between executive, legislative, and judicial misdeeds. In the executive realm, the measures also differentiate between bribery and embezzlement, and between corruption at the highest echelons of the executive (rulers/cabinet) and in the public sector at large. The measures thus tap into several types of corruption: both "petty" and "grand"; both bribery and theft; both corruption aimed at influencing law making and that affecting implementation. Underlying all six indicators are notions of public office, private gain, and the use of the former for the latter. A Bayesian factor analysis of the six indicators at the level of country-year demonstrates the coherence of the index: they all map to the same conceptual construct.

V-Dem data on corruption are not without weaknesses, yet they have several strengths compared to the main alternatives. First, they have extensive temporal and geographical coverage, as pointed out, which fits our needs. Second, while other datasets collect information on public sector or bureaucratic corruption excluding the executive, legislative, and judicial branches, V-Dem measures capture a broader conceptualization of corruption, thus strengthening the index's content validity. Third, CPI and CC are "polls of polls" that aggregate information from different sources. This inevitably multiplies biases and measurement errors by including those of each original source into the two indexes. V-Dem, on the other hand, avoids this problem because it produces its own original data on corruption. McMann et al. (2016) confirmed the validity of the V-Dem corruption data across countries

---

[5] See www.v-dem.net/en/ for data and documentation.

and over time. However, we also conducted our analyses by employing CPI and CC as robustness checks and the main results are corroborated.

Our dependent variables are thus the V-Dem's indicator for *Political Corruption*, which aggregates the six indicators briefly illustrated previously, and the indicator for *Executive Corruption* obtained by averaging the point estimates from a Bayesian factor analysis model of the indicators for executive bribery and executive embezzlement. We decided to focus specifically on corruption in executive authorities because sub-Saharan countries mostly adopt presidential systems often characterized by strong presidents and quite weak legislative assemblies. The directionality of both indicators runs from less corruption to more corruption. Both political and executive corruption indexes range from 0 to 1 and have average values around 0.61 (1960–2018). This is higher than the world average for the same period, which is around 0.49 for both measures, indicating that corruption south of the Sahara is more common than in other world regions. But there are also substantial cross-country variations. Botswana, Cape Verde, and Namibia generally exhibit low levels of both political and executive corruption, not much higher than in Western European and North American countries. On the contrary, Gabon, Nigeria, and Congo-Brazzaville are among the African countries that have very high average values for both political and executive corruption for 1960–2018.

The line chart plotted in Figure 8.5 displays the longitudinal trend of the indexes of political (solid line) and executive (dashed line) corruption. After initially falling during the first postindependence years, average values for both indexes – particularly for corruption in the executive branch – increased steadily from the mid-1960s to the mid-1970s. In the late 1970s, the region experienced a second period of decline in corruption levels that, however, again increased from the end of the 1970s and over the subsequent 20 years. From the late 1990s, political corruption stopped rising and stabilized at an average of 0.66. While since the mid-1960s executive corruption had remained higher than political corruption, on the other hand, it began to decrease from the end of the century. Since 2014, both political and executive corruption have sharply declined.

The bar chart in Figure 8.5 shows that, in line with our expectations, political corruption stopped rising and executive corruption started to

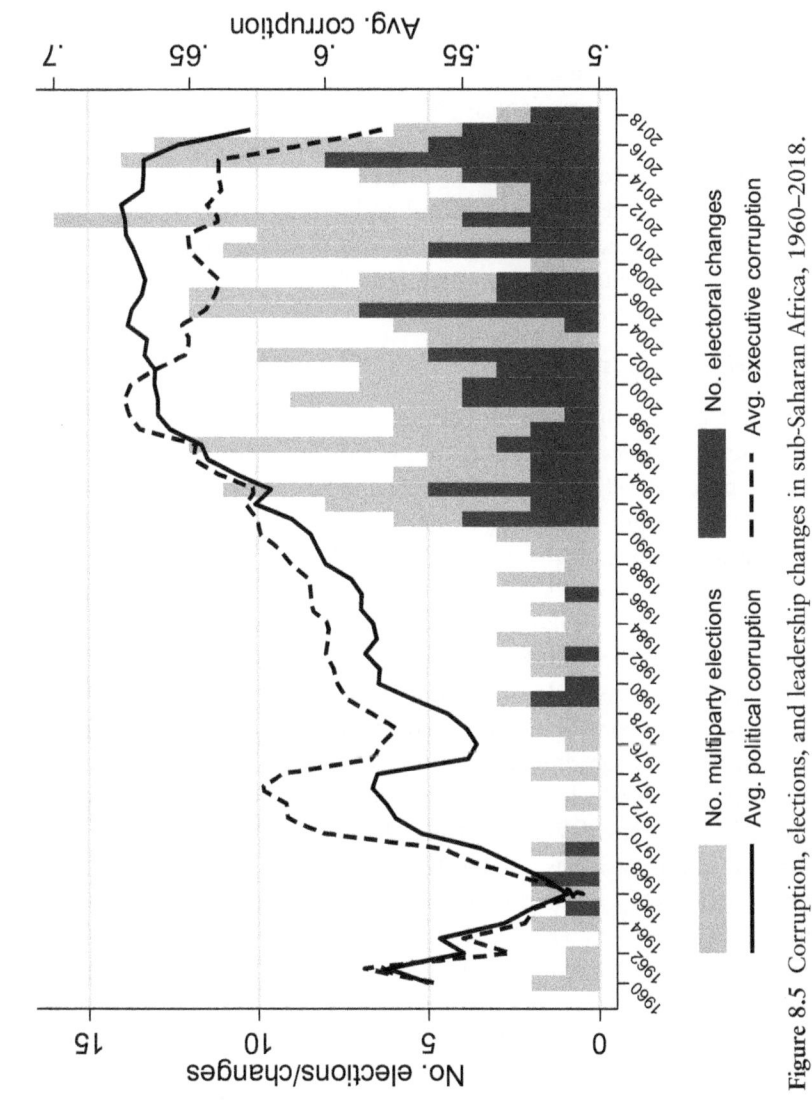

Figure 8.5 Corruption, elections, and leadership changes in sub-Saharan Africa, 1960–2018.
Source: ALC and V-Dem

decline in the period when multiparty elections and electoral changes in the region had become more common than during the previous three decades. Figure 8.6 displays the average levels of both political (dark gray) and executive (light gray) corruption by ways in which leaders took office by decades. Overall, leaders elected in fully democratic countries are associated with lower levels of both types of corruption than non-elected leaders. This is particularly evident since the 1990s. In the latter decades, democratic leaders also tended to perform better than leaders elected in regimes failing to meet minimal democratic standards. Average levels of political and executive corruption associated with these leaders are not significantly different from those under leaders that came to power through non-electoral means.

Empirical Analysis

We control the validity of our research hypotheses by including in the empirical analyses a number of potentially confounding factors, including the level of economic development (measured through the natural logarithm of GDP per capita), the size of the government (government expenditure as a share of GDP), and economic freedom (imports of goods and services as a share of GDP). We also consider the possible impact of the rents obtained from natural resources and of official development aid. Both variables are entered as shares of GDP/GNI. All these controls are drawn from the World Bank's WDI. Moreover, we control for political stability through a 0–10 scale measuring the magnitude of interstate and civil conflicts and political violence in general (data from the Center for Systemic Peace, *Major Episodes of Political Violence 1946–2017*). Finally, we include three time-invariant variables – namely, ethnolinguistic fractionalization, British colonial legacy and a dummy coded "1" for states that have a federal structure – as well as a dummy coded "1" for all the years after 1989 to account for temporal dynamics. We also run our analyses by substituting time-invariant variables with country fixed effects and the post-1990 dummy with dummies for each decade or year fixed-effects. The main results did not change. Brief descriptions and descriptive statistics for all control variables are reported in Table A4 in the appendix.

Table 8.3 shows the results for political and executive corruption, respectively, by only reporting regressions coefficients associated with

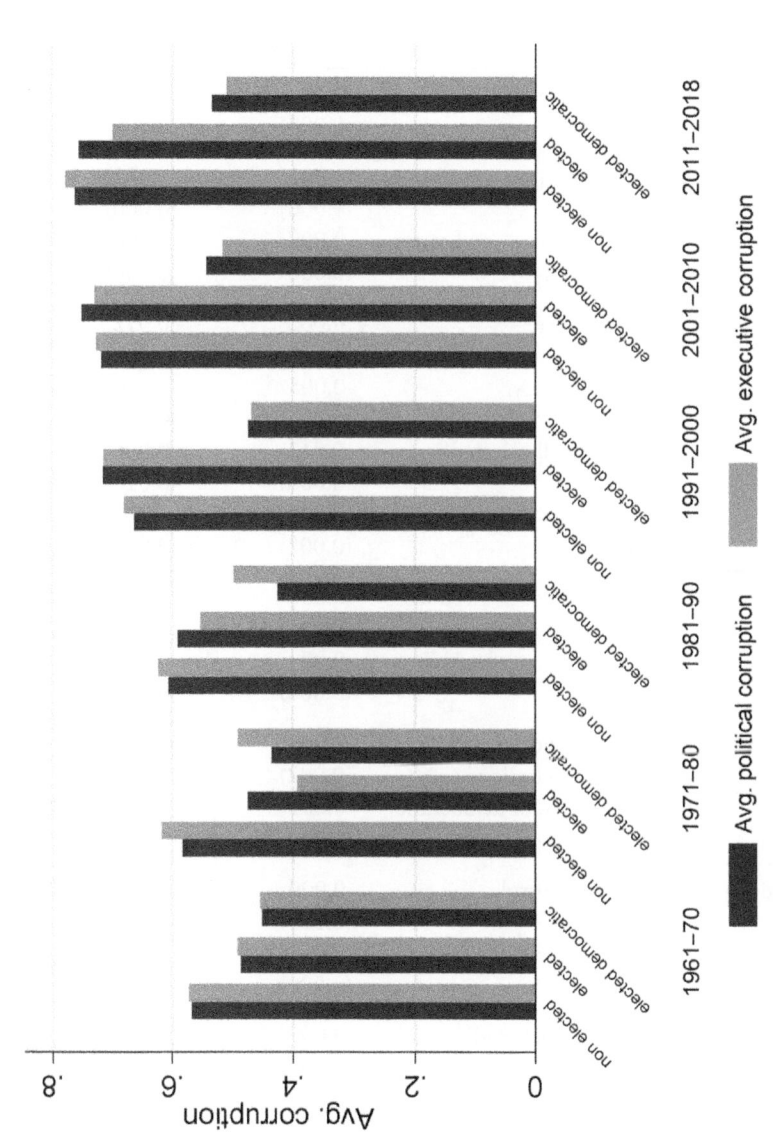

Figure 8.6 Political and executive corruption under non-elected, elected, and democratic leaders in sub-Saharan Africa, by decade.
Source: ALC and V-Dem

Table 8.3 *Summary of main regression results for corruption control (political corruption and executive corruption)*

Model		Δ Political corruption	Δ Executive corruption
Model 1	Leader duration $_{(t-1)}$	−0.000	0.000
		(0.000)	(0.000)
Model 2	Leader duration $_{(t-1)}$	−0.001**	−0.001**
		(0.000)	(0.000)
	Leader duration $_{(t-1)}$ * Leader duration $_{(t-1)}$	0.000***	0.000**
		(0.000)	(0.000)
Model 3	Δ elected leader	0.002	−0.012**
		(0.004)	(0.005)
	Elected leader $_{(t-1)}$	−0.005**	−0.004
		(0.002)	(0.003)
	Δ democratically elected leader	0.012*	−0.006
		(0.006)	(0.010)
	Democratically elected leader $_{(t-1)}$	−0.008***	−0.002
		(0.002)	(0.004)
Model 4	Δ cumulative no. of elections	−0.000	−0.006***
		(0.001)	(0.002)
	Cumulative no. of elections $_{(t-1)}$	−0.002***	−0.001**
		(0.000)	(0.001)
Model 5	Δ cumulative no. of democratic elections	0.000	−0.011***
		(0.002)	(0.003)
	Cumulative no. of democratic elections $_{(t-1)}$	−0.001**	0.000
		(0.000)	(0.001)
Model 6	Δ executive control	−0.000	0.000
		(0.000)	(0.000)
	Executive control $_{(t-1)}$	0.000***	0.000
		(0.000)	(0.000)
Model 7	Δ incumbent reelected	0.009*	−0.005
		(0.005)	(0.006)
	Incumbent reelected $_{(t-1)}$	−0.004*	−0.001
		(0.002)	(0.003)
	Δ electoral succession	0.002	−0.015**
		(0.005)	(0.007)

Table 8.3 (*cont.*)

Model		Δ Political corruption	Δ Executive corruption
	Electoral succession $_{(t-1)}$	−0.010***	−0.009**
		(0.003)	(0.004)
	Δ electoral alternation	0.001	−0.015*
		(0.006)	(0.008)
	Electoral alternation $_{(t-1)}$	−0.006**	−0.002
		(0.003)	(0.004)
Model 8	Δ multiparty regime – no alternation	0.007	−0.016***
		(0.005)	(0.006)
	Multiparty regime – no alternation $_{(t-1)}$	−0.005**	−0.003
		(0.002)	(0.003)
	Δ multiparty regime – one alternation	−0.007	−0.030***
		(0.006)	(0.008)
	Multiparty regime – one alternation $_{(t-1)}$	−0.006*	−0.002
		(0.003)	(0.004)
	Δ multiparty regime – more alternation	0.010	0.004
		(0.010)	(0.016)
	Multiparty regime – more alternation $_{(t-1)}$	−0.007**	−0.002
		(0-004)	(0.006)

Notes: Controls are omitted. Complete regression results in the appendix. Panel-corrected standard errors (PCSE) in parentheses. * $p < 0.1$; ** $p < 0.05$; *** $p < 0.01$.

our key explanatory factors for ease of presentation. Full regression results can be found in Table A11 and the Table A12 in the appendix. Overall, our findings support most of the research hypotheses we advanced. But there are interesting differences with regard to the temporal dynamic of the association between leadership changes and the two types of corruption. The effects of our explanatory factors on executive corruption are mostly significant only in the short term, whereas their impact on political corruption becomes manifest in the long period.

The positive association between leaders' duration in office and corruption postulated in HP2 is not supported by the evidence, neither for political nor for executive corruption. The non-linear relationship between leaders' tenure and corruption imagined in HP2.1 is only partially confirmed. We do find, in line with our expectations, that both political and executive corruption are higher under leaders who have been in office for more than 20 years. With regard to executive corruption, we detected no significant associations with shorter tenures. Levels of political corruption, on the other hand, are significantly lower for leaders who have been in office for no more than ten years.

As postulated by HP3, leaders elected under nondemocratic conditions are associated with lower levels of both political and executive corruption when compared to unelected leaders. However, for executive corruption the beneficial effect of multiparty elections is only significant in the year in which an elected leader comes to office, whereas the effects on political corruption only emerge in the long period. Democratic leaders too are significantly associated with lower levels of political corruption when compared to unelected leaders. However, a Wald test between the regression coefficients of leaders elected in an undemocratic setting and democratically elected leaders did not prove that the latter outperform the former in fighting political corruption.

We expected that the higher the number of multiparty elections a country held since independence the lower the level of corruption (HP4), and that a similar negative association should also hold for elections deemed democratic (HP4.1). Both hypotheses were confirmed by the results of our analyses on political as well as executive corruption. We again detected some differences with regard to the timing of the impact of our two explanatory factors on the two types of corruption. For political corruption, the cumulative number of elections, and of democratic elections, only produces a significant impact in the long period. For executive corruption, the effect of the cumulative number of elections short of democracy is manifest in both the short and the long term, whereas that of democratic elections is only significant in the short run and does not persist over longer periods.

Rather surprisingly, the association between the (higher) competitiveness of elections and (lower) levels of corruption that we hypothesized in HP5 is only significant for the aggregate index of political corruption – that is, the higher the share of votes (seats) obtained by the sitting president (parliamentary government), the higher the level of political corruption – but not for the estimate of corruption in the executive branch.

HP6 conjectured that leaders assuming office in an electoral succession will be associated with lower corruption levels than both unelected leaders and incumbents that are reelected. The hypothesis found empirical support in our data. While, when compared to the other two types of leaders, "successors" only exhibit significantly better performances in containing political corruption if we consider a long time horizon, the improvements they are associated with in a country's fight against executive corruption starts in the year they are elected and endures in subsequent years.

Our findings only partially confirmed HP7, which assumed that opposition leaders winning an election outperform both unelected leaders as well as incumbents that are reelected. "Alternators" are in fact associated with significantly lower levels of corruption than unelected leaders, but not when they are compared to incumbents that are confirmed in office. As with some of the previous models, there is again a distinctive temporal impact of electoral alternation on political and executive corruption, respectively. The impact on executive corruption is significant, though weak, only in year t, but it then dissipates in the following years. On the contrary, political corruption exhibits a significant effect only when we consider a longer time horizon.

Partial confirmation is also found for HP7.1, postulating an effect of cumulated political alternations on corruption. Both in countries that experienced only one episode of electoral alternation and those that accumulated two or more turnovers, levels of political corruption tend to be lower when compared to one-party or no-party/military regimes. The significance of the regression coefficients of the lagged values of these two variables shows that these effects can only be detected in the year after a new alternation occurred. However, regimes that passed the "two turnovers test" do not display levels of political corruption that are significantly lower than those of regimes that experienced only one episode of alternation. In the last model of Table 8.3, the significance of the regression coefficients of the variable "multiparty regime – one alternation," taken in first-difference, indicates that when a political regime experiences its first episode of alternation it displays a significantly lower level of executive corruption compared to non-multiparty regimes. This beneficial effect vanishes in the next year. Multiparty regimes that experience more than one electoral alternation, however, do not present lower levels of executive corruption compared to non-multiparty regimes.

A Synopsis of Key Empirical Findings

African political leaders – particularly the way they reach and retain office – are empirically linked to a range of development outcomes. We hereafter sum up the main results of the investigations we carried out on the impact of leadership dynamics on economic growth, social welfare, stateness, and control of corruption south of the Sahara, as presented and discussed in more detail in Chapters 5, 7, and the present one.

Economic growth visibly appears to respond to the conditions under which government leaders are selected in Africa. For a country's economic progress, soldiers' takeovers in the region have not paid off when compared to the performance of non-coup leaders, nor have rulers' longer stays in office proved beneficial when compared to shorter tenures. Elected power-holders – even those who run under highly questionable, nondemocratic conditions – are associated with better economic results. This is all the more the case for countries with longer track records with the use of national elections and for those where such votes were held under more competitive conditions. Except for the role of successions and alternations – which, on the aggregate, do not prove to be a relevant factor – elections as a method for selecting and holding African leaders somewhat more accountable do essentially alter the latter's incentives and ultimately contribute to improving economic performances, as we anticipated.

When we move beyond growth and turn to measures that are meant to account for a country's social welfare progress or regression – namely, public health spending, school enrollment, life expectancy, and child mortality – the adjustment of performances to modified leadership dynamics appears to be slower, taking place in the long term rather than more straightaway. This is not surprising given the nature of most health and education indicators. On the other hand, a leader's length of tenure in office is not clearly related to welfare changes in the way we anticipated. But a country's longer, cumulative experience with elections as a way of "choosing" its rulers is, as is in part the actual competitiveness of voting processes. Democratically elected leaders, in particular, are related to welfare improvements across the board, regardless of the measures one looks at among the ones we examined. Elected leaders at large also exhibit predominantly beneficial effects, albeit in a less comprehensive manner. Contrary to what we found when examining growth, our welfare output and outcome indicators are also responsive to leadership changes through both succession and alternation. In all, the way a country selects its leaders does have a relevant impact on the social welfare of its people.

The buildup of state capacity – that is, ensuring political order and a functioning administration – are key components of development processes in often poor and fragile contexts such as those of sub-Saharan Africa. State consolidation was thus our third empirical focus and we found very substantial support for our starting hypotheses. While extensive stays in office become detrimental for the capacity of a state when too long (more than 15 years), a leader's being elected – particularly when this comes as a result of comparatively competitive and democratic contests, as well as when taking office as a successor or an alternator – typically works as a state strengthening factor. How long leaders sit at the top, on the other hand, is not systematically related to increased levels of political nor executive corruption – syndromes that are in direct contradiction to the well-functioning of the public sector apparatus. But there are indications that both types of toxic practices are more common under leaders who have been in power for 20 years or more and – in the case of the broader phenomenon of political corruption – lower for those who have been in office for less than a decade. Unelected leaders, in particular, tend to preside over more venal systems when compared to elected ones (even where the latter take or retain office through votes are not free and fair), although the latter also appear to allow the diffusion of executive corruption once they move out of an early honeymoon period (political corruption at large tends to spread at a later stage). The actual extent of competition at the polls is not *per se* a factor. But the longer a country's history with elections, the more democratic its politics, and the more frequent election-based leadership rotation (particularly with successors rather than alternators), the less corrupt habits are allowed to expand in and corrode the public sphere.

Analysts and observers have long been divided between those who ignore or write off political leadership as a relevant factor for development and those who suspect, hint, or openly argue the exact contrary, if virtually always without producing any rigorous evidence. We tried to address the issue starting from scratch, by conceiving and compiling an original leaders' dataset and setting out to employ it for systematic testing of the leadership-development hypothesis. The evidence is rich and ultimately compelling. Rulers do indeed make a difference across a range of dimensions and empirical measures of progress. The dynamics of political leadership matter for Africa's development.

9 | *Autocrats, Hegemons, Democrats, and Transients*

Across Africa, the multiparty reforms of the 1990s ushered in a new politico-institutional scenario that was vastly different from what had been in place before. At least to an extent – as we illustrated in this work – African rulers had to "adapt or die": in relatively more open political settings, they were now to take the job of delivering development rather more seriously in terms of their prospects for political survival. Virtually all of them were subjected to a higher degree of public scrutiny over their government performances and had to face some potential competition. Anecdotally, the photo opportunity of president John Magufuli, "the Bulldozer," little more than a month after he had been voted into office, cleaning rubbish from the streets of Dar-es-Salaam – hardly something you could have expected from most autocrats of the past such as, say, Jomo Kenyatta, Mengistu Haile Mariam, Gnassingbé Eyadéma, or Moussa Traoré – well illustrates the extent to which, even under the politically "safe" conditions guaranteed by a hegemonic party such as the Chama Cha Mapinduzi, an elected ruler would likely be much better aware that he needs to show he is at work and will deliver. Thus, while all too often democratic formalities proved little more than a façade, with political survival risks actually kept to a minimum, in many cases more substantial implications emerged. As environmental pressures changed, the political behavior of some leaders responded, and, in a number of countries, contributed to improved development performances. We now want to complete the conceptual and empirical analyses carried out in previous chapters by deriving and outlining an up-to-date account of distinct kinds of contemporary African leaders.

A New Typology for African Leaders

In the early 1980s, Jackson and Rosberg (1982, 1984) outlined a typology of political leadership in postcolonial Africa that rapidly became widely influential. The authors, as we have already seen in Chapter 1, argued that the continent had seen the emergence of an overarching leadership style, dubbed "personal rule" and essentially revolving around an authoritarian exercise of power aimed at political survival, with the largest room for informal and neo-patrimonial practices in a context lacking significant institutional and political constraints for the individuals at the top. As much as the conceptualization and theoretical implications of Jackson and Rosberg's work fitted and helped the understanding of the politics of the time, however, they gradually lost their usefulness due to the important transformations that most African polities underwent after the latter decade of the twentieth century. Not only have institutions become more important in structuring the political game and leadership dynamics on the continent (cf. Posner and Young 2007, 2018), but Jackson and Rosberg's categorization of leaders as "princes," "prophets," "autocrats," and "tyrants" is no longer as helpful in highlighting the key features shared by some African rulers but not by others. Today, there are few tyrants and even fewer prophets. The key divides are now those between unelected and elected rulers, between leaders who control electoral outcomes and those who cannot or do not want to, or between office-holders who take over from their party predecessors and those who emerge from the ranks of election-winning oppositions. Moreover, Jackson and Rosberg's implicit but crucial argument about a generalized development failure of Africa's postcolonial leaderships would be even more difficult to apply to the power-holders of the past three decades.

Thus, we hereafter propose a revised and rather straightforward typology of African leaders, one that we deem more useful for the continent's recent, present, and future scenarios. The typology builds on the same underlying perspective that we adopted in previous chapters, it complements our econometric analyses and allows us to sketch a simple map for understanding where individual leadership stories belong.

The criteria that we employ to distinguish different leaders are depicted in the diagram in Figure 9.1 below. First, length of stay in office. Since our underlying focus is on the *impact* of political leadership, we set apart leaders that only remained in power for less than one year from the rest of the pack. Due to their short duration in office, we deem these interim or "transient" leaders to have a very limited chance

A New Typology for African Leaders   257

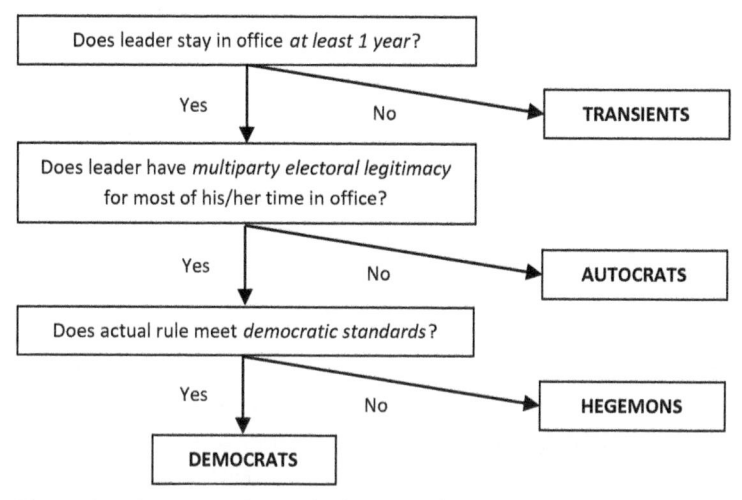

```
┌─────────────────────────────────────────┐
│ Does leader stay in office at least 1 year? │
└─────────────────────────────────────────┘
         Yes │    │ No
             │    └─────────────► ┌───────────┐
             │                    │ TRANSIENTS│
             ▼                    └───────────┘
┌─────────────────────────────────────────┐
│ Does leader have multiparty electoral   │
│ legitimacy for most of his/her time in  │
│ office?                                 │
└─────────────────────────────────────────┘
         Yes │    │ No
             │    └─────────────► ┌───────────┐
             │                    │ AUTOCRATS │
             ▼                    └───────────┘
┌─────────────────────────────────────────┐
│ Does actual rule meet democratic        │
│ standards?                              │
└─────────────────────────────────────────┘
         Yes │    │ No
             │    └─────────────► ┌───────────┐
             ▼                    │ HEGEMONS  │
      ┌───────────┐               └───────────┘
      │ DEMOCRATS │
      └───────────┘
```

Figure 9.1 A new typology of African leaders: criteria (I).
Note: elected leaders include those who constitutionally "inherit" an electoral mandate following the voluntary resignation or the natural death of an incumbent elected leader.

of significantly affecting a country's economic or socioeconomic progress. Some three dozen leaders (or about 10 percent of the total), for example, spent less than a month in office, most of them serving for no more than ten days. Take the case of Carmen Pereira, who served as Guinea-Bissau's acting president for just three days, in 1984, as the country adopted a new constitution. This was enough to qualify her as Africa's first female leader, but it unlikely allowed her to actually pull any strings. Neither did the numerous other heads of state that were also very briefly in power in Bissau, in later times, have much more chance to do so, namely Ansumane Mané (7 days), Veríssimo Correia Seabra (14), Mamadu Ture Kuruma (29), Raimundo Pereira (two stints, 94 and 189 days), Malam Bacai Sanhá (in his early stay, only about nine months). We do believe, however, that some transient leaders may have room to make a difference with regard to certain specific political processes and outcomes, as we explain below.

Secondly, among all the remaining leaders who held sway for at least one year, we separate those that were elected (under a multiparty system) from unelected ones. The latter category includes not only the likes of military rulers, but also the heads of the one-party regimes that were so abundant in postcolonial decades, regardless of whether or not such regimes allowed voters to cast ballots for the sole party allowed. We label "autocrats" all members of this group. Some of them, and in particular many of the first power-holders who were in charge at independence, initially started off under encouraging auspices as elected rulers (such was the case of Grégoire Kayibanda of Rwanda, Leabua Jonathan in Lesotho, Sylvanus Olympio in Togo, Modibo Keïta in Mali, Julius Nyerere in Tanzania, or Milton Obote in Uganda, for instance) before closing down most avenues for political participation and competition and turning their countries into dictatorships. Others oversaw adjustments in the opposite direction, as they were only legitimized by a multiparty election long after first having taken their oath (as with Kenya's Daniel arap Moi, Ghana's Jerry Rawlings, or Uganda's Yoweri Museveni). In our typology, to decide whether a specific ruler ultimately remains an autocrat, we simply look at what prevails in terms of number of years, i.e., the amount of time he or she served as unelected office-holder versus the years during which he/she could count on an electoral mandate. Gnassingbé Eyadéma, for example, only spent the last 13 (1993–2005) of his total 39 years in office (since 1967) as an elected leader, which is not sufficient for his case to move out of the category of autocrats. After all, this was a case where authoritarian continuities were particularly evident:

none excelled Eyadéma for using force to direct the democratisation [sic] process. From 1990 until his re-election in 1993 he sanctioned the organisation by the Togolese army of what he called, according to a leaked confidential document, 'acts of intimidation ... [that must be careful to] spill as little blood as possible'. This policy entailed their persistent verbal and physical assaults on opposition leaders, their seizure of the reformist Prime Minister appointed by the National Conference, their regular takeover of the state television and radio to broadcast their own (and Eyadéma's) point of view, and periodic rampages through the capital. When things got out of control they led to political assassinations and the murders of southerners, who were deemed by the northern controlled army to be the chief instigators of the democratisation movement. Invariably, after each illegal outburst, Eyadéma ordered the return to barracks of the army personnel involved, while calling for democrats to compromise to avoid further clashes. In this way he was able slowly to regain most of the powers that the National Conference had stripped him of, and reduced the Prime Minister from his great rival to something close to a figurehead/ally. (Baker 1998:123)

Table 9.1 *A new typology of African leaders: criteria (II)*

		Multipartism	
		Elected	Unelected
Degree of democracy	Polity2 < 6	Hegemon	Autocrat
	Polity2 ≥ 6	Democrat	–

Note: elected leaders include those who constitutionally "inherit" an electoral mandate following the voluntary resignation or the natural death of an incumbent elected leader.

In other cases, the distinct phases of a ruler's period in power had him longer under a formally reformed environment. Joaquim Chissano, for example, became head of state in single-party Mozambique in 1986, but later gained an electoral term in 1994. Ultimately, if closely, he spent less time in office as an unelected ruler (1986–1994) than as an elected president (1994–2005), and we thus count him according to his latter status.

Once we have identified elected leaders, we split them into two groups – namely "democrats" and "hegemons" – based on whether or not they ruled under conditions that met the minimum requirements of democracy. Both hegemons and democrats are leaders operating within multiparty frameworks for most of their time in office, but hegemons do not normally allow any serious political and electoral challengers to emerge, whereas democrats by and large do. Of course, over time most countries are subject to democratic advances and setbacks, which may occur under the watch of the same power-holder. We therefore consider a leader's entire tenure (including the years as unelected leader, if any) and look at whether his or her country's Polity2 score average remains below 6, implying that he or she qualifies as a hegemon, or reaches 6 or more, making him or her a democrat. Thus, once brief leadership spells are set apart, the remaining cases are classified according to the two said criteria – openness to multipartism and degree of democracy – as shown in Table 9.1, presenting our new typology of leaders.

If we were blind to the brevity of interim leaders' duration in office, we would see them fall into one of the remaining three groups (namely, autocrats, hegemons, and democrats). In a sense, interim leaders are drawn from across the spectrum of the abovementioned categories, to which they initially belong. Yet we want to separate these "transient" leadership experiences from the rest. That of transitional leaders is an understudied topic. From our perspective, they play a peculiar role. Due to their short stay in office, it is generally difficult to attribute development outcomes – whether good or bad – to their rule. But we may still expect them to be closely associated with certain specific developments, such as the resolution of a conflict or a multiparty transition, largely having to do with their country's political events, rather than with economic or social improvements. We shall clarify this below.

Finally, as many as 37 leaders – or about 10 percent of the total – are peculiar in that they served two (at times even three) distinct stints in office. Olusegun Obasanjo and Muhammadu Buhari of Nigeria are two good illustrations. Both held office as military autocrats in the late 1970s and early 1980s, respectively, but each of them came back to power some 20–30 years later as an elected president – Obasanjo as a hegemon, due to the country's limited democracy score, and Buhari as a democrat, having reached the presidency after an electoral alternation. The same happened to Didier Ratsiraka and Mathieu Kérékou, who first ruled Madagascar and Benin, respectively, as soldiers for almost 20 years and then, after a few years' interlude, were again at the helm for another stint, this time around as "democrats." David Dacko of the Central African Republic and Pierre Buyoya of Burundi, by contrast, were also twice in office, but in both cases they figure as unelected autocrats. For these and similar cases, we chose to count the two leadership spells separately (i.e., Obasanjo I and Obasanjo II, Buyoya I and Buyoya II).

Trending Leaders

Table 9.2 illustrates the empirical distribution of cases across our fourfold typology of African leaders as transients, autocrats, hegemons, and democrats.[1] Out of a total 360 leaders that reached power between 1960 and 2018, there were as many as 92 transient leaders, that is, leaders who held office for less than one year. This amounts to one quarter (25.5 percent) of all cases, a very substantial percentage.

---

[1] See also Table A13 in the appendix on the occurrence of each of the four types of leaders in individual sub-Saharan countries.

Table 9.2 *Four categories of African leaders: empirical distribution*

	N of leaders N	N of leaders %	Country-years in office N	Country-years in office %	Avg. years in office
Transients	92	25.5	28	1	0.3
Autocrats	119	33	1,276	49.5	10.7
Hegemons	65	18.1	755	29.4	11.6
Democrats	84	23.4%	518	20.1	6.2
	360	100	2,577	100	7.2

Source: ALC dataset

When we turn to the total share of the time they held sway, however, the reason why it is worth setting them apart as a group becomes clearer. Their average stay in office was a mere 0.3 years. All together, these leaders only remained at the helm of one or another sub-Saharan country for a total 28 country-years out of 2,577 country-years, that is, little more than 1 percent. At the opposite end, a dozen long-standing African rulers singularly held office for more than that, from Gambia's Dawda Jawara (29 years) to emperor Haile Selassie of Ethiopia (33) or Cameroon's Paul Biya (34 and counting).

Note that our definition of transient leaders – which is strictly based on a length-of-tenure measure – only partly overlaps with the common understanding of interim or transitional office-holder. It includes, for example, the first brief stint in power of Siaka Stevens, who was regularly sworn in as prime minister following Sierra Leone's legislative election of 1967, and could have been reasonably expected to remain in office for a substantial period of time, but was in fact overthrown by a coup only six days later. On the other hand, the likes of Michel Kafando (Burkina Faso), Dioncounda Traoré (Mali), Manuel Serifo Nhamadjo (Guinea-Bissau), or Gyude Bryant (Liberia) were chosen by their countries as caretakers, that is, interim rulers only tasked with rapidly transiting the nation back to electoral rule and then leaving office; yet completing the job took them more than one year and they are thus excluded from among our transients.

Seven leaders who only came to office in the second half of 2017 had not yet served one year as of June 30, 2018 (the last date covered by our dataset), even though their tenure continued. They include prominent figures such as Angola's João Lourenço, Ethiopia's Abiy Ahmed, and South Africa's Cyril Ramaphosa, alongside Zimbabwe's Emmerson Mnangagwa, Botswana's Mokgweetsi Masisi, Liberia's George Weah, and Sierra Leone's Julius Maada Bio. Since we already know that all of them endured for more than one year, we opted for a case-by-case assessment, based on their country's Polity2 trends and on our knowledge of political events, to move each of them into one of the non-interim categories. Eventually, Lourenço, Abiy, and Mnangagwa were reclassified as hegemons, whereas Ramaphosa, Masisi, Weah, and Maada Bio as democrats.

Autocrats represent by far the largest category, one-and-a-half times as numerous as the next group (namely, democrats). Their 119 cases account for nearly half (49.5 percent) of all country-years in independent Africa (1,276 out of 2,577), each dictator spending, on average, almost 11 years in power. Little short of one third – i.e., 35 leaders – were in charge across sub-Saharan Africa at the time of their country's independence without being backed by a multiparty election mandate (or, when they did obtain electoral legitimacy, this was only for a limited time). Of those unelected leaders that gained authority at a later stage, one third or so (36) did so in a peaceful manner, whereas another third (40) used violence. Eight more – four who had emerged peacefully and four who had used violence – subsequently earned one or more electoral terms, which, however, lasted less than the period of their unelected tenure.

All but one of the "personal rulers" selected by Jackson and Rosberg (1982) as epitomes of their leaders' types fall into our (unelected) autocrats category – regardless of whether the authors originally labeled them princes, tyrants, prophets, etc. – from Léopold Senghor (Senegal) to Jomo Kenyatta (Kenya), Haile Selassie (Ethiopia), Sobhuza II (Swaziland/eSwatini), William Tubman and William Tolbert (Liberia), Gaafar Nimeiry (Sudan), Félix Houphouët-Boigny (Côte d'Ivoire), Ahmadou Ahidjo (Cameroon), Omar Bongo (Gabon), Hastings Banda (Malawi), Joseph Mobutu (Congo-Zaire), Ahmed Sékou Touré (Guinea), Julius Nyerere (Tanzania), Francisco Macías Nguema (Equatorial Guinea), and Idi Amin Dada (Uganda). The only exception is Kwame Nkrumah, who turns out to be an elected hegemon according to our criteria.[2] The fact that

---

[2] Ghana's first president obtained a direct electoral mandate in 1960, if through a controversial ballot held alongside a referendum on a new

virtually all the remaining leaders are autocrats is largely the effect of our choice of contrasting unelected leaders – the archetypical figure of the postindependence era examined by the two authors – with those backed by multiparty electoral mandates, who came to represent a substantial majority after 1990. But it is also a further proof of the current need to dig in a direction different from Jackson and Rosberg's if we want to improve our understanding of the diversity of contemporary African power-holders.

Elected leaders, as pointed out, include both those who stayed in office under essentially nondemocratic conditions and those who ruled more democratically. The two groups are of more or less comparable size. The 65 hegemons represent some 18.1 percent of the total number of leaders, as against 84 democrats accounting for 23.4 percent. But the average hegemon typically held office for twice as long as the average democrat, that is, almost 12 years as against little more than six years. This results in a considerably longer overall presence of hegemonic rule in the region (755 country years out of 2,577, or 29.4 percent) when compared to democratic rule (518 country years, or 20.1 percent of the total).

Hegemons are also a somewhat more heterogeneous lot. Almost half of them (31) came to office directly through the vote, in virtually all cases during a transition toward a multiparty regime. Of these, a majority of 21 took over from a predecessor who either belonged to the same party or sponsored the new leader's rise to power. The remaining 10 are a more surprising, somewhat "out-of-place" collection of leaders who ran for and won office as opposition candidates, thus embodying the kind of alternation in government that is so often considered the hallmark of a functioning democratic regime, and yet failed to oversee or promote a satisfactory democratic progress in their country. Most of the other half (27), consisting of leaders who were not directly elected into office, is rather evenly split between those who

---

constitution. Ghanaians found the following question on their ballots: "Do you accept Kwame Nkrumah or Joseph Boakye Danquah as the first President under the new Constitution?" Nkrumah obtained 1,016,076 votes (or 89 percent) against Danquah's 124,623 (10.9 percent). A second referendum, in 1964, left his Convention People's Party as the country's sole legal party and the only one fielding candidates in the legislative election of the following year. Since Nkrumah himself was ousted in 1966, however, he ultimately spent more time as an elected leader (1960–1964), than as one that we consider unelected due to the single-party system (1964–1966).

reached power regularly and peacefully (13), and those who did it irregularly through violence (14). In either case, these takeovers were subsequently legitimized by popular votes, and for a longer period, but still running short of democratic requirements. Five more cases consist of postindependence leaders who had their mandate legitimized by voters just prior to or shortly after independence, if again under conditions that did not meet democratic standards. The last two are power-holders who replaced elected predecessors following their resignations but had yet to obtain an autonomous electoral mandate (i.e., Abiy Ahmed of Ethiopia and Emmerson Mnangagwa of Zimbabwe.) [3]

Democrats are rather more homogenous. For the most, they gained power the moment they won an election (63 out of 84). As many as two-thirds of them did so by successfully challenging the ruling group (40 alternators), with the remaining ones replacing an outgoing leader belonging to their own party (23 successors). It is only in one-fourth of all cases that democrats took advantage of a regime transition that introduced multipartism to win office (14 successors, 6 alternators). Besides the stated 63, an additional 6 were regularly handed power following an incumbent leader's resignation or death in office, and only subsequently obtained their own electoral mandate. Seven of our democrats were put in charge when colonial rule came to an end following their pre-independence electoral success, including Seretse Khama in Botswana and Sam Nujoma in Namibia. The last batch of 8 democratic leaders followed in the footsteps of elected predecessors who had resigned or passed away while in office; they were yet to obtain an autonomous electoral mandate.

When we turn to diachronic trends, the impressive changes in the relative weight of the four categories over time reveals much about the major shifts in Africa's political leadership dynamics and landscape. Figure 9.2 shows the absolute number of autocrats, hegemons, democrats, and transients for every year across the entire 1960–2018 period.[4] The steady increase of the total on the left side of the graph results from more countries gradually obtaining independence, until

---

[3] Emmerson Mnangagwa won Zimbabwe's first post-Mugabe presidential election on July 30, 2018.

[4] The overall number of leaders in the figure occasionally appears to be higher than the overall number of independent sub-Saharan states due, in some countries, to the presence of one or more transient leaders in a single year.

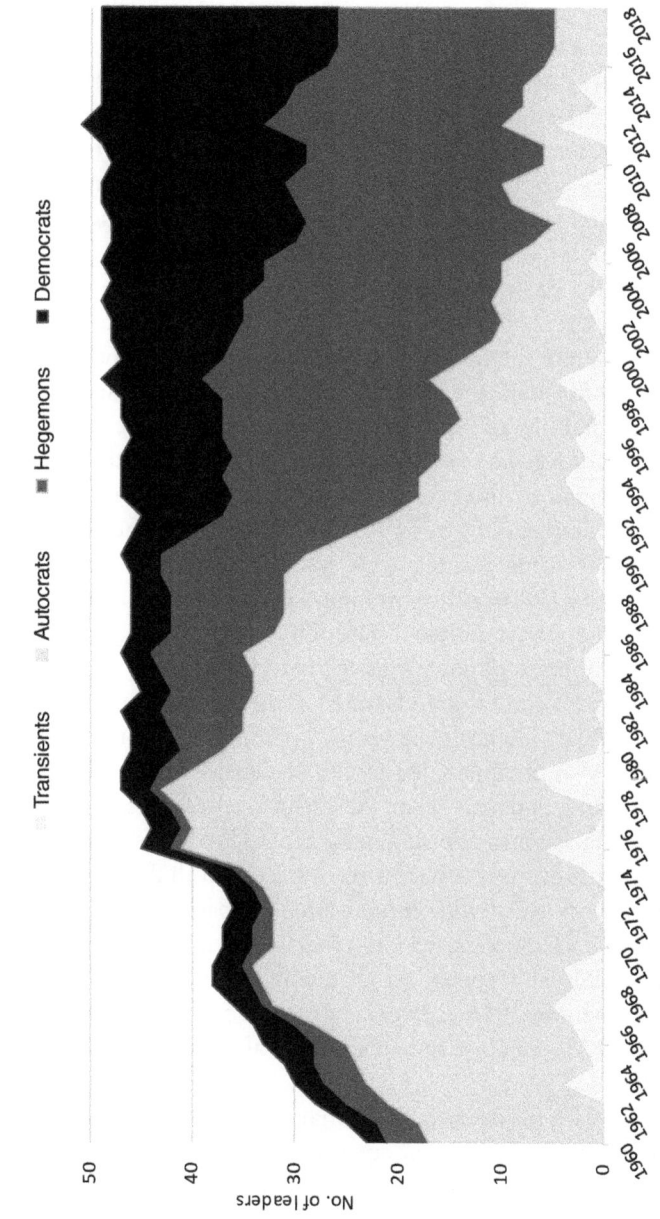

Figure 9.2 Types of leaders in Africa, 1960–2018 (Data as of June 30, 2018).
Source: ALC dataset

virtual stability is reached from around 1980. This goes hand in hand with the massive upsurge in the number of autocrats, whose number expands impressively and peaks at 41 out of 45 states in 1977. The founding fathers of independence, who gradually enter the graph, include as many as 35 autocrats (with many of them elected to office just prior to the end of colonialism, but then steering their countries towards dictatorship), and only 7 hegemons, 5 democrats, and 2 transients. Unelected dictators thus appear to take the lion's share of the distinct areas depicted in the figure also due to the fact that they combine their large overall number with a long average duration in office. After the peak, their tally drops steadily across the subsequent four decades, except for two minor short and limited bouts before and after 2010. While the number of transient leaders remains relatively low and uninfluential, the decline of full-fledged autocrats opens the doors to the parallel rise of hegemons, starting from the early 1980s, and of democrats, from the early 1990s. The reason why the number of hegemons begins to increase at an earlier-than-expected stage (i.e., before the widespread diffusion of multiparty reforms across the continent) is that some leaders who had initially come to office as unelected in the 1980s, either through a single party or through arms, organized and won multiparty elections in the subsequent decade. Since each of them is ultimately assigned to the category he predominantly belongs to, several are classified as hegemons (namely, Cameroon's Paul Biya, Guinea's Lansana Conté, Mauritania's Maaouya Ould Taya, Mozambique's Joaquim Chissano, Burkina Faso's Blaise Compaoré, and Sudan's Omar Al-Bashir). After around 1995, the presence of hegemonic rule stabilizes, as Africa always counts no less than 20 chief executives – with a record 25 in both 2001 and 2002 – who had mainly ruled with formal electoral backing in a nondemocratic context. Democrats, on the other hand, increase steadily from the early 1990s and appear to gradually catch up with hegemons, overtaking them in 2015 (22 versus 21), and reaching an even higher maximum of 23 – or close to half of the total – for every single year in 2016–2018.

Thus, by 2018, the overwhelming majority of African countries were led by elected rulers, somewhat equally split into hegemons and democrats, if with a slight prevalence of the latter. The governments of only five countries remained in the hands of full-fledged autocratic rulers. These were quite a heterogeneous lot. Two such autocrats represent late instances of forms of rule largely belonging to the past. One is Mswati III of newly renamed eSwatini (formerly Swaziland), who has long been the last absolute monarch in the sub-Saharan region, and one of only ten remaining across the world, all but Brunei Darussalam and eSwatini itself located in the Middle East or North Africa. With its reluctance to ever use elections and its reliance on a highly pervasive and repressive state apparatus, on the other hand, Isaias Afwerki's Eritrea also displays a number of features that were more commonly seen in past dictatorships. An additional two cases, on the other hand, would more likely hold multiparty elections of some kind if conditions allowed. Yet both Somalia, whose process of rebuilding authority remains hostage to the country's never-ending conflict, and South Sudan, whose recent secession from the north was quickly followed by a descent into new cycles of violence, are governed by rulers who can only claim indirect electoral legitimacy at best. Mohamed Abdullahi "Farmajo" Mohamed was voted into office by a 184-majority in the 328-strong electoral college consisting of the country's parliamentarians, themselves chosen by some 14,000 clan delegates. Only a tiny fraction of the Somali population was thus involved in the process. Salva Kiir Mayardit's original mandate as president of the southern region, on the other hand, was formally obtained in the context of the 2010 election in pre-partition Sudan, that is, before the country's southern citizens decided to secede, and was thus not meant to have a mandate for national leadership but for subregional government. The last case is Yoweri Museveni's. While Uganda's former rebel does currently lead an electoral authoritarian regime similar to many others on the continent, overall he spent more time as unelected head of state (during 1986–2006 he only won so-called no-party elections, which do not satisfy our standards for electoral terms of office) than as an elected president (since 2006).

New Leaders, Better Outcomes?

To test the impact of different types of leaders on their countries' socioeconomic and political performance, we regressed the indicators of development already investigated in Chapters 7 and 8 on two distinct dummy variables, one coded "1" for hegemons and one coded "1" for democrats. Autocrats are taken as the reference category, while transients are excluded from this analysis since, as we pointed out, we assume that their short duration gives them a much smaller chance of affecting development progress, except for some more specific processes that we examine below. The models reported in Table 9.3 have

Table 9.3 Regression results of performance indicators on leader's type (transients excluded)

	Economic growth		Social welfare				Stateness	Corruption	
	GDP growth	GDP per capita growth	Δ Primary school enrolment	Δ Secondary school enrolment	Δ Health spending	Δ Life expectancy at birth	Δ Under-5 mortality rate	Δ State capacity	Δ Political corruption	Δ Executive corruption
Dep. var. $_{t-1}$	0.207*** (0.040)	0.201*** (0.040)	−0.019*** (0.005)	−0.023** (0.009)	−0.086*** (0.031)	−0.012** (0.005)	−0.012*** (0.002)	−0.109*** (0.018)	−0.022*** (0.006)	−0.017*** (0.006)
Reference category = Autocrat										
Δ Hegemon					0.125 (0.110)			0.077** (0.032)	0.023*** (0.005)	0.012 (0.007)
Hegemon $_{t-1}$	1.408*** (0.411)	1.352*** (0.401)	0.247 (0.258)	0.064 (0.181)	0.0805* (0.0464)	0.119*** (0.035)	−0.521** (0.223)	0.011 (0.014)	0.006*** (0.002)	0.006** (0.002)
Δ Democrat					0.126 (0.129)			0.134*** (0.034)	−0.002 (0.006)	−0.010 (0.009)
Democrat $_{t-1}$	1.878*** (0.504)	1.780*** (0.492)	0.454 (0.378)	0.580*** (0.210)	0.100 (0.0666)	0.276*** (0.050)	−0.950*** (0.248)	0.042** (0.017)	−0.003 (0.002)	0.005 (0.003)
Wald test	1.42	1.29	.39	4.48**	.14	8.85***	2.35	3.94**	18.4***	2.19
Democrat vs Hegemon										
Constant	1.234 (2.582)	0.886 (2.487)	5.546** (2.655)	−2.800 (2.001)	0.0388 (0.300)	0.369 (0.351)	0.349 (1.663)	−0.336*** (0.083)	0.004 (0.008)	−0.004 (0.009)
N	1,382	1,382	1,314	823	705	1,597	1,580	1,346	1,486	1,486
Countries	42	42	42	42	42	42	42	41	42	42
R^2	0.129	0.125	0.065	0.094	0.075	0.117	0.210	0.111	0.060	0.036

Note: For each dependent variable, all controls used in models discussed in Chapters 7 and 8 are included. Regression coefficients of control variables are omitted.
* p < 0.1; ** p < 0.05; *** p < 0.01.

the same specifications as those described in the previous two chapters (the lagged dependent variable model for economic growth and the ECM for social welfare, state consolidation and corruption) and, in particular, they employ the same control variables. For ease of presentation and discussion of the regression results, the coefficients for control variables are omitted from the table. Except for models investigating economic growth and social welfare outputs and outcomes (for which we deem more time to be necessary before results attributable to political leaders can make their appearance), the remaining models include the variables *Hegemon* and *Democrat* not only at time *t–1*, but also in first difference (Δ). As already clarified for some explanatory factors in Chapters 7 and 8, the dichotomous nature of the variables *Hegemon* and *Democrat* implies that the first difference (Δ) represents the discrete change in the value assumed by these variables at time *t* compared to time *t–1*. This choice allows us to focus more specifically on the potentially immediate shock effect produced by the entry of a leader that we classify with a different status (a hegemon or a democrat replacing an autocrat) on the dependent variables in that same year.

The first two models show that, in line with our overall framework, both democrats and hegemons perform better than autocrats' in enhancing the economic growth trajectories of their countries. However, a Wald test shows no significant differences between the regression coefficients of democrats and hegemons, implying that, on average, the former do not outperform the latter in fostering economic development.

Besides growth, the advancement of citizens' well-being is also affected by a country's leadership. Starting from improvements in education, regression results show that while neither democrats nor hegemons significantly affect primary school enrolment levels, democrats are positively and significantly associated with higher secondary school enrolment rates. When we turn to leaders' accomplishments in enhancing health, hegemons only display marginally higher levels of health expenditure when compared to autocrats, while being a democrat does not appear to significantly influence health spending. But both democrats and hegemons outperform autocratic leaders in terms of health outcomes, contributing to increase their citizens' life expectancy at birth and to decrease the rate of child mortality. In terms of life expectancy at birth, moreover, democrats tend to outpace hegemons too.

State consolidation indicators display similar trends. Here we also look at the immediate effect possibly produced by the advent of a new type of leader (a hegemon or a democrat displacing an autocrat). Both the entry of a democrat and of a hegemon are significantly associated with the strengthening of the administrative and extractive capacities of their political regimes. However, while the positive effect of hegemons is evident only in the short period, democrats display a positive impact on state consolidation both as an immediate effect related to their rise to office as well as in the medium and long terms. Furthermore, democrats appear to outperform hegemons in strengthening their political regime's bureaucratic apparatus alongside the said dimensions.

Finally, the results we obtained on corruption lead us back to what we already discussed in the previous chapter. Hegemons tend to be associated with higher levels of political and executive corruption than autocrats as well as – at least for what concerns "political" corruption – democrats (see the significant value of the Wald test in the column reporting the model on political corruption). The emerging picture is broadly in line with the existing literature on the impact of democratic openings, which shows how regimes featuring the simultaneous presence of autocratic and democratic features – i.e., so-called hybrid regimes – tend to display higher levels of political corruption than both democratic and closed authoritarian systems (Montinola and Jackman 2002; Pellegata 2013). However, our analyses also shows that democratic leaders are not significantly associated with lower levels of political and executive corruption when compared to their autocratic peers. This result suggests that, while leaders who contest multiparty elections – particularly democratically elected officeholders – do contribute to the consolidation of the bureaucratic apparatus of their countries, they are not as effective in reducing the widely spread corrupt practices that have affected many sub-Saharan public sectors since independence.

Fast Service: Transient Leaders as Fixers

Transient or interim leaders, as shown previously, constitute a very substantial share of Africa's leaders – namely, a quarter of the total – and yet they only covered a flimsy one-hundredth of overall country-years. This imbalance is a direct result of the very criteria for their selection, that is, each of them is by definition one of the power-holders that held authority for the shortest periods of time. Even when they are added together, these short spells only amount to so much. Furthermore, transient leaders are also a rather heterogeneous group whose members, as already pointed out, would easily fall into any one of the other three categories if we simply disregarded the shortness of their stay in office. So why single them out? What makes them different, if anything? While their transience in power is a strong reason for believing such office-holders had the smallest chance of meaningfully affecting their countries' economic and socioeconomic progress, we ultimately decided not to exclude them from the econometric analyses we carried out in previous chapters since we cannot fully rule out the developmental impact of this group of leaders. In addition, omitting them would technically require us to ignore the country-year their interlude falls in, implying that we would likewise disregard that same year from the period covered by other leaders in power before or after them. We did test whether removing them from our analyses changed our findings, but the latter were confirmed.

But there are also reasons for taking a closer look at this set of short-term power-holders. What we expect of transient leaders is a particularly strong association with certain political occurrences. Many of them were handed power at exceptional junctures featuring unusual degrees of political uncertainly, fluidity, or some kind of domestic political transition. Indeed, a substantial share of interim rulers was raised to office precisely tasked with transiting their country towards first or new elections, post-conflict reconciliation, or some other sought-for scenario. Yusuf Lule, Godfrey Binaisa, and Paulo Muwanga, for example, all served as interim leaders in Uganda after the infamous Idi Amin was deposed, in 1979, as the country was steered toward a parliamentary election (which would ultimately turn out to be highly contentious). Goukouni Oueddei's first and brief spell in office, also in 1979, came as Chad's warring factions agreed to form a government of national unity aimed at reconciling the north and south of the country (after a short interlude, Goukouni returned to head the unity government for a second time, until he was finally ejected by Hissène Habré's coup in 1982). For a month, in early 1991, Leonel Mário d'Alva became acting head of state of São Tomé and Príncipe as the small island state awaited the swearing in of its first directly elected president, Miguel Trovoada. In Madagascar, former prime minister Norbert

Table 9.4 *Transient leaders: regular versus* **irregular exit from power**

	Regular exit		Irregular exit		
	N	%	N	%	Total
1960–1989	31	63.3	18	36.7	49
1990–2018	36	83.7	7	16.3	43
1960–2018	67	72.8	25	27.2	92

Source: ALC dataset

Ratsirahonana also acted as head of state, between late 1996 and early 1997, following the impeachment of Albert Zafy, until a new president was eventually voted in. Nigeria's chief of defence staff Abdulsalami Abubakar, on the other hand, "inherited" the top job from military dictator Sani Abacha, whose sudden death, in 1998, opened the way to the country's renewed, quick, and successful attempt at transitioning to multiparty rule. Empirically, as these and other cases suggest, it is reasonable to expect an empirical link between these kinds of short-term leadership spells and such political developments as the introduction of multiparty elections, democratic improvements, conflict resolution, and political stability.

It seems safe to assume, however, that the violent ejection of an interim leader amounts to an abrupt interruption of any course of action possibly aimed at the abovementioned political outcomes. The very possibility of accomplishing any task his or her leadership might have been meant to complete is simply prevented. Accordingly, we expect transients to actually improve the political performance of their country only if they end up leaving office in essentially regular, orderly ways. The latter was the case for a large majority of them – almost two-thirds in 1960–1989, and more than four-fifths after 1990 – as opposed to only a minority that was irregularly or violently thrown out (Table 9.4). Unsurprisingly, Table 9.4 also shows that, while the share of transients who were violently ousted from office halves with the advent of multipartism (1990–2018) compared to the first three postindependence decades dominated by one-party regimes, the share of interims who accomplished their tasks and regularly handed over power to a successor officeholder increased from 63.3 percent to 83.7 percent.

Fast Service: Transient Leaders as Fixers

Table 9.5 *The association between transient leaders and political performance: regression results*

	Multiparty election for the executive	Δ Level of democracy	Δ Internal violence
Dep. var. $_{t-1}$		−0.130***	−0.162***
		(0.016)	(0.021)
Transient (irregular exit)	−1.302	−2.397***	0.439**
	(1.063)	(0.425)	(0.177)
Transient $_{t-1}$ (irregular exit)	0.035	−2.900***	−0.034
	(0.691)	(0.592)	(0.242)
Transient (regular exit)	1.413***	1.260***	0.027
	(0.374)	(0.3034)	(0.091)
Transient $_{t-1}$ (regular exit)	0.984**	2.114***	0.218*
	(0.393)	(0.425)	(0.131)
Constant		−0.797***	0.666***
		(0.267)	(0.205)
Country fixed effects	Yes	Yes	Yes
Year dummies	Yes	Yes	Yes
N	2428	2374	2345
Countries	46	47	47
R^2		0.157	0.1139
Log Likelihood	−664.845		

Note: the first model was estimated through a conditional fixed-effects logistic regression, the remaining three through the Error Correction Model (ECM) with panel corrected standard errors.
* $p < 0.1$; ** $p < 0.05$; *** $p < 0.01$.

We chose three dependent variables as proxies for political tasks possibly assigned to an interim leader. These dependent variables reveal the occurrence of a multiparty election in country *i* at time *t*, the year-on-year change in a country's Polity2 score, and the same kind of variation in the magnitude of intra-state episodes of violence.

Table 9.5 below reports the results of three statistical models regressing our three dependent variables on two dichotomous *explanans* that identify whether the leader in power in country *i* at time *t* (in models with Polity2 and internal violence as dependent variables this is identified by the discrete change of the independent variables between the value at time *t* and the value of time *t–1*) and at time *t–1* was a transient who would eventually leave in a regular way or one whose tenure would be interrupted by violent means. Given the dichotomous nature of the dependent variable revealing the occurrence of an election, the first model was estimated through a multilevel logistic regression with standard errors clustered at the country level, while the remaining two models were run using the ECM technique with panel-corrected standard errors. All the models include country and year fixed-effects. Our main results did not change when we tested the same models by excluding autocrats, under the assumption that they have worse political performances than all other leaders, transients included. We thus do not present this latter set of results.

In line with our hypotheses, the empirical results show that, whereas transients who would regularly leave office are positively and significantly associated with the occurrence of multiparty elections in the very same year or in the following one, transients ultimately ousted by irregular/violent means display no significant effect on such a dependent variable. Interestingly, the positive association of transients with a regular exit from power on the occurrence of multiparty elections disappears when we took our independent variables in longer time lags ($t–3$ and $t–5$). This appears to further confirm the idea that short-duration leaders were often meant to complete a specific and temporary task, quickly leading toward the opening of a new political phase, and new elections in particular.

Compared to the other types of leaders who remained in power for more than one year, transients who experienced a regular exit from office are also positively and significantly associated with an increase in the level of democracy of their country, as measured by the Polity2 score. This positive contribution is evident in both the short and the long period, as stressed by the significance of regression coefficients for *Transient (regular exit)* and *Transient (regular exit)$_{t-1}$*, respectively. This seems to indicate that transients, while only acting as heads of state/government for a short time, tend to positively contribute to a country's process of democratization beyond their own short mandate. On the contrary, transients who were deposed through violent means tend to be significantly associated with a decrease in their country's Polity2 score.

When we turn to the magnitude of civil conflicts, the results do not entirely support our expectations. They indicate that, on average, "regular" transients do not display significant effects in terms of decreasing intra-state violence, and their spells in office can be followed by increases in violence in the year following their departure. This may possibly point to returns to conflicts after an interim period. The tenure of "irregular" transients (i.e., those who experience an irregular exit from power), however, appears to be more strongly and immediately associated with an increase in the magnitude of ethnic and civil violence.

The Battle for Leadership

African politics was notoriously dominated by an extremely high degree of personalization of power during the early decades after independence. This reflected on the great attention researchers and observers paid to individual personalities as the cornerstones of national political systems (cf. Cohen 2015). To understand Malawi, you needed to learn about its *deus ex machina* Hastings Banda. To get a clue about what was going on in Guinea, you had to come to terms with Ahmed Sékou Touré's political protagonism. Four-fifths of Africa's "twentennials" – the 36 leaders who have stayed in office for two decades or more – reached power in the 1960s, 1970s, or 1980s. Coups, as pointed out, were the other side of this disproportionate stability and, as matter of fact, many coup-makers quickly proved themselves difficult to remove from office.

Scholarly attention since the last decade of the twentieth century, on the other hand, was much more heavily directed toward the politico-institutional arrangements and electoral processes of the "new" regimes that had emerged from the Third Wave democratic reforms that had already swept other parts of the world and also arrived to the sub-Saharan region. Presidents and other executive power-holders remained pivotal figures, as anywhere else, yet the focus was now more often on their coming to terms with the broader institutional setup because they needed to deal with a new environment made up of legal oppositions, embryonic legislative bodies, and other autonomous institutions, constitutional norms, and constraints. If anything, power handovers were becoming more common and most countries had embarked on processes of gradual political institutionalization, if with substantial variations across the region.

Our approach fully acknowledges the growing role of institutions in Africa's political landscape. But we also stress the added value of accounting for individual leadership experiences within a given politico-institutional setup. Reformed institutional settings led to new types of political figures, usually somewhat more constrained and development- or at least performance-oriented. In this chapter, we thus revisited Jackson and Rosberg's (1982, 1984) classic reading of Africa's "personal rulers" to account for the region's key political developments of recent decades from a political leadership perspective. Besides a group of time-limited passers-by or fixers – whom we dubbed "transient leaders" and were occasionally far from inconsequential – completing an up-to-date typology that could embrace all African leaders since independence based on what today appear to be the most relevant and analytically valuable differentiating features led us to isolate three groups. Virtually unchallenged dictatorial rulers (i.e., autocrats), experienced and enduring election manipulators (hegemons) and popularly-mandated and potentially more responsible executives (democrats). The historical trend highlights a clear decline of the former, and appears to tell us that the battle ahead will pitch the latter two types against each other.

10 | *Leaders to Come*

Sixty years of politics and development in independent Africa show that leaders do matter for the progresses and failures of countries in the region. How sub-Saharan office-holders reach power affects how they will behave and what they will do – if, of course, not in any deterministic manner – and ultimately contributes to shaping the development trajectories of their nations and the well-being of their fellow citizens. In the simplest possible terms, this is the main takeaway from this study.

Yet the journey we embarked upon was longer and complex. Two were our starting points. One was exactly the common sense but largely untested idea that the vicissitudes of Africa's development have something to do with its rulers. The other was the recognition that a clear divide separated a postcolonial political epoch – dominated by highly personalistic politics, long overstays in office, and abrupt military takeovers – from a subsequent, post-1990 era during which multi-party elections, organized under vastly different conditions regarding actual respect for freedoms and rule of law, became the new political currency. Our work, in particular, aimed at understanding the possible connection between the said leaders development nexus and the evolution of African leadership. We conjectured that the various and changing ways in which leaders have reached power in Africa across the decades has potentially important implications for the advancement (or lack thereof) of individual countries.

But there we hit a snag. There were not enough nor suitable data to investigate these issues in the way we thought they deserved to be addressed. We thus decided to build our own collection of data from scratch, one that would fit our needs and would also allow other scholars to investigate related matters. This resulted in the Africa Leadership Change (ALC) dataset, an innovative venture both from a conceptual point of view, in line with our relatively unusual emphasis on leaders and the modes of power transfers, as well as from an empirical perspective, creating and bringing together a wealth of detailed and fragmented information that would not otherwise be available in any similar breadth of coverage.

Using the ALC data, we then undertook a first task, that of a comprehensive and detailed mapping of the nature of all political leadership stints and transfers, and related trends, in 49 sub-Saharan states from 1960 to 2018. This enabled us not just to fully quantify the extent to which multiparty elections, which had quickly become a rarity in postcolonial Africa, had come to dominate the continent's political landscape over recent decades – a transformation whose details had already been systematized by other researchers. But the ALC dataset allowed us to go into much more detail by also accounting for the exact incidence of crucial occurrences such as electoral successions and electoral alternations, that is, leadership handovers in the context of ruling party continuity as opposed to government turnovers. Both successions and alternations have increasingly come to represent major parts of the ways in which leadership is passed on. Unsurprisingly, even under the new political arrangements many power-holders have not been keen to hand over power. Thorough data on presidential term limits, however, show the real extent to which African rulers have been able to overcome this type of constitutional constraint and have started again to overstay their time in office. While the media have rightly brought into the spotlight the numerous and disquieting cases where limits have been removed, the fact is that these remain a minority of instances. Moreover, as Africa's new political frameworks made rotation in power more frequent, the average tenure of political leaders declined. This was in spite of the fact that military coups – which, by nature, are a way of suddenly cutting short a sitting ruler's service – had meanwhile become much rarer than they had been at any previous moment in the continent's political history. Overall, our mapping effort confirmed that, in terms of the ways leaders rotated in office, pre- and post-1990 Africa have been two worlds apart.

We could now directly address the core of our argument and assess the extent of its empirical foundations, or the lack thereof: do different types of leaders, identified on the basis of how they reach office, produce different development performances in Africa? The focus of our empirical investigations would span distinct selected components of a country's economic, social, and political progress – namely economic growth, social welfare, state consolidation, and control of corruption.

The evidence we unveiled turned out to be largely in line with what our framework predicted. Elections in Africa are far from inconsequential, as is still often claimed by too many observers. Across the spectrum, and contrary to supporters of the "good coup" thesis, military coup-makers have mainly proved ineffective and mostly deleterious for their countries. Leaders who stayed too long in power also showed poor results along the majority of our indicators, notably in terms of economic expansion.

Elected leaders almost systematically outperformed their unelected peers. This held true even where basic democratic conditions were absent: mandates obtained under the new multiparty frameworks most often proved enough to start altering leaders' incentives and, through them, their performances. Better democratic circumstances, a higher degree of competitiveness, a country's longer experience with voting, the advent of an electoral successor, and that of an electoral alternator, however, were all factors that tended to further add to the performance of leaders who gained office through the ballot box.

African rulers have thus changed. Understanding them requires identifying proper distinctions based on up-to-date key features, something we did by outlining a new typology of the continent's contemporary power-holders. Today, besides the marginal role of interim or transient leaders, sub-Saharan Africa exhibits a massively reduced presence of all-out autocrats. The bulk of the region's office-holders now consists of elected hegemons – whose incidence seems to have somewhat stabilized over the past 20 years – and of a gradually growing number of democratically elected rulers. The increased prevalence of the latter two categories is connected to the widespread use of elections and has gone hand in hand with the capacity of these power-holders to improve their countries' development performances. As Africa changed its leaders, the new leaders brought with them broader progress, and began to change Africa.

Africa's Coming Leaders and Development Scenario

The implications of the new leadership dynamics for the continent's prospects are vast and deep. By directly affecting the selection, survival and demise of rulers – and thus indirectly impacting on their behavior – certain politico-institutional arrangements have proven to support development performances better than alternative setups tend to do.

This might have been of little comfort, had the more constructive environments and more development-oriented leaderships been a thing of the past, a feature of the hopeful early years of postcolonial Africa. Luckily, however, this is not the case but rather the opposite is true. The politico-institutional mechanisms and processes that make the emergence of better leaders – itself never an easy task – a little more likely have become more common over the past three decades, compared to the preceding 30 years. With all its ups and downs, Africa has thus mostly been moving in the right *direction*. Democratic progresses have been fragile, incomplete, or stop-and-go, and yet they deserve to be acknowledged more than many observers would normally concede. We maintain that, when at the end of the Cold War the region first embraced multiparty institutions molded on the democratic model, African countries started a journey that was never meant to be short or trouble-free, one that continues to this day. The payoffs have been economic and social as well as in political ameliorations.

The direction of progress has thus mostly been a favorable one. But there is another side to the prospects for leaders and development in Africa, one that becomes evident against the backdrop of broader political events elsewhere in the world. The idea and practice of liberal democracy has notoriously come under intensifying stress over the past decade or so (e.g., Foa and Mounk 2017; The Economist 2018; Foreign Affairs 2018; Freedom House 2018; Galston 2018; Lührmann et al. 2018). As a whole, the sub-Saharan region has largely, albeit not uniformly, shown a remarkable degree of resilience, mostly sticking to its recent democratic gains and trying to resist sliding back. Yet as challenges continue to lie ahead for democracy worldwide, Africa and its leaderships will not be spared forever. The weakening of the democratization movement and the rise of the influence of authoritarian global powers will likely translate into frailer support for the region's democratic efforts and actors, for its electoral institutions and pluralist processes, and possibly even into external pulls and domestic pushes toward nondemocratic options. To the extent that the democratic improvements experienced south of the Sahara will not be safeguarded, neither will the region's recent development progresses. The backsliding of political openings might again affect the selection processes, the quality and the commitment of Africa's rulers, this time in a less favorable developmental direction. A lot is still at stake.

*Appendix*

Table A1 Leadership changes in African countries, 1960–2018 (Data as of June 30, 2018): basic data

Country	Leaders (Interim)*	Avg. duration in office°	Multiparty elections	Electoral changes	Alternations	Peaceful non-electoral changes	Violent changes
Angola	3 (0)	14.22	3	1	0	1	0
Benin	19 (9)	5.62	6	4	4	7	5
Botswana	5 (0)	10.36	10	0	0	4	0
Burkina Faso	9 (2)	8.16	6	1	0	1	6
Burundi	12 (4)	6.86	4	3	2	4	5
Cameroon	2 (0)	29.27	5	0	0	1	0
Cape Verde	5 (1)	10.67	6	3	3	1	0
Central African Rep.	10 (2)	8.85	6	2	1	1	5
Chad	8 (3)	11.49	5	0	0	2	3
Comoros	19 (10)	4.54	6	5	3	6	6
Congo, Dem. Rep.	4 (0)	14.51	2	0	0	1	2
Congo, Rep.	11 (4)	8.33	4	1	1	5	3
Cote d'Ivoire	5 (1)	14.36	5	2	2	1	1
Djibouti	2 (0)	20.52	5	1	0	0	0
Equatorial Guinea	2 (0)	24.87	4	0	0	0	1
Eritrea	1 (0)	25.12	0	0	0	0	0
eSwatini	2 (0)	24.92	0	0	0	1	0
Ethiopia	8 (2)	12,83	5	0	0	4	3
Gabon	5 (2)	18.88	6	1	0	2	0
Gambia, The	3 (0)	18.62	11	1	1	0	1

282

Ghana	13 (2)	5.97	10	5	3	2	5
Guinea	7 (2)	14.7	5	1	0	3	2
Guinea-Bissau	16 (7)	4.79	5	4	1	5	5
Kenya	4 (0)	13.78	6	2	2	1	0
Lesotho	10 (1)	5.88	7	5	3	1	3
Liberia	8 (1)	9.64	5	3	2	2	2
Madagascar	11 (3)	7.35	5	4	3	3	2
Malawi	5 (0)	11.09	5	3	2	1	0
Mali	8 (1)	8.29	5	3	1	1	3
Mauritania	10 (4)	9.19	6	2	0	1	6
Mauritius	8 (0)	6.16	10	5	5	2	0
Mozambique	4 (0)	10.76	5	2	0	1	0
Namibia	3 (0)	9.43	5	2	0	0	0
Niger	9 (1)	7.15	6	3	1	1	4
Nigeria	15 (4)	5.33	8	4	1	4	5
Rwanda	4 (1)	18.58	3	0	0	1	2
São Tomé and Príncipe	6 (1)	8.58	6	4	2	1	0
Senegal	4 (0)	14.46	7	2	2	1	0
Seychelles	4 (1)	13.7	6	0	0	2	1
Sierra Leone	14 (4)	5.62	7	4	3	3	6
Somalia	12 (4)	6.03	1	1	1	7	1
South Africa	9 (1)	7.4	13	3	1	5	0
South Sudan	1 (0)	6.98	0	0	0	0	0
Sudan	9 (2)	8.26	6	2	0	3	3

Table A1 (*cont.*)

Country	Leaders (Interim)*	Avg. duration in office°	Multiparty elections	Electoral changes	Alternations	Peaceful non-electoral changes	Violent changes
Tanzania	5 (0)	11.44	5	3	0	1	0
Togo	8 (4)	14.43	6	1	0	3	2
Uganda	9 (5)	13.51	4	1	0	3	5
Zambia	7 (1)	8.94	9	4	2	2	0
Zimbabwe	2 (0)	19.11	6	0	0	1	0

Notes: * Leaders that return in office in a different period of time are counted twice. °Interim leaders are excluded.
Source: ALC dataset

Table A2 *Terms limits in Africa*

	Chief executive	Term limits (max) *(then* / *now)*	Term duration *(current)*	Since	Respected / Violated / Failed Violation	When	How	What then	Notes	Wording of Constitution
Angola	Pres	Yes (2) / Yes (2)	5	2010	Not met yet	–	–	–	Indirectly elected executive presidency (leader of most-voted party at legislative election), not subject to parliamentary confidence (2010 Constitution). In 2017 Dos Santos voluntarily stepped down. Term limits already in 1992 Constitution, but no election in 1992–2012.	2010, art. 113.2: "Each citizen may serve up to two terms of office as President of the Republic."
Benin	Pres	Yes (2) / Yes (2)	5	1990	Resp / Resp	2006 / 2016	–	Alternation (Kérékou → Yayi Boni) / Alternation (→Talon)		1990, art. 42: "The President of the Republic shall be elected … for a mandate of five years, renewable only one time. In any case, no one shall be able to

285

Table A2 (*cont.*)

	Chief executive	Term limits (max) *(then /now)*	Term duration *(current)*	Since	Respected / Violated / Failed Violation	When	How	What then	Notes	Wording of Constitution
										exercise more than two presidential mandates."
Botswana	Parl	Yes (2) / Yes (2)	5	1997	Resp / Resp	2008 / 2018	–	Succession (Mogae → Khama) / Succession (→ Masisi)	Indirectly elected executive presidency.	1966 [amended 1997], art. 34.1: "The President shall ... hold office for an aggregate period not exceeding 10 years beginning from the date of his or her first assumption of office of President."
Burkina Faso	Pres	Yes (2) / Yes (2)	5	1991	Viol / Viol / FailedViol	1997 / 2005 / 2014	Parliament / Court	Run&Won (Compaoré) / Run&Won (Compaoré) / Alternation (→ Kaboré)	Term limits removed by parliament in 1997, reintroduced in 2000 (from 7 to 5y terms), but bypassed by court decision on non-retroactivity in 2005. Failed violation in 2014 amid popular riots.	2015, art .37: "The President of Burkina Faso is elected for five years ... He is re-eligible one time."
Burundi	Pres	Yes (2) / Yes (2)	5	2005	Viol	2015	Court	Run&Won (Nkurunziza 2015)	Bid to extend term limits fails qualified majority in parliament in 2014, but allowed by court. Oppositions boycotted elections, popular riots.	2005, art. 96: "The President of the Republic is elected ... for a term of five years renewable one time."

Country								
Cameroon	Pres	Yes (2) / No	7	1996	Viol	2008	Parliament	Run&Won (Biya 2011)	Term limits removed by parliament in 2008. Small opposition party walked out of parliament and violent protests left dozens dead.	2008, art. 6.2: "The President of the Republic shall be elected for a term of office of 7 (seven) years. He shall be eligible for re-election."
Cape Verde	Parl	n.a.	n.a.	n.a.	n.a.	n.a.	n.a.	n.a.	Executive power shared by prime minister and a directly elected president. No term limit for prime minister, two-term limit (5y each) for president.	2010, art. 146.1: "The President of the Republic may not be a candidate for a third term within five years immediately following the end of his second consecutive term."
Central African Republic	Pres	Yes (2) / Yes (2)	6	1995	Not met yet	–	–	–	Term limits reintroduced by both 2004 and 2015 constitutions, but never met due to coups.	2016, art. 35: "The duration of the mandate of the President of the Republic is of five (5) years. The mandate is renewable one sole time."
Chad	Pres	Yes (2) / No	5	1996	Viol	2005	Referendum	Run&Won (Déby 2006)	Term limits removed by referendum in 2005.	2015, art. 61: "The President is elected for a mandate of five years … He is re-eligible."
Comoros	Pres	Yes (1)	5	n.a.	n.a.	n.a.	n.a.	n.a.	Presidency rotated every 4y among the three islands between 2001 and 2018.	2009, art.13: "The presidency shall rotate among the islands."

287

Table A2 (*cont.*)

	Chief executive	Term limits (max) *(then / now)*	Term duration *(current)*	Since	Respected / Violated / Failed Violation	When	How	What then	Notes	Wording of Constitution
Congo, Rep.	Pres	Yes (2) / Yes (3)	7	2002 / 2015	Viol / Not met yet	2015 / n.a.	Referendum	Run&Won (Sassou Nguesso 2016) / n.a.	Two-term limits both in 1992 and 2002 constitutions, but amendment by referendum in 2015 allowed a third term.	2015, art .65: "The President of the Republic is elected for a mandate of five (5) years renewable two (2) times."
Congo, Dem. Rep.	Pres	Yes (2) / Yes (2)	5	2005	Resp	[2019]	–	Alternation (Kabila → Tshisekedi)	Term limit met in 2016, but elections delayed until late 2018.	2011, art. 70: "The President of the Republic is elected ... for a mandate of five years renewable a single time. At the end of his mandate, the President of the Republic remains in [his] functions until the effective installation of the newly elected President."
Côte d'Ivoire	Pres	Yes (2) / Yes (2)	5	2000	Not met yet	–	–	–	Term limits only introduced by 2000 and then again by 2016 constitutions. No elections between 2000 and 2010.	2016, art. 55 "The President of the Republic is elected for five years ... He may be re-elected only once."

Country	System	Run&Won	Year 1	Year 2	2010	Parliament	Run&Won (Guelleh 2011)	Notes	Citation
Djibouti	Pres	Yes (2) / No 5	1992	Viol	2010	Parliament	Run&Won (Guelleh 2011)	Term limits removed in 2010, with duration reduced from 6y to 5y.	2010, art. 24: "The President of the Republic is elected for five years … by majority ballot in two rounds. He is re-eligible."
Equatorial Guinea	Pres	No / Yes (2) 7	2011	Not met yet	–	–	–	Term limits introduced in 2012 but do not apply retrospectively. A third term is allowed after a gap term.	2012, art. 36: "The President of the Republic is elected for a term of seven years renewable with the possibility of being reelected … limited to two consecutive periods, not … for a third mandate until alternation is produced."
Eritrea	Non elect.	n.a.	n.a.	n.a.	n.a.	n.a.	n.a.	Term limits introduced by 1997 constitution (i.e., executive president elected by parliament), but constitution never enforced and no national elections.	1997, art .41: "The term of office of the President shall be five years … No person shall be elected to hold the office of President for more than two terms."
eSwatini	Mon	n.a.	n.a.	n.a.	n.a.	n.a.	n.a.		
Ethiopia	Parl	n.a.	n.a.	n.a.	n.a.	n.a.	n.a.	Ceremonial president indirectly elected with term limits (6y term).	1994, art. 70.4: "The term of office of the President shall be six years. No person shall be elected President for more than two terms."

Table A2 (*cont.*)

	Chief executive	Term limits (max) (*then* / *now*)	Term duration (*current*)	Since	Respected / Violated / Failed Violation	When	How	What then	Notes	Wording of Constitution
Gabon	Pres	Yes (2) / No	7	1991	Viol	2003	Parliament	Run&Won (Bongo 2005)	Term limits lifted in 2003 by parliament.	2003, art. 9: "The President of the Republic is elected for a presidential term of seven (7) years ... The President is re-electable."
Gambia	Pres	No / No	5	–	–	–	–	–		1996, art. 64.1: "The term of office of an elected President shall, subject to subsection (3) and (6), be for a term of five years."
Ghana	Pres	Yes (2) / Yes (2)	4	1992	Resp / Resp	2000 / 2008	–	Alternation (Rawlings → Kufour) / Alternation (→ Mills)		1992, art. 66.2: "A person shall not be elected to hold office as President ... for more than two terms."
Guinea	Pres	Yes (2) / Yes (2)	5	1992 / 2010	Viol / Not met yet	2001 / n.a.	Referendum	Run&Won (Conté 2003) / n.a.	Term limits lifted in 2001 (with terms extended from 5y to 7y), reintroduced in 2010.	2010, art.27: "The duration of his mandate is five years, renewable one time. In any case, no one may exercise more than two presidential mandates, consecutive or not."

Country	Regime	Term limits	Term length	Year	Respected?	Year removed	Mode	Notes	Constitutional text
Guinea-Bissau	Pres	Yes (2) / Yes (2)	5	1993	Not met yet	–	–	–	1984 (amended 1996), art.66: "1. The term for the President ... is of five years. 2. The President ... may not run for a third consecutive mandate."
Kenya	Pres	Yes (2) / Yes (2)	5	1992	Resp / Resp	2002 / 2013	–	Alternation (Moi → Kibaki) / Alternation (→ Kenyatta)	Semi-presidential at best (Constitution 1984/1996, art. 103: "The government is politically accountable to the President ... and before the National Popular Assembly")
Lesotho	Parl	n.a.	n.a.	n.a.	n.a.	n.a.	–	n.a.	2010, art 142.2: "A person shall not hold office as President for more than two terms."
Liberia	Pres	Yes (2) / Yes (2)	6	1986	Resp	2018	–	Alternation (J.Sirleaf → Weah)	Term limits introduced as 1992 amendments to 1969 constitution and confirmed by new 2010 constitution.
Madagascar	Pres	Yes (2) / Yes (2)	5	1992	Not met yet	–	–	–	No term limits for either the monarch nor the prime minister.
Malawi	Pres	Yes (2) / Yes (2)	5	1994	FailedViol	2002	Parliament	Succession (Muluzi → B.Mutharika)	1986, art. 50: "The president ... shall hold office for a term of six years ... No person shall serve as President for more than two terms."
									2010, art. 45: "The President ... is elected ... for a mandate of five years renewable one sole time."
									Muluzi's bid to remove term limits rejected by parliament in 2002.
									1994, art. 82: "The President shall hold office for five years ... The President ... may serve in their respective capacities a maximum of two consecutive terms."

No elections between 1986–1997 and 1998–2006.

Term limits both in the 1992 and 2010 constitutions.

Table A2 (*cont.*)

	Chief executive	Term limits (max) *(then / now)*	Term duration *(current)*	Respected / Violated / Failed Violation	Since	When	How	What then	Notes	Wording of Constitution
Mali	Pres	Yes (2) / Yes (2)	5	Resp	1992	2002	–	Alternation (Konaré → Touré)	Konaré regularly stepped down, but Touré ousted by a coup shortly before meeting term limits.	1992, art. 30: "The President of the ... He shall be re-eligible only once."
Mauritania	Pres	No / Yes (2)	5	Not met yet	2006	–	–	–		1991 (as amended 2006), art.26 and art. 28: "The President ... is elected for five years" and is "re-eligible one sole time."
Mauritius	Parl	n.a.	n.a.	n.a.	n.a.	n.a.	n.a.	n.a.	No term limits for ceremonial head of state elected by parliament.	1968, art. 28.2: "The President shall be elected by the Assembly ... hold office for a term of 5 years and shall be eligible for re-election."
Mozambique	Pres	Yes (2) / Yes (2)	5	Resp / Resp	1990	2005 / 2014	–	Succession (Chissano → Guebuza) / Succession (→ Nyusi)	Term limits both in 1990 (two reelections, additional only after a gap term) and 2004 (two terms) constitutions.	2004, art. 147: "The term of the office of the President of the Republic shall be five years ... The President of the Republic may be re-elected only once."

292

Namibia	Pres	Yes (2) / Yes (2)	5	1990	Viol / Resp / Resp	1999 / 2005 / 2014	Parliament	Run&Won (Nujoma 2005) / Succession (→ Pohamba) / Succession (→ Geingob)	Third term only allowed for "first" president Nujoma (who had initially been elected by constituent assembly) by parliament in 2005.	1990, art. 29.3: "A person shall hold office as President for not more than two terms," art. 134.3: "the first President of Namibia may hold office as President for three terms."
Niger	Pres	Yes (2) / Yes (2)	5	1999	FailedViol	2009	Court / Parliament / Military	Alternation (→ Issoufou)	Tandja's 2009 failed bid to abolish term limits of 1992 constitution: wins election but military ousts him. New constitution and 2011 election.	2010, art. 47: "The President of the Republic is elected … for a mandate of five years, renewable one sole time."
Nigeria	Pres	Yes (2) / Yes (2)	4	1999	FailedViol	2006	Parliament	Succession (Obasanjo → Yar'Adua)	Obasanjo's bid for third term rejected by parliament.	1999, art. 137.1: "A person shall not be qualified for election to the office of President if … he has been elected to such office at any two previous elections."
Rwanda	Pres	Yes (2) / Yes (2)	7	2003 / 2015	Viol	2015	Parliament & Referendum	Run&Won (Kagame 2017)	Two terms reduced from 7y to 5y by 2015 reform, but a transitional 7y term was added, followed by new count	2015, art. 101 "The President … is elected for a five (5) year term … may be re-elected once"; art. 172: "The

293

Table A2 (cont.)

Chief executive	Term limits (max) (then / now)	Term duration (current)	Since	Respected / Violated / Failed Violation	When	How	What then	Notes	Wording of Constitution
								potentially allowing Kagame two further 5y terms.	"President ... in office at the time this revised Constitution comes into force continues to serve the term of office ... considering ... the particular challenges of Rwanda's tragic history and ... the desire to lay a firm foundation for sustainable development, a seven (7) year presidential term of office is established and shall follow the completion of the term of office referred to in the first paragraph of this article. The provisions of Article 101 ... shall take effect after the seven (7) year term of office referred to in the second paragraph of this article."

São Tomé e Príncipe	Pres	Yes (2) / Yes (2)	5	1990	Resp / Resp	2001 / 2011	Succession (Trovoada → de Menezes) / Alternation (→ Pinto da Costa)	Two-term limit, but additional non-successive mandates allowed. Semi-presidential at best (Constitution 1975/1990, art. 101: "The Government is politically responsible before the President of the Republic and the National Assembly")	1975/1990, art. 75: "The President of the Republic is elected for five years. . . . The number of successive mandates of the President must not exceed two."
Senegal	Pres	Yes (2) / Yes (2)	5	1991 / 2001	FailedViol / FailedViol	1998 / 2012	Court / Court	Run&Lost (Diouf → Wade) / Run&Lost (Wade → Sall)	Term limits and duration repeatedly changed, but protests led to election defeats. Limits removed in 1998 by Diouf (but lost 2000 election); re-introduced in 2001 by Wade (from 5y to 7y terms in 2008); lifted by Wade in 2012 (but lost 2012 election). Since 2016, from 7y to 5y.	2016, art. 27 "The duration of the mandate of the President of the Republic is of five years. No one may exercise more than two consecutive mandates."
Seychelles	Pres	Yes (2) / Yes (3)	5	1993	Not met yet	–	–	–	René resigned in 2003 before term limit, with vice president Michel taking over and later elected.	1993, art. 52: "President shall hold office for a term of five years . . . A person shall hold office as President . . . for not more than three terms."

Table A2 (cont.)

	Chief executive	Term limits (max) *(then / now)*	Term duration *(current)*	Since	Respected / Violated / Failed Violation	When	How	What then	Notes	Wording of Constitution
Sierra Leone	Pres	Yes (2) / Yes (2)	5	1991	Resp / Resp	2007 / 2018	–	Alternation (Kabbah → Koroma) / Alternation (→ Bio)	After 1992 coup, 1991 constitution was reinstated in 1996.	1991, art. 46: "No person shall hold office as President for more than two terms of five years each whether or not the terms are consecutive."
Somalia	Non elect.	–	n.a.	n.a.	n.a.	n.a.	n.a.	n.a.	President indirectly elected by federal parliament (selected by elders and community representatives) under transitional constitution of 2012.	2012, art. 91: "The President of the Federal Republic of Somalia shall hold office for a term of four (4) years."
South Africa	Parl	Yes (2) / Yes (2)	5	1996	Not met yet	–	–	–	Indirectly elected executive presidency. Both Mbeki and Zuma served but did not complete their second term.	1996, art. 88: "No person may hold office as President for more than two terms, but when a person is elected to fill a vacancy … the period between that election and the next election of a President is not regarded as a term."
South Sudan	Non elect.	–	n.a.	n.a.	n.a.	n.a.	n.a.	n.a.	No term limits in transitional constitution of 2011. No elections yet.	2011, art. 100: "The tenure of the office of the President of the Republic of South

296

Country	Office	Term limits	Year adopted	Respected/Violated	Year reached	Outcome	Notes	Constitutional text
Sudan	Pres	Yes (2) / Yes (2)	5	1998 / 2005	Viol / Not met yet	2005	Election delayed	Stayed (Bashir 2005) / Run&Won (Bashir 2010)	Two-term limits in both 1998 and 2005 constitutions. But transitional government 2005–2010 following new constitution (without new election), and terms counted anew since 2010.	Sudan shall be five years." 2005, art. 57: "The tenure of office of the President of the Republic shall be five years ... may be re-elected for one more term only."
Tanzania	Pres	Yes (2) / Yes (2)	5	1995	Resp / Resp / Resp	1995 / 2005 / 2015	–	Succession (Mwinyi → Mkapa) / Succession (→ Kikwete) / Succession (→ Magufuli)		1977/1995, art. 40: "No person shall be elected more than twice to hold the office of President," art. 42: "the person elected as President ... shall hold the office for a period of five years."
Togo	Pres	Yes (2) / No	5	1992	Viol	2002	Parliament	Run&Won (Eyadéma 2003)	Term limit removed in 2003.	2007, art. 59: "The President of the Republic is elected ... for a mandate of five (5) years. He is re-eligible."
Uganda	Pres	Yes (2) / Yes	5	1995	Viol	2005	Parliament	Run&Won (Museveni 2006)	Term limits removed by parliament in 2005, reintroduced in 2017.	1995/2017, art.105: "A person shall not hold office as President for more than two terms."

Table A2 (*cont.*)

	Chief executive	Term limits (max) *(then / now)*	Term duration *(current)*	Since	Respected / Violated / Failed Violation	When	How	What then	Notes	Wording of Constitution
Zambia	Pres	Yes (2) / Yes (2)	5	1991	FailedViol	2001	Parliament	Succession (Chiluba → Mwanawasa)	Chiluba's bid for term limit removal rejected by his own party and oppositions.	1991, art. 35: "Every President shall hold office for a period of five years . . . no person who has twice been elected as President shall be eligible for re-election."
Zimbabwe	Pres	No / Yes (2)	5	2013	Not met yet	–	–	–	Mugabe pushed to resign in 2018, Mnangagwa elected in 2018.	2013, art. 91: "A person is disqualified for election as President . . . if he or she has already held office as President . . . for two terms, whether continuous or not," art. 95: "terms of office are five years."

Notes: the table refers to term limits for the chief executive (i.e., including presidents in formal semi-presidential systems such as Congo, Dem. Rep., Guinea-Bissau, Senegal, or São Tomé e Príncipe, but not for ceremonial heads of state in parliamentary systems). "N.a." means "not applicable." Unless differently specified, data refer to the 2018 situation. Form of government: Eritrea, Somalia, and South Sudan are yet to hold direct elections; eSwatini is an absolute monarchy.

Source: based on data by Andrea Cassani, Albert Trithart, and various other sources

Table A3 *Leadership change as an explanatory factor: summary and descriptive statistics of independent variables*

Variable	Description	Obs.	Mean	St. Dev.	Min.	Max.	Share of obs.	Hypothesis
Coup	Dummy coded 1 if the country experienced one (or more) coup at time t	2561			0	1	3.31%	HP 1
Violent takeover	Dummy coded 1 if incumbent leader at time t took power in a violent/irregular way	2561			0	1	18.39%	HP 1.1
Duration (no interim)	Number of years a leader has been in power at time t	2545	8.902	8.232	0	41.120		HP 2
Duration² (no interim)	Squared number of years a leader has been in power at time t	2545	147.01	247.86	0	1690.9		HP 2.1
Non-elected leader	Dummy coded 1 if incumbent leader at time t took power in an irregular or a peaceful but non-electoral way	2561			0	1	52.19%	HP 3 & 3.1 (reference category)
Elected leader	Dummy coded 1 if incumbent leader at time t took power through a multiparty election	2561			0	1	27.85%	HP 3
Democratically elected leader	Dummy coded 1 if incumbent leader at time t took power	2561			0	1	19.96%	HP 3.1

Table A3 (*cont.*)

Variable	Description	Obs.	Mean	St. Dev.	Min.	Max.	Share of obs.	Hypothesis
Number of multiparty elections	through a multiparty election in a democratic setting Total number of elections a country held, over the years, at time t	2575	1.749	2.405	0	13		HP 4
Number of democratic multiparty elections	Total number of democratic elections a country held, over the years, at time t	2575	.758	1.650	0	11		HP 4.1
Executive control	Total vote share obtained by leader at presidential election or total seats share obtained by ruling party/coalition at legislative election	2514	78.597	30.776	.512	100		HP 5
Non-elected leader	Dummy coded 1 if incumbent leader at time t took power in an irregular or a peaceful but non-electoral way	2561			0	1	52.05%	HP 6 & 7 (reference category)

Incumbent reelected	Dummy coded 1 if incumbent leader at time t was reelected through a multiparty election	2561	0	1	21.49% HP 6 & 7 (residual category)
Electoral succession	Dummy coded 1 if incumbent leader at time t took power via an electoral succession	2561	0	1	15.63% HP 6
Electoral alternation	Dummy coded 1 if incumbent leader at time t took power via an electoral alternation	2561	0	1	10.82% HP 7
Non-multiparty regimes	Dummy coded 1 if at time t political regime was not open to multipartism	2574	0	1	49.26% HP 7.1 (reference category)
Multiparty regimes – no alternation	Dummy coded 1 if at time t a multiparty regime was in place that never experienced alternation	2574	0	1	32.87% HP 7.1 (residual category)
Multiparty regimes – one alternation	Dummy coded 1 if at time t a multiparty regime was in place that experienced one alternation only	2574	0	1	11.11% HP 7.1
Multiparty regimes – more alternations	Dummy coded 1 if at time t a multiparty regime was in place that experienced more than one alternation	2574	0	1	6.76% HP 7.1

Source: ALC dataset

Table A4 *Dependent variables and controls: definitions and descriptive statistics*

Variable	Definition	Obs.	Mean	St. Dev.	Min.	Max.	Share of obs.
Dependent variables							
GDP growth	Annual percentage growth rate of GDP at market prices based on constant local currency *Source*: World Development Indicators	2222	3.989	7.755	−51.030	149.973	
GDP per capita growth	Annual percentage growth rate of GDP per capita based on constant local currency *Source*: World Development Indicators	2222	1.316	7.390	−50.230	140.511	
Public health spending	Public health expenditure as a % of GDP (including donations from international agencies and nongovernmental organizations) *Source*: World Development Indicators	935	2.492	1.287	.044	9.087	
Primary school enrollment	Gross ratio of enrollment rate in primary school, regardless of age *Source*: World Development Indicators	1767	82.623	32.247	7.86349	207.234	

Secondary school enrollment	Gross ratio of enrollment rate in secondary school, regardless of age *Source*: World Development Indicators	1354	27.748	22.462	1.004	115.971
Life expectancy at birth	The number of years a newborn infant would live if prevailing patterns of mortality at the time of its birth were to stay the same throughout its life *Source*: World Development Indicators	2406	51.303	8.250	21.612	74.353
Under-5 mortality rate	Probability per 1,000 that a newborn baby will die before reaching age five *Source*: World Development Indicators	2.338	156.037	79.271	13.5	443.5
Political corruption	Expert based composite index that aggregates six distinct types of corruption that cover both different areas and levels of the polity realm,	2524	.613	.212	.131	.976

Table A4 (cont.)

Variable	Definition	Obs.	Mean	St. Dev.	Min.	Max.	Share of obs.
	distinguishing between executive, legislative and judicial corruption *Source*: VDem Dataset						
Executive corruption	Expert based indicator measuring how routinely do members of the executive, or their agents, engage in corruption activities *Source*: VDem Dataset	2525	.615	.247	.054	.976	
State capacity index	Aggregate index of 24 different indicators measuring the three core functions of a state: extractive capacity, coercive capacity and administrative capacity *Source*: Hanson and Sigman (2013)	2031	−.813	.629	−3.512	1.317	

Controls: geographic and demographic variables

Population growth	Annual growth rate (%) of total population *Source*: World Development Indicators	2472	2.585	1.127	−6.184	11.813	

(log)Population	Natural logarithm of total population Source: World Development Indicators	2424	15.344	1.513	11.010	19.015
Population<14	Population between the ages 0 to 14 as a percentage of the total population Source: World Development Indicators	2520	43.657	4.416	18.387	50.231
Landlocked	Dummy coded 1 for countries without sea coasts Source: Authors	2526			0	1	32.58%
(log)Land area	Natural logarithm of total country's area Source: World Development Indicators	2501	12.029	2.039	6.131	14.680
Controls: macroeconomic and financial variables						
(log)GDP per capita	Natural logarithm of GDP per capita (constant 2010 $) Source: World Development Indicators	2181	6.834	.969	4.751	9.920
GDP growth	Annual percentage growth rate of GDP at market prices based on constant local currency Source: World Development Indicators	2222	3.989	7.755	−51.030	149.973

Table A4 (*cont.*)

Variable	Definition	Obs.	Mean	St. Dev.	Min.	Max.	Share of obs.
Government spending	General government consumption expenditure as a % of GDP *Source*: World Development Indicators	2048	15.741	7.868	0	84.508	
Gross capital formation	Gross capital formation (% of GDP) *Source*: World Development Indicators	1782	20.356	14.98402	−2.424	219.069	
Natural resources rents	Total natural resources rents (% of GDP) *Source*: World Development Indicators	1953	11.862	12.408	0	89.166	
Net ODA (% GNI)	Net official development assistance received as a % of GNI *Source*: World Development Indicators	2123	10.891	11.767	−.260	181.103	
Imports	Imports of goods and services as a share of GDP *Source*: World Development Indicators	2155	40.640	30.186	2.982	424.817	

Trade	Trade is the sum of exports and imports of goods and services measured as a share of GDP *Source*: World Development Indicators	2155	69.793	43.788	6.320	531.734
Controls: political and sociocultural variables						
Conflict involvement	Total summed magnitudes of all (societal and interstate) conflict and episodes of violence in which the state at time t is involved *Source*: Center for Systemic Peace: Major Episodes of Political Violence	2408	.729	1.678	0	10
Federalism	Dummy coded 1 for federal states *Source*: Quality of Government Dataset	2395			0	1	15.70%
Life expectancy at birth	The number of years a newborn infant would live if prevailing patterns of mortality at the time of its birth were to stay the same throughout its life *Source*: World Development Indicators	2406	51.303	8.250	21.612	74.353

Table A4 (*cont.*)

Variable	Definition	Obs.	Mean	St. Dev.	Min.	Max.	Share of obs.
Ethnolinguistic fractionalization	Indicator measuring ethnic, religious and linguistic fractionalization *Source:* Alesina et al. (2003)	2258	.718	.192	.180	.952	
British colonial legacy	Dummy coded 1 for former British colonies *Source:* Quality of Government Dataset	2575			0	1	39.42
Trend variables							
Post 1990	Dummy for years following 1990 *Source:* Authors	2575			0	1	54.25%

Table A5 *Regression results for public health spending*

	Δ Public health expenditure	Δ Public health expenditure	Δ Public health expenditure	Δ Public health expenditure	Δ Public health expenditure	Δ Public health expenditure	Δ Public health expenditure	Δ Public health expenditure
Public health expenditure (t-1)	−0.251*** (0.046)	−0.275*** (0.051)	−0.257*** (0.046)	−0.259*** (0.046)	−0.253*** (0.046)	−0.251*** (0.046)	−0.255*** (0.046)	−0.255*** (0.046)
Leader duration (t-1)	0.004 (0.003)	0.016** (0.007)						
Leader duration (t-1) * Leader duration (t-1)		−0.000** (0.000)						
Δ elected leader			0.066 (0.071)					
Elected leader (t-1)			0.143** (0.070)					
Δ democratically elected leader			0.175 (0.117)					
Democratically elected leader (t-1)			0.210** (0.096)					
Δ cumulative no. of elections				0.022 (0.021)				

309

Table A5 (*cont.*)

	Δ Public health expenditure	Δ Public health expenditure	Δ Public health expenditure	Δ Public health expenditure	Δ Public health expenditure	Δ Public health expenditure	Δ Public health expenditure
Cumulative no. of elections (t-1)			0.037** (0.018)				
Δ cumulative no. of democratic elections				−0.025 (0.039)			
Cumulative no. of democratic elections (t-1)				0.012 (0.030)			
Δ executive control					0.001 (0.001)		
Executive control (t-1)					−0.002 (0.001)		
Δ incumbent reelected						0.075 (0.084)	
Incumbent reelected (t-1)						0.148* (0.076)	
Δ electoral succession						0.119 (0.089)	
Electoral succession (t-1)						0.194** (0.088)	

310

Δ electoral alternation						0.063 (0.098)	
Electoral alternation (t-1)						0.168** (0.083)	
Δ multiparty regime – no alternation							0.165* (0.095)
Multiparty regime – no alternation (t-1)							0.156** (0.077)
Δ multiparty regime – one alternation							−0.039 (0.106)
Multiparty regime – one alternation (t-1)							0.201** (0.087)
Δ multiparty regime – more alternation							−0.077 (0.138)
Multiparty regime – more alternation (t-1)							0.104 (0.097)
Δ Population < 14	−0.115 (0.141)	−0.135 (0.140)	−0.130 (0.141)	−0.123 (0.140)	−0.114 (0.140)	−0.133 (0.140)	−0.127 (0.140)	−0.150 (0.141)
Population < 14 (t-1)	−0.061*** (0.017)	−0.066*** (0.017)	−0.058*** (0.017)	−0.049*** (0.018)	−0.058*** (0.019)	−0.058*** (0.017)	−0.058*** (0.017)	−0.062*** (0.017)

311

Table A5 (cont.)

	Δ Public health expenditure	Δ Public health expenditure	Δ Public health expenditure	Δ Public health expenditure	Δ Public health expenditure	Δ Public health expenditure	Δ Public health expenditure	Δ Public health expenditure
Δ (log)GDP per capita	−0.285 (1.252)	−0.294 (1.245)	−0.579 (1.274)	−0.488 (1.301)	−0.436 (1.279)	−0.541 (1.275)	−0.567 (1.280)	−0.338 (1.289)
(log)GDP per capita (t-1)	0.074 (0.119)	0.095 (0.117)	0.039 (0.122)	−0.013 (0.137)	0.071 (0.117)	0.093 (0.114)	0.033 (0.124)	0.054 (0.123)
Δ GDP growth	0.002 (0.012)	0.002 (0.012)	0.003 (0.012)	0.002 (0.012)	0.003 (0.012)	0.004 (0.012)	0.003 (0.012)	0.002 (0.012)
GDP growth (t-1)	0.008 (0.012)	0.007 (0.012)	0.007 (0.012)	0.007 (0.012)	0.008 (0.012)	0.009 (0.012)	0.007 (0.012)	0.007 (0.012)
Δ government expenditure	0.037*** (0.008)	0.038*** (0.008)	0.034*** (0.007)	0.034*** (0.007)	0.034*** (0.007)	0.035*** (0.008)	0.034*** (0.007)	0.034*** (0.007)
Government expenditure (t-1)	0.010* (0.006)	0.011* (0.005)	0.009 (0.005)	0.009* (0.005)	0.010* (0.005)	0.009* (0.005)	0.009 (0.006)	0.009* (0.005)
Δ natural resources rents	−0.012*** (0.004)	−0.012*** (0.004)	−0.012*** (0.004)	−0.012*** (0.004)	−0.012*** (0.004)	−0.013*** (0.004)	−0.012*** (0.004)	−0.012*** (0.004)
Natural resources rents (t-1)	−0.004 (0.003)	−0.004 (0.003)	−0.003 (0.003)	−0.004 (0.003)	−0.004 (0.003)	−0.005* (0.003)	−0.003 (0.003)	−0.003 (0.003)
Δ conflict involvement	−0.056* (0.029)	−0.054* (0.029)	−0.039 (0.029)	−0.050* (0.028)	−0.050* (0.029)	−0.046 (0.031)	−0.042 (0.029)	−0.044 (0.028)

Conflict involvement $_{(t-1)}$	−0.025 (0.024)	−0.024 (0.024)	−0.015 (0.026)	−0.033 (0.024)	−0.032 (0.024)	−0.032 (0.026)	−0.018 (0.026)	−0.021 (0.025)
Country dummies	Yes	Yes	Yes	Yes	Yes	Yes	Yes	Yes
Constant	2.749* (1.423)	2.827** (1.393)	2.855* (1.473)	3.037** (1.468)	2.772* (1.429)	2.904** (1.474)	2.895** (1.460)	2.922** (1.455)
N	758	758	770	770	770	760	770	770
Countries	46	46	46	46	46	45	46	46
R^2	0.214	0.217	0.215	0.212	0.209	0.212	0.214	0.218

Notes: Coefficients of country dummies are not shown. Panel-corrected standard errors (PCSE) in parentheses. * $p < 0.1$; ** $p < 0.05$; *** $p < 0.01$

Table A6 *Regression results for primary school enrollment*

	Δ Primary school enrollment	Δ Primary school enrollment	Δ Primary school enrollment	Δ Primary school enrollment	Δ Primary school enrollment	Δ Primary school enrollment	Δ Primary school enrollment	Δ Primary school enrollment
Primary school enrollment $_{(t-1)}$	−0.019*** (0.006)	−0.020*** (0.006)	−0.020*** (0.006)	−0.020*** (0.006)	−0.019*** (0.006)	−0.019*** (0.006)	−0.021*** (0.006)	−0.021*** (0.006)
Leader duration $_{(t-1)}$	−0.013 (0.016)	−0.117** (0.049)						
Leader duration $_{(t-1)}$ * Leader duration $_{(t-1)}$		0.004** (0.002)						
Δ elected leader			0.522 (0.624)					
Elected leader $_{(t-1)}$			0.540 (0.418)					
Δ democratically elected leader			0.810 (0.845)					
Democratically elected leader $_{(t-1)}$			1.014** (0.416)					
Δ cumulative no. of elections				−0.101 (0.196)				
Cumulative no. of elections $_{(t-1)}$				−0.060 (0.060)				

314

Δ cumulative no. of democratic elections	0.090 (0.317)	
Cumulative no. of democratic elections (t-1)	−0.018 (0.062)	
Δ executive control		−0.009 (0.011)
Executive control (t-1)		−0.009* (0.005)
Δ incumbent reelected		0.609 (0.657)
Incumbent reelected (t-1)		0.617 (0.423)
Δ electoral succession		0.698 (0.734)
Electoral succession (t-1)		0.539 (0.427)
Δ electoral alternation		0.742 (0.983)
Electoral alternation (t-1)		1.516*** (0.510)
Δ multiparty regime – no alternation		0.559 (0.686)

Table A6 (*cont.*)

	Δ Primary school enrollment	Δ Primary school enrollment	Δ Primary school enrollment	Δ Primary school enrollment	Δ Primary school enrollment	Δ Primary school enrollment	Δ Primary school enrollment	Δ Primary school enrollment
Multiparty regime – no alternation (t-1)								0.612 (0.381)
Δ multiparty regime – one alternation								1.358 (1.213)
Multiparty regime – one alternation (t-1)								0.807 (0.535)
Δ multiparty regime – more alternation								0.141 (1.678)
Multiparty regime – more alternation (t-1)								1.890*** (0.571)
Δ (log)Population	8.382 (20.747)	7.558 (20.660)	3.660 (20.516)	6.376 (20.307)	6.532 (20.318)	4.571 (20.420)	3.681 (20.455)	5.354 (20.483)
(log)Population (t-1)	−0.095 (0.135)	−0.092 (0.135)	−0.097 (0.132)	−0.081 (0.134)	−0.099 (0.134)	−0.113 (0.150)	−0.118 (0.142)	−0.116 (0.136)
Δ (log)GDP per capita	−11.303 (15.518)	−12.354 (15.568)	−13.577 (15.442)	−10.834 (15.424)	−11.933 (15.401)	−12.380 (15.503)	−14.399 (15.406)	−14.265 (15.374)
(log)GDP per capita (t-1)	−0.443** (0.206)	−0.436** (0.203)	−0.528*** (0.201)	−0.399* (0.208)	−0.438** (0.201)	−0.539*** (0.209)	−0.496** (0.202)	−0.495** (0.197)

Δ GDP growth	0.194	0.205	0.211	0.192	0.201	0.203	0.221	0.218
	(0.148)	(0.149)	(0.147)	(0.147)	(0.147)	(0.148)	(0.146)	(0.146)
GDP growth (t-1)	0.261*	0.275*	0.273*	0.261*	0.269*	0.266*	0.284*	0.280*
	(0.148)	(0.149)	(0.147)	(0.147)	(0.147)	(0.148)	(0.146)	(0.146)
Δ natural resources rents	0.016	0.016	0.017	0.012	0.013	0.009	0.016	0.018
	(0.037)	(0.037)	(0.036)	(0.036)	(0.036)	(0.038)	(0.036)	(0.036)
Natural resources rents (t-1)	0.022	0.021	0.031*	0.021	0.023	0.022	0.030*	0.030*
	(0.016)	(0.016)	(0.016)	(0.015)	(0.016)	(0.016)	(0.016)	(0.016)
Δ net ODA (%GNI)	−0.015	−0.014	−0.017	−0.015	−0.015	−0.017	−0.015	−0.017
	(0.030)	(0.030)	(0.030)	(0.030)	(0.030)	(0.030)	(0.030)	(0.030)
Net ODA (%GNI) (t-1)	0.002	0.003	−0.001	0.003	0.003	0.001	−0.001	0.000
	(0.019)	(0.019)	(0.019)	(0.018)	(0.018)	(0.019)	(0.018)	(0.019)
Δ conflict involvement	−0.323	−0.311	−0.344	−0.333	−0.331	−0.433*	−0.343	−0.330
	(0.241)	(0.241)	(0.236)	(0.237)	(0.237)	(0.258)	(0.236)	(0.235)
Conflict involvement (t-1)	−0.217*	−0.202*	−0.181	−0.220*	−0.209*	−0.213*	−0.173	−0.166
	(0.112)	(0.112)	(0.114)	(0.114)	(0.112)	(0.112)	(0.114)	(0.113)
Ethnolinguistic fractionalization (t-1)	0.186	0.078	0.173	0.209	0.167	0.357	0.100	0.124
	(0.774)	(0.785)	(0.771)	(0.763)	(0.766)	(0.834)	(0.784)	(0.765)
British colonial legacy (t-1)	0.148	0.144	0.054	0.207	0.170	0.018	0.190	0.189
	(0.324)	(0.326)	(0.329)	(0.326)	(0.333)	(0.332)	(0.323)	(0.320)
Post 1990 (t-1)	0.868**	0.792**	0.410	1.012***	0.869**	0.628*	0.333	0.328
	(0.341)	(0.351)	(0.430)	(0.386)	(0.354)	(0.368)	(0.425)	(0.430)

Table A6 (*cont.*)

	Δ Primary school enrollment	Δ Primary school enrollment	Δ Primary school enrollment	Δ Primary school enrollment	Δ Primary school enrollment	Δ Primary school enrollment	Δ Primary school enrollment	Δ Primary school enrollment
Constant	5.345**	5.791**	5.845**	4.804*	5.300**	6.952**	6.017**	5.930**
	(2.701)	(2.706)	(2.632)	(2.708)	(2.628)	(2.971)	(2.788)	(2.684)
N	1,326	1,326	1,337	1,337	1,337	1,297	1,337	1,337
Countries	42	42	42	42	42	42	42	42
R^2	0.063	0.067	0.067	0.064	0.063	0.063	0.069	0.070

Notes: Panel-corrected standard errors (PCSE) in parentheses. * $p < 0.1$; ** $p < 0.05$; *** $p < 0.01$

Table A7 *Regression results for secondary school enrollment*

	Δ Secondary school enrollment	Δ Secondary school enrollment	Δ Secondary school enrollment	Δ Secondary school enrollment	Δ Secondary school enrollment	Δ Secondary school enrollment	Δ Secondary school enrollment	Δ Secondary school enrollment
Secondary school enrollment (t-1)	−0.021** (0.009)	−0.022** (0.009)	−0.024** (0.010)	−0.024** (0.010)	−0.025** (0.010)	−0.024** (0.010)	−0.025*** (0.010)	−0.026*** (0.010)
Leader duration (t-1)	−0.012 (0.008)	−0.097*** (0.026)						
Leader duration (t-1) * Leader duration (t-1)		0.003*** (0.001)						
Δ elected leader			0.059 (0.331)					
Elected leader (t-1)			0.332* (0.191)					
Δ democratically elected leader			−0.148 (0.315)					
Democratically elected leader (t-1)			0.811*** (0.213)					
Δ cumulative no. of elections				−0.010 (0.082)				
Cumulative no. of elections (t-1)				0.069 (0.045)				
Δ cumulative no. of democratic elections					0.002 (0.113)			

Table A7 (*cont.*)

	Δ Secondary school enrollment	Δ Secondary school enrollment	Δ Secondary school enrollment	Δ Secondary school enrollment	Δ Secondary school enrollment	Δ Secondary school enrollment	Δ Secondary school enrollment
Cumulative no. of democratic elections (t-1)				0.121** (0.051)			
Δ executive control					−0.002 (0.006)		
Executive control (t-1)					−0.008*** (0.003)		
Δ incumbent reelected						0.190 (0.326)	
Incumbent reelected (t-1)						0.447** (0.180)	
Δ electoral succession						−0.015 (0.333)	
Electoral succession (t-1)						0.521** (0.206)	
Δ electoral alternation						−0.374 (0.521)	
Electoral alternation (t-1)						1.306*** (0.261)	
Δ multiparty regime – no alternation							0.129 (0.303)

Multiparty regime – no alternation (t-1)								0.497*** (0.170)
Δ multiparty regime – one alternation								–0.698 (0.672)
Multiparty regime – one alternation (t-1)								0.550** (0.247)
Δ multiparty regime – more alternation								0.206 (0.673)
Multiparty regime – more alternation (t-1)								1.452*** (0.350)
Δ (log)Population	7.206 (13.066)	7.036 (13.128)	1.405 (12.843)	4.463 (12.984)	4.626 (12.931)	4.575 (12.680)	2.577 (12.993)	1.629 (12.892)
(log)Population (t-1)	0.052 (0.092)	0.069 (0.091)	0.081 (0.089)	0.034 (0.089)	0.086 (0.094)	0.054 (0.098)	0.050 (0.091)	0.067 (0.092)
Δ (log)GDP per capita	–7.152 (11.282)	–7.922 (11.148)	–7.429 (11.239)	–8.820 (11.341)	–8.275 (11.312)	–7.400 (11.110)	–7.800 (11.277)	–8.474 (11.317)
(log)GDP per capita (t-1)	0.365** (0.155)	0.410*** (0.153)	0.333** (0.152)	0.327** (0.150)	0.341** (0.154)	0.295** (0.150)	0.365** (0.153)	0.374** (0.154)
Δ GDP growth	0.093 (0.109)	0.102 (0.108)	0.092 (0.108)	0.108 (0.109)	0.103 (0.109)	0.093 (0.107)	0.097 (0.109)	0.103 (0.109)
GDP growth (t-1)	0.111 (0.109)	0.121 (0.107)	0.106 (0.108)	0.124 (0.109)	0.118 (0.109)	0.106 (0.107)	0.111 (0.109)	0.115 (0.109)
Δ natural resources rents	–0.043** (0.019)	–0.044** (0.019)	–0.038* (0.019)	–0.041** (0.019)	–0.040** (0.019)	–0.039** (0.020)	–0.039** (0.019)	–0.039** (0.019)
Natural resources rents (t-1)	–0.000 (0.009)	–0.002 (0.009)	0.007 (0.009)	0.002 (0.009)	0.005 (0.009)	0.004 (0.010)	0.004 (0.009)	0.003 (0.009)
Δ net ODA (%GNI)	–0.029* (0.015)	–0.029* (0.016)	–0.029* (0.015)	–0.031** (0.015)	–0.030* (0.016)	–0.032** (0.016)	–0.026* (0.015)	–0.026* (0.015)

Table A7 (*cont.*)

	Δ Secondary school enrollment	Δ Secondary school enrollment	Δ Secondary school enrollment	Δ Secondary school enrollment	Δ Secondary school enrollment	Δ Secondary school enrollment	Δ Secondary school enrollment	Δ Secondary school enrollment
Net ODA (%GNI) (t-1)	-0.025***	-0.024***	-0.027***	-0.027***	-0.027***	-0.027***	-0.026***	-0.025***
	(0.009)	(0.009)	(0.009)	(0.009)	(0.009)	(0.009)	(0.008)	(0.008)
Δ conflict involvement	0.065	0.067	0.054	0.067	0.051	0.112	0.063	0.078
	(0.102)	(0.104)	(0.097)	(0.100)	(0.099)	(0.103)	(0.097)	(0.098)
Conflict involvement (t-1)	-0.014	0.000	-0.015	-0.008	-0.027	-0.018	-0.007	-0.012
	(0.057)	(0.057)	(0.055)	(0.056)	(0.055)	(0.055)	(0.056)	(0.055)
Ethnolinguistic fractionalization (t-1)	-0.497	-0.675	-0.582	-0.553	-0.545	-0.378	-0.559	-0.507
	(0.400)	(0.411)	(0.387)	(0.401)	(0.399)	(0.400)	(0.387)	(0.383)
British colonial legacy (t-1)	0.010	-0.040	-0.119	0.001	-0.062	-0.106	-0.026	0.003
	(0.181)	(0.175)	(0.174)	(0.170)	(0.171)	(0.167)	(0.174)	(0.172)
Post 1990 (t-1)	0.685***	0.603***	0.384**	0.556***	0.581***	0.493**	0.320*	0.343*
	(0.187)	(0.193)	(0.184)	(0.177)	(0.178)	(0.194)	(0.182)	(0.180)
Constant	-1.949	-1.993	-2.094	-1.437	-2.285	-0.786	-1.901	-2.224
	(2.041)	(1.997)	(1.976)	(1.954)	(2.067)	(2.025)	(2.014)	(2.026)
N	828	828	834	834	834	803	834	834
Countries	42	42	42	42	42	42	42	42
R^2	0.085	0.099	0.101	0.086	0.090	0.092	0.109	0.106

Notes: Panel-corrected standard errors (PCSE) in parentheses. * $p < 0.1$; ** $p < 0.05$; *** $p < 0.01$

Table A8 *Regression results for life expectancy at birth*

	Δ Life expectancy at birth	Δ Life expectancy at birth	Δ Life expectancy at birth	Δ Life expectancy at birth	Δ Life expectancy at birth	Δ Life expectancy at birth	Δ Life expectancy at birth	Δ Life expectancy at birth
Life expectancy at birth (t-1)	−0.009* (0.006)	−0.009* (0.006)	−0.013** (0.006)	−0.015*** (0.006)	−0.014** (0.005)	−0.010* (0.006)	−0.012** (0.006)	−0.013** (0.005)
Leader duration (t-1)	−0.001 (0.002)	−0.011** (0.005)						
Leader duration (t-1) * Leader duration (t-1)		0.000* (0.000)						
Δ elected leader			−0.038 (0.059)					
Elected leader (t-1)			0.070 (0.049)					
Δ democratically elected leader			0.127** (0.060)					
Democratically elected leader (t-1)			0.277*** (0.054)					
Δ cumulative no. of elections				0.038** (0.019)				
Cumulative no. of elections (t-1)				0.077*** (0.015)				
Δ cumulative no. of democratic elections					0.055* (0.031)			

Table A8 (*cont.*)

	Δ Life expectancy at birth	Δ Life expectancy at birth	Δ Life expectancy at birth	Δ Life expectancy at birth	Δ Life expectancy at birth	Δ Life expectancy at birth	Δ Life expectancy at birth	Δ Life expectancy at birth
Cumulative no. of democratic elections (t-1)				0.085*** (0.015)				
Δ executive control					0.000 (0.001)			
Executive control (t-1)					−0.001 (0.001)			
Δ incumbent reelected						−0.022 (0.068)		
Incumbent reelected (t-1)						0.106** (0.047)		
Δ electoral succession						0.051 (0.073)		
Electoral succession (t-1)						0.226*** (0.056)		
Δ electoral alternation						0.100 (0.073)		
Electoral alternation (t-1)						0.214*** (0.058)		
Δ multiparty regime – no alternation							0.017 (0.068)	
Multiparty regime – no alternation (t-1)							0.113** (0.045)	

Δ multiparty regime – one alternation							0.067 (0.083)
Multiparty regime – one alternation (t-1)							0.304*** (0.060)
Δ multiparty regime – more alternation							0.221* (0.124)
Multiparty regime – more alternation (t-1)							0.335*** (0.077)
Δ (log)Population	3.711 (4.190)	3.592 (4.177)	2.360 (4.253)	3.853 (4.203)	2.709 (4.215)	2.227 (4.279)	2.326 (4.258)	2.662 (4.225)
(log)Population (t-1)	0.011 (0.020)	0.012 (0.020)	0.017 (0.018)	-0.002 (0.017)	0.034* (0.019)	0.015 (0.021)	0.006 (0.019)	0.009 (0.019)
Δ (log)GDP per capita	-4.912* (2.807)	-4.994* (2.801)	-5.699* (2.910)	-6.061** (2.880)	-6.011** (2.890)	-5.871** (2.914)	-5.764** (2.918)	-5.887** (2.901)
(log)GDP per capita (t-1)	0.002 (0.030)	0.001 (0.029)	-0.007 (0.031)	-0.029 (0.030)	-0.014 (0.029)	0.011 (0.031)	-0.002 (0.030)	0.007 (0.029)
Δ GDP growth	0.059** (0.027)	0.060** (0.027)	0.068** (0.029)	0.070** (0.028)	0.070** (0.028)	0.069** (0.029)	0.068** (0.029)	0.070** (0.028)
GDP growth (t-1)	0.069** (0.027)	0.070** (0.027)	0.074*** (0.028)	0.076*** (0.028)	0.077*** (0.028)	0.076*** (0.028)	0.074*** (0.028)	0.076*** (0.028)
Δ natural resources rents	-0.001 (0.003)	-0.001 (0.003)	-0.001 (0.003)	-0.001 (0.003)	-0.001 (0.003)	-0.002 (0.003)	-0.001 (0.003)	-0.002 (0.003)
Natural resources rents (t-1)	0.002 (0.001)	0.001 (0.001)	0.003*** (0.001)	0.004*** (0.001)	0.004*** (0.001)	0.001 (0.001)	0.002** (0.001)	0.002** (0.001)
Δ net ODA (%GNI)	0.002 (0.002)	0.002 (0.002)	0.001 (0.002)	0.001 (0.002)	0.002 (0.002)	0.002 (0.002)	0.002 (0.002)	0.001 (0.002)
Net ODA (%GNI) (t-1)	0.003* (0.002)	0.003* (0.002)	0.003* (0.002)	0.004** (0.002)	0.004** (0.002)	0.004** (0.002)	0.003** (0.002)	0.003* (0.002)

Table A8 (*cont.*)

	Δ Life expectancy at birth	Δ Life expectancy at birth	Δ Life expectancy at birth	Δ Life expectancy at birth	Δ Life expectancy at birth	Δ Life expectancy at birth	Δ Life expectancy at birth	Δ Life expectancy at birth
Δ conflict involvement	−0.003 (0.022)	−0.003 (0.022)	−0.023 (0.025)	−0.020 (0.025)	−0.030 (0.025)	−0.026 (0.026)	−0.022 (0.025)	−0.019 (0.025)
Conflict involvement (t-1)	0.001 (0.011)	0.002 (0.011)	0.010 (0.011)	0.015 (0.011)	0.001 (0.011)	0.007 (0.011)	0.012 (0.011)	0.014 (0.011)
Ethnolinguistic fractionalization (t-1)	0.112 (0.131)	0.105 (0.131)	0.088 (0.127)	0.035 (0.128)	0.098 (0.123)	0.099 (0.130)	0.082 (0.128)	0.042 (0.129)
British colonial legacy (t-1)	−0.082** (0.035)	−0.082** (0.035)	−0.124*** (0.034)	−0.146*** (0.035)	−0.167*** (0.040)	−0.094*** (0.036)	−0.099*** (0.033)	−0.098*** (0.033)
Post 1990 (t-1)	0.067 (0.105)	0.058 (0.105)	−0.006 (0.104)	−0.096 (0.096)	−0.010 (0.100)	0.051 (0.107)	−0.029 (0.106)	−0.050 (0.105)
Constant	0.167 (0.384)	0.219 (0.370)	0.329 (0.351)	0.860** (0.339)	0.145 (0.350)	0.194 (0.419)	0.404 (0.361)	0.375 (0.356)
N	1,616	1,616	1,636	1,636	1,636	1,590	1,636	1,636
Countries	42	42	42	42	42	42	42	42
R^2	0.093	0.095	0.114	0.143	0.132	0.089	0.107	0.117

Notes: Panel-corrected standard errors (PCSE) in parentheses. * $p < 0.1$; ** $p < 0.05$; *** $p < 0.01$

Table A9 *Regression results for under-5 mortality rate*

	Δ Under-5 mortality rate	Δ Under-5 mortality rate	Δ Under-5 mortality rate	Δ Under-5 mortality rate	Δ Under-5 mortality rate	Δ Under-5 mortality rate	Δ Under-5 mortality rate	Δ Under-5 mortality rate
Under-5 mortality rate (t-1)	−0.012*** (0.003)	−0.012*** (0.003)	−0.014*** (0.003)	−0.015*** (0.003)	−0.013*** (0.003)	−0.013*** (0.003)	−0.014*** (0.003)	−0.014*** (0.003)
Leader duration (t-1)	0.016 (0.012)	0.048 (0.035)						
Leader duration (t-1) * Leader duration (t-1)		−0.001 (0.001)						
Δ elected leader			0.565 (0.469)					
Elected leader (t-1)			−0.558* (0.326)					
Δ democratically elected leader			−0.632 (0.629)					
Democratically elected leader (t-1)			−1.352*** (0.329)					
Δ cumulative no. of elections				0.037 (0.137)				
Cumulative no. of elections (t-1)				−0.261*** (0.060)				
Δ cumulative no. of democratic elections					−0.189 (0.191)			

Table A9 (*cont.*)

	Δ Under-5 mortality rate	Δ Under-5 mortality rate	Δ Under-5 mortality rate	Δ Under-5 mortality rate	Δ Under-5 mortality rate	Δ Under-5 mortality rate	Δ Under-5 mortality rate
Cumulative no. of democratic elections (t-1)				−0.279*** (0.071)			
Δ executive control					−0.001 (0.008)		
Executive control (t-1)					0.009** (0.004)		
Δ incumbent reelected						0.375 (0.544)	
Incumbent reelected (t-1)						−0.634** (0.319)	
Δ electoral succession						0.038 (0.483)	
Electoral succession (t-1)						−1.342*** (0.334)	
Δ electoral alternation						−0.356 (0.610)	
Electoral alternation (t-1)						−1.258*** (0.401)	
Δ multiparty regime – no alternation							−0.155 (0.524)
Multiparty regime – no alternation (t-1)							−0.729** (0.314)
Δ multiparty regime – one alternation							−0.479 (0.671)

Multiparty regime – one alternation (t-1)							−2.076***
							(0.396)
Δ multiparty regime – more alternation							0.289
							(0.992)
Multiparty regime – more alternation (t-1)							−1.414***
							(0.460)
Δ (log)Population	−245.980***	−245.606***	−222.162***	−225.877***	−221.481***	−221.708***	−222.691***	−222.356***
	(34.835)	(34.832)	(36.854)	(36.867)	(36.656)	(37.352)	(36.892)	(36.857)
(log)Population (t-1)	0.041	0.039	−0.023	0.033	−0.081	−0.026	0.032	0.014
	(0.126)	(0.126)	(0.120)	(0.123)	(0.123)	(0.145)	(0.128)	(0.121)
Δ (log)GDP per capita	−171.558***	−171.379***	−157.456***	−155.879***	−155.157***	−155.945***	−157.198***	−155.320***
	(26.918)	(26.938)	(28.353)	(28.366)	(28.291)	(28.350)	(28.397)	(28.454)
(log)GDP per capita (t-1)	0.820***	0.827***	0.817***	0.871***	0.837***	0.761***	0.805***	0.771***
	(0.165)	(0.163)	(0.181)	(0.178)	(0.180)	(0.189)	(0.177)	(0.169)
Δ GDP growth	1.572***	1.570***	1.412***	1.396***	1.388***	1.394***	1.409***	1.388***
	(0.261)	(0.261)	(0.277)	(0.277)	(0.277)	(0.278)	(0.278)	(0.279)
GDP growth (t-1)	1.464***	1.461***	1.345***	1.329***	1.319***	1.323***	1.343***	1.320***
	(0.259)	(0.259)	(0.273)	(0.272)	(0.272)	(0.273)	(0.273)	(0.274)
Δ natural resources rents	−0.012	−0.012	−0.009	−0.010	−0.010	−0.007	−0.008	−0.006
	(0.022)	(0.021)	(0.022)	(0.021)	(0.021)	(0.023)	(0.021)	(0.022)
Natural resources rents (t-1)	−0.019**	−0.018**	−0.024***	−0.024***	−0.027***	−0.018**	−0.022**	−0.020**
	(0.008)	(0.008)	(0.009)	(0.009)	(0.009)	(0.009)	(0.008)	(0.008)
Δ net ODA (%GNI)	0.050**	0.050**	0.059***	0.058***	0.057***	0.056***	0.057***	0.060***
	(0.020)	(0.020)	(0.021)	(0.021)	(0.021)	(0.021)	(0.021)	(0.021)
Net ODA (%GNI) (t-1)	−0.008	−0.008	−0.018	−0.021	−0.021	−0.022	−0.019	−0.015
	(0.014)	(0.014)	(0.015)	(0.014)	(0.015)	(0.015)	(0.015)	(0.014)

Table A9 (*cont.*)

	Δ Under-5 mortality rate	Δ Under-5 mortality rate	Δ Under-5 mortality rate	Δ Under-5 mortality rate	Δ Under-5 mortality rate	Δ Under-5 mortality rate	Δ Under-5 mortality rate	Δ Under-5 mortality rate
Δ conflict involvement	0.698***	0.696***	0.901***	0.896***	0.929***	0.983***	0.898***	0.885***
	(0.183)	(0.184)	(0.208)	(0.208)	(0.208)	(0.223)	(0.209)	(0.209)
Conflict involvement (t-1)	0.376***	0.373***	0.296***	0.296***	0.340***	0.333***	0.282***	0.268***
	(0.080)	(0.080)	(0.079)	(0.081)	(0.081)	(0.085)	(0.080)	(0.079)
Ethnolinguistic fractionalization (t-1)	−0.790	−0.771	−0.440	−0.275	−0.522	−0.573	−0.430	−0.120
	(1.187)	(1.183)	(1.195)	(1.193)	(1.193)	(1.250)	(1.199)	(1.203)
British colonial legacy (t-1)	0.058	0.059	0.211	0.226	0.306	0.169	0.125	0.127
	(0.218)	(0.219)	(0.218)	(0.221)	(0.227)	(0.229)	(0.216)	(0.223)
Post 1990 (t-1)	−0.973*	−0.941*	−0.533	−0.453	−0.678	−0.816	−0.418	−0.262
	(0.508)	(0.511)	(0.542)	(0.500)	(0.504)	(0.512)	(0.540)	(0.542)
Constant	−4.150**	−4.339**	−2.882	−4.013**	−2.202	−3.379	−3.641*	−3.316*
	(1.992)	(1.980)	(2.000)	(2.022)	(1.968)	(2.379)	(2.048)	(1.912)
N	1,598	1,598	1,618	1,618	1,618	1,571	1,618	1,618
Countries	42	42	42	42	42	42	42	42
R^2	0.317	0.317	0.314	0.315	0.312	0.305	0.313	0.319

Notes: Panel-corrected standard errors (PCSE) in parentheses. * $p < 0.1$; ** $p < 0.05$; *** $p < 0.01$

Table A10 *Regression results for state consolidation*

	Δ State capacity index	Δ State capacity index	Δ State capacity index	Δ State capacity index	Δ State capacity index	Δ State capacity index	Δ State capacity index
State capacity index $_{(t-1)}$	−0.107*** (0.018)	−0.109*** (0.019)	−0.107*** (0.018)	−0.110*** (0.018)	−0.107*** (0.018)	−0.115*** (0.018)	−0.108*** (0.018)	−0.105*** (0.018)
Leader duration $_{(t-1)}$	−0.001* (0.001)	0.002 (0.002)						
Leader duration $_{(t-1)}$ * Leader duration $_{(t-1)}$		−0.000* (0.000)						
Δ elected leader			0.056** (0.023)					
Elected leader $_{(t-1)}$			0.023 (0.015)					
Δ democratically elected leader			0.099*** (0.032)					
Democratically elected leader $_{(t-1)}$			0.055*** (0.019)					
Δ cumulative no. of elections				0.007 (0.009)				
Cumulative no. of elections $_{(t-1)}$				0.008** (0.004)				
Δ cumulative no. of democratic elections					0.013 (0.014)			

331

Table A10 (*cont.*)

	Δ State capacity index	Δ State capacity index	Δ State capacity index	Δ State capacity index	Δ State capacity index	Δ State capacity index	Δ State capacity index
Cumulative no. of democratic elections (t-1)				0.007 (0.004)			
Δ executive control					−0.001*** (0.000)		
Executive control (t-1)					−0.001*** (0.000)		
Δ incumbent reelected						0.034 (0.028)	
Incumbent reelected (t-1)						0.020 (0.017)	
Δ electoral succession						0.085*** (0.033)	
Electoral succession (t-1)						0.051*** (0.016)	
Δ electoral alternation						0.133*** (0.034)	
Electoral alternation (t-1)						0.056** (0.022)	
Δ multiparty regime – no alternation							0.032 (0.027)

Multiparty regime – no alternation (t-1)							0.024* (0.015)
Δ multiparty regime – one alternation							0.102*** (0.039)
Multiparty regime – one alternation (t-1)							0.041** (0.020)
Δ multiparty regime – more alternation							0.177*** (0.065)
Multiparty regime – more alternation (t-1)							0.062** (0.030)
Δ (log)GDP per capita	0.192** (0.092)	0.188** (0.091)	0.189** (0.090)	0.203** (0.091)	0.209** (0.090)	0.171* (0.092)	0.189** (0.090)	0.201** (0.090)
(log)GDP per capita (t-1)	0.044*** (0.011)	0.046*** (0.011)	0.039*** (0.011)	0.037*** (0.011)	0.040*** (0.011)	0.035*** (0.011)	0.039*** (0.011)	0.039*** (0.011)
Δ natural resources rents	−0.001 (0.001)	−0.001 (0.001)	−0.000 (0.001)	−0.000 (0.001)	−0.000 (0.001)	−0.001 (0.001)	−0.000 (0.001)	−0.000 (0.001)
Natural resources rents (t-1)	−0.002*** (0.001)	−0.001** (0.001)	−0.001* (0.001)	−0.001** (0.001)	−0.001** (0.001)	−0.001** (0.001)	−0.001** (0.001)	−0.001** (0.001)
Δ trade	−0.002*** (0.000)	−0.002*** (0.000)	−0.002*** (0.000)	−0.002*** (0.000)	−0.002*** (0.000)	−0.002*** (0.000)	−0.002*** (0.000)	−0.002*** (0.000)
Trade (t-1)	0.000 (0.000)	0.000 (0.000)	0.000 (0.000)	0.000 (0.000)	0.000 (0.000)	0.000 (0.000)	0.000 (0.000)	0.000 (0.000)
(log)Land area (t-1)	0.002 (0.003)	0.001 (0.003)	0.002 (0.003)	0.003 (0.003)	0.003 (0.003)	0.001 (0.003)	0.001 (0.003)	0.003 (0.003)

Table A10 (*cont.*)

	Δ State capacity index	Δ State capacity index	Δ State capacity index	Δ State capacity index	Δ State capacity index	Δ State capacity index	Δ State capacity index	Δ State capacity index
Ethnolinguistic fractionalization $_{(t-1)}$	−0.020 (0.029)	−0.014 (0.029)	−0.029 (0.028)	−0.032 (0.028)	−0.023 (0.028)	−0.011 (0.030)	−0.033 (0.028)	−0.034 (0.027)
British colonial legacy $_{(t-1)}$	0.020** (0.010)	0.020** (0.010)	0.018* (0.010)	0.017 (0.010)	0.018* (0.011)	0.018* (0.010)	0.020* (0.010)	0.022** (0.011)
Post 1990 $_{(t-1)}$	−0.052*** (0.016)	−0.050*** (0.016)	−0.076*** (0.018)	−0.072*** (0.018)	−0.061*** (0.017)	−0.074*** (0.016)	−0.079*** (0.018)	−0.078*** (0.018)
Constant	−0.347*** (0.083)	−0.371*** (0.084)	−0.322*** (0.081)	−0.317*** (0.083)	−0.342*** (0.082)	−0.218*** (0.083)	−0.311*** (0.081)	−0.333*** (0.081)
N	1,361	1,361	1,378	1,378	1,378	1,357	1,378	1,378
Countries	41	41	41	41	41	41	41	41
R^2	0.100	0.103	0.111	0.104	0.102	0.115	0.115	0.109

Notes: Panel-corrected standard errors (PCSE) in parentheses. * $p < 0.1$; ** $p < 0.05$; *** $p < 0.01$

Table A11 *Regression results for political corruption*

	Δ Political corruption	Δ Political corruption	Δ Political corruption	Δ Political corruption	Δ Political corruption	Δ Political corruption	Δ Political corruption
Political corruption (t-1)	−0.019*** (0.007)	−0.018*** (0.007)	−0.019*** (0.007)	−0.022*** (0.007)	−0.019*** (0.007)	−0.019*** (0.007)	−0.021*** (0.007)	−0.017** (0.007)
Leader duration (t-1)	−0.000 (0.000)	−0.001** (0.000)					
Leader duration (t-1) * Leader duration (t-1)		0.000*** (0.000)					
Δ elected leader			0.002 (0.004)				
Elected leader (t-1)			−0.005** (0.002)				
Δ democratically elected leader			0.012* (0.006)				
Democratically elected leader (t-1)			−0.008*** (0.002)				
Δ cumulative no. of elections				−0.000 (0.001)			
Cumulative no. of elections (t-1)				−0.002*** (0.000)			
Δ cumulative no. of democratic elections					0.000 (0.002)		
Cumulative no. of democratic elections (t-1)					−0.001** (0.000)		

Table A11 (*cont.*)

	Δ Political corruption	Δ Political corruption	Δ Political corruption	Δ Political corruption	Δ Political corruption	Δ Political corruption	Δ Political corruption
Δ executive control				−0.000 (0.000)			
Executive control (τ-1)				0.000*** (0.000)			
Δ incumbent reelected					0.009* (0.005)		
Incumbent reelected (τ-1)					−0.004* (0.002)		
Δ electoral succession					0.002 (0.005)		
Electoral succession (τ-1)					−0.010*** (0.003)		
Δ electoral alternation					0.001 (0.006)		
Electoral alternation (τ-1)					−0.006** (0.003)		
Δ multiparty regime – no alternation							0.007 (0.005)
Multiparty regime – no alternation (τ-1)							−0.005** (0.002)
Δ multiparty regime – one alternation							−0.007 (0.006)

Multiparty regime – one alternation (t-1)							−0.006*
							(0.003)
Δ multiparty regime – more alternation							0.010
							(0.010)
Multiparty regime – more alternation (t-1)							−0.007**
							(0.004)
Δ (log)GDP per capita	−0.016	−0.015	−0.008	−0.008	−0.011	−0.010	−0.008	−0.008
	(0.013)	(0.013)	(0.013)	(0.013)	(0.013)	(0.013)	(0.013)	(0.013)
(log)GDP per capita (t-1)	0.000	−0.000	0.001	0.002*	0.001	0.002	0.001	0.001
	(0.001)	(0.001)	(0.001)	(0.001)	(0.001)	(0.001)	(0.001)	(0.001)
Δ government expenditure (%GDP)	0.000	0.000	0.000	0.000	0.000	0.000	0.000	0.000
	(0.000)	(0.000)	(0.000)	(0.000)	(0.000)	(0.000)	(0.000)	(0.000)
Government expenditure (% GDP) (t-1)	0.000	0.000	0.000	−0.000	0.000	0.000	0.000	0.000
	(0.000)	(0.000)	(0.000)	(0.000)	(0.000)	(0.000)	(0.000)	(0.000)
Δ imports (%GDP)	0.000	0.000	−0.000	−0.000	−0.000	−0.000	−0.000	−0.008
	(0.000)	(0.000)	(0.000)	(0.000)	(0.000)	(0.000)	(0.000)	(0.013)
Imports (%GDP) (t-1)	−0.000**	−0.000**	−0.000**	−0.000**	−0.000**	−0.000**	−0.000**	−0.000**
	(0.000)	(0.000)	(0.000)	(0.000)	(0.000)	(0.000)	(0.000)	(0.000)
Δ natural resources rents	0.000	0.000*	0.000	0.000	0.000	0.000	0.000	0.000
	(0.000)	(0.000)	(0.000)	(0.000)	(0.000)	(0.000)	(0.000)	(0.000)
Natural resources rents (t-1)	0.000	0.000	0.000	0.000	0.000	0.000	0.000	0.000
	(0.000)	(0.000)	(0.000)	(0.000)	(0.000)	(0.000)	(0.000)	(0.000)
Δ net ODA (%GNI)	0.000	0.000	0.000	0.000	0.000	0.000	0.000	0.000
	(0.000)	(0.000)	(0.000)	(0.000)	(0.000)	(0.000)	(0.000)	(0.000)

Table A11 (*cont.*)

	Δ Political corruption	Δ Political corruption	Δ Political corruption	Δ Political corruption	Δ Political corruption	Δ Political corruption	Δ Political corruption	Δ Political corruption	Δ Political corruption
Net ODA (%GNI) (t-1)	0.000***	0.000***	0.000***	0.000***	0.000***	0.000***	0.000***	0.000***	0.000***
	(0.000)	(0.000)	(0.000)	(0.000)	(0.000)	(0.000)	(0.000)	(0.000)	(0.000)
Δ conflict involvement	−0.000	−0.000	−0.001	−0.001	−0.001	−0.001	−0.001	−0.001	−0.001
	(0.001)	(0.001)	(0.001)	(0.001)	(0.001)	(0.001)	(0.001)	(0.001)	(0.001)
Conflict involvement (t-1)	0.001*	0.001*	0.001	0.001	0.001*	0.001*	0.001	0.001	0.001
	(0.001)	(0.001)	(0.001)	(0.001)	(0.001)	(0.001)	(0.001)	(0.001)	(0.001)
Post 1990 (t-1)	−0.000	−0.001	0.004**	0.005***	0.001	0.002	0.004**	0.004**	
	(0.001)	(0.001)	(0.002)	(0.002)	(0.002)	(0.002)	(0.002)	(0.002)	
Ethnolinguistic fractionalization (t-1)	0.004	0.004	0.002	0.004	0.002	0.001	0.004	0.003	
	(0.005)	(0.005)	(0.004)	(0.004)	(0.004)	(0.004)	(0.005)	(0.004)	
British colonial legacy (t-1)	−0.001	−0.001	−0.001	−0.000	−0.001	−0.001	−0.001	−0.001	
	(0.002)	(0.001)	(0.002)	(0.002)	(0.002)	(0.002)	(0.002)	(0.002)	
Federal state (t-1)	−0.002	−0.002	−0.001	−0.002	−0.001	−0.002	−0.001	−0.001	
	(0.002)	(0.002)	(0.002)	(0.002)	(0.002)	(0.002)	(0.002)	(0.002)	
Constant	0.012	0.016*	0.006	0.002	0.006	−0.003	0.007	0.006	
	(0.008)	(0.008)	(0.009)	(0.009)	(0.009)	(0.010)	(0.009)	(0.009)	
N	1,503	1,503	1,522	1,522	1,522	1,498	1,522	1,522	
Countries	42	42	42	42	42	41	42	42	
R^2	0.033	0.036	0.044	0.042	0.035	0.040	0.045	0.044	

Notes: Panel-corrected standard errors (PCSE) in parentheses. * $p < 0.1$; ** $p < 0.05$; *** $p < 0.01$

Table A12 *Regression results for executive corruption*

	Δ Executive corruption	Δ Executive corruption	Δ Executive corruption	Δ Executive corruption	Δ Executive corruption	Δ Executive corruption	Δ Executive corruption	Δ Executive corruption
Executive corruption (t-1)	−0.015*** (0.006)	−0.016*** (0.006)	−0.017*** (0.007)	−0.020*** (0.007)	−0.018*** (0.007)	−0.018*** (0.007)	−0.021*** (0.007)	−0.017*** (0.007)
Leader duration (t-1)	0.000 (0.000)	−0.001** (0.000)						
Leader duration (t-1) * Leader duration (t-1)		0.000** (0.000)						
Δ elected leader			−0.012** (0.005)					
Elected leader (t-1)			−0.004 (0.003)					
Δ democratically elected leader			−0.006 (0.010)					
Democratically elected leader (t-1)			−0.002 (0.004)					
Δ cumulative no. of elections				−0.006*** (0.002)				
Cumulative no. of elections (t-1)				−0.001** (0.001)				
Δ cumulative no. of democratic elections					−0.011*** (0.003)			
Cumulative no. of democratic elections (t-1)					0.000 (0.001)			

Table A12 (*cont.*)

	Δ Executive corruption	Δ Executive corruption	Δ Executive corruption	Δ Executive corruption	Δ Executive corruption	Δ Executive corruption	Δ Executive corruption
Δ executive control			0.000 (0.000)				
Executive control (t-1)			0.000 (0.000)				
Δ incumbent reelected					−0.005 (0.006)		
Incumbent reelected (t-1)					−0.001 (0.003)		
Δ electoral succession					−0.015** (0.007)		
Electoral succession (t-1)					−0.009** (0.004)		
Δ electoral alternation					−0.015* (0.008)		
Electoral alternation (t-1)					−0.002 (0.004)		
Δ multiparty regime – no alternation							−0.016*** (0.006)
Multiparty regime – no alternation (t-1)							−0.003 (0.003)
Δ multiparty regime – one alternation							−0.030*** (0.008)

Multiparty regime – one alternation (t-1)							−0.002 (0.004)
Δ multiparty regime – more alternation							0.004 (0.016)
Multiparty regime – more alternation (t-1)							−0.002 (0.006)
Δ (log)GDP per capita	−0.013 (0.016)	−0.013 (0.016)	−0.006 (0.016)	−0.004 (0.016)	−0.008 (0.016)	−0.007 (0.016)	−0.004 (0.016)	−0.006 (0.016)
(log)GDP per capita (t-1)	0.001 (0.001)	0.001 (0.001)	0.002 (0.001)	0.003** (0.001)	0.002 (0.001)	0.002 (0.001)	0.002* (0.001)	0.002 (0.001)
Δ government expenditure (%GDP)	0.001** (0.000)	0.001** (0.000)	0.001** (0.000)	0.001** (0.000)	0.001** (0.000)	0.001** (0.000)	0.001** (0.000)	0.001** (0.000)
Government expenditure (%GDP) (t-1)	0.000 (0.000)	0.000* (0.000)	0.000 (0.000)	0.000 (0.000)	0.000 (0.000)	0.000 (0.000)	0.000 (0.000)	0.000 (0.000)
Δ imports (%GDP)	−0.000 (0.000)	−0.000 (0.000)	−0.000 (0.000)	−0.000 (0.000)	−0.000 (0.000)	−0.000 (0.000)	−0.000 (0.000)	−0.000 (0.000)
Imports (%GDP) (t-1)	−0.000*** (0.000)	−0.000*** (0.000)	−0.000*** (0.000)	−0.000*** (0.000)	−0.000*** (0.000)	−0.000*** (0.000)	−0.000*** (0.000)	−0.000*** (0.000)
Δ natural resources rents	0.000* (0.000)	0.000* (0.000)	0.000 (0.000)	0.000 (0.000)	0.000 (0.000)	0.000 (0.000)	0.000 (0.000)	0.000 (0.000)
Natural resources rents (t-1)	0.000 (0.000)	0.000 (0.000)	0.000 (0.000)	0.000 (0.000)	0.000 (0.000)	0.000 (0.000)	0.000 (0.000)	0.000 (0.000)
Δ net ODA (%GNI)	−0.000 (0.000)	−0.000 (0.000)	0.000 (0.000)	0.000 (0.000)	0.000 (0.000)	0.000 (0.000)	0.000 (0.000)	0.000 (0.000)
Net ODA (%GNI) (t-1)	0.000** (0.000)	0.000** (0.000)	0.000*** (0.000)	0.000*** (0.000)	0.000*** (0.000)	0.000*** (0.000)	0.000* (0.000)	0.000*** (0.000)

Table A12 (*cont.*)

	Δ Executive corruption	Δ Executive corruption	Δ Executive corruption	Δ Executive corruption	Δ Executive corruption	Δ Executive corruption	Δ Executive corruption	Δ Executive corruption
Δ conflict involvement	−0.001	−0.001	−0.002	−0.002	−0.002	−0.002	−0.002	−0.002
	(0.002)	(0.002)	(0.002)	(0.002)	(0.002)	(0.002)	(0.002)	(0.002)
Conflict involvement (t-1)	0.001	0.001	0.000	0.000	0.000	0.000	0.000	0.000
	(0.001)	(0.001)	(0.001)	(0.001)	(0.001)	(0.001)	(0.001)	(0.001)
Post 1990 (t-1)	−0.003	−0.004*	0.001	0.002	−0.001	−0.001	0.001	−0.000
	(0.002)	(0.002)	(0.003)	(0.003)	(0.002)	(0.002)	(0.003)	(0.003)
Ethnolinguistic fractionalization (t-1)	0.002	0.002	0.002	0.003	0.002	0.001	0.003	0.002
	(0.006)	(0.006)	(0.006)	(0.006)	(0.006)	(0.006)	(0.006)	(0.006)
British colonial legacy (t-1)	0.003	0.003	0.001	0.002	0.001	0.002	0.002	0.001
	(0.002)	(0.002)	(0.002)	(0.002)	(0.002)	(0.002)	(0.002)	(0.002)
Federal state (t-1)	−0.002	−0.002	−0.001	−0.001	−0.001	−0.001	−0.001	−0.001
	(0.003)	(0.003)	(0.004)	(0.004)	(0.004)	(0.004)	(0.004)	(0.004)
Constant	0.002	0.007	−0.000	−0.004	−0.000	−0.006	−0.001	−0.001
	(0.009)	(0.009)	(0.010)	(0.009)	(0.009)	(0.011)	(0.009)	(0.009)
N	1,503	1,503	1,522	1,522	1,522	1,498	1,522	1,522
Countries	42	42	42	42	42	41	42	42
R²	0.028	0.030	0.032	0.038	0.038	0.030	0.035	0.045

Notes: Panel-corrected standard errors (PCSE) in parentheses. * $p < 0.1$; ** $p < 0.05$; *** $p < 0.01$

Table A13 *Types of leaders across African countries*

Country	Autocrats	Hegemons	Democrats	Transients
Angola	1	2	0	0
Benin	6	0	4	9
Botswana	0	0	5	0
Burkina Faso	5	1	1	2
Burundi	7	1	0	4
Cameroon	1	1	0	0
Cape Verde	1	0	3	1
Central African Republic	5	2	1	2
Chad	4	1	0	3
Comoros	3	3	3	10
Congo, Dem. Rep.	2	2	0	0
Congo, Rep.	5	2	0	4
Côte d'Ivoire	1	3	0	1
Djibouti	1	1	0	0
Equatorial Guinea	1	1	0	0
Eritrea	1	0	0	0
eSwatini	2	0	0	0
Ethiopia	3	3	0	2
Gabon	1	2	0	2
Gambia, The	0	2	1	0
Ghana	3	2	5	3
Guinea	2	2	0	3
Guinea-Bissau	5	1	3	7
Kenya	2	0	2	0
Lesotho	3	0	6	1
Liberia	3	2	2	1
Madagascar	4	0	4	3
Malawi	1	1	3	0
Mali	4	1	2	1
Mauritania	3	3	0	4
Mauritius	0	0	8	0
Mozambique	1	3	0	0
Namibia	0	0	3	0
Niger	4	2	2	1
Nigeria	5	3	3	4
Rwanda	2	1	0	1
São Tomé and Príncipe	1	0	4	1

Table A13 (*cont.*)

Country	Autocrats	Hegemons	Democrats	Transients
Senegal	1	1	2	0
Seychelles	1	0	2	1
Sierra Leone	4	2	4	4
Somalia	6	0	2	4
South Africa	0	4	4	1
South Sudan	1	0	0	0
Sudan	4	1	2	2
Tanzania	2	3	0	0
Togo	3	1	0	4
Uganda	3	1	0	5
Zambia	1	2	3	1
Zimbabwe	0	2	0	0
Total	*119*	*65*	*84*	*92*

Source: ALC dataset

References

Aborisade, Richard A. and Aliyyu, Nurudeen B. (2018) Corruption and Africa. In Akanle, Olayinka and Adésìnà, Jìmí Olálékan (eds.), *The Development of Africa: Issues, Diagnoses and Prognoses*. London: Springer, pp. 227–254.

Acemoglu, Daron and Robinson, James (2012) *Why Nations Fail: The Origins of Power, Prosperity, and Poverty*. New York: Crown Business.

Acemoglu, Daron, Johnson, Simon, and Robinson, James (2001) The colonial origins of comparative development: An empirical investigation. *The American Economic Review*, 91(5), pp. 1369–1401.

Agbese, Pita Ogaba (2004) Soldiers as rulers: Military performance. In Kieh, G. K. and Agbese, P. O. (eds.), *The Military and Politics in Africa: From Engagement to Democratic and Constitutional Control*. Aldershot: Ashgate, pp. 57–90.

Ahlquist, John and Levi, Margaret (2011) Leadership: What it means, what it does, and what we want to know about it. *Annual Review of Political Science*, 14, pp. 1–24.

Alesina, Alberto, Özler, Sule, Roubini, Nouriel, and Swagel, Phillip (1996) Political instability and economic growth. *Journal of Economic Growth*, 1(2), pp. 189–211.

Alesina, Alberto, Devleeschauwer, Arnaud, Easterly, William, Kurlat, Sergio, and Wacziarg, Romain (2003) Fractionalization. *Journal of Economic Growth*, 8, pp. 155–194.

Alt, James and Lassen, David (2014) Enforcement and public corruption: Evidence from the American States. *The Journal of Law, Economics, and Organization*, 30(2), pp. 306–338.

Anderson, Cristopher J. and Yulia, V. Tverdova (2003) Corruption, political allegiances and attitudes toward government in contemporary democracies. *American Journal of Political Science*, 47(1), pp. 91–109.

Andersson, Staffan and Heywood, Paul M. (2009) The politics of perception: Use and abuse of Transparency International's approach to measuring corruption. *Political Studies*, 57(4), pp. 746–767.

Arriola, Leonardo (2009) Patronage and political stability in Africa. *Comparative Political Studies*, 42(10), pp. 1339–1362.

Ayoob, Mohammed (2001) State making, state breaking, and state failure. In Crocker, Chester A., Hampson, Fen Osler, and Aall, Pamela (eds.), *Turbulent Peace: The Challenges of Managing International Conflict*. Washington, DC: United States Institute of Peace Press, ch. 9.

Bach, Daniel (2011) Patrimonialism and neopatrimonialism: Comparative trajectories and readings. *Commonwealth & Comparative Politics*, 49(3), pp. 275–294.

Bäck, Hanna and Hadenius, Axel (2008) Democracy and state capacity: Exploring a J-shaped relationship. *Governance*, 21, pp. 1–24.

Baker, Bruce (1998) The class of 1990: How have the autocratic leaders of sub-Saharan Africa fared under democratization. *Third World Quarterly*, 19(1), pp. 115–127.

Barro, Robert (2003) Determinants of economic growth in a panel of countries. *Annals of Economics and Finance*, 4, pp. 231–274.

Bates, Robert (2008a) *When Things Fell Apart: State Failure in Late-Century Africa*. Cambridge: Cambridge University Press.

(2008b) State failure. *Annual Review of Political Science*, 11, pp. 1–12.

Bates, Robert and Block, Steven (2013) Revisiting African agriculture: Institutional change and productivity growth. *Journal of Politics*, 75(2), pp. 372–384.

Bates, Robert, Block, Steven, Fayad, Ghada, and Hoeffler, Anke (2012) The new institutionalism and Africa. *Journal of African Economies*, 22(4), pp. 499–522.

Bayart, Jean-François (1993) *The State in Africa: The Politics of the Belly*. London: Longman.

Beck, Nathaniel and Katz, Jonathan (1995) What to do (and not to do) with time-series-cross-section data in comparative politics. *American Political Science Review*, 89(3), pp. 634–647.

Beck, Thorsten, Clarke, George, Groff, Alberto, Keefer, Philip, and Walsh, Patrick (2001) New tools and new tests in comparative political economy: The Database of Political Institutions. *World Bank Economic Review*, 15(1), pp. 165–176.

Beerbohm, Eric (2015) Is democratic leadership possible? *American Political Science Review*, 109(4), pp. 639–652.

Bell, David (2014) Political leadership. *Government and Opposition*, 49(1), pp. 139–158.

Bermeo, Nancy (2016) On democratic backsliding. *Journal of Democracy*, 27(1), pp. 5–19.

Berry, Christopher and Fowler, Anthony (2018) *Leadership or Luck? Randomization Inference for Leader Effects*. mimeo, April 2018.

Besley, Timothy and Case, Anne (1995) Does electoral accountability affect economic policy choices? Evidence from gubernatorial term limits. *Quarterly Journal of Economics*, 110(3), pp. 769–798.

Bienen, Henry and van de Walle, Nicolas (1989) Time and power in Africa. *American Political Science Review*, 83(1), pp. 19–34.

Blake, Charles H. and Martin, Christopher (2006) The dynamics of political corruption: Re-examining the influence of democracy. *Democratization* 13, pp. 1–14.

Blondel, Jean (1987) *Political Leadership: Towards a General Analysis*. London: Sage.

(2014) What have we learned? In Rhodes, R. A. W. and 't Hart, Paul (eds.), *The Oxford Handbook of Political Leadership*. Oxford: Oxford University Press, pp. 705–716.

Blondel, Jean and Thiebault, Jean-Luis (eds.) (2010) *Political Leadership, Parties and Citizens: The Personalisation of Leadership*. London: Routledge.

Blundo, Giorgio and de Sardan, Jean-Pierre Olivier (2006) *Everyday Corruption and the State: Citizens and Public Officials in Africa*. London: Zed Publishing.

Bollen, Kenneth and Jackman, Robert (1985) Political democracy and the size distribution of income. *American Sociological Review* 50(4), pp. 438–457.

Booth, David (2011) *Governance for Development in Africa: Building on What Works*. Africa Power & Politics Programme, Policy Brief n. 1. London: Overseas Development Institute.

Brady, David and Spence, Michael (eds.) (2010a) *Leadership and Growth*. World Bank Publications, Washington, DC.

Brady, David and Spence, Michael (2010b) Leadership and politics: A perspective from the commission on growth and development, in Brady, David and Spence, Michael (eds.), *Leadership and Growth*. World Bank Publications, Washington, DC.

Bratton, Michael and van de Walle, Nicolas (1994) Neopatrimonial regimes and political transitions in Africa. *World Politics*, 46(4), pp. 453–489.

(1997) *Democratic Experiments in Africa. Regime Transitions in Comparative Perspective*. Cambridge, Cambridge University Press.

Bratton, Michael, (2004) The alternation effect in Africa. *Journal of Democracy*, 15(4), pp. 147–158.

(2008) Do free elections foster capable government? The democracy-governance connection in Africa. *Afrobarometer, Working Paper N.* 104, 331–354.

Brown, David (1999) Reading, writing and regime types: Democracy's impact on primary school enrolment. *Political Research Quarterly* 52 (4), 681–707.

Brown, David and Mobarak, Ahmed Mushfiq (2009) The transforming power of democracy: regime type and the distribution of electricity. *American Political Science Review*, 103(2), pp. 193–213.

Brown, David and Hunter, Wendy (2004) Democracy and human capital formation: Education spending in Latin America, 1980 to 1997. *Comparative Political Studies*, 37(7), pp. 842–864.

Brownlee, Jason (2007) Hereditary succession in modern autocracies. *World Politics*, 59, pp. 595–628.

Bueno de Mesquita, Bruce, Morrow, James D., Siverson, Randolph M., and Smith, Alastair (2002) Political institutions, policy choice and the survival of leaders. *British Journal of Political Science*, 32, pp. 559–590.

Bueno de Mesquita, Bruce, Smith, Alastair, Siverson, Randolph M., and Morrow, James D. (2003) *The Logic of Political Survival*. Cambridge, MA: Institute of Technology.

Bunce, Valerie (1980) Changing leaders and changing policies. The impact of elite succession on budgetary priorities in democratic countries. *American Journal of Political Science*, 24(3), pp. 373–395.

(1981) *Do New Leaders Make a Difference? Executive Succession and Public Policy Under Capitalism and Socialism*. Princeton, NJ: Princeton University Press.

Burns, James MacGregor (1978) *Leadership*. New York: Harper & Row.

Carbone, Giovanni (2008) *No-Party Democracy? Ugandan Politics in Comparative Perspective*. Boulder, CO: Lynne Rienner.

(2009) The consequences of democratization. *Journal of Democracy*, 20(2), pp. 123–137.

(2011) Democratic demands and social policies: The politics of health reform in Ghana. *Journal of Modern African Studies*, 49(3), pp. 381–408.

Carbone, Giovanni and Cassani, Andrea (2016) Nigeria and democratic progress by elections in Africa. *Africa Spectrum*, 51(3), pp. 33–59.

Carbone, Giovanni, Memoli, Vincenzo, and Quartapelle, Lia (2016) Are lions democrats? The impact of democratization on economic growth in Africa, 1980–2010. *Democratization*, 23(1), pp. 27–48.

Carlyle, Thomas (1841) *On Heroes, Hero Worship, and the Heroic in History*. London: James Fraser.

Carothers, Thomas (2007) How democracies emerge: The 'sequencing' fallacy. *Journal of Democracy*, 18, 12–27.

Carter, Danielle (2011) Sources of state legitimacy in contemporary South Africa: A theory of political goods. *Afrobarometer Working Papers*, 134.

Cassani, Andrea (2014) Hybrid what? Partial consensus and persistent divergences in the analysis of hybrid regimes. *International Political Science Review*, 35(5), pp. 542–558.

Cederman, Lars-Erik, Wimmer, Andreas, and Min, Brian (2010) Why do ethnic groups rebel? New data and analysis. *World Politics*, 62(1), pp. 87–119.
Central Intelligence Agency (1986, 23 September) *The significance of foreign involvement in Third World coups*. Memorandum of the Foreign Subversion and Instability Center. Washington, DC: Central Intelligence Agency.
Charron, Nicholas and Victor Lapuente (2010) Does democracy produce quality of government? *European Journal of Political Research*, 49, pp. 443–470.
Chazan, Naomi, Lewis, Peter, Mortimer, Robert, Rothchild, Donald, and Stedman, Steven (1999) *Politics and Society in Contemporary Africa*. Boulder, CO: Lynne Rienner.
Cheeseman, Nic (2010) African elections as a vehicle for change. *Journal of Democracy*, 21(4), pp. 139–153.
  (2015) *Democracy in Africa. Successes, Failures, and the Struggle for Political Reform*. Cambridge: Cambridge University Press.
  (2016, 3 November) *Democracy in Africa: Elections, term limits and political change*. Seminar, NASP PhD Program in Political Studies, Università degli Studi di Milano.
Cheeseman, Nic and Klaas, Brian (2018) *How to Rig an Election*. New Haven and London: Yale University Press.
Cheeseman, Nic, Reyntjens, Filip, and Collord, Michaela (2018) War and democracy. The legacy of conflict in East Africa. *Journal of Modern African Studies*, 56(1), pp. 31–61.
Cheibub, José Antonio (1998) Political regimes and the extractive capacity of governments. Taxation in democracies and dictatorships. *World Politics*, 50, 349–376.
Cheibub, Jose Antonio, Gandhi, Jennifer, and Vreeland, James Raymond. (2010) Democracy and dictatorship revisited. *Public Choice*, 143(1–2), pp. 67–101.
Chong, Alberto (2004) Inequality, democracy, and persistence: Is there a political Kuznets curve? *Economics and Politics*, 16, (2), 189–212.
Clapham, Christopher (1969) Imperial leadership in Ethiopia. *African Affairs*, 68(271), pp. 110–120.
  (1998) Degrees of statehood. *Review of International Studies*, 24, 143–157.
Cohen, Herman (2015) *The Mind of the African Strongman. Conversations with Dictators, Statesmen, and Father Figures*, Washington, DC: New Academia Publishing.
Collier, David and Levitsky, Steven (1997) Democracy with adjectives: Conceptual innovation in comparative research. *World Politics*, 49(3), pp. 430–451.

Collier, Paul (2008, 22 June) Let us now praise coups. *Washington Post.*
Collier, Paul and Gunning, Jan (1999) Why has Africa grown slowly? *Journal of Economic Perspectives*, 13(3), pp. 3–22.
Collier, Paul and Hoeffler, Anke (2005) *Coup Traps: Why Does Africa Have so Many Coups d'état?* Centre for the Study of African Economies, University of Oxford.
Collier, Paul, Hoeffler, Anke, and Söderbom, Måns (2008) On the duration of Civil War. *Journal of Peace Research*, 45, 461–478.
Connell, Dan and Smyth, Frank (1998) Africa's new bloc. *Foreign Affairs*, 77(2), pp. 95–106.
Corrales, Javier and Penfold, Michael (2014) Manipulating term limits in Latin America. *Journal of Democracy*, 25(4), pp. 157–168.
de Boef, Suzanna and Keele, Luke (2008) Taking time seriously. *American Journal of Political Science*, 53(1), 184–200.
de Waal, Alex (2018) *Mass Starvation. The History and Future of Famine.* New York: Wiley.
Decalo, Samuel (1973) Military coups and military regimes in Africa. *Journal of Modern African Studies*, 11(1), pp. 105–127.
  (1976) *Coups and Army Rule in Africa: Studies in Military Style.* New Haven, CT: Yale University Press.
  (1990) *Coups and Army Rule in Africa: Motivations and Constraints*, 2nd ed. New Haven, CT: Yale University Press.
Derpanopoulos, George, Frantz, Erica, Geddes, Barbara, and Wright (2016) Are coups good for democracy? *Research and Politics*, 3(1), pp. 1–7.
Diamond, Larry (2002) Thinking about hybrid regimes. *Journal of Democracy*, 13(2), pp. 21–35.
Dulani, Boniface (2015, 25 May) *African publics strongly support term limits, resist leaders' efforts to extend their tenure.* Afrobarometer, No. 30.
Easterly, William and Levine, Ross (1997) Africa's growth tragedy: Policies and ethnic divisions. *Quarterly Journal of Economics*, 12(4), pp. 1203–1250.
Easterly, William and Pennings, Steven (2018) *Shrinking Dictators: Assessing the Growth Contribution of Individual National Leaders*, mimeo.
Elbadawi, Ibrahim and Sambanis, Nicholas (2002) How much war will we see? Explaining the prevalence of Civil War. *Journal of Conflict Resolution*, 46, 307–334.
Elgie, Robert (2015) *Studying Political Leadership. Foundations and Contending Accounts.* Basingstoke: Palgrave Macmillan.
Ellingsen, Tanja (2000) Colorful community or ethnic witches' brew? Multi-ethnicity and domestic conflict during and after the Cold War. *Journal of Conflict Resolution*, 44, pp. 228–249.

Englebert, Pierre (2000) *State Legitimacy and Development in Africa*. Boulder, CO: Lynne Rienner.
Fearon, James and Laitin, David (2003) Ethnicity, insurgency and civil war. *American Political Science Review*, 97, pp. 75–90.
Feng, Yi (1997) Democracy, political stability and economic growth. *British Journal of Political Science*, 27(3), pp. 391–418.
Ferraz, Claudio and Finan, Frederico (2011) Electoral accountability and corruption: Evidence from the audits of local governments. *American Economic Review*, 101(4), pp. 1274–1311.
Foa, Roberto Stefan and Mounk, Yascha (2017) Democratization. The signs of deconsolidation. *Journal of Democracy*, 28(1), pp. 5–15.
Foreign Affairs (2018) Is democracy dying? A global report.
Freedom House (2017) *Freedom in the World 2017. Populists and Autocrats: The Dual Threat to Global Democracy*, Washington, DC: Freedom House.
 (2018) *Freedom in the World 2018. Democracy in Crisis*, Washington, DC: Freedom House.
Galston, William (2018) The populist challenge to liberal democracy. *Journal of Democracy*, 29(2), pp. 5–19.
Gastil, Robert D. (1985) *Freedom in the World: Political Rights and Civil Liberties*. Westport, CT: Greenwood Press.
Gerring, John, Knutsen, Carl Henrik, Skaaning, Svend-Erik, Teorell, Jan, Coppedge, Michael, Lindberg, Staffan I., and Maguire Matthew (2016) *Electoral democracy and human development*. V-Dem Institute Working Paper.
Gerring, John (2005) Causation. A unified framework for the social sciences. *Journal of Theoretical Politics*, 17(2), pp. 163–198.
Gerschewski, Johannes (2013) The three pillars of stability: Legitimation, repression, and co-optation in autocratic regimes. *Democratization*, 20(1), pp. 13–38.
Gilley, Bruce (2006) The meaning and measure of state legitimacy: Results for 72 countries. *European Journal of Political Research*, 45, pp. 499–525.
Gleditsch, Nils Petter, Wallensteen, Peter, Eriksson, Mikael, Sollenberg, Margareta, and Strand, Håvard (2002) Armed conflict 1946-2001: A new dataset. *Journal of Peace Research*, 39(5), pp. 615–637.
Goemans, Henk, Gleditsch, Kristen, and Chiozza, Giacomo (2009) Introducing Archigos: A dataset of political leaders. *Journal of Peace Research*, 46(2), pp. 269–283.
Goldsmith, Arthur A. (2001) Risk, rule and reason. Leadership in Africa. *Public Administration and Development*, 21, pp. 77–87.
 (2004) Predatory versus developmental rule in Africa. *Democratization*, 11(3), pp. 98–110.

Govea, Rodger and Holm, John (1998) Crisis, violence and political succession in Africa. *Third World Quarterly*, 19(1), pp. 129–148.
Gray, Clive and McPherson, Malcolm (2001) The leadership factor in African policy reform and growth. *Economic Development and Cultural Change*, 49(4), pp. 707–740.
Greenstein, Fred (1969) *Personality and Politics*. Chicago, IL: Markham Publishing Company.
   (2004) *The Presidential Difference: Leadership Style from FDR to G.W. Bush*. Princeton, NJ: Princeton University Press.
Hanson, Jonathan and Sigman, Rachel (2013) Leviathan's latent dimensions: Measuring state capacity for comparative political research. Unpublished manuscript. Available at SSRN: https://ssrn.com/abstract=1899933.
Harding, Robin and Stasavage, David (2014) What democracy does (and doesn't do) for basic services: School fees, school inputs, and African elections. *The Journal of Politics*, 76(1), pp. 229–245.
Harkness, Kristen (2017) Military loyalty and the failure of democratization in Africa: How ethnic armies shape the capacity of presidents to defy term limits. *Democratization*, 24(5), pp. 801–818.
Harms, Philipp and Zink, Stefan (2003) Limits to redistribution in a democracy: A survey. *European Journal of Political Economy*, 19, (4), pp. 651–668.
Hegre, Håvard, Ellingsen, Tanja, Gates, Scott, and Gleditsch, Nils P. (2001) Toward a democratic civil peace? Democracy, political change, and civil war, 1816–1992. *American Political Science Review*, 95, pp. 33–48.
Herbst, Jeffrey (1990) The structural adjustment of politics in Africa. *World Development*, 18(7), pp. 949–958.
   (2000) *States and Power in Africa. Comparative Lessons in Authority and Control*. Princeton, NJ: Princeton University Press.
Hickey, Sam, Lavers, Tom, Niño-Zarazúa, Miguel, and Seekings, Jeremy (2018)*The negotiated politics of social protection in sub-Saharan Africa*, WIDER Working Paper 34.
Horowitz, Shale, Hoff, Karla, and Milanovic, Branko (2009) Government turnover: Concepts, measures and applications. *European Journal of Political Research*, 48(1), pp. 107–129.
Hughes, Arnold and May, Roy (1988) The politics of succession in Black Africa. *Third World Quarterly*, 10(1), pp. 1–22.
Huntington, Samuel P (1968) *Political Order in Changing Societies*. New Haven, CT: Yale University Press.
Huntington, Samuel (1991) *The Third Wave: Democratization in the Late Twentieth Century*. Norman, OK: University of Oklahoma Press.

Hyde, Susan D. and Marinov, Nikolay (2012) Which elections can be lost? *Political Analysis*, 20(2), pp. 191–201.

Hyden, Goran (2012) *African Politics in Comparative Perspective*, 2nd ed. Cambridge: Cambridge University Press.

Jackman, Robert (1978) The predictability of coups d'état: A model with African data. *American Political Science Review*, 72, pp. 1262–1275.

Jackson, Robert H. (1990) *Quasi-States: Sovereignty, International Relations and the Third World*. Cambridge: Cambridge Studies in International Relations.

Jackson, Robert H. and Rosberg, Carl G. (1984) Personal rule: Theory and practice in Africa. *Comparative Politics*, 16(4), pp. 421–442.

(1982) *Personal Rule in Black Africa. Prince, Autocrat, Prophet, Tyrant*. Berkeley/Los Angeles/London: University of California Press.

Jackson, Robert and Rosberg, Carl (1982b) Why Africa's weak states persist: The empirical and the juridical in statehood. *World Politics*, 35(1), pp. 1–24.

Jenkins, Craig and Kposowa, Augustine (1990) Explaining military coups d'état: Black Africa, 1957-1984. *American Sociological Review*, 55, pp. 861–875.

Johnson, Thomas, Slater, Robert, and McGowan, Pat (1984) Explaining African military coups d'état, 1960–1982. *American Political Science Review*, 78(3), pp. 622–640.

Jones, Benjamin (2009) National leadership and economic growth. In Durlauf, Steven and Blume, Lawrence (eds.), *The New Palgrave Dictionary of Economics*, Online Edition. New York: Palgrave Macmillan.

Jones, Benjamin and Olken, Benjamin (2005) Do leaders matter? National leadership and growth since World War II. *Quarterly Journal of Economics*, 120(3), pp. 835–864.

Kaplan, Robert (1997) Was democracy just a moment? *The Atlantic*, December.

Khapoya, Vincent (1988) Moi and beyond: Towards peaceful succession in Kenya? *Third World Quarterly*, 10(1), pp. 54–66.

Kasfir, Nelson (1976) *The Shrinking Political Arena. Participation and Ethnicity in African Politics, with a Case Study of Uganda*. Berkeley and Los Angeles, CA: University of California Press.

Kaufmann, Daniel, Kraay, Aart, and Mastruzzi, Massimo (2006) Measuring governance using cross-country perceptions data. In Rose-Ackerman, Susan (ed.) *International Handbook on the Economics of Corruption*. Northampton: Edward Elgar Publishing, pp. 52–104.

Keefer, Philip (2007) The poor performance of poor democracies. In Boix, Carles and Stoke, Susan (eds.), *The Oxford Handbook of Comparative Politics*. New York: Oxford University Press, pp. 886–909.

Keefer, Philip and Khemani, Stuti (2005) Democracy, public expenditure, and the poor: Understanding political incentives for providing public services. *The World Bank Research Observer*, 20(1), pp. 1–27.

Kelsall, Tim (2013) *Economic growth and political succession: A study of two regions*. Working Paper n. 1, Developmental Regimes in Africa Project, London.

Kempe, Ronald H. (1999) Corruption and development in Africa. In H. Kempe, Ronald and Bornwell C., Chikulo (eds.), *Corruption and Development in Africa Lessons from Country Case-Studies*. Basingstoke: Macmillan Press, pp. 17–39.

Kendall-Taylor, Andrea and Frantz, Erica (2016) When dictators die. *Journal of Democracy*, 27(4), pp. 159–171.

Khan, Mushtaq H. (2005) Markets, states and democracy: Patron–client networks and the case for democracy in developing countries. *Democratization*, 12(5), pp. 704–724.

Kim, Nam Kyu (2016) Revisiting economic shocks and coups. *Journal of Conflict Resolution*, 60(1), pp. 3–31.

Kjær, Anne and Therkildsen, Ole (2011) *Elections in Africa: Mixed blessings for growth and poverty alleviation*, DIIS Policy Brief.

(2013) Elections and landmark policies in Tanzania and Uganda. *Democratization* 20(4), pp. 592–614.

Korolev, Alexander (2016) Regime responsiveness to basic needs: A dimensional approach. *Studies in Comparative International Development*, 51, pp. 434–455.

Kramon, Eric (2018) *Money for votes. The causes and consequences of electoral clientelism in Africa*. New York: Cambridge University Press.

Lake, David A. and Baum, Matthew A. (2001) The invisible hand of democracy: Political control and the provision of public services. *Comparative Political Studies*, 34(6), pp. 587–621.

Lambsdorff, Johan G. (2006) Measuring corruption: The validity and precision of subjective indicators. In Sampford, Charles, Shacklock, Arthur, Connors, Carmel, and Galtung, Fredrik (eds.), *Measuring Corruption*. Burlington: Ashgate, pp. 81–100.

Lasswell, Harold (1930) *Psychopathology and Politics*. Chicago, IL: Chicago University Press.

(1948) *Power and Personality*. New York: Norton.

Leff, Nathaniel H. (1964) Economic development through bureaucratic corruption. *American Behavioral Scientist*, 8, pp. 291–303.

Levi, Margaret. (2002) The state of the study of the state. In Katznelson, Ira, and Milner, Helen, (eds.), London, New York: Apsa/Norton, pp. 33–55.

Levitsky, Steven and Way, Lucan (2010) *Competitive Authoritarianism: Hybrid Regimes After the Cold War*. Cambridge: Cambridge University Press.

Lindberg, Staffan (2003) It's our time to "chop." Do elections in Africa feed neo-patrimonialism rather than counteract it? *Democratization*, 10, pp. 121–140.

(2006) The surprising significance of African elections. *Journal of Democracy*, 17(1), p. 139.

(2006) *Democracy and Elections in Africa*. Baltimore, MD: The Johns Hopkins University Press.

Lindberg, Staffan (ed.) (2009) *Democratization by Elections: A New Mode of Transition*. Baltimore, MD: The Johns Hopkins University Press.

(2010) What accountability pressures do MPs in Africa face and how do they respond? Evidence from Ghana. *Journal of Modern African Studies*, 48(1), pp. 117–142.

Lindberg, Staffan and Clark, John (2008) Does democratization reduce the risk of military intervention in politics in Africa? *Democratization*, 15(1), pp. 86–105.

Linz, Juan and Alfred, Stepan (1996) *Problems of Democratic Transition and Consolidation*. Baltimore, MD: Johns Hopkins University Press.

Londregan, John and Poole, Keith (1990) Poverty, the coup trap, and the seizure of executive power. *World Politics*, 42(2), pp. 151–183.

Lupia, Arthur (2003) Delegation and its perils. In Strøm, Kaare, Mu̇'ller, Wolfgang C., and Bergman, Torbjorn (eds.), *Delegation and Accountability in Parliamentary Democracies*. Oxford, New York: Oxford University Press, pp. 33–54.

Lührmann, Anna, Mechkova, Valeriya, Dahlum, Sirianne, Maxwell, Laura, Olin, Moa, Sanhueza Petrarca, Constanza, Sigman, Rachel, Wilson, Matthew C., and Lindberg, Staffan I. (2018) State of the world 2017: Autocratization and exclusion? *Democratization*, 25(8), pp. 1321–1340.

Luttwak, Edward (1968) *Coup d'état. A Practical Handbook*. Cambridge: Harvard University Press.

Lyne de Ver, Heather (2008) *Leadership, politics and development: A survey of the literature*. Background Paper n. 3, Development Leadership Programme.

Maltz, Gideon (2007) The case for presidential term limits. *Journal of Democracy*, 18(1).

Marinov, Nikolay and Goemans, Hein (2013) Coups and democracy. *British Journal of Political Science*, 44, pp. 799–825.

Marshall, Monty G. and Marshall, Donna Ramsey (2017a) *Coup d'état events, 1946–2016*. Vienna: Centre for Systemic Peace.

(2017b) *Coup d'état events, 1946–2016. Codebook.* Vienna: Centre for Systemic Peace.
Marshall, Monty G. and Gurr, Ted Robert (2003) *Peace and conflict 2003: A global survey of armed conflicts, self-determination movements and democracy.* Center for International Development and Conflict Management, University of Maryland.
Marshall, Monty, Jaggers, Keith, and Gurr, Ted Robert (2013) *Polity IV project: Political regime characteristics and transitions, 1800–2013: Dataset users' manual.* Vienna: Centre for Systemic Peace.
Mattes, Robert (2008) *The material and political bases of lived poverty in Africa: Insights from the Afrobarometer.* Afrobarometer, WP 98.
Mauro, Paolo (1995) Corruption and growth. *Quarterly Journal of Economics,* 110(3), pp. 681–712.
Mayhew, David (2008) Incumbency advantage in U.S. presidential elections: The historical record. *Political Science Quarterly,* 123(2), pp. 201–228.
Mazrui, Ali (1967) The monarchical tendency in African political culture. *British Journal of Sociology,* 18, pp. 231–250.
  (1970) Leadership in Africa: Obote of Uganda. *International Journal,* 25 (3), pp. 538–564.
  (1977) *Soldiers and kinsmen in Uganda. The making of a military ethnocracy,* Beverly Hills, CA: Sage.
  (1995) Political leadership in Africa: Seven styles and four traditions. In d'Orville, Hans (ed.), *Political leadership for Africa. Essays in Honour of Olusegun Obasanjo.* New York: Africa Leadership Foundation, pp. 161–164.
  (2007) Pan-Africanism, democracy and leadership in Africa: The continuing legacy for the new millennium. Binghamton, NY: Institute of Global Cultural Studies.
Mazzuca, Sebastián and Munck, Gerardo (2014) State or democracy first? Alternative perspectives on the state-democracy nexus. *Democratization,* 21(7), pp. 1221–1243.
Mbaku, John M. (2010) *Corruption in Africa. Cause, Consequences and Cleanups.* Plymouth: Lexington Books.
McGowan, Patrick (2003) African military coups d'état, 1956–2001: Frequency, trends and distribution. *Journal of Modern African Studies,* 41, pp. 339–370.
  (2005) Coups and conflict in West Africa, 1955–2004. Part I: Theoretical perspectives. *Armed Forces and Society,* 32(1), pp. 5–23.
  (2006) Coups and conflict in West Africa, 1955–2004. Part II: Empirical findings. *Armed Forces and Society,* 32(2), pp. 234–253.
McGuire, Martin and Olson, Mancur (1996) The economics of autocracy and majority rule: The invisible hand and the use of force. *Journal of Economic Literature,* 34, pp. 72–96.

McKie, Kristin (2017) The politics of institutional choice across Sub-Saharan Africa: Presidential term limits. *Studies in Comparative International Development*, 52, pp. 436–456.

McMann, Kelly, Pemstein, Daniel, Seim, Brigitte Teorell, Jan, and Lindberg, Staffan (2016) Strategies of validation: Assessing the varieties of democracy corruption data. *V-Dem Working Paper Series*. Available at: www.v-dem.net/en/ (accessed September 24, 2019).

Médard, Jean-François (2005) France and sub-Saharan Africa. A privileged relationship. In Engel, Ulf and Olsen, Gorm Rye (eds.), *Africa and the North. Between Globalization and Marginalization*. London: Routledge, pp. 38–54.

(1991) L'état néopatrimonial en Afrique noire. In Médard, Jean-François (ed.), *États d'Afrique noire: Formation, mécanismes et crises*, Paris: Karthala, pp. 323–353.

(1979) L'état sous-développé au Cameroun. In CEAN (eds.), *Année africaine 1977*. Paris: Pédone, pp. 35–84.

(1979) *L'état au Cameroun*. Paris: Presses de la Fondation nationale des sciences politiques.

Melber, Henning (2015) From Nujoma to Geingob: 25 years of presidential democracy. *Journal of Namibian Studies*, 18, pp. 49–65.

Meltzer, Allan H. and Richard, Scott F. (1981) A rational theory of the size of government. *Journal of Political Economy* 89(5), pp. 914–927.

Miller, Andrew (2011) Debunking the myth of the good coup d'état in Africa. *African Studies Quarterly*, 12(2), pp. 45–70.

Miller, Michael (2015) Electoral authoritarianism and human development. *Comparative Political Studies*, 48(12), pp. 1526–1562.

Mkandawire, Thandika (2001) Thinking about developmental states in Africa. *Cambridge Journal of Economics*, 25, pp. 289–313.

Montinola, Gabriella R. and Jackman, Robert W. (2002) Sources of corruption: A cross-country study. *British Journal of Political Science*, 32(1), pp. 147–170.

Mulligan, Casey, Gil, Ricard, and Sala-i-Martin, Xavier (2004) Do democracies have different public policies than non-democracies. *Journal of Economic Perspectives*, 18, pp. 51–74.

Musella, Fortunato and Webb, Paul (2015) The revolution of personal leaders. *Italian Political Science Review/Rivista Italiana di Scienza Politica*, 45(3), pp. 223–226.

Ndulu, Benno and O'Connell, Stephen (eds.) (2008) *The Political Economy of Economic Growth in Africa, 1960–2000*. Cambridge: Cambridge University Press, pp. 3–75.

Nelson, Joan (2007) Elections, democracy and social services. *Studies in Comparative International Development*, 41, pp. 79–97.

Ngolet, François (2000) Ideological manipulations and political longevity: The power of Omar Bongo in Gabon since 1967. *African Studies Review*, 43(2), pp. 55–71.

Nohlen, Dieter, Krennerich, Michael, and Thibaut, Bernhard (eds.) (1999) *Elections in Africa. A Data Handbook*. Oxford: Oxford University Press.

Norris, Pippa (2012) *Making Democratic Governance Work. How Regimes Shape Prosperity, Welfare and Peace*. Cambridge: Cambridge University Press.

Nye, Joseph S. (2008) *The Powers to Lead*. Oxford: Oxford University Press.

Olivier de Sardan, Jean-Pierre (1999) A moral economy of corruption in Africa? *The Journal of Modern African Studies*, 37(1), pp. 25–52.

Olson, Mancur (1993) Dictatorship, Democracy and Development. *American Political Science Review*, 87(3), pp. 567–576.

Ottaway, Marina (1999) *Africa's New Leaders. Democracy or State Reconstruction?* Washington, DC: Carnegie Endowment for International Peace.

Paige, Glenn (1977) *The Scientific Study of Leadership*. New York: The Free Press.

Pellegata, Alessandro (2011) Cacciare i Mascalzoni. Alternanza e Corruzione Politica. In Pasquino, Gianfranco and Valbruzzi, Marco (eds.), *Il Potere dell'Alternanza. Teorie e Ricerche sui Cambi di Governo*. Bologna: Bononia University Press, pp. 37–61.

(2013) Constraining Political Corruption: An Empirical Analysis of the Impact of Democracy. *Democratization*, 20(7), pp. 1195–1218.

Poggi, Gianfranco (1992) *Lo stato. Natura, sviluppo, prospettive*. Bologna: Il Mulino.

Poguntke, Thomas and Webb, Paul (2015) Presidentialization and the politics of coalition: lessons from Germany and Britain. *Italian Political Science Review/Rivista Italiana di Scienza Politica*, 45(3), pp. 249–275.

(2005) *The Presidentialization of Politics. A Comparative Study of Modern Democracies*. Oxford: Oxford University Press.

Posner, Daniel and Young, Daniel (2007) The institutionalization of political power in Africa. *Journal of Democracy*, 18(3), pp. 126–140.

(2018) Term limits: Leadership, political competition and the transfer of power. In Cheeseman, Nic (ed.), *Institutions and Democracy in Africa. How the Rules of the Game Shape Political Developments*. New York: Cambridge University Press, pp. 260–277.

Powell, Jonathan (2014) An assessment of the 'democratic' coup theory. Democratic trajectories in Africa, 1952–2012. *African Security Review*, 23(3), pp. 1–12.

Powell, Jonathan, Lasley, Trace, and Schiel, Rebecca (2016) Combating coups d'état in Africa, 1950–2014. *Studies in Comparative International Development*, 51, pp. 482–502.

Powell, Jonathan and Thyne, Clayton (2011) Global instances of coups from 1950 to 2010: A new dataset. *Journal of Peace Research*, 48(2), pp. 249–259.

Price, Robert (1974) Politics and culture in contemporary Ghana: The big-man, small-boy syndrome. *Journal of African Studies*, 1(2), pp. 173–204.

Przeworski, Adam, Michael Alvarez, José Antonio Cheibub, and Fernando Limongi (2000) *Democracy and Development: Political Institutions and Well-Being in the World, 1950–1990*. Cambridge: Cambridge University Press.

Radelet, Steven (2010) Successful stories from emerging Africa. *Journal of Democracy*, 21(4), pp. 87–101.

Reyntjens, Filip (2016) The struggle over term limits in Africa. A new look at the evidence. *Journal of Democracy*, 27(3), pp. 61–68.

Rhodes, R.A.W. and 't Hart, Paul (2014) Puzzles of political leadership. In Rhodes, R.A.W. and 't Hart, Paul (eds.), *The Oxford Handbook of Political Leadership*. Oxford: Oxford University Press, pp. 1–21.

Ridde, Valery and Morestin, Florence (2011) A scoping review of the literature on the abolition of user fees in health care services in Africa. *Health Policy and Planning*, 26, pp. 1–11.

Rodrik, Dani (2016) An African growth miracle? *Journal of African Economies*, 27(1), pp. 1–18.

Roessler, Philip (2011) The enemy within. Personal rule, coups and civil war in Africa. *World Politics*, 63(2), pp. 300–346.

Flora, Peter, Stein, Kuhnle, and Derek, Urwin (eds.) (1999) *State Formation, Nation-Building and Mass Politics in Europe. The Theory of Stein Rokkan*. Oxford, Oxford University Press.

Rose-Ackerman, Susan (1999) *Corruption and Government: Causes, Consequences and Reforms*. Cambridge, UK: Cambridge University Press.

(2001) Political corruption and democratic structures. In Jain, Arvind (ed.), *The Political Economy of Corruption*, pp. 35–62.

Ross, Michael (2006) Is democracy good for the poor? *American Journal of Political Science*, 50, pp. 860–874.

Rotberg, Robert (2004) Strengthening African leadership. *Foreign Affairs*, 83(4), pp. 14–18.

(2013) *Africa Emerges*. London: Polity.

Rothstein, Bo (2009) Creating political legitimacy: Electoral democracy versus quality of government. *American Behavioral Scientist*, 53, pp. 311–330.

Rothstein, Bo and Teorell, Jan (2008) What is quality of government? A theory of impartial government institution. *Governance*, 21(2), pp. 165–190.

Saad, Lydia (2013, 18 January) Americans call for term limits, end to electoral college. *Gallup* (www.gallup.com).

Sachs, Jeffrey D. and Warner, Andrew M. (1997) Sources of slow growth in African economies. *Journal of African Economies*, 6(3), pp. 335–376.

Sandbrook, Richard and Oelbaum, Jay (1999) *Reforming the political kingdom: Governance and development in Ghana's Fourth Republic.* Accra: Centre for Democracy and Development.

Sandholtz, Wayne and Koetzle, William (2000) Accounting for corruption: Economic structure, democracy, and trade. *International Studies Quarterly* 44(1), pp. 31–50.

Schacther, Ruth (1961) Single-party systems in West Africa. *American Political Science Review*, 55(2), pp. 264–307.

Schedler, Andreas (ed.) (2006) *Electoral authoritarianism. The dynamics of unfree competition.* Boulder, CO: Lynne Rienner.

Schmitter, Philippe (2005) Democratization and state capacity. Paper presented at the X Congreso Internacional del CLAD sobre la Reforma del Estado y de la Administración Pública, Santiago, Chile, October 18–21.

Scott, James C. (1972) *Comparative Political Corruption.* Englewood Cliffs: Prentice-Hall.

Seekings, Jeremy (2014) *Are African welfare states different? Welfare state-building in Anglophone African in comparative.* Perspective, Paper presented at the workshop on social policy and regimes of social welfare in Africa. Switzerland: University of Fribourg.

Seligson, Mitchell A. (2002) The impact of corruption on regime legitimacy: A comparative study of four Latin American countries. *Journal of Politics* 64(2), pp. 408–433.

Sen, Amartya (1994, January 10) An argument on the primacy of political rights. Freedoms and needs. *New Republic*, pp. 31–38.

Siegle, Joseph T., Weinstein, Michael M., and Halperin, Morton H. (2004) Why democracies excel. *Foreign Affairs*, 83(5), pp. 57–71.

Sil, Rudra and Chen, Cheng (2004) State legitimacy and the (in)significance of democracy in post-Communist Russia. *Europe-Asia Studies*, 56, pp. 347–368.

Sklar, Richard, Onwudire, Ebere, and Kew, Darren (2006) Nigeria: Completing Obasanjo's legacy. *Journal of Democracy*, 17(3), pp. 100–115.

Skowronek, Stephen (1997) *The Politics Presidents Make. Leadership from John Adams to Bill Clinton.* Cambridge, MA: Harvard University Press.

Slater, Dan (2008) Can leviathan be democratic? Competitive elections, robust mass politics and state infrastructural power. *Studies in Comparative International Development*, 43, pp. 252–272.

Snyder, Jack (2000) *From Voting to Violence: Democratization and nationalist conflict*, New York: Norton.

Souaré, Issaka (2014) The African Union as a norm entrepreneur on military coups d'état in Africa (1952–2012): An empirical assessment. *Journal of Modern African Studies*, 52(1), pp. 69–94.

Stasavage, David (2005a) Democracy and education spending in Africa. *American Journal of Political Science*, 49(2), pp. 43–58.

(2005b) The role of democracy in Uganda's move to Universal Primary Education. *Journal of Modern African Studies*, 43(1), pp. 53–73.

Sung, Hung-En (2004) Democracy and Political Corruption: A Cross-national Comparison. *Crime, Law and Social Change* 41(2), pp. 179–193.

Svolik, Milan (2012) *The Politics of Authoritarian Rule*. Cambridge: Cambridge University Press.

Sylla, Lanciné (1982) Succession of the charismatic leader: The Gordian knot of African politics. *Daedalus*, 111(2), pp. 11–28.

Tansey, Oisín (2017) The fading of the anti-coup norm. *Journal of Democracy*, 28(1), pp. 144–156.

Teorell, Jan, Dahlberg, Stefan, Holmberg, Sören, Rothstein, Bo, Hartmann, Felix, and Svensson, Richard (2015) The quality of government standard dataset. Version Jan 15. University of Gothenburg: The Quality of Government Institute.

The Economist (2018) *A manifesto for renewing liberalism.*

Theron, Monique (2011) African trends and transformation: The profiles of Sub-Saharan African executive heads of state since independence. *Developmental Leadership Program, Research Paper 17.*

(2012) Emerging and non-emerging African countries: A statistical exploration of the leadership factor. *Developmental Leadership Program, Research Paper 19.*

Thies, Cameron G. (2004) State building, interstate and intrastate rivalry: A study of post-colonial developing country extractive efforts, 1975–2000. *International Studies Quarterly*, 48, pp. 53–72.

Thomson, Alex (2000) *An Introduction to African Politics*. London: Routledge.

Tilly, Charles (1990) *Coercion, Capital and European States, AD 990-1992*. Oxford: Blackwell Publishers.

Timmons, Jeffrey F. (2010) Taxation and representation in recent history. *Journal of Politics*, 72, pp. 191–208.

Treisman, Daniel (2000) The causes of corruption: A cross-national study. *Journal of Public Economics*, 76(3), pp. 399–458.

Tull, Denis and Simons, Claudia (2017) The institutionalisation of power revisited: presidential term limits in Africa. *Afrika Spectrum*, 52(2), pp. 79–102.

van de Walle, Nicholas (2001) *African Economies and the Politics of Permanent Crisis, 1979–1999*. Cambridge: Cambridge University Press.

(2002) Africa's range of regimes. *Journal of Democracy*, 13(2), pp. 66–80.
van de Walle, Nicolas (2012) The path from neopatrimonialism. Democracy and clientelism in Africa today. In Bach, Daniel and Gazibo, Mamoudou (eds.), *Neopatrimonialism in Africa and Beyond*. London: Routledge, pp. 111–123.
Varol, Ozan (2012) The democratic coup d'état. *Harvard International Law Journal*, 53(2), pp. 291–356.
Varshney, Ashutosh (2000) Why have poor democracies not eliminated poverty? A suggestion. *Asian Survey* 40(5), pp. 718–736.
Verzichelli, Luca (2011) Leadership. In Badie, B., Berg-Schlosser, D., and Morlino, L. (eds.), *International Encyclopedia of Political Science*. Thousand Oaks, CA: SAGE Publications, pp. 1408–1411.
Wang, Erik and Xu, Yiqing (2018) Awakening Leviathan: The effect of democracy on state capacity. *Research & Politics*, pp. 1–7.
Weghorst, Keith and Lindberg, Staffan (2013) What drives the swing voter in Africa? *American Journal of Political Science*, 57(3), pp. 717–734.
Wells, Alan (1974) The coup d'état in theory and practice: Independent Black Africa in the 1960s. *American Journal of Sociology*, 79(4), pp. 871–887.
Yates, Douglas (2017) Dynastic rule in Equatorial Guinea. *African Journal of Political Science and International Relations*, 11(12), pp. 339–359.
Zolberg, Aristide R. (1968) The structure of political conflict in the new states of tropical Africa. *American Political Science Review*, 62(1), pp. 70–87.

Index

Note: Locators in *italics* refer to figures. Locators with a 't' refer to tables. Locators with an 'n' refer to footnotes.

Abdelaziz, Mohamed Ould (Mauritania) 106t, 158
accountability 3, 5–6, 33–34, 43–44, 156–57, 240–41
"Addis Charter" (African Charter on Democracy, Elections and Governance) 138
Africa Leadership Change (ALC) dataset 67, 282t
  advantages 63, 68–69
  and *Archigos* dataset 72–74, 75t
  defining and coding of variables 62–68
  and other datasets 74–77
  purpose and focus 62, 62n, 68
  rationale 60–62
African Charter on Democracy, Elections and Governance ("Addis Charter") 138
African Union (formerly Organization of African Unity) 5, 135–39
Afwerki, Isaias (Eritrea) 24, 83t, 86t, 166
Agostinho Neto, António (Angola) 19, 82t, 92
Aguiyi-Ironsi, Johnson (Nigeria) 27, 124
Ahidjo, Ahmadou (Cameroon) 28, 83t, 84, 86t, 92, 96, 262
Ahlquist, J. 12–13
Ahmed, Abiy (Ethiopia) 261, 264
Akyüz, Y. 189
ALC *see* Africa Leadership Change (ALC) dataset
Algiers Declaration 137
alternation
  and accountability 5, 33–34, 43, 51

corruption and 240–41, 251
democracy and 48–51, *49*, 70t, 72, 154, 158–59, *159*
elections in Africa and 4, *115*
electoral 65–66, 114, *115*, 282t
impact of 43–44
measuring impact of 181, 183–84, 206–7, 224–25, 238, 252–53
America *see* United States of America
Amin, Idi (Uganda) 18–19, 27, 127–28, 150, 262
Angola
  coups and military takeovers 133
  elections 71t, 95t, 99t
  fate of founding father 82t
  leadership change 75–76t, 90t, 92–93, 118–19, 180, 282t
  leadership types 343t
  political party system 80, 96, 193
  term limits 152t, 164t, 165n, 167, 285t
  see also Santos, José Eduardo dos
Aptidon, Hassan Gouled (Djibouti) 80, 83t, 86t
Archigos 2, 61, 72–74, 75–76t, 77
Argentina 149–50, 160
ASEAN (Association of Southeast Asian Nations) 136
autocrats
  development performance of 22–23, 55, 267–70, 268t
  early typology 18
  elections 96
  empirical definition 257–59, *257*, 259t
  empirical distribution 261t, 262–67, *265*, 279, 343t

363

autocrats (cont.)
  retaining power 45–46, 112, 168
  succession and 172
Bäck, H. 229
Baker, B. 101–2, 258
Banda, Hastings Kamuzu (Malawi)
  ethnic strife and factionalism 18
  fate of founding father 66, 80, 83t, 150
  influence 275
  leadership style 17–18, 262
  legitimacy 134
  tenure 30–31, 86t, 150
  term limits 151
Banda, Joyce 31
Barre, Mohamed Siad (Somalia) 64, 86t
Barro, R. 188
Barrow, Adama (The Gambia) 72, 118
al-Bashir, Omar (Sudan)
  ascent to power 127
  leadership type 266
  tenure 86t, 166
  term limits 152t, 164t, 165n, 297t
Bates, R. 53, 229
Baum, M. 42, 52, 210
Beck, N. 185–86
Bédié, Henri Konan 73
Beerbohm, E. 7
Benin
  coups and military takeovers 27–28, 91, 107, 123–24, 123n
  elections 70t, 95t, 99t, 103
  fate of founding father 81t
  leadership changes 75–76t, 90t, 91, 111, 167–68, 282t
  leadership type 343t
  term limits 152t, 159, 164t, 285–86t
  see also Kérékou, Mathieu
Bermeo, N. 142
Berry, C. 23
Bertelsmann Transformation Index (BTI) 231
Bienen, H. 29, 132
"big man" politics 15, 17, 31, 85
Bio, Julius Maada (Sierra Leone) 262
Biya, Paul (Cameroon)
  ascent to power 28
  elections 96, 101
  ethnic strife and factionalism 97–101
  leadership type 266
  tenure 86t, 166, 261
  term limits 164t, 287t
Blair, Tony (UK) 85, 155
Block, S. 53
Blondel, J. 11–12, 41
Bokassa, Jean-Bédel (Central African Republic) 17, 19, 27, 132, 150
Bolivia 160
Bonaparte, Napoleon (France) 150
Bongo, Omar (Gabon)
  elections 96
  ethnic strife and factionalism 97–101
  hereditary succession 173–74
  influence 85–87
  leadership type 18, 262
  legitimacy 16
  tenure 18, 28, 84, 86t, 111–12, 150–51, 173
  term limits 151, 164t, 290t
Booth, D. 192–94
Botswana
  corruption 244
  coups and military takeovers 133
  democracy 94
  development and growth 211, 232
  elections 94, 95t, 99t, 109, 116
  fate of founding father 82t
  leadership changes 66, 90t, 282t
  leadership type 343t
  term limits 164t, 165n, 286t
  see also Khama, Ian; Khama, Seretse
Bozizé, François (Central African Republic) 106t, 125, 142–43
Brady, D. 36
Bratton, M. 44, 227, 239
Brazil 150, 160
Britain see United Kingdom
Brown, D. 210
Brownlee, J. 172
BTI (Bertelsmann Transformation Index) 231
Bueno de Mesquita, B. 11, 36, 39–40, 112
Buhari, Muhammadu (Nigeria) 16, 88, 260
Bunce, V. 11, 21, 37–38, 54
Burkina Faso

coups and military takeovers 27–28, 88–89, 105, 106t, 121, 123n, 126, 136–37, 139, 143t
  elections 70t, 95t, 99t, 143
  fate of founding fathers 81t
  leadership changes 75–76t, 86t, 90t, 282t
  leadership type 266, 343t
  term limits 152t, 161–63, 163–64t, 165n, 166, 286t
  see also Compaoré, Blaise; Sankara, Thomas
Burma 120
Burns, J.M. 9
Burundi
  coups and military takeovers 27–28, 123n, 127, 136, 141
  elections 66, 70–71t, 95t, 99t, 102, 118
  fate of founding father 81t
  leadership changes 75–76t, 90t, 282t
  leadership type 343t
  role of military 80, 139, 169–70
  term limits 152t, 161–63, 163–64t, 165n, 286–87t
Buyoya, Pierre (Burundi) 127, 260

Cameroon
  coups and military takeovers 89
  elections 30, 95t, 96, 99t
  ethnic strife and factionalism 97–101
  fate of founding father 83t
  leadership change 28, 75–76t, 86t, 90t, 91, 282t
  leadership type 262, 266, 343t
  political party system 80, 95
  role of military 170
  term limits 118, 152t, 152–53, 163–64t, 287t
  see also Ahidjo, Ahmadou; Biya, Paul
Cape Verde
  corruption 244
  coups and military takeovers 89
  elections 66, 70t, 95t, 99t, 103
  fate of founding father 83t
  leadership changes 75–76t, 90t, 282t
  leadership type 343t
  term limits 152t, 152–53, 164t, 165n, 287t

Carbone, G. 116–18, *116–17*
Carlyle, Thomas 8
Carothers, T. 227
Cassani, A. 116–18, *116–17*
CC (Control of Corruption) index 242–43
CCM (Chama Cha Mapinduzi), Tanzania 29, 94–95, 255
Central African Republic
  coups and military takeovers 106t, 123n, 125, 139, 143t, 196
  development and growth 232
  elections 70–71t, 95t, 99t, 142
  fate of founding father 81t
  foreign influence 64, 132
  leadership changes 75–76t, 90t, 282t
  leadership type 343t
  role of military 27, 123
  term limits 152t, 164t, 287t
  see also Bokassa, Jean-Bédel
Chad
  coups and military takeovers 64, 123n, 196
  development and growth 232
  elections 95t, 99t, 118
  ethnic strife and factionalism 97–101, 271
  fate of founding father 81t, 128
  leadership changes 90t, 282t
  leadership type 343t
  term limits 152t, 163–64t, 287t
  see also Déby, Idriss
Chama Cha Mapinduzi (CCM), Tanzania 29, 94–95, 255
charismatic leaders 7–9, 16, 18, 87
Charron, N. 229
child mortality
  impact of coups on 146t, 148
  impact of leaders on 24–25, 147t, 212–16, *214*, *217*, 252–53, 269
  measuring 223–25, 302t
  regression tables 220t, 327t
Chissano, Joaquim (Mozambique) 31, 64, 164t, 259, 266, 292t
Clapham, C. 15
Clark, J. 105, 126n, 135
"coerced resignations" 126
Cole, B. 69n
Collier, P. 125, 127, 140, 191

Comoros
  coups and military takeovers 27–28, 91, 123n, 123
  democratization 118
  elections 66, 70t, 95t, 99t
  fate of founding father 81t
  foreign influence 132, 141
  leadership changes 65, 75–76t, 90t, 282t
  leadership type 343t
  political party system 97
  term limits 159, 164t, 165n, 287t
Compaoré, Blaise (Burkina Faso)
  ascent to power 89
  leadership type 266
  tenure 85, 86t, 124
  term limits 162, 164t, 165n
competitiveness
  corruption and 241, 245, 247, 250
  development performance and 176, 180–81, 206, 213–16, 214, 217, 224, 252–53
  electoral mechanism 51–52, 57
  measuring 53n, 182–83
  negative consequences 56–57, 228–29
  state consolidation and 228–29, 233–34, 234–53, 235–38
Congo-Brazzaville (Republic of the Congo)
  corruption 244
  coups and military takeovers 27, 123n, 123, 139, 196
  elections 71t, 95t, 99t, 102
  fate of founding father 81t
  leadership changes 75–76t, 90t, 282t
  leadership type 343t
  role of military 170
  term limits 152t, 163–64t, 165n, 166, 288t
  see also Sassou Nguesso, Denis
Congo-Kinshasa (Democratic Republic of the Congo)
  coups and military takeovers 27, 89–90, 123, 123n, 196
  development and growth 232
  dynastic succession 93, 173
  elections 95t, 97, 99t
  fate of founding father 81t
  leadership changes 28, 75–76t, 90t, 282t

leadership type 262, 343t
  term limits 152t, 164t, 165n, 288t
  see also Mobutu Sese Seko, Joseph-Desiré
Conté, Lansana (Guinea) 86t, 150–51, 173, 266
Control of Corruption (CC) index 242–43
corruption
  coups and 144–48, 146t
  definition 241–42
  explanatory factors/explaining 239–41
  leadership and 147t, 240–41, 244–46, 245, 246–51, 247, 253, 270
  measuring 185–87, 242–44, 246
  regression tables and descriptive statistics 248t, 302t, 335t, 339t
Corruption Perceptions Index (CPI) 242–43
Côte d'Ivoire
  coups and military takeovers 105, 123n, 123–24
  democracy 72
  development and growth 193–94
  elections 71t, 95t, 96, 99t
  fate of founding father 82t
  foreign influence 134
  leadership changes 73, 75–76t, 90t, 282t
  leadership type 343t
  political party system 95, 97
  term limits 151–52, 152t, 164t, 289t
  see also Houphouët-Boigny, Felix
coups d'état
  causal and inhibiting factors 27, 88, 128–35
  condemnation and sanctioning of 135–41
  definition of 121n, 125–28
  democratizing effect of 139–44, 143t
  global incidence of 120–21, 122, 133–34
  incidence in Africa 27, 88–89, 103–5, 104, 108t, 123, 123n
  incidence in Africa since 2000 105, 106t, 108t, 124–25, 196
  leaders' overstay and 1, 79, 123–24, 275

Index

research on 133–35
socioeconomic impact of 144–48, 146–47t
types 128
violence and 64, 80, 127–28
CPI (Corruption Perceptions Index) 242–43

Daar, Aden Abdulle Osman (Somalia) 82t, 84
Dacko, David (Central African Republic) 64, 81t, 132, 260
Déby, Idriss (Chad) 64, 86t, 97–101, 112, 166, 196
Decalo, S. 130, 132, 134, 144
"democratic coups" 140–42
Democratic Republic of the Congo (DRC) *see* Congo-Kinshasa
democrats
 corruption control 270
 development performance of 22–23, 267–70, 268t
 empirical definition 257, 259t, 259–60
 empirical distribution 261t, 263–66, 265, 279, 343t
 entry into power 264
 in typology 6
development aid and economic growth 189
Development Leadership Programme 25
dictators *see* autocrats
Diouf, Abdou (Senegal) 64, 155–56, 164t, 165n, 295t
Djibouti
 elections 71t, 95t, 99t
 fate of founding father 83t
 leadership changes 75–76t, 90t, 91, 282t
 leadership type 343t
 role of military 170
 term limits 118, 152t, 163–64t, 289t
 see also Aptidon, Hassan Gouled
dynastic succession 171–74

Easterly, W. 22–23, 190
economic growth
 coups and 129, 144–48, 146t, 196
 elected leaders and 47, 57, 147t

elections and elected leadership *195*, 196–97, *198*, 199–207, 252
explanations for slow 188–94
leaders' impact on 20–26, 35–37, 252
measuring leaders' impact on 176–77, 185–87, 194, 197–207, 200t, 203t, 302t
new leaders' focus 19
education *see* school enrollment
Egypt 120–21, 126, 136–37, 141–42
elections
 accountability of leaders 3, 5–6, 33–34, 44, 240–41
 achievements/events related to 116–19, *116–17*
 benefits of 4, 26, 31, 43, 47, 52–53, 279
 datasets on 74–77
 definitions of variables 65–66
 democratization and manipulation of 96–103, 99t
 incidence of multiparty 1–2, 4, 30, 60, 79, *98*, 277
 leadership change and 48–51, *49*
 non-multiparty elections 28–29, 94–96, 95t
 outcomes of 113–14, *115*
 skepticism regarding benefits of 192–93
 steps in electoral mechanism 51–52
Elections and democracy in Africa dataset 74
endowments and economic growth 190
Englebert, P. 190, 192
Equatorial Guinea
 coups and military takeovers 123n, 127
 elections 30, 95t, 99t
 fate of founding father 82t
 hereditary succession 174
 leadership changes 90t, 91, 111, 282t
 leadership type 343t
 term limits 118, 152t, 162, 164t, 165n, 166–67, 289t
 see also Nguema, Francisco Macías; Obiang, Teodoro Nguema Mbasogo

Eritrea
  development and growth 24
  elections 95t, 99t, 109, 116–18, 165n
  fate of founding father 83t
  leadership changes 28, 90–91, 90t, 282t
  leadership type 267, 343t
  term limits 164t, 289t
  see also Afwerki, Isaias
eSwatini
  coups and military takeovers 133
  elections 95t, 99t, 109, 116–18
  fate of founding father 82t
  leadership changes 28, 76t, 90t, 91, 282t
  leadership type 63, 165n, 171, 262, 266–67, 343t
  legitimacy of leadership 134
  term limits 164t
Ethiopia
  coups and military takeovers 123n, 196
  elections 95t, 99t
  fate of founding father 81t
  leadership changes 66, 75–76t, 86t, 90t, 173, 282t
  leadership type 262, 343t
  political party system 96, 165n
  term limits 118, 164t, 165n, 289t
  see also Haile Selassie I
Europe 9–10, 85
European Union 139
Executive Index of Electoral Competition 53n
Eyadéma, Gnassingbé (Togo)
  ascent to power 27, 89–90, 124, 137
  elections 101
  ethnic strife and factionalism 97–101, 130–31
  hereditary succession 173
  leadership style 258
  legitimacy 16
  tenure 84, 86t, 150–51
  term limits 164t

founding fathers 14–16, 29, 79–80, 81t, 84, 266
Fowler, A. 23
Franck, R. 24

Franco, Francisco (Spain) 85, 120
Freedom House index 61, 68
Freedom in the World Index 61
FRELIMO (Frente de Libertação de Moçambique) 30, 92, 193–94

Gabon
  corruption 244
  dynastic succession 93, 172–74
  elections 30, 71t, 95t, 96, 99t, 125
  ethnic strife and factionalism 97–101
  fate of founding father 82t
  foreign influence 63–64, 126, 134
  leadership changes 28, 75–76t, 86t, 90t, 282t, 290t
  leadership type 262, 343t
  term limits 118, 152t, 163–64t, 165n
  see also Bongo, Omar
Gambia, The
  coups and military takeovers 105, 123n, 127, 139, 141
  democracy 72
  elections 95t, 99t, 118
  fate of founding father 82t, 86t, 91
  leadership changes 71t, 90t, 91, 282t
  leadership type 50n, 50–51, 343t
  term limits 152t, 164t, 290t
  see also Jammeh, Yahya
GDP *see* economic growth
Germany 85
Gerring, J. 47
Ghana
  coups and military takeovers 27–28, 80, 89, 107, 123n, 142
  democracy 69, 159
  development and growth 210–11
  elections 70t, 99t, 103, 262–63n
  ethnic strife and factionalism 97–101
  fate of founding father 81t
  leadership changes 75–76t, 90t, 125, 173, 282t
  leadership type 16–17, 343t
  political party system 96
  term limits 152t, 159, 164t, 290t
  see also Nkruma, Kwame; Rawlings, Jerry
Glewwe, P. 189
Goemans, Hein 140–41
Goemans, Henk 61, 72

Index

Goldsmith, A.A. 25–26, 55, 91
Gore, C. 189
Govea, R. 32–33, 41
governance, and economic growth 190–94
Gowon, Yakubu (Nigeria) 27, 124
"Great Man" theories 7–8
Greenstein, F. 14, 37
Guéï, Robert (Côte d'Ivoire) 123–24
Guinea
  coups and military takeovers 106t, 123n, 137, 139, 143t
  elections 71t, 95t, 99t
  ethnic strife and factionalism 97–101
  fate of founding father 82t
  leadership changes 75–76t, 86t, 90t, 150–51, 173, 282t
  leadership type 262, 266, 343t
  term limits 152t, 163–64t, 290t
  see also Touré, Ahmed Sékou
Guinea-Bissau
  coups after 2000 105, 106t, 125, 136, 139, 143t
  coups and military takeovers 27–28, 91, 123n
  elections 70–71t, 95t, 99t
  fate of founding father 82t
  interim leaders 64, 257, 261
  leadership changes 72, 75–76t, 90, 173, 282t
  leadership type 343t
  term limits 152t, 164t, 291t

Habyarimana, Juvénal (Rwanda) 27, 84, 86t, 96–101
Hadenius, A. 229
Haile Selassie I (Ethiopia) 15, 18, 81t, 86t, 261–62
Haiti 35, 136, 141, 172
Hanson, J. 231
Harare Summit (1997) 137
health expenditure *see* public health expenditure
hegemons
  corruption control 270
  development performance of 267–70, 268t
  empirical definition 257, 259t, 259–60, 263–64

empirical distribution 261t, 264–66, 265, 279, 343t
entry into power 263–64
and multiparty systems 6
hereditary succession 171–74
Hickey, S. 211
Hoeffler, A. 125, 127
Holm, J. 32–33, 41
Horowitz, S. 54, 241
Houphouët-Boigny, Felix (Côte d'Ivoire)
  elections 96
  fate of founding father 82t, 111
  influence 15–23
  leadership style 16, 18, 262
  tenure 84–85, 86t, 89, 150–51
  term limits 151
Hughes, A. 92
Huntington, S.P. 226
hybrid regimes 69–72, 209, 211, 241, 270
Hyde, S. 74–77

ICRG (International Country Risk Guide) 230–31
interim leaders *see* transient leaders
investment and economic growth 188–89
Isaias Afwerki *see* Afwerki, Isaias

Jackman, R. 126
Jackson, R.H. 17–18, 20–23, 32, 226, 255–56, 262–63
Jammeh, Yahya (The Gambia)
  ascent to power 91, 118, 127
  leadership style 50, 88
  tenure 25, 72, 84, 86t
Janowitz, M. 130
Jawara, Dawda (The Gambia) 82t, 86t, 91, 261
Jenkins, C. 124, 126, 130
Johnson Sirleaf, Ellen (Liberia) 164t, 192
Jones, B. 21–22
Jugnauth, Pravind Kumar (Mauritius) 173

Kabila, Joseph (Congo-Kinshasa) 164t, 165n, 173, 196
Kagame, Paul (Rwanda)
  ascent to power 63, 85, 196

Kagame, Paul (Rwanda) (cont.)
  leadership 24, 55
  tenure 86t
  term limits 161–62, 164t, 165n
Kaplan, R. 226
Katz, J. 185–86
Kaunda, Kenneth (Zambia) 15, 29, 66, 80, 83t, 86t, 102
Keefer, P. 55
Kelsall, T. 192–94
Kenya
  development and growth ,193, 194
  elections 62–63, 95t, 96, 99t, 118
  electoral alternation 66, 70–71t, 103
  fate of founding father 82t
  hereditary succession 172–73
  leadership changes 75–76t, 90t, 125, 150–51, 169–70, 282t
  leadership type 262, 343t
  military and coups 134
  political parties 29
  term limits 151–52, 152t, 159, 164t, 291t
  see also Kenyatta, Jomo; Moi, Daniel arap
Kenya African National Union (KANU) 29, 96
Kenyatta, Jomo (Kenya)
  ethnic strife and factionalism 18
  fate of founding father 82t
  hereditary succession 172–73
  leadership style 16, 18, 29, 262
Kenyatta, Uhuru (Kenya) 172–73
Kérékou, Mathieu (Benin)
  ascent to power 27
  leadership style 28–29, 102, 260
  tenure 91, 114, 150–51
  term limits 164t
Khama, Ian (Botswana) 172–73
Khama, Seretse (Botswana) 23–24, 82t, 94, 264
Khan, M.H. 56
Khemani, S. 55
Kibaki, Mwai (Kenya) 62–63, 66, 164t
Kiir Mayardit, Salva (South Sudan) 83t, 267
Kjær, A. 52–53, 211
Kolingba, André (Central African Republic) 102, 132

Korolev, A. 56–57
Kposowa, A. 124, 126, 130

Lake, D. 42, 52, 210
Lapuente, V. 229
Latin America 10, 136, 149–50, 160
leadership
  definition 13, 62–63
  development performance of 19, 25–26, 35–37
  focus of research on 7–12
leadership change
  development and mode of 44–46, 52–54
  frequency in Africa 90–91, 90t, 107–13, 109–10, 112t
  modes of 104, 113
  studying impact of 33–34, 38–41
  summary statistics 299t
"leadership trap" 1, 29–30
Lesotho
  coups and military takeovers 89, 123n, 142
  elections 70t, 95t, 99t
  fate of founding father 82t
  form of government 165n, 171
  leadership changes 65, 75–76t, 90t, 282t
  leadership type 258, 343t
  term limits 164t, 291t
Levi, M. 12–13, 228
Levine, R. 190
Liberia
  coups and military takeovers 89, 123n, 128
  elections 70t, 95t, 97, 99t, 118
  fate of founding father 82t, 86t
  interim leaders 261
  leadership changes 75–76t, 90t, 92, 150–51, 282t
  leadership type 18, 262–63, 343t
  term limits 164t, 165n, 291t
life expectancy (at birth) 147t, 213–16, 214, 217, 223–25, 269
  impact of coups on 146t, 148
  regression tables 220–22t, 323t
life presidents 79–80, 150–51
Lindberg, S. 74–77, 105, 126n, 135
Linz, J. 226

Index

Lissouba, Pascal (Congo-Brazzaville) 102
Lomé Declaration (2000) 138
Lourenço, João (Angola) 19–23, 118–19, 174, 180, 261
Luttwak, E. 125

McGowan, P. 88–89, 105, 133, 135, 144, 191
McGuire, M. 55
Machel, Samora (Mozambique) 64, 82t, 92
Machiavelli, Niccolò 7
Macías Nguema *see* Nguema, Francisco Macías
McKie, K. 151, 169
Madagascar
  coups and military takeovers 89, 105, 106t, 123n, 137, 143, 143t
  elections 66, 70t, 95t, 99t, 118
  fate of founding father 82t
  interim leaders 271–72
  leadership changes 75–76t, 90t, 102, 282t
  leadership type 343t
  term limits 152t, 164t, 291t
Malawi
  coups and military takeovers 133
  democracy 170
  development and growth 193, 211
  dynastic succession 173
  elections 50, 70t, 95t, 99t, 103
  fate of founding father 66, 83t, 150
  leadership changes 66, 75–76t, 90t, 173, 282t
  leadership type 343t
  single- or multiparty system 80
  term limits 152t, 164t, 167, 291t
  see also Banda, Hastings Kamuzu
Mali
  attempts at democracy 30, 89–90, 118, 123n, 125, 139–40, 143t
  coups and military takeovers 27, 87–88, 105, 106t
  development and growth 211
  elections 70t, 95t, 99t
  fate of founding father 81t
  interim leaders 261
  leadership changes 30–31, 75–76t, 90t, 142, 282t

leadership type 258, 343t
term limits 152t, 159, 164t, 292t
Mandela, Nelson (South Africa) 17, 24–25, 63, 168
Marinov, N 74–77, 140–41
Marshall, D. 126
Marshall, M. 69n, 126
Masisi, Mokgweetsi (Botswana) 262
Mauritania
  coups and military takeovers 27–28, 89, 105, 106t, 123n, 125, 140, 143t
  coups sanctioned 137, 139
  elections 71t, 95t, 99t, 143
  ethnic strife and factionalism 97–101
  fate of founding father 81t
  leadership changes 65, 75–76t, 87t, 89, 90t, 282t
  leadership type 343t
  term limits 152t, 158, 164t, 167, 292t
Mauritius
  elections 70–71t, 95t, 99t, 109, 114, 116
  fate of founding father 82t
  form of government 165n
  hereditary succession 173
  leadership changes 75–76t, 90t, 282t
  leadership type 343t
  term limits 164t, 292t
May, R. 92
Mazrui, A. 16
Mazzuca, S. 228
M'ba, Leon (Gabon) 63–64, 82t, 126
Meles Zenawi *see* Zenawi, Meles
Merkel, Angela (Germany) 85, 155
methodology of current research 58–59, 184–88
Mexico 50, 150, 156–57
Michel, James (Seychelles) 167
Micombero, Michel (Burundi) 25, 84
military centrality theories 130
military interventions *see* coups de'état
Miller, A. 142
Mkandawire, T. 19
Mkapa, Benjamin (Tanzania) 31
Mnangagwa, Emmerson (Zimbabwe) 121n, 262, 264, 264n
Mobarak, A.M. 210

Mobutu Sese Seko, Joseph-Desiré (Congo-Kinshasa)
  ascent to power 27–28, 85, 124, 128, 137
  ethnic strife and factionalism 97–101
  influence 35
  leadership style 18, 262–63
  legitimacy 16
  tenure 86t, 89–90
Moi, Daniel arap (Kenya)
  elections 96
  ethnic strife and factionalism 97–101
  leadership style 17, 29
  legitimacy 258
  tenure 31, 86t, 169
  term limits 151
Mozambique
  coups and military takeovers 133
  development and growth 193–94, 210–11
  elections 30, 71t, 95t, 99t, 102
  fate of founding father 82t
  leadership changes 66, 75–76, 90t, 92, 124–25, 282t
  leadership type 343t
  political parties 96
  term limits 152t, 164t, 292t
  see also Chissano, Joaquim
Mswati III (eSwatini) 28, 63, 86t, 266–67
Mugabe, Robert (Zimbabwe)
  dynastic succession 174
  fate of founding father 83t, 121n, 166
  leadership style 140
  tenure 86t
Muluzi, Bakili (Malawi) 31, 66, 170
Munck, G. 228
Musella, F. 7, 32
Museveni, Yoweri (Uganda)
  ascent to power 24, 196
  hereditary succession 174
  leadership type 267
  legitimacy 258
  tenure 84, 86t, 166
  term limits 164t
Musharraf, Pervez (Pakistan) 120, 127
Mutharika, Bingu wa (Malawi) 31, 66, 173
Mutharika, Peter (Malawi) 31, 173

Namibia
  corruption 244
  coups and military takeovers 133
  democratization 118
  development and growth 19–23, 232
  elections 70t, 95t, 99t, 109
  leadership changes 75–76, 90t, 102–3, 282t
  leadership type 343t
  political party system 97
  term limits 152t, 163–64t, 165n, 293t
  see also Nujoma, Sam
NELDA (*National Elections across Democracy and Autocracy*) 74–77
Nguema, Francisco Macías (Equatorial Guinea) 15–23, 82t, 150, 174, 262
Niger
  coups and military takeovers 27–28, 89, 105, 106t, 123n, 125, 128, 141
  coups and regime change 139–40, 142, 143t
  elections 70t, 95t, 99t
  fate of founding father 81t
  leadership changes 65–66, 75–76, 90t, 282t
  leadership type 343t
  term limits 152t, 161–63, 164t, 293t
Nigeria
  corruption 244
  coups and military takeovers 27–28, 30, 87–89, 107, 123n, 124
  democracy 72
  elections 70t, 95t, 97, 99t, 103
  fate of founding father 81t
  leadership changes 65, 75–76, 90t, 91, 272, 282t
  leadership type 16, 260, 343t
  role and impact of military 80, 88, 123, 127
  term limits 152t, 164t, 167, 293t
  see also Obasanjo, Olusegun
Nimeiry, Gaafar (Sudan) 27, 262
Nkrumah, Kwame (Ghana) 15–16, 18, 81t, 150, 262–63n, 262
Nkurunziza, Pierre (Burundi) 66, 161–63, 164t, 165n
Nordlinger, E. 144

Index

Nujoma, Sam (Namibia)
  fate of founding father 83t, 102–3, 162
  leadership type 264
  legacy 19–23
  tenure 165n, 169
  term limits 164t
Nyerere, Julius (Tanzania)
  elections 96
  fate of founding father 83t
  leadership type 16, 18, 29, 258, 262
  tenure 86t, 92

OAS (Organization of American States) 136
Obama, Barack (USA) 107
Obasanjo, Olusegun (Nigeria)
  influence 137–38
  leadership type 260
  tenure 31
  term limits 164t, 167
Obiang Nguema Mbasogo, Teodoro (Equatorial Guinea) 28, 85, 86t, 111, 124, 151, 166, 174
Obote, Milton (Uganda) 16, 81t, 258
Olivier de Sardan, J-P. 239
Olken, B. 21–22
Olson, M. 55
Olympio, Sylvanus (Togo) 27, 80, 81t, 123, 258
Organization of African Unity *see* African Union
Organization of American States (OAS) 136

Paige, G. 9
Pakistan 120, 127
patriarchal leaders 16
Pellegata, A. 241
Pennings, S. 22–23
Pereira, Carmen (Guinea-Bissau) 64, 257
personal leadership
  in Africa 17–19, 79–80, 255–56, 275
  change in Africa away from 31, 151
  development and 20–21, 23–26
  renewed personalization 9, 31–32, 280
Pinochet, Augusto (Chile) 35, 55, 120

Pohamba, Hifikepunye (Namibia) 19–23, 102–3, 164t
Polity datasets 61, 68, 69n
population growth and economic growth 189
Posner, D. 31–33, 151, 158
Powell, J. 126–27, 134, 136, 139–41
presidents for life 79–80, 150–51
"princes" 18–19
Príncipe *see* São Tomé and Príncipe
promissory coups d'état 143
'prophets" 18–19
Przeworski, A. 61
public health expenditure
  impact of coups on 145, 146t, 148
  impact of leaders on 56, 147t, 212, 214, 216–25, 217, 252–53, 269
  measuring 212–16, 302t
  regression tables 220–22t, 309t

"Quality of Government" dataset 219–30

Radelet, S. 24, 192
Rainer, I. 24
Rajoelina, Andry (Madagascar) 102, 106t, 143
Ramaphosa, Cyril (South Africa) 174, 262
Rangolaam, Navin (Mauritius) 172–73
Ratsiraka, Didier (Madagascar) 102, 260
Ravalomanana, Marc (Madagascar) 66, 106t
Rawlings, Jerry (Ghana)
  ascent to power 27, 128
  ethnicity and factionalism 97–101
  leadership type 17, 63, 73, 88
  legitimacy 258
  term limits 164t
René, France-Albert (Seychelles) 86t, 111
Republic of the Congo *see* Congo-Brazzaville (Republic of the Congo)
Roosevelt, Franklin D. (USA) 149
Rosberg, C.G. 17–18, 20–23, 32, 255–56, 262–63
Rotberg, R. 23–24, 94

Rwanda
  coups and military takeovers 27, 123n, 196
  elections 95t, 96–97, 99t, 118, 211
  fate of founding father 81t
  leadership changes 84, 90t, 282t
  leadership type 258, 343t
  political party system 96
  role of military 169–70
  term limits 152t, 162, 163–64t, 166, 293t
  see also Habyarimana, Juvénal; Kagame, Paul

Sacks, A. 228
Sankara, Thomas (Burkina Faso) 27, 88–89, 128
Santos, José Eduardo dos
  hereditary succession 174
  legacy 19–23
  tenure 28, 85, 86t, 91, 166
  term limits 167, 285t
São Tomé and Príncipe
  democratization 118
  elections 95t, 99t
  fate of founding father 83t
  interim leaders 271
  leadership changes 90t, 282t
  leadership type 343t
  term limits 152t, 164t, 295t
Sassou Nguesso, Denis (Congo-Brazzaville) 87t, 102, 164t, 165n, 196
Schacther, R. 29
school enrollment
  impact of coups on 145, 146t, 148
  impact of leaders on 24–25, 147t, 214, 216–25, 217, 252–53, 269
  measuring impact of 212–16, 302t
  regression tables 220–22t, 314t, 319t
  social impact of 56, 212
Schumpeter, J. 50
Security Council of UN 136
Sékou Touré see Touré, Ahmed Sékou
selectorate theory 39–40
Senegal
  coups and military takeovers 89, 134
  elections 70t, 95t, 99t, 103, 116
  fate of founding father 82t, 93–94
  hereditary succession 172–74

  leadership changes 64, 66, 75–76t, 90t, 92, 282t
  leadership type 343t
  term limits adopted 152t, 167, 295t
  term limits manipulated 161–63, 163–64t, 165n, 166
  see also Senghor, Léopold
Senghor, Léopold (Senegal) 15
  ethnic strife and factionalism 18
  fate of founding father 64, 82t, 93–94
  leadership type 18, 262
  tenure 87t, 92
Seychelles
  coups and military takeovers 89, 123n
  elections 95t, 99t
  fate of founding father 81t
  leadership changes 75–76t, 86t, 90t, 111, 282t
  leadership type 343t
  term limits 152t, 164t, 165n, 167, 295t
Siegle, J.T. 47
Sierra Leone
  coups and military takeovers 27–28, 87–89, 123n, 136–37, 141–42
  democracy 72, 118
  dynastic succession 93
  elections 65, 70t, 95t, 99t, 114
  fate of founding father 82t
  leadership changes 75–76t, 90t, 92, 103, 282t
  leadership type 262, 343t
  political party system 96
  term limits 159, 164t, 296t
  see also Stevens, Siaka
Sigman, R. 231
Simons, C. 157–58
el-Sisi, Abdel Fattah (Egypt) 121, 136
Sobhuza II (eSwatini) 18, 28, 82t, 262
social welfare
  coups and 144–48, 146t
  democracy and 208–12
  elections and elected leadership 33–34, 147t, 213–16, 214, 217, 223–25, 252–53
  ethnicity 24–25
  leaders' impact on 55, 177, 252–53

Index

measuring leaders' impact on 185–87, 216–25, 220t, 309t
Somalia
  coups and military takeovers 123, 123n
  democracy 226, 267
  development and growth 232
  elections 70–71t, 95t, 99t, 109, 114, 116–18
  fate of founding father 82t
  leadership changes 84, 86t, 90t, 282t
  leadership type 343t
  term limits 164t, 296t
South Africa
  coups and military takeovers 133
  democracy 63, 118
  development and growth 232
  dynastic succession 174
  elections 70t, 95t, 99t
  fate of founding father 80, 81t
  interim leaders 111
  leadership changes 75–76t, 90t, 282t
  leadership type 343t
  term limits 164t, 165n, 296t
  see also Mandela, Nelson
South Sudan
  democracy 267
  development and growth 41
  elections 95t, 109, 116–18
  fate of founding father 83t
  independence 184, 267
  leadership changes 90–91, 90t, 282t
  leadership type 343t
  term limits 152t, 164t, 296t
Spence, M. 36
state capacity
  definitions 226–27, 253
  democracy and 228–29, 233–34, 235–38
  leadership, development and 38–39, 41, 225, 253
  leadership type and 18, 20–23
  measuring 229–35, 236t, 268t, 302t
State Capacity Index 231–32
state consolidation
  coups and 145, 146t
  definition of state 226–27
  elections and elected leaders 147t, 232–35, 233–34, 235–38, 253, 270

  factors influencing 225–30
  lack of state capacity and 41
  measuring 185–87, 230–38
  regression tables 236t, 268t, 331t
state intervention and economic growth 189
Stepan, A. 226
Stevens, Siaka (Sierra Leone) 72, 84, 92, 261
Strøm, K. 180–81
succession
  democracy and electoral 49, 69–72, 70t, 158–59, *159*
  dynastic 171–74
  electoral 65–66, 114, *115*
  impact of 37, 40–41, 54, 177–78
  measuring impact of 180–81, 183, 206, 224, 251–53
  research on 10–12, 21–22, 32–33
  successful 92–93
Sudan
  coups and military takeovers 27, 123n, 127, 142
  elections 70t, 95t, 99t
  fate of founding father 82t
  leadership changes 75–76t, 86t, 90t, 282t
  leadership type 18, 262, 266, 343t
  term limits 152t, 162, 163–64t, 165n, 297t
Svolik, M. 45, 55
Swaziland *see* eSwatini
Sylla, L. 15, 87, 93

Talon, Patrice (Benin) 168–72
Tandja, Mamadou (Niger) 106t, 161, 164t
Tanzania
  coups and military takeovers 133
  democracy 72, *159*
  development and growth 52–53, 210–11
  elections 70t, 95t, 96, 99t, 102
  fate of founding father 83t
  leadership changes 75–76t, 90t, 124–25, 282t
  leadership type 343t
  legitimacy of leaders 134
  political parties 29, 94–96

Tanzania (cont.)
  term limits 159, 164t, 169–70, 297t
  see also Nyerere, Julius
Taylor, Charles (Liberia) 97
tenure of leaders
  changing trends in 107–13, 110, 112t
  definition 63
  impact of 85–87, 178–79, 220–22t, 223, 249–50, 252
  mode of entry into power and 113
  presidents for life 79–80, 150–51
  single-party rule and 28–29
  syndrome of overstay 28, 85–87, 86t
  see also term limits
term limits
  adoption in Africa 150–53, 152t, 153, 158–59, 170, 278
  democracy and 116–17, 155–72, 159, 168–69
  and multiparty elections 158–59, 159
  strategies for bypassing 162–63, 163t
  success of bypassing attempts 163–68, 164t, 165n, 285t
  worldwide adoption of 149–50
Thailand 48–50, 120–23, 136
Therkildsen, O. 52–53, 211
Thyne, C. 126–27, 134, 139–40
Togo
  coups and military takeovers 27, 80, 89–90, 123, 123n
  dynastic succession 93, 172–73
  elections 71t, 95t, 99t
  ethnic strife and factionalism 130–31
  fate of founding father 81t
  leadership changes 27, 75–76t, 90t, 282t
  leadership type 258, 343t
  term limits 118, 152t, 163–64t, 297t
  see also Eyadéma, Gnassingbé
Tolbert, William (Liberia) 18, 128, 262
Touré, Ahmed Sékou (Guinea)
  fate of founding father 15–23, 82t
  influence 275
  leadership style 262
  tenure 86t, 150–51
Touré, Amadou Toumani (Mali) 106t, 125, 139–40, 164t, 165n

transformational leaders 8–9
transient leaders
  development performance of 53–54, 259–60, 273t
  empirical definition 63–64, 256–57, 257, 259t, 261
  empirical distribution 260–62, 261t, 264n, 264–66, 265, 343t
  political performance and mode of exit 272–73t, 273–75
  political role of 271–72
Transparency International 242
Traoré, Moussa (Mali) 27, 84–101, 86t, 89–90, 139–40
Tubman, William (Liberia) 18, 82t, 86t, 92, 150–51, 262
Tull, D. 157–58
types of leaders
  criteria for identifying new 257, 259t
  development performance of elected 267–70, 268t
  early classifications 8–9, 16–19
  empirical distribution of 260–67, 261t, 265
  need for new 255–56
  value of new typology 275–76
  see also transient leaders
"tyrants" 18–19

Uganda
  coups and military takeovers 27, 123n, 127–28, 196
  development and growth 52–53, 210–11
  elections 71t, 95t, 97, 99t, 118
  fate of founding father 81t
  hereditary succession 174
  interim leaders 271
  leadership changes 75–76t, 90t, 282t
  leadership type 16, 258, 343t
  political parties 96
  term limits 152t, 161, 163–64t, 166, 169–70, 297t
  see also Amin, Idi; Museveni, Yoweri
UN Security Council (UNSC) 136
United Kingdom 9–23, 85
United States of America 9, 85, 149

V-Dem (Varieties of Democracy project) 243–44
Vall, Ely Ould Mohamed (Mauritania) 89, 105, 106t, 143
Varieties of Democracy project (V-Dem) 243–44
Varol, O. 141
Verwoerd, Hendrik (South Africa) 80, 81t
Vieira, João Bernardo (Guinea-Bissau) 64, 106t, 173

Wade, Abdoulaye (Senegal)
  ascent to power 25, 66
  hereditary succession 172–74
  term limits 162–63, 164t, 165n
Walle, N. van de 29, 239
Wang, E. 229
WDI (World Development Indicators) 194
Weah, George (Liberia) 118, 262
Webb, P. 7, 32
Weber, Max 7–8
Wells, A. 133
WGI (Worldwide Governance Indicators) 230
Wolfensohn, Jim 238
World Development Indicators (WDI) 194
Worldwide Governance Indicators (WGI) 230

Xu, Y. 229

Young, D. 31–33, 151, 169

Zaire *see* Congo-Kinshasa (Democratic Republic of the Congo)
Zambia
  coups and military interventions 133–34, 139
  development and growth 211
  elections 50, 70t, 95t, 96, 99t, 103
  fate of founding father 66, 83t
  leadership changes 66, 75–76t, 90t, 125, 173, 282t
  leadership type 343t
  term limits 152t, 164t, 167, 298t
  see also Kaunda, Kenneth
Zenawi, Meles (Ethiopia) 24, 63, 86t, 173, 196
Zida, Yacouba Isaac (Burkina Faso) 89, 106t, 121
Zimbabwe
  coups and military takeovers 121n, 133, 139
  development and growth 211
  dynastic succession 174
  elections 95t, 99t, 109
  fate of founding father 83t
  leadership changes 90t, 91, 282t
  leadership type 343t
  role of military 121n
  term limits 152t, 164t, 167, 298t
  see also Mnangagwa, Emmerson; Mugabe, Robert
Zuma, Jacob (South Africa) 174